READINGS ON EQUAL EDUCATION
(Formerly *Educating the Disadvantaged*)

READINGS
ON EQUAL
EDUCATION

Volume 21

PUBLIC POLICY AND EQUAL
EDUCATIONAL OPPORTUNITY

SCHOOL REFORMS, POSTSECONDARY
ENCOURAGEMENT, AND STATE POLICIES ON
POSTSECONDARY EDUCATION

Volume Editor and Series Editor
Edward P. St. John

AMS PRESS, INC.
NEW YORK

READINGS ON EQUAL EDUCATION
VOLUME 21
Public Policy and Equal Educational Opportunity
School Reforms, Postsecondary Encouragement, and State Policies on Postsecondary Education

Copyright © 2006 by AMS Press, Inc.
All rights reserved

ISSN 0270-1448
Set ISBN 0-404-10100-3
Volume 21 ISBN 0-404-10121-6
Library of Congress Catalog Card Number 77-83137

All AMS Books are printed on acid-free paper that meets the guidelines for performance and durability of the Committee on Production Guidelines for Book Longevity of the Council on Library Resources.

AMS PRESS, INC.
63 FLUSHING AVENUE – UNIT #221
BROOKLYN NAVY YARD, BLDG. 292, SUITE 417
BROOKLYN, NY 11205-1005, USA

Manufactured in the United States of America

CONTENTS

VOLUME 21

CONTRIBUTORS' NOTES

DEBORAH FAYE CARTER is associate professor of education in the Center for the Study of Higher and Postsecondary Education at the University of Michigan School of Education. Dr. Carter's research interests focus on access and equity issues in higher education, particularly as they relate to race and socioeconomic status. Her book, *A Dream Deferred? Examining the Degree Aspirations of African American and White College Students,* was published by Routledge Falmer in 2001. Her current research projects include a study on first-year student transition to college and college student retention. She received her Ph.D. from the University of Michigan in 1997.

ANNA S. CHUNG is a Ph.D. candidate in economics at Indiana University, Bloomington and research associate for the Indiana Project on Academic Success. Her dissertation research on students in for-profit postsecondary institutions has been supported by grants from the American Educational Research Association and the National Association of Student Financial Aid Administrators. She has also been awarded the Cameron Fincher Fellowship by the Association for Institutional Research for the best dissertation proposal of the year. Her other research on the economics of education focuses on the effects of public policy on access to higher education, labor market outcomes for students, and utilizing economic indicators in assessment of education policies.

CHOONG-GEUN CHUNG is statistician at the Center for Evaluation and Education Policy (CEEP) at Indiana University, Bloomington. His research interests are statistical models for school reform, access and persistence in higher education, and issues in minority representation in special education.

SUZANNE E. ECKES is assistant professor in educational leadership and policy studies at Indiana University. She has a master's degree in education from Harvard University and a J.D./Ph.D. from University of Wisconsin, Madison. Her research interests include desegregation, affirmative action, Title IX, teachers' privacy rights, and charter schools.

AMON EMEKA is assistant professor of sociology at the University of Southern California and an affiliate of the University of Washington Beyond High School project, which provided the data summarized in the chapter he co-authored. His scholarly work revolves around processes of socioeconomic status attainment among racial and ethnic minorities in the U.S., with a special interest in the experiences of Black immigrants and their American-born children.

JACOB P. K. GROSS is a doctoral student in education policy studies at Indiana University and research associate for the Indiana Project on Academic Success. He focuses on higher education policy, particularly access, retention, and persistence of low-income and historically marginalized groups. His other research interests include critical whiteness and the impacts of economic globalization on domestic education policies.

CHARLES HIRSCHMAN is Boeing International Professor in the department of sociology and the Daniel J. Evans School of Public Affairs at the University of Washington. He received his Ph.D. from the University of Wisconsin and then taught at Duke University and Cornell University before joining the faculty at the University of Washington. He is the author of *Ethnic and Social Stratification in Peninsular Malaysia* (American Sociological Association, 1975), the co-editor of *Southeast Asian Studies in the Balance: Reflections from America* (Association for Asian Studies, 1992), and *The Handbook of International Migration: The American Experience* (Russell Sage Foundation, 1999), and has written more than 100 articles and book chapters on demography, race and ethnicity, social stratification, and Southeast Asia. He is the current president of the Population Association of America.

CAROL-ANNE HOSSLER is clinical associate professor in the W. W. Wright School of Education at Indiana University, Bloomington. A former classroom teacher and building principal, her research interests include beginning teachers and the induction years, mentoring, and the development of professional learning communities in schools. Dr. Hossler has focused on professional collaboration throughout her career, has received grants in this area, and has worked as a consultant in the Accelerated Schools. In addition, she directs the Indiana University Mentor Institute. She also coordinates a community partnership with a local food pantry and the developmentally disabled.

SHOUPING HU is associate professor in the department of educational leadership and policy studies at Florida State University. He holds a B.S. in geography and completed two years of graduate study in higher education at Peking University. He has an M.A. in economics and a Ph.D. in higher education from Indiana University. His research focuses on postsecondary participation, college student learning, and higher education finance and policy. Dr. Hu's work has appeared in the *Journal of Higher Education, Research in Higher Education, Review of Higher Education, Journal of College Student Development, Educational Evaluation and Policy Analysis, Education Policy Analysis Archives,* and *Journal of Student Financial Aid.* His most recent publication is the ASHE higher education report *Beyond Grade Inflation: Grading Problems in Higher Education* (Jossey-Bass, 2005).

KIM K. METCALF is director of Assessment and Gifted/Talented Programs with the Monroe County Community School Corporation, Indiana. He moved to this position after serving as associate professor of education and director of the Indiana Center for Evaluation at Indiana University. Dr. Metcalf received his Ph.D. in teacher education and educational research from The Ohio State University. His research has focused on teacher effectiveness, evaluation methodology, and school choice. He is a contributor to the *Handbook of Research on Teacher Education* and co-author of *The Act of Teaching* and has published his work on school choice in a range of professional and scholarly journals throughout the world. Dr. Metcalf's work has been recognized by the Association of Teacher Educators and the U.S. General Accounting Office and in 2004 the American Evaluation Association awarded him the Outstanding Evaluation Award for his longitudinal study of the voucher program in Cleveland, Ohio.

GLENDA DROOGSMA MUSOBA is assistant professor of education at Florida International University. Previously she was policy analyst and associate director of the Indiana Project on Academic Success at Indiana University. She has a Ph.D. in higher education from Indiana University. Her research interests include higher education access and equity, persistence in higher education, education policy, K-16 education reform, and social justice.

KELLI M. PAUL is a doctoral candidate at Indiana University in educational psychology with a specialization in inquiry methodology. She has an M.S. in educational psychology with a specialization in inquiry methodology from Indiana University. Her dissertation research focuses on comparing statistical models for analyzing longitudinal data. Her research interests include school choice and vouchers, quantitative research methods, and statistics. She was a research assistant/statistician on the evaluation of the Cleveland Scholarship and Tutoring Program from 2001-2004.

KELLY E. RAPP (ktrapp@indiana.edu) is an affiliate of the Center for Evaluation and Education Policy (CEEP) at Indiana University, where she previously worked as a research associate. She is working toward her Ph.D. in educational psychology with an emphasis on inquiry methodology. Ms. Rapp collaborates as a part of CEEP's Educational Options Team, specifically researching university sponsorship of charter schools, the racial composition of charter school student bodies, and alternative schools. She is co-editor of *The Principal's Legal Handbook* (Education Law Association).

EDWARD P. ST. JOHN is Algo D. Henderson Collegiate Professor of Education at the Center for the Study of Higher and Postsecondary Education at the University of Michigan. He recently published *Refinancing the College Dream: Access, Equal Opportunity, and Justice for Taxpayers* (Johns Hopkins University Press, 2003) and co-edited *Incentive-Based Budgeting in Public Universities* (Edward Elgar, 2002) and *Reinterpreting Urban School Reform: Have Urban Schools Failed, or Has the Reform Movement Failed Urban Schools?* (SUNY Press, 2003). He holds an Ed.D. from Harvard and M.Ed. and B.S. degrees from the University of California, Davis.

WILLIAM E. SEDLACEK is professor of education and assistant director of the Counseling Center at the University of Maryland. His research interests include race, gender, and multicultural issues in higher education. He has specialized in developing alternative measures to tests and grades that predict student success. His most recent book is *Beyond the Big Test: Noncognitive Assessment in Higher Education* (Jossey-Bass, 2004).

HUNG-BIN SHEU is a doctoral student in counseling psychology at the University of Maryland. He is interested in multicultural issues and has conducted research on career development and subjective well-being of racial/ethnic minorities as well as multicultural counseling competency and training.

ADA B. SIMMONS is executive associate director of the Center for Evaluation and Education Policy (CEEP) at Indiana University, Bloomington. Prior to her current appointment, she was Research Analyst in the campus's institutional research office. Her research focuses on issues of educational equity, such as minority disproportionality in special education and access and attainment of underrepresented groups in higher education. She holds an Ed.D. from Indiana University.

INTRODUCTION

PUBLIC POLICY AND EQUAL EDUCATIONAL OPPORTUNITY: SCHOOL REFORMS, POSTSECONDARY ENCOURAGEMENT, AND STATE POLICIES ON POSTSECONDARY EDUCATION

Edward P. St. John

Researchers and policy makers who are concerned about reducing inequalities in educational opportunity in states and in the nation as a whole must also contend constructively with the intended effects of accountability and other reforms initiated with the aim of improving achievement. Unfortunately, research that focuses exclusively on equity is frequently overlooked in debates about education reform, while research that ignores equity receives excessive attention (Fitzgerald, 2004). While the education reforms in the 1960s and 1970s focused on equalizing opportunity to attain an education for students from low-income and minority families, the reforms of the past two decades have focused on raising standards and improving education for all students. The long-standing policy goal of equalizing opportunity should be considered when assessing the effects of the new reforms. Yet it is also important to build an understanding of the intended effects the new reforms have on achievement outcomes while also considering the equity effects of these reforms. Balanced research of this type is vitally important as a source of information for policy development. The chapters in this volume of the *Readings on Equal Education (REE)* series demonstrate balanced approaches to policy research. Before introducing the chapters in this volume, it is important to focus explicitly on critical tasks facing researchers and policy makers who are concerned about equal educational opportunity.

The Equity Agenda in Education Policy Research

This volume extends the equity agenda of the *REE* series by introducing a comprehensive, balanced framework for assessing the effects of public finance and education policies both on equity and on achievement. Before introducing this framework, which has guided the solicitation and development of chapters for this volume, I revisit the critical tasks of balanced policy research, which I introduced in *REE Volume 20* and which now guide the agenda for the series (St. John, 2004a, 2004c).

Task 1 is to assess the impact of interventions and policies on equal educational opportunity. With the shift in focus on education reform to measures of student achievement as central outcomes, it is easy to overlook the long-standing intent of equal opportunity when designing and evaluating educational programs and public and private finance strategies. Volume 20 of *REE* focused on the Gates Millennium Scholars Program, a private grant program with the goal of improving opportunity for low-income students of color (Merkowitz, 2004; Wilds, 2004). The chapters in this volume further this agenda by providing reviews and new research on reforms intended to improve achievement, including a few programs that use balanced approaches also focusing on equalizing opportunity.

Task 2 is to examine effects of interventions and policies on excellence and efficiency as well as equity. Since the national education reform agenda over the past two decades has focused on excellence and efficiency rather than on equity, it is equally important to examine how reforms influence excellence outcomes. Not only is it important to examine reforms such as accountability systems that focus on achievement outcomes, but it is also important to examine the reforms that focus primarily on equalizing opportunity, such as the GMS programs. The authors in this volume further extend this balanced approach to policy research by examining a range of reforms in both K-12 and higher education.

Task 3 is to rethink the role of policy when considering implications of policy research. When a balanced approach is used in education policy research, it is possible to engage in a process of rethinking strategies, with an emphasis on illuminating workable changes in education and finance policies that use balanced approaches in improving educational opportunity—strategies that emphasize equity and excellence in their design and implementation. When research focuses only on equity or only on achievement outcomes, it is too easy to make recommendations that would either create inequalities or discourage academic improvement and competitiveness among some groups. For example, when education policies promote preparation and there is not adequate need-based grant aid, then large numbers of qualified low-income students can be denied the opportunity for college enrollment (Fitzgerald, 2004; Lee, 2004). In other words, it is crucial that we seek a better balance in the redesign of education reform and the financial strategies that support education systems and students who enroll in them. *REE Volume 21* carries forward the agenda of using a balanced approach for assessing the effects of policies aimed at education and the financing of education.

The agenda of assessing reforms using a balanced approach and looking across these assessments to inform the policy decisions at the state and the federal levels requires a comprehensive framework. This volume uses the Framework for Assessing Policy Influences on Educational Opportunity (Figure 1) introduced in *Refinancing the College Dream* (St. John, 2003) to make progress toward this aim. The framework examines the outcomes of education in its social and economic contexts, in the students' family contexts, and in the role of policy in influencing improvement in three spheres of opportunity: achievement and equity outcomes of K-12 education, transitions from high school to college, and academic success and attainment in college.

Figure 1. Framework for Assessing Policy Influences on Educational Opportunity: Linking Education Policy to Educational Outcomes

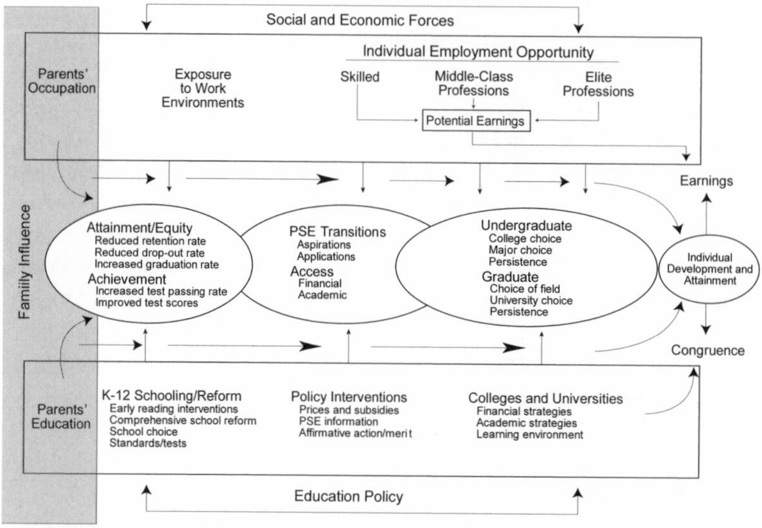

Source: E. P. St. John, *Refinancing the College Dream: Access, Equal Opportunit y, and Justice for Taxpayers,* Johns Hopkins, 2003.

In addition to identifying the spheres of opportunity, the framework provides a way to look across education systems at the role and influence of education and finance policies. Although there are pressures to promote accountability within all three spheres, just as there are globally in education policy, researchers and policy makers tend to limit their analysis to a single sphere. Before we can construct a vantage point on these cross-cutting issues, it is necessary to build a detailed understanding of policies within each sphere. While access to graduate programs should also be considered using a balanced framework, this volume does not include such studies. Solicited for this volume were chapters on specific reforms in K-12 education, encouragement programs that facilitate transitions to postsecondary education, and academic success in undergraduate education. This volume examines policies and interventions related to each of these spheres of educational opportunity and, as a conclusion, looks across these studies to reflect on the future of education reform.

School Reforms

The first sphere of educational opportunity addresses education reforms that can influence student achievement and test scores. As illustrated in Figure 1, it is important to take into account students' family contexts when assessing the effects of K-12 reforms on both achievement and equity outcomes. It is also important to consider racial/ethnic and income differences in attainment, along with effects on achievement (test scores and other outcomes). Four chapters in Section I examine the effects of reforms.

The first two chapters review the major initiatives related to school choice. In Chapter 1, Suzanne E. Eckes and Kelly E. Rapp review the research on charter schools, a school choice scheme that is being tested in a number of states. Eckes, an assistant professor at Indiana University, is a legal and policy researcher who is currently directing a study of charter schools in Indiana. This chapter provides a review of prior research on charter schools, drawing from analyses she conducted at the Indiana Center for Evaluation and Education Policy. In Chapter 2, Kim K. Metcalf and Kelli M. Paul examine the research on school vouchers, with a detailed review of the Cleveland program. They look at both the achievement and equity effects of that program, revealing some of the program's unintended effects that have received too little attention in the policy debates about vouchers.

The second two chapters in Section I provide new research evidence that explores complexities of educational improvement, considering both the achievement and equity features, as well as outcomes of school reforms. In Chapter 3, Glenda Droogsma Musoba, a policy researcher at Indiana University, examines the effects of state accountability policies and school funding on student SAT scores, using a national sample of responses to the College Board's questionnaires that accompany SAT exams and state policy indicators (developed by St. John, Musoba, & Chung, 2004) in a two-level analysis. Her chapter addresses the question: Do K-12 reforms or school funding have a more substantial association with student achievement and college preparation, as measured by SAT scores? Then, in Chapter 4, a research team from Indiana University presents results from an evaluation study of Michigan's Comprehensive School Reform (CSR) program, using teacher survey responses. This chapter focuses on the relationships between classroom practices and classroom outcomes.

Postsecondary Encouragement

The second sphere in the framework (Figure 1) focuses on transitions from high school to postsecondary education. In theory, three types of strategies can encourage students to make these transitions: subsidizing the cost of attendance through tuition subsides (i.e., funding colleges) or through student aid for low-income students; providing opportunities for students to complete college preparatory curricula (i.e., to meet admission requirements); and using affirmative action and other policies that focus on overcoming inequalities in admissions. Comprehensive encouragement programs combine features of all three aspects of the college transition process. Three of the chapters in Section II examine different outcomes related to the comprehensive encouragement program, Washington State Achievers (WSA) Program, funded by the Bill & Melinda Gates Foundation. The final chapter in Section II examines another comprehensive encouragement program, Twenty-First Century Scholars, for its effects on persistence and degree completion after four years.

The WSA Program supports education reform in 16 high schools that serve low-income students in the state of Washington and also provides scholarships for 500 students from these schools. Students who are selected for WSA awards receive guaranteed scholarship support for enrollment in a Washington college after high school graduation. The students studied in these chapters had opportunities to apply for scholarships but did not have the benefit of school reforms because the high school reforms had not been implemented in time to affect the educational opportunities of the students who graduated in the first few years of the program. In Chapter 5, Amon Emeka, of the University of Southern California, and Charles Hirschman, of the University of Washington, examine the characteristics of students selected for the WSA program, using social capital theory. Their study conducted surveys of high school students in Tacoma, Washington, a population that includes students in schools with WSA funding and schools that were not funded. Then, in Chapter 6, William Sedlacek and Hung-Bin Sheu, both of the University of Maryland, examine the academic behaviors of WSA awardees. These analyses use a survey of the initial cohort of recipients. In Chapter 7, in collaboration with Shouping Hu, of Florida State University, I examine the effects of WSA selection—that is, of receiving a guarantee for an aid award—on college applications and college enrollment. These analyses used Hirschman's surveys of Tacoma high school students.

Chapter 8 presents a study of the long-term effects of the Twenty-First Century Scholars Program, a comprehensive postsecondary encouragement program in Indiana. Prior studies of that program have focused on college enrollment and persistence during the first year after college (Musoba, 2004; St. John, 2004b; St. John, Musoba, Simmons, & Chung, 2002). While the early research on this program has informed policy decisions in states, especially the development of state grant programs,[1] this is the

---

[1] The research on the Twenty-First Century Scholars Program was the focal point of a session hosted by the National Governors Associated (NGA) in 2002 and was presented at another national meeting on state grant programs, also in 2002. These meetings, along with the report

first study to examine the long-term effects. With colleagues at Indiana University—Jacob P. K. Gross, Glenda Droogsma Musoba, and Anna S. Chung—I present analyses of the impact of scholars awards on persistence and degree attainment after four years.

State Policies on Postsecondary Education

The third sphere of the comprehensive framework (Figure 1) focuses on college success. To consider equity outcomes of government and institutional policies and practices, it is important to look at differences in these outcomes across racial/ethnic and/or income groups. Since race can no longer be considered as a variable in college admissions, it is especially important to examine income differences in access and persistence. Theoretically, college success can be influenced by school reforms, public finance strategies, and state higher education accountability policies. The two chapters in Section III examine the relationships between education policies and postsecondary outcomes in three different ways.

First, in Chapter 9, in collaboration with Choong-Geun Chung of Indiana University, I present a reanalysis of the National Education Longitudinal Study (NELS) of the high school class of 1992, focusing on the role and influence of state finance policies on access and persistence. The reanalysis of NELS was necessary because of the serious statistical errors made by the National Center for Education Statistics (NCES) in their research using this database (Becker, 2004; Fitzgerald, 2004; Heller, 2004). Not only did NCES demonstrate omitted variable bias when they failed to examine the direct effects of student financial aid on access and persistence (Becker, 2004), but they also demonstrated selection bias in screening prepared students out of their analyses. The

published by Lumina Foundation for Education (St. John, Musoba, Simmons, & Chung, 2002), have brought national visibility to this program.

reanalysis used the state finance policy indictors (developed by St. John, Chung, Musoba, & Simmons, 2004) in a two-level model to assess the effects of state finance policies on college choice and persistence.

Chapter 10 presents analyses of college persistence by college students in the Indiana high school class of 2000, focusing on differences across racial/ethnic groups. This chapter was written in collaboration with Deborah F. Carter, a colleague at the University of Michigan, and Choong-Geun Chung and Glenda Droogsma Musoba of Indiana University. These analyses used a longitudinal database on students in the 2000 Indiana high school cohort, a database developed from records of student SAT questionnaires and enrollment records of public and private colleges in the state. The chapter examines the effects of high school preparation, college major choices, and student aid on continuous college enrollment during the first two years after high school.

Conclusion

In combination, these analyses provide a comprehensive view of the role and influence of public finance on education policy. In the concluding chapter, I summarize the studies in the context of the three spheres of educational opportunity, as well as look across the spheres using the three critical tasks noted above as organizing frames. This view across the education systems provides new visibility into the consequences of accountability processes, privatization schemes, public finance strategies, and educational practices.

References

Becker, W. E. (2004). Omitted variables and sample selection in studies of college-going decisions. In E. P. St. John (Ed.), *Readings on equal education: Vol. 19. Public policy and college access: Investigating the federal and state roles in equalizing postsecondary opportunity* (pp. 65-86). New York: AMS Press, Inc.

Fitzgerald, B. (2004). Federal financial aid and college access. In E. P. St. John (Ed.), *Readings on equal education: Vol. 19. Public policy and college access: Investigating the federal and state roles in equalizing postsecondary opportunity* (pp. 1-28). New York: AMS Press, Inc.

Heller, D. E. (2004). NCES research on college participation: A critical analysis. In E. P. St. John (Ed.), *Readings on equal education: Vol. 19. Public policy and college access: Investigating the federal and state roles in equalizing postsecondary opportunity* (pp. 29-64). New York: AMS Press, Inc.

Lee, J. B. (2004). Access revisited: A preliminary reanalysis of NELS. In E. P. St. John (Ed.), *Readings on equal education: Vol. 19. Public policy and college access: Investigating the federal and state roles in equalizing postsecondary opportunity* (pp. 87-96). New York: AMS Press, Inc.

Merkowitz, D. R. (2004). Opportunity answered: Summary research findings on the Gates Millennium Scholars Program. In E. P. St. John (Ed.), *Readings on equal education: Vol. 20. Improving access and college success for diverse students: Studies of the Gates Millennium Scholars Program* (pp. 1-22). New York: AMS Press, Inc.

Musoba, G. D. (2004). Postsecondary encouragement for diverse students: A reexamination of the Twenty-First Century Scholars Program. In E. P. St. John (Ed.), *Readings on equal education: Vol. 19. Public policy and college access: Investigating the federal and state roles in equalizing postsecondary opportunity* (pp. 153-180). New York: AMS Press, Inc.

St. John, E. P. (2003). *Refinancing the college dream: Access, equal opportunity, and justice for taxpayers.* Baltimore, MD: Johns Hopkins University Press.

St. John, E. P. (2004a). Conclusions and implications. In E. P. St. John (Ed.), *Readings on equal education: Vol. 20. Improving access and college success for diverse students: Studies of the*

Gates Millennium Scholars Program (pp. 265-282). New York: AMS Press, Inc.

St. John, E. P. (2004b). The impact of financial aid guarantees on enrollment and persistence: Evidence from research on Indiana's Twenty-First Century Scholars and Washington State Achievers Programs. In D. E. Heller & P. Marin (Eds.), *State merit scholarship programs and racial inequality* (pp. 124-140). Cambridge, MA: The Civil Rights Project, Harvard University.

St. John, E. P. (2004c). Introduction. In E. P. St. John (Ed.), *Readings on equal education: Vol. 20. Improving access and college success for diverse students: Studies of the Gates Millennium Scholars Program* (pp. xvii-xxv). New York: AMS Press, Inc.

St. John, E. P., Chung, C. G., Musoba, G. D., & Simmons, A. B. (2004). Financial access: The impact of state financial strategies. In E. P. St. John (Ed.), *Readings on equal education: Vol. 19. Public policy and college access: Investigating the federal and state roles in equalizing postsecondary opportunity* (pp. 109-129). New York: AMS Press, Inc.

St. John, E. P., Musoba, G. D., & Chung, C. G. (2004). Academic access: The impact of state education policies. In E. P. St. John (Ed.), *Readings on equal education: Vol. 19. Public policy and college access: Investigating the federal and state roles in equalizing postsecondary opportunity* (pp. 131-151). New York: AMS Press, Inc.

St. John, E. P., Musoba, G. D., Simmons, A. B., & Chung, C. G. (2002). *Meeting the access challenge: Indiana's Twenty-First Century Scholars Program.* New Agenda Series, Vol. 4, No. 4. Indianapolis: Lumina Foundation for Education.

Wilds, D. J. (2004). Foreword. In E. P. St. John (Ed.), *Readings on equal education: Vol. 20. Improving access and college success for diverse students: Studies of the Gates Millennium Scholars Program* (pp. v-viii). New York: AMS Press, Inc.

SECTION I

School Reforms

CHAPTER 1

CHARTER SCHOOL RESEARCH: TRENDS AND IMPLICATIONS[1]

Suzanne E. Eckes and Kelly E. Rapp

The charter school movement has experienced tremendous growth from its recent beginnings in 1991. Although some view this movement as an answer to the nation's education problems, others argue that charter schools will damage the public school system by diverting resources. In 2004, there were around 3,000 charter schools in operation, and the results so far have been mixed. Charter schools have been the focus of several studies that often reach conflicting conclusions. For example, some studies find achievement gains for students attending charter schools, while others find no improvement. This chapter will help policy makers better understand what has been learned about charter schools and why some research questions remain unsettled.

Following a brief contextual overview of charter schools, this chapter first describes charter schools through an examination of relevant policy considerations. Specifically, equity, leadership,

[1] This research was supported in part by the Educational Options Division of the Indiana Department of Education. However, all opinions expressed in the chapter are those of the authors and not necessarily those of the Indiana Department of Education.

management, and new developments are discussed. Additionally, the performance of charter schools is addressed through evaluation research on parent satisfaction, impacts on districts, innovations, and achievement and accountability. In so doing, the chapter analyzes the quality of the charter school research and makes recommendations for further investigation.

Overview

A charter school is a publicly funded, tuition-free school of choice that has greater autonomy than traditional public schools (Eckes & Plucker, 2004). What sets charter schools apart from other schools is their charter, which is a performance contract that establishes each school and details the school's mission and goals. Charter schools are most often new schools that were not in existence before the charter was granted, but it is also common for a traditional public or private school to convert to charter school status.

Functioning as a public school, a charter school receives a charter from a public agency, usually a state or local school board (Heubert, 1997). The entity that issues the charter is known as a sponsor or authorizer and plays a key role in the charter school system. The sponsor serves as the public's primary formal agent for holding charter schools accountable for their performance (D. Bulkley, 2001; Vergari, 2001). State legislatures have generally permitted the following four public entities to serve as charter school sponsors: (1) school districts, (2) state boards or departments of education, (3) other public entities, including cities or counties, and (4) new public boards created specifically for serving as charter school sponsors (Vergari, 2001).

The first charter school law was passed in 1991 in Minnesota (Minnesota, 1991), and the first charter school was established there in 1992. From 1991 to the present, the charter school movement has experienced tremendous growth. Today it is estimated that there are nearly 3,000 charter schools (Center for Education Reform, 2004). Charter schools enroll about 1.5 percent of public school students (Hoxby, 2004). While 41 states, the District of Columbia, and Puerto Rico have adopted charter school legislation, Arizona, California, Florida, Michigan, and Texas have more than half of all charter schools (U.S. Charter Schools, n.d.). States with no charter school laws include Alabama, Kentucky, Maine, Montana, Nebraska, North Dakota, South Dakota, Vermont, and West Virginia.

One of the main reasons for founding charter schools was to seek an alternative vision of schooling that could not be realized in the traditional public schools (RPP International, 2000). Specifically, in order to have the flexibility to be innovative, charter schools are free from some state laws and rules that apply to traditional public schools. There is significant variation in charter schools across states because the state laws that dictate most aspects of charter schools—including funding, student and staff recruitment, and charter attainment status—differ. Although the details vary by state, there are some generalizations that can be made about charter schools. For example, charter schools are not typically confined to the constraints of traditional public school requirements, such as certain bureaucratic and union rules. In some states, such flexibility includes the freedom to hire teachers according to their own standards and to adopt specific curriculums (Kafer, 2003). Some charter schools may even create their own calendar or length of school day (Ryan & Heise, 2002).

The charter school policy innovation is a reform that is aimed at altering the accountability arrangements in public education (Mintrom & Vergari, 1997). When a charter is issued, there is a defined limited term of operation; most charters are granted for three to five years. As a result, if a charter school fails to meet the provisions of its charter, the sponsor may take steps to close the school. Finn, Manno, and Vanourek (2000) have described this type of accountability as "public marketplaces in which a school's clients and stakeholders reward its successes, punish its failures, and send it signals about what needs to change" (p. 127). Indeed, it is much easier for sponsors to revoke the charters of charter schools than it is for authorities to close traditional public schools.

While there is controversy surrounding the charter school movement, charter schools have attracted bipartisan support (Cobb & Glass, 1999; Haft, 1998; Parker, 2001; Peterson, 1998; U.S. Department of Education, 2004a). Both Republicans and

Democrats have backed the federal government in approving financial support for establishing charter schools and for acquiring operational facilities. Bill Clinton's 1997 State of the Union Address called for the creation of 3,000 charter schools by the year 2002. Likewise, George W. Bush has proposed $700 million in spending for charter schools (Frankenberg, Lee, & Orfield, 2003). In addition to support from the federal government, several states have also contributed large amounts of public funds to support charter schools. For example, Arizona appropriated $600 million for charter school funding (Good & Braden, 2000), which was one of the largest appropriations in the country.

The debate over school choice generally involves liberals favoring more limited reform and conservatives favoring a more expansive reform leading to increased privatization and expanded individual control over educational choices (Haft, 1998). Overall, however, charter schools appeal to both political conservatives and political moderates. Political conservatives consider charter schools as a step toward vouchers; conversely, political moderates view charters as a way of averting the use of vouchers (Townley, 2000). As policy makers started paying attention to charter schools, the market metaphor for choice and competition became an essential part of the discussion (Wells, 2002). Free market advocates believe that charter schools will either stimulate weaker public schools to improve or will drive them out of the education process (Haft, 1998). More specifically, these advocates argue that the existence of charter schools promotes competition between charter and traditional public schools and provides a more market-based rationale for accountability. In so doing, charter schools could encourage systemic change by providing more educational choices, creating competitive market forces (RPP International, 2001).

Populations Served: Equity Issues

Charter schools provide additional choices for families who want to leave their assigned school but want to remain within the public school system (Rich, 2002). When choosing a public school, market enthusiasts claim that parents seek the best schools regardless of their racial composition. Accordingly, charter schools may provide additional opportunities for poor and minority students (see Green, 2001; Nathan, 1996; Peterson, 1998) and as a result should foster racial integration (see Chubb & Moe, 1999; Finn, 1990; Reinhard & Lee, 1991). As such, offering parents increased school choice via charter schools has taken center stage in national education debates over the relationship between choice and desegregation (Saporito & Lareau, 1999).

On the other hand, when charter school legislation was first introduced some critics expressed concerns that school choice might lead to further racial and ethnic segregation (Cobb & Glass, 1999; Hocschild & Scovronick, 2003; Horn & Mirกn, 1999; Howe, Eisenhart, & Betebenner, 2001). Further, some observers feared that charter schools would provide school officials the means to help White parents escape from racially desegregated public schools (Elmore, 1988; Fitzgerald, Harris, Huidekoper, & Mani, 1998; Green, 2001). In response to such concerns, 19 states adopted policies requiring the racial composition of charter schools to reflect the racial population of surrounding school districts (Frankenberg & Lee, 2003).

Statistical evidence does not support the concern that charter schools will lead to "White flight"; in fact, few charter schools have a disproportionately high percentage of White students (Frankenberg & Lee, 2003; National Center for Education Statistics [NCES], 2002). On the contrary, many charter schools have a disproportionately high percentage of racial minorities (Eckes & Rapp, 2005; Green, 2001). For example, charter school data reveals that the percentage of African American students in charter schools is 20 percent higher than in traditional public schools, and the discrepancy is 13 percent when comparing Hispanic students in charter versus traditional public schools (NCES, 2002).

Data regarding the segregation in charter schools is generalized. In other words, there are some charter schools that enroll a higher percentage of White students than the surrounding public schools, and there are some that have greater racial integration than public schools (Cobb & Glass, 1999). However, in general, charter schools are typically more racially segregated than public schools (Eckes & Rapp, 2005; Frankenberg & Lee, 2003). In fact, 12 charter schools have been identified by the U.S. Department of Education (2004a) as having a high level of segregation. Wamba and Ascher (2003) argue that one explanation for the segregation is that courts do not always order equity plans in charter schools. Although some states such as California and South Carolina require that the charter school's student body reflect the diversity of the school district population, this requirement is often not enforced. Additionally, cultural identity may play a role in the establishment of charter schools, as seen in ethnic-centered schools established to address the educational needs of African American students, and this can contribute to racial segregation of charter schools as well. Reid and Johnson (2001) note how the school choice movement has been embraced by minority parents.

The *Milwaukee Journal Sentinel* reported in March 2004 that over 200 Afrocentric schools have opened in the United States since 1996 (Sykes, 2004). Parker (2001) highlights that in Lansing, Michigan, African Americans make up 33 percent of the school district, yet the Afrocentric charter school is almost completely African American. Likewise, in Saginaw, Michigan, only 13 percent of the students in the school district are Hispanic, yet the charter school is overwhelmingly Hispanic (Parker, 2001). Ethnocentric charter schools may contribute to the higher proportion of minority students attending charter schools.

Such generalized data reflects that charter schools are more segregated than public schools, but it is difficult to determine whether charter schools have a higher percentage of poor students enrolled. This is due to the fact that charter schools often do not participate in free and reduced-lunch programs, which are a common indicator of students' socioeconomic status (Wells, Holme, Lopez, & Cooper, 2000). However, about one in four charter schools specifically established their charter to serve at-risk students (RPP International, 2000). At least 12 state statutes offer priority to charter schools that serve impoverished minority students (Ryan & Heise, 2002).

In addition to equity concerns regarding racial and economic integration, critics also worry that charter schools "skim" the most talented students from the traditional public schools ("The Limits of Choice," 1996). Indeed, some states allow charter schools to use selective criteria when admitting the student body. For example, one New York district permits charter schools to "screen applicants on the basis of test scores, interviews, and teacher comments" (p. 2008). Interestingly, a growing number of charter schools are choosing to gear their curriculum toward gifted students (Eckes & Plucker, 2005). Charter elementary and high schools with missions specifically aimed at serving a gifted and talented population have been formed or proposed in several states, including California, Colorado, Delaware, North Carolina, Ohio, and Pennsylvania (Hoagie's, n.d.). Stargate School, a chartered K-8 school in Colorado, "was founded specifically to meet and exceed academic and socio-emotional requisites of this population, identified by the State of Colorado as 'special needs children'" (Stargate, n.d.). Similarly, the mission statement of a North Carolina charter school reads: "The Metrolina Regional Scholars' Academy is a nondiscriminatory, public charter school that provides a differentiated, exceptionally challenging education for children of extremely high academic or intellectual ability, ages 4 to 13" (Metrolina, n.d.). A few virtual or online charter schools have also been created to target the gifted population. Overall, however, the number of charter schools specifically designed for gifted students is quite small.

In addition to charter schools focused on the gifted there are some charter schools that specifically target students with disabilities. Even though some charter schools target this population, some still fear that charter schools may avoid recruiting students with special needs. Under law, charter schools are required to provide students with disabilities a free appropriate public education (Heubert, 1997; McKinney, 1996; U.S. Department of Education, 2000). Specifically, charter school leaders must address equitable enrollment of students with disabilities, among other things (U.S. Department of Education, 1998). In so doing, charter schools must examine the interplay between federal law, state law, and their individual charter contract to understand fully their responsibilities in serving special needs students (Mead, 2002).

Despite these requirements, however, McKinney (1996) revealed that only 4 percent of students enrolled in charter schools received special education services. Other studies have found slightly higher percentages (RPP International & the University of Minnesota, 1997). A 2000 national study of charter schools and students with disabilities in 15 states revealed parents were generally encouraged to enroll their special needs children in charter schools. Parents at a few of the charter schools, however, reported that charter school staff attempted to dissuade parents from enrolling their child because of the child's disability (U.S. Department of Education, 2000). It is important to note that the parents interviewed in this study were parents of the students who are or who were enrolled at the charter school. As such, the number of parents who have been counseled out of the visited schools is not known.

Other obstacles regarding serving students with special needs included difficulties in developing special education programs within the charter school. A few of the schools reported not developing a special education program until the second or third year because of difficulties associated with starting a school. In addition to charter school start-up difficulties, there was sometimes confusion about a charter school's responsibility in serving students with special needs (U.S. Department of Education, 2000).

Most public charter schools admit students via a random lottery when determining which students will be allowed to attend a charter school, a process which may help prevent skimming. Under a lottery system, charter schools have the opportunity to enhance equity by providing poor families with opportunities for school choice that were previously available only to wealthy families who could afford private school tuition (Vergari, 2003).

Charter School Leadership and Governance

The importance of effective leadership in schools has been well documented (Dressler, 2001), and charter schools are no different. Dressler (2001) writes that "effective schools are led by principals who have a clear vision of where they are going, who are knowledgeable enough about teaching and education to help teachers and students work toward desired ends, and who are able to protect schools from the kinds of demands that make it difficult for schools to operate on a professional basis" (p. 177). Drake and Roe (1999) observed that "the principal's major task is to make a positive difference as evidenced in the learning of students, teachers, parents, and all associated with the school" (p. 169).

Specific to charter school leadership, Dressler (2001) argues, "If we accept the premise that charter schools provide an opportunity to experience fundamental change, such change must also include ideas for what principals do and how they are prepared" (p. 174). Sarason (1999) stresses that the leaders of charter schools hold demanding and stressful positions because most charter school leaders have never created a new setting, and there has been nothing in their professional backgrounds to prepare them for this challenge.

Sarason (1999) also notes the positive and negative aspects of the fact that charter school leaders are self-selected. Although "the person is critical of the existing state of affairs, has developed a vision of an alternative school, has mustered support, and knows the difference between an ego trip and dedication to a vision" (p. 381), there is a negative impact "if the person is in it for personal glory, can only see clear sailing ahead, has little or no inkling of the predictable problems ahead, has vastly underestimated the time and energy required, and who by virtue of the staff he or she has selected assumes that what initially is a happy family will always remain so" (p. 381).

In addition to Dressler's (2001) and Sarason's (1999) work, the literature reveals few studies focused specifically on charter school leadership. In one study, Lane (1998) identified five areas that require the attention of charter school leaders. Specifically, charter school leaders must have expertise in start-up logistics, curriculum and assessment, governance and management, community and public relations, and regulatory issues. The study noted that the basic difficulty facing charter school founders involves a lack of expertise in one or more of these areas. In his study, Lane identifies the barriers to charter school development and what charter school leaders need to know to overcome these barriers. Similarly, Smith and Willcox (2004) note that charter school leaders rarely receive adequate funding for facilities. As such, in addition to running a school, charter leaders must also scrape together funding from foundations and other donors to build a permanent facility for their students. Indeed, charter school leaders often face greater obstacles than traditional public schools. Such obstacles should be considered when comparing charter schools with traditional public schools.

An integral component of the leadership at a charter school is the teachers, and various studies describe the characteristics of charter school teachers. Freed from the rules and regulations that may serve as barriers to change in the public school system, charter schools have the opportunity to be more innovative than traditional schools, making different choices about fundamental practices, including the selection of teachers.

The Education Policy Center at Michigan State University (Burian-Fitzgerald & Harris, 2004) used data from the National Center for Educational Statistics (NCES) for the 1999-2000 school year to compare several characteristics of traditional and charter public school teachers in order to determine whether and in what ways charter school teachers differ from their peers in noncharter schools. Examining certification, years of experience, and undergraduate college selectivity, the researchers found evidence that charter school administrators are innovative in their hiring practices; therefore, teachers in charter and traditional public schools differ on several measurable characteristics that may affect student learning. Results of this study indicated that charter schools appear to place more of an emphasis on the selectivity of a teacher's undergraduate institution and less on certification and experience when making hiring decisions (Burian-Fitzgerald & Harris, 2004). Indeed, the National Study of Charter Schools reports that charter school teachers are less likely to be certified than their peers in district-operated public schools (RPP International, 1999).

Additional findings of the research at Michigan State University indicate that more innovation is observed in the hiring practices of charter schools when there are multiple authorizing entities, when certification requirements are flexible, and when charter administrators are not bound by local collective bargaining agreements (Burian-Fitzgerald & Harris, 2004). The increased autonomy of charter schools over traditional public schools raises questions about adherence to collective bargaining agreements. Many states do not require charter schools to be bound by the district collective bargaining agreements which outline work rules, compensation, job security, and benefits (Education Commission of the States [ECS], 2003). The presence of multiple employers of public school teachers in an area may cause union leaders to generate new roles for the union that work with the policies of charter schools (ECS, 2003).

For-Profit Management and Charter Schools

Private management companies, also referred to as educational management organizations (EMOs), are for-profit firms that are increasingly providing administrative and educational services to charter schools in need of assistance with the overwhelming demands of opening a new school (Chubb, 2003; Plank, Arsen, & Sykes, 2000). Nationwide, approximately 12 percent of charter schools use EMOs (Walk, 2003) for their expertise in choosing a site, setting up payrolls, hiring teachers, training staff, and developing curriculum and instruction methods (Harrington-Lueker, 2002; Plank et al., 2000; Walk, 2003). Most states require charter holders to be nonprofit organizations, but the laws do not prohibit charter schools from contracting with for-profit companies for comprehensive management services (Chubb, 2003). Although there are many advantages to contracting with a management company (The Brown Center on Education Policy, 2003; Chubb, 2003; Walk, 2003), the emergence of EMOs in the charter movement raises concerns that the profit motive will lead firms to cut costs at the expense of educational quality (Dykgraaf & Lewis, 1998; Lacireno-Paquet, Holyoke, Moser, & Henig, 2002; Plank et al., 2000; Zollers & Ramanathan, 1998) or that the freedom of educators to practice site-based, or decentralized, management will be threatened (K. E. Bulkley, 2002; Dykgraaf & Lewis, 1998; Harrington-Lueker, 2002).

An underlying premise of the charter school movement is that the concepts of a free market will generate new and improved public education, and the emergence of EMOs provides supporting evidence for this assumption (Chubb, 2003; Walk, 2003). Proponents of EMOs claim that they encourage competition by increasing the number of schools and introducing new investors and entrepreneurs into public education (The Brown Center on Education Policy, 2003; K. E. Bulkley, 2002). The free market approach depends on parents' ability to choose the schools their children attend (Conn, 2002); therefore, management companies are driven to serve their students well. Otherwise, parents will pull their children from the charter school and the EMO might risk losing its contract (Walk, 2003). The profit strategy of the EMOs is to provide a better education than is provided by other public schools, thus encouraging students to enroll in the EMO-managed schools and establishing a strong reputation which will ensure future contracts (Walk, 2003).

Other advantages to contracting with an EMO include their vast resources and buying power. Charter schools can reduce costs by offering a curriculum provided by the EMOs rather than expending the resources to develop a new one. The EMOs can also save the charter schools money by making large-scale purchases of supplies and equipment (Walk, 2003). Additionally, a recent study that examined test score data over a three-year period at 90 EMO-managed charter schools, primarily in Michigan, found that these schools made greater gains in student achievement than other charter schools (The Brown Center on Education Policy, 2003). The EMO-operated charter schools in this study targeted low-achieving students and thus had significantly lower standardized test scores than other charter schools and regular public schools; however, charter schools run by EMOs registered significantly larger gains from 2000-2002 than both non-EMO charters and regular public schools (The Brown Center on Education Policy, 2003).

Although the previously mentioned Brown Center on Education Policy study revealed that charter schools that use EMOs serve a larger proportion of African American children and low-income children and are more likely to be located in urban communities (The Brown Center on Education Policy, 2003), some researchers contend that when for-profit companies run charter schools, they try to increase profits by avoiding high-cost, or disadvantaged, students (Lacireno-Paquet et al., 2002; Metzger, 2003; Plank et al., 2000). This difference may be explained by the size of the EMO. Lacireno-Paquet (2004) found that small EMOs (those that manage between three and ten charter schools) serve significantly lower percentages of minority students. Schools that do not serve high-cost students (those with severe handicaps or limited English proficiency students, for example) may succeed in generating profits for their EMOs (Plank et al., 2000). Other ways in which EMOs and their charter schools can increase profits include providing fewer services such as transportation and special education (Dykgraaf & Lewis, 1998; Plank et al., 2000). Zollers and Ramanathan (1998) assert that the profit motive leads EMOs to ignore special education law and to treat students with more complicated disabilities as financial liabilities, often counseling them out of their schools. Specifically, the standardized curriculum and instruction methods used by the EMOs to benefit from economy of scale are not conducive to students with special needs (Zollers & Ramanathan, 1998).

The centralized bureaucracy of the private management companies concerns charter school advocates who envision the movement as an opportunity for grassroots community organizations to provide alternatives to top-down schools run by distant public school districts (Dykgraaf & Lewis, 1998; Harrington-Lueker, 2002). Rather than decentralizing education, or leaving the decisions about a school up to the personnel most involved with the school, the emergence of EMOs threatens to homogenize the charter school movement as EMOs identically manage their schools (K. E. Bulkley, 2002; Dykgraaf & Lewis, 1998; Harrington-Lueker, 2002; Metzger, 2003). K. E. Bulkley (2002) found that more decisions are made outside of an EMO-managed charter school than a charter school that does not work with a management company. Additionally, Dykgraaf and Lewis (1998) describe a management group that uses a generic parent handbook and parent committee structure and an identical calendar and curriculum in all of its schools, thwarting the innovation and individuality promoted by the charter movement. Researchers conclude that further study and policy clarification are needed to determine the benefits of for-profit management companies and protect the charter movement from potential harms of working with them (The Brown Center on Education Policy, 2003; K. E. Bulkley, 2002; Conn, 2002; Dykgraaf & Lewis, 1998; Lacireno-Paquet, 2004; Metzger, 2003; Plank et al., 2000; Walk, 2003).

New Directions: Cyber Charter Schools

In the five years since former U.S. Secretary of Education William Bennett helped develop "virtual charter schools" that provide educational programs to charter schools via the Internet (Kafer, 2003), the number of these schools has rapidly increased. Currently there are 60 such cyber charter schools operating in 15 states, serving over 16,000 students, or roughly 2 percent of the nationwide charter school student population (Huerta & Gonzalez, 2004). Cyber charter schools, like traditional charter schools, are independent public schools created through formal agreements with a sponsoring agency and operating free from most regulations governing schools. However, instruction is delivered through alternative, non-classroom-based mediums (Huerta & Gonzalez, 2004), and the cyber charters typically provide students with a computer, a curriculum, textbooks, and Internet access for no charge (Cook, 2002). Typically, cyber charter schools are able to cross district boundaries and enroll students from multiple districts, and they are composed predominantly of previously home-schooled students (Bogden, 2003; Cook, 2002; Huerta & Gonzalez, 2004). A study of Ohio's 23 cyber charter schools revealed that they serve mostly secondary level students and are composed of a smaller percentage (21%) of minority students than traditional charter schools in Ohio (80%) (Legislative Office of Education Oversight [LOEO], 2004). Despite these smaller studies, there are no comprehensive studies that have analyzed a wide sample of cyber charters (Huerta & Gonzalez, 2004).

Among the benefits of cyber charter schools is the ability to serve a wide range of students, such as students who are homebound for medical reasons, who are employed, or who are incarcerated. Students who do not feel comfortable in traditional classrooms, such as highly creative students or gay and lesbian students, may benefit from the option of a cyber charter school as well. Cyber charter schools also offer home-schooling families the option of public financing for a program that relieves parents of much of the instructional burden but with little loss of autonomy. Additionally, cyber charters can offer innovative curriculum choices and can personalize the pace and content of instruction (Bogden, 2003).

The most significant policy issue that cyber charter schools raise is the question of funding. Charter schools can potentially claim 75 percent or more of a state's per-pupil allocation for each student who enrolls in the school (Conn, 2002). However, because they don't require extensive facilities or other services such as transportation or food, costs per pupil at cyber charter schools are low in relation to traditional education costs, making cyber charters potentially profitable and attractive for private management companies (Conn, 2002; Cook, 2002; Harrington-Lueker, 2002).

Allowing cyber charter schools to draw enrollments across district boundaries creates funding problems when districts are charged based on a portion of their per-pupil expenditures for students who are no longer under their supervision (Bogden, 2003; Cook, 2002; Huerta & Gonzalez, 2004). This dilemma led to legal action in Pennsylvania in 2001 when districts refused to pay bills from cyber charter schools for the per-pupil allocations of the students they had lost. The state's education commissioner started withholding funds from the districts to pay the cyber charters, and the districts were not allowed to appeal this decision. This situation resulted in legislation that reimburses public school districts up to 30 percent of the per-student funding lost when area students enroll in cyber charters (Bogden, 2003; Cook, 2002). Additionally, many cyber charter students were formally home-schooled and therefore not previously covered by public dollars. Since the enrollment of these students into cyber charters causes unexpected new obligations to public school budgets, Colorado's charter school law specifically bans online schools from enrolling previously home-schooled students (Bogden, 2003).

Bogden (2003) and Huerta and Gonzalez (2004) contend that appropriate per-pupil funding allocations need to be determined for cyber charter schools. Although online education can cost substantially less to operate because facilities, a large amount of faculty, transportation, and food services are not necessary, new costs of high technology, such as maintaining an intranet, do emerge (Bogden, 2003; Cook, 2002; Huerta & Gonzalez, 2004). In addition to financial accountability, cyber charter schools must be held responsible for student performance and program quality (Bogden, 2003; Huerta & Gonzalez, 2004). Cyber charters often contract with EMOs, and there have been complaints of corruption, conflict of interest, and withholding computers and special education services (Bogden, 2003; Cook, 2002; Huerta & Gonzalez, 2004). Measures need to be implemented to ensure that students rather than their parents are completing the work and that cyber charter schools are reporting accurate enrollment figures and using the best practices in instruction and assessment (Bogden, 2003). In Ohio, local school districts are sponsoring their own cyber charter schools, making it easier to monitor accountability. Additionally, when school districts operate cyber charters this expands educational opportunities in their districts and helps to retain students who might drop out of school or leave the district for another traditional or cyber charter school (LOEO, 2004).

Impact on Parents and Districts

Few comprehensive, nationwide studies of parent satisfaction with charter schools have been conducted recently. However, what research has been done indicates a positive response, and several indicators of market satisfaction—such as waiting lists for charter schools—support the conclusion that parents and students are often satisfied with charter schools (RPP International, 2000). Additionally, The Center for Education Reform (2003) summarizes a study of New York's charter schools in June of 2003 in which 65 percent of charter school parents reported that their child previously attended a traditional public school. When asked to grade their current charter schools, 42 percent of New York charter school parents assigned their school an A grade overall (51% assigned an A for quality of instruction), compared to only 21 percent who gave the same grade to their child's previous school. The most common reply (33%) to a question about what their previous school did better than their charter school was "nothing" (Center for Education Reform, 2003).

Studies conducted in Arizona charter schools also indicate parent satisfaction with charter schools. A survey of parents with children in charter schools administered during the 2001-2002 academic year revealed that 66.9 percent of Arizona charter school parents assigned their charter schools an A or A+ rating, an increase from a 64 percent result a year earlier. When compared to the satisfaction of parents with traditional public schools in Arizona, the percentage of parents giving charter schools a grade of A or above is much greater than the 38 percent of Arizona's traditional public school parents who gave their schools similar grades in May 2000. The quality of academics at a charter school influenced the parents' grading more than the quality of after school programs, technology, or building facilities. Finally, the report concluded that parents tend to make informed decisions about where to have their children educated (Center for Education Reform, 2003).

A previous Arizona study (Gifford & Keller, 1996) investigated reasons why parents and students elected to leave a previous school and why they selected a specific charter school. Primarily, charter school parents removed their child from a traditional public school because of dissatisfaction with curriculum. Teacher attitude and class sizes were also popular choices; parents considered these same three reasons when selecting a specific charter school.

Charter schools offer parents a chance to have a voice in their child's education by creating or influencing decisions at their child's school. This sense of parental ownership and intimate connection to the school seems to outweigh low student achievement and problems with school management for many charter schools parents. Parental empowerment may explain why parents continue to support charter schools and claim that they offer a superior education to their public school equivalents, although the data on charter school achievement is mixed. Even though the research suggests that some charter schools are stronger than others, many parents continue to support charter schools, even those with poor achievement records and issues with school management.

For example, at the James Academy of Excellence in South Carolina, the school district withdrew its support of the charter school after it foresaw problems with school operations and the school building itself. Even as teachers at the school raised their concerns about disorganization and lack of a clear curriculum, parents were steadfast in their support of the school (Bruce, 2004). Parents seemed willing to overlook these serious foundational issues in favor of simply having an educational option for their children, despite the fact that this option has not been proven successful. An *Atlanta Journal-Constitution* letter to the editor ("In Children's Interest," 2004) asserts, "Eventually charter schools may be synonymous with academic excellence. Now it's enough that they stand for public school choice."

Although studies in the area of parent satisfaction with charter schools are not fully developed, research on voucher programs provide guidance. To illustrate, voucher studies show that vouchers may not actually provide a better education for students, yet many parents still hold the idea that voucher programs are better choices for their children. Goldhaber (2001) notes that parents base some schooling decisions on nonacademic characteristics of a school, such as the socioeconomic status of the students attending. Additionally, parents may be attracted to personal attention or stricter discipline guidelines. Further, studies regarding vouchers suggest that parents may choose voucher programs over public schools because of fear that promised public school improvements will not happen in time to benefit their children (Reid & Johnson, 2001).

Research findings about systemic effects of charter schools on schools districts have been mixed. Bulkley and Fisler (2002) cite several studies that have found little evidence of major district changes to improve the quality of traditional public schools in response to competition by charter schools. However, in a study of

49 school districts in five states (RPP International, 2001), evidence that charter schools had affected their district's budget, operations, and/or educational offerings was found in every instance. Nearly half of all district leaders perceived that charter schools had negatively affected their budget by taking revenues associated with students who transferred out of the district schools and into the charter schools. When legislation enables districts to recover funding lost from students that choose charter schools, however, negative financial impact is mitigated (RPP International, 2001). Other common responses to the charter schools included increased marketing and public relations efforts by the districts and the creation of new programs similar to those offered by the charter schools (Bulkley & Fisler, 2002).

Innovations in Curriculum and Instruction

One of the promises of the charter school movement is that, due to the increased autonomy they enjoy in comparison to traditional public schools, charter schools can experiment with many educational innovations. Charter school advocates argue that this flexibility has the potential to improve student performance through the development of high quality teaching and learning. Additionally, charter schools tend to attract pioneering educators who try new approaches to education that can be applied to the larger public education system if deemed effective. Specifically, the autonomy of charter schools appeals to innovative educators and allows them to implement these ideas effectively (Griffin & Wohlstetter, 2001; U.S. Department of Education, 2004b). However, there is a dearth of wide-scale research examining the pedagogy in charter schools; therefore, far less is known about what happens inside charter school classrooms than is known about how charter schools are organized and governed (Bulkley & Fisler, 2002).

Bulkley and Fisler (2002) describe a study in Michigan which concluded that charter schools were somewhat more likely to engage in curricular innovations than other public schools. Characteristics of innovative charter schools were motivation, lack of constraints, and an inclusive deliberative process within the school. Although some of the most innovative practices in Michigan were taking place in charter schools, the study noted, many charter schools were not engaging in new practices but instead were creating variations of practices already common in the traditional public school community (Bulkley & Fisler, 2002). Additionally, a report from the U.S. Department of Education (2004b) highlighting eight of the most successful charter schools in the United States recorded innovations in terms of creative organization, scheduling, curriculum, and instruction.

An earlier study (Griffin & Wohlstetter, 2001), which investigated instructional and organizational issues—including the design of an instructional program—faced in the start-up years of 17 charter schools across the United States observed in the charter school organizers a strong desire to create their own instructional program. However, this is a time-consuming task that conflicts with the demands of getting the charter school up and running quickly. Therefore, the researchers found that charter schools were using instructional programs that often featured curricula developed by educators outside the school. In the sample of charter schools in this study, slightly less than one-third of the schools (5 out of 17) were connected with national reform efforts and had instructional programs that were developed outside the school by education reformers. Other charter schools developed their instructional programs by putting together pieces from both original and pre-made sources.

Additionally, in this study, innovative instruction in the charter schools—whose enrollments ranged from 80 to 1,300 students—was characterized by low student/faculty ratios, small class size, and personalized learning, regardless of the educational level or the size of the charter school. Furthermore, personalized learning was emphasized and several of the schools featured individualized learning plans for all students. Instructional programs within charter schools tended to be interdisciplinary and focused on integrating the school with the community, often through applied projects (Griffin & Wohlstetter, 2001).

Achievement and Accountability

Charter school accountability has tended to focus on student achievement and fiscal management, and some charter schools have been successful in these regards while many others have had problems. This range in charter school quality can be explained by the lack of a uniform design among the large number of schools in operation (Rich, 2002). The threat of competition and failure force charter schools and their sponsors to maintain high standards of accountability, closely examining these issues.

When a charter school fails to meet the standards of accountability, there is the possibility that the charter could be revoked or not renewed. Revocation is the withdrawal of a school's charter during its term, while renewal relates to the decision by a charter-granting authority to enter into a new contract once the term of an existing contract expires (Mead, 2003). More than 6 percent of the total number of charter schools have been closed (Vergari, 2003). Although the rate of charter school closures has been compared favorably with the rate of small business closures, such closures present hardships for students. Additionally, there are several legal issues to consider during a revocation or nonrenewal of a charter.

Student Achievement

Despite the attention on student achievement as an accountability measure, there are few comprehensive studies involving student achievement in charter schools (Ryan & Heise, 2002; Walk, 2003). One explanation for the lack of data could relate to the fact that charter schools are fairly new. The data that does exist, however, is both contradictory and inconclusive (Mulholland, 1999; Ryan & Heise, 2002). Although the research indicates varied results (D. Bulkley, 2001; Horn & Mirᴎn, 1999; RPP International, 1999; Vergari, 2003), there is some evidence of success. For example, Holland and Soifer (2002) argue that charter schools nationwide have demonstrated impressive results. These researchers cite a 2000 Colorado Department of Education study that found charter schools perform 10 percent to 16 percent above state averages on standardized tests. Other successful studies

Holland and Soifer discuss include isolated incidents in various states, including Massachusetts and California.

Likewise, Ryan and Heise (2002) found promising results when they examined a 1999 Arizona study which concluded that charter school students were not performing very differently from Arizona's traditional public school students. Ryan and Heise (2002) noted that the researchers in Arizona, however, found that students enrolled in charter schools for two or three consecutive years had an advantage over those students who enrolled in Arizona's traditional public schools during this same time period. In a recent study comparing the reading and mathematics proficiency of charter school students to students in traditional public schools, charter school students were 4 percent more likely to be proficient in reading and 2 percent more likely to be proficient in math on their state's exams. This study compared charter school students to students in neighboring schools and covered 99 percent of fourth grade students enrolled in charter schools nationwide (Hoxby, 2004).

Conversely, a Brookings Institution study of ten states from 1999 to 2001 reported that charter school test scores were lower than traditional public schools (Brown Center on Education Policy, 2002). Most recently, the first national comparison of test scores among students in charter schools was released by the U.S. Department of Education. This report demonstrates that students attending charter schools are performing about a half year behind students attending traditional public schools in math and reading (Schemo, 2004). According to an American Federation of Teachers report, charter school students had lower achievement on the National Assessment of Educational Progress (NAEP) in both fourth and eighth grades as compared to traditional public school students (Nelson, Rosenberg, & Van Meter, 2004).

Advocates for charter schools argue that the lower levels of student achievement can be explained. The Center for Education Reform (2002) documented that charter schools have been successful in educating students who have been poorly served by the traditional public school system, including a large numbers of students from low-achieving backgrounds (Paige, 2004). Further, there are usually several start-up problems with new charter schools that are not considered.

As noted, charter schools are held to an elevated standard of accountability to the public regarding student achievement; however, few charter school authorizers have revoked the charter because of poor student achievement. Rather, these closures have generally resulted from fiscal or managerial problems in the schools (SRI International, 2002; Vergari, 2001).

Revocation

When it becomes necessary to revoke or not to renew a charter, state statutes vary over the details of these procedures. Generally, state statutes will allow for the revocation of a charter if there is a material violation of provisions of the charter, a failure to make reasonable progress toward the required educational objectives of the charter, a failure to comply with fiscal accountability procedures or fiscal management, or for a violation of any laws that have not been exempted by the charter (Wall, 1998). While the guidelines for revocation are generally clearly laid out, oftentimes the procedures upon closure or for appealing the closure are not as evident (Eckes & Plucker, 2004). However, some states have provided clarity on this issue. In Kansas, for example, there is legislation requiring the charter to contain a provision specifying "the manner in which contracts of employment and status of certified employees of the district who participate in the operation of the [charter] school will be dealt with upon nonrenewal or revocation of the charter . . . . " (Kan. Stat. Ann., 1996).

A recent case in Missouri further illustrates the need for policy clarification regarding revocation and renewal procedures. The School District of Kansas City, MO, agreed in 1999 to serve as the sponsor of Westport Community Secondary School in a charter agreement that did not expressly state its duration, although a Missouri state statute specified that a charter agreement may be no less than five years. From the time the charter commenced, the district did not obtain or commission an audit of Westport's performance or provide to Westport any reports alleging performance deficiencies (*School District of Kansas City*, 2004).

Five years after the charter school had been in operation, the district voted not to approve Westport's charter renewal application, effectively terminating the charter agreement. As a result, Westport initiated a lawsuit with the circuit court claiming that its due process rights were violated and that it was entitled to a hearing. In granting a preliminary injunction, the circuit court found that "the charter school statute is unclear and ambiguous in some respects" (*Westport Community*, 2004, p. 4) and that "the statute provides no guidance for the procedure of renewing or amending an existing charter" (p. 5). Therefore, because Westport Community Secondary School was not provided with the statutorily required process, the court decided that the district had no basis on which to deny the Westport renewal. An appeals court in Missouri, however, ruled in the district's favor regarding the closure of the Westport charter school (*School District*, 2004). The appeals court found that proper procedures had been followed. As a result of such cases, some have argued that state legislatures need to be more specific in drafting statutes on charter school revocation, renewal, and the appeal process (Eckes & Plucker, 2004). In doing so, state legislatures should ensure that statutes are constitutional, especially regarding due process and contracts.

Quality of the Research and Future Directions

The verdict is still out on charter schools. Much of the research on facets of charter schools is in early stages, and what evidence does exist on the performance of charter schools must be interpreted with caution. Specifically, there are several hurdles in assessing student achievement in charter schools—one of the main indicators used to judge school performance—including methodological problems regarding sample size, control groups, and selection bias (Vergari, 2003). As such, data regarding student achievement in charter schools is open to criticism. Further, Hoxby (2003) argues that asking about student achievement is the wrong question unless the achievement at the charter school can be compared to a regular public school with similar resources. If such comparisons are not made, she contends, the data is not credible. In the ideal studies, charter school students would be compared to students attending traditional public schools who had applied to the charter school but were rejected due to space. Therefore, we cannot say with certainty whether charter schools are more successful in improving student achievement than traditional public schools and, as such, none of the studies discussed in this chapter should be viewed as providing the definitive answer.

Additionally, the political climate regarding charter schools is highly charged, making objective understanding of the research difficult. Conflicting charter evaluation studies could be attributed to opposing positions using research as political ammunition to reach the desired conclusions (Center on Education Policy, 2000). In addition to politically motivated research, other challenges relate to designing an objective charter school study, as some questions will be difficult to answer no matter which method is used (see generally, Center on Education Policy). Currently, it is a challenge to determine how charter schools have affected the educational market, but as charter schools expand, it will be possible for studies to examine whether charter school competition spurs improvement in traditional public schools.

Accordingly, more high-quality studies that move beyond focusing primarily on student achievement would help reconcile the current contradictions in the research. Specifically, issues of equity and the impact of charter schools on traditional public schools as well as the innovations being implemented in charter school need more attention. Additionally, concerns over charter school management and the implications of cyber charters need to be further studied. The extensive body of research on the voucher program may be a useful resource for the design of more effective charter school studies. Finally, many other nations have choice programs, and a rigorous review of the international choice research could increase the domestic knowledge base.

There is still much to be learned about charter schools. Charter schools are a fairly recent phenomenon; therefore, they are still in their early stages of implementation. As charter schools mature, current findings will be challenged and new questions will emerge. As such, at this time it is difficult to determine the impact charter schools have had on student achievement, equity, and other areas. Although charter schools are not necessarily the panacea that some had hoped for, they have had a significant impact on education, and future evolutions of the movement should continue to do so.

References

Bodgen, J. (2003). Cyber charter schools: A new breed in the education corral. *The State Education Standard, 4*(3), 33-37.

The Brown Center on Education Policy. (2002). *The Brown Center Report on American education: How well are American students learning?* (Vol. 1, No. 3). Washington, DC: The Brookings Institution.

The Brown Center on Education Policy. (2003). *The 2003 Brown Center Report on American education: How well are American students learning?* (Vol. 1, No. 4). Washington, DC: The Brookings Institution.

Bruce, A. L. (2004, August 20). Parents, students try to save charter school. Dorchester District 2 officials withdrew support for James Academy of Excellence. *The Post and Courier* (Charleston, SC), 1B.

Bulkley, D. (2001, October 1). Educational performance and charter school authorizers: The accountability bind. *Education Policy Analysis Archives, 9*(37). Available at http://epaa.asu.edu/apaa/v9n37.html.

Bulkley, K. E. (2002, November). *Recentralizing decentralization? Educational management organizations and charter schools' education programs.* Paper presented at the Annual Meeting of the University Council for Educational Administration, Rutgers, NJ.

Bulkley, K. E., & Fisler, J. (2002). *A decade of charter schools: From theory to practice* (CPRE Policy Briefs RB-35). Philadelphia, PA: Consortium for Policy Research in Education.

Burian-Fitzgerald, M., & Harris, D. (2004). *Teacher recruitment and teacher quality: Are charter schools different?* (Policy Report No. 20). East Lansing: Michigan State University, The Education Policy Center.

Center for Education Reform. (2002). *Charter schools 2002: Results from CER's annual survey of America's charter schools.* Washington, DC: Author. Available at http://edreform.com/_upload/survey2002.pdf.

Center for Education Reform. (2003). *What the research reveals about charter schools: Summary and analyses of the studies.* Washington, DC: Author. Available at http://209.183.221.111/_upload/research.pdf.

Center for Education Reform. (2004). *Charter schools.* Available at www.edreform.com/index.cfm?fuseAction=state Stats&pSectionID=15&cSectionID=44.

Center on Education Policy. (2000). *School vouchers: What we know and don't know . . . and how we could learn more.* Washington DC: Author. Available at www.ctredpol.org/vouchers/schoolvouchers.pdf.

Chubb, J. E. (2003). Ignoring the market. *Education Next, 3*(2), 80-83.

Chubb, J. E., & Moe, T. (1990). *Politics, markets, and America's schools.* Washington, DC: The Brookings Institution.

Cobb, C. D., & Glass, G. V. (1999, January 14). Ethnic segregation in Arizona charter schools. *Education Policy Analysis Archives, 7*(1). Available at http://epaa.asu. edu/epaa/v7n1.

Conn, K. (2002). When school management companies fail: Righting educational wrongs. *Journal of Law and Education, 31*(3), 245-269.

Cook, G. (2002). *The cyber charter challenge. American School Board Journal, 189*(9). Available at www.asbj.com/2002/09/0902ASBJS2.pdf.

Drake, T., & Roe, W. (1999). *The principalship* (5th ed.). Upper Saddle River, NJ: Prentice Hall.

Dressler, B. (2001). Charter school leadership. *Education and Urban Society, 33*(2), 170-185.

Dykgraaf, C. L., & Lewis, S. K. (1998). For-profit charter schools: What the public needs to know. *Educational Leadership, 56*(2), 51-53.

Eckes, S. E., & Plucker, J. (2004). *Charter revocations: Legal considerations concerning procedure* (Education Policy

Briefs Vol. 2, No. 5). Bloomington: Indiana University, Center for Evaluation and Education Policy.

Eckes, S. E., & Plucker, J. (2005). Charter schools and gifted education: Legal obligations. *Journal of Law and Education, 34*(3), 1-24.

Eckes, S. E., & Rapp, K. (2005). *Racial segregation in charter schools: Legal and other influences on the current reality.* Manuscript submitted for publication.

Education Commission of the States. (2003). *Collective bargaining and teachers unions in a charter district.* Denver, CO: Author. Available at www.ecs.org/ clearinghouse/49/71/4971.pdf.

Elmore, R. F. (1988). Choice in public education. In W. L. Boyd & C. T. Kerchner (Eds.), *The politics of excellence and choice in education: 1987 yearbook of the Politics of Education Association* (pp. 79-98). New York: Falmer Press.

Finn, C. (1990). Why we need choice. In W. L. Boyd & H. J. Walberg (Eds.), *Choice in education: Potential and problems* (pp. 3-20). Berkeley, CA: McCutchan Publishing Corporation.

Finn, C., Manno, B., & Vanourek, G. (2000). *Charter schools in action: Renewing public education.* Princeton, NJ: Princeton University Press.

Fitzgerald, J., Harris, P., Huidekoper, P., & Mani, M. (1998, January). *1997 Colorado charter schools evaluation study: The characteristics, status and student achievement data of Colorado charter schools.* Denver, CO: The Clayton Foundation.

Frankenberg, E., & Lee, C. (2003). *Charter schools and race: A lost opportunity for integrated education.* Cambridge, MA: Harvard University, The Civil Rights Project. Available at www.civilrightsproject.harvard.edu/research/deseg/Charter_ Schools03.pdf.

Frankenberg, E., Lee, C., & Orfield, G. (2003). *A multiracial society with segregated schools: Are we losing the dream?* Cambridge, MA: Harvard University, The Civil Rights Project. Available at www.civilrightsproject.harvard.edu/research/reseg 03/AreWeLosingtheDream.pdf.

Gifford, M., & Keller, T. (1996). *Arizona's charter schools: A survey of parents* (Arizona Issue Analysis No. 140). Phoenix, AZ: The Goldwater Institute.

Goldhaber, D. (2001). *School choice as education reform: What do we know?* ERIC Digest No. 165. (ERIC Document Reproduction Service No. ED455342).

Good, T. L., & Braden, J. S. (2000). Charter schools: Another reform failure or a worthwhile investment? *Phi Delta Kappan, 81*(10), 745-750.

Green, P. C., III. (2001). Racial balancing provisions and charter schools: Are charter schools out on a constitutional limb? *Brigham Young University Education and Law Journal, 2001,* 65-84.

Griffin, N. C., & Wohlstetter, P. (2001). Building a plane while flying it: Early lessons from developing charter schools. *Teachers College Record, 103*(2), 336-365.

Haft, W. (1998). Charter schools and the nineteenth century corporation: A match made in the public interest. *Arizona State Law Journal, 30,* 1023-1089.

Harrington-Lueker, D. (2002). Charters, 10 years in. *American School Board Journal, 189*(11), 20-26.

Heubert, J. (1997, Summer). Schools without rules? Charter schools, federal disability law and the paradoxes of deregulation. *Harvard Civil Rights–Civil Liberties Law Review, 32,* 301-353.

Hoagie's Gifted Education Page. (n.d.). *Schools for the gifted.* Available at www.hoagiesgifted.org/schools.htm.

Hocschild, J. L., & Scovronick, N. (2003). *The American dream and the public schools.* New York: Oxford University Press.

Holland, R., & Soifer, D. (2002). How school choice benefits the urban poor. *Howard Law Journal, 45,* 337-374.

Horn, J., & Mir⬚n, G. (1999). *Evaluation of the Michigan public school academy initiative.* Kalamazoo: Western Michigan University, The Evaluation Center.

Howe, K., Eisenhart, M., & Betebenner, D. (2001). School choice crucible: A case study of Boulder Valley. *Phi Delta Kappan, 83*(2), 137-146.

Hoxby, C. (2003). School choice and school competition: Evidence from the United States. *Swedish Economic Policy Review, 10.* Available at http://econweb.fas.harvard.edu/faculty/hoxby/papers/hoxby_SEPR.pdf.

Hoxby, C. (2004). *A straightforward comparison of charter schools and regular public schools in the United States.* Available at http://econweb.fas.harvard.edu/faculty/hoxby/papers/hoxbyall charters.pdf.

Huerta, L. A., & Gonzalez, M. (2004). *Cyber and home school charter schools: How states are defining new forms of public schooling.* Available at www.ncspe.org/publications_files/Paper87.pdf.

In children's interest, look past numbers . . . (2004, August 20). [Letter to the editor]. *The Atlanta Journal–Constitution,* 20A.

Kafer, K. (2003). School choice in 2003: An old concept gains new life. New York University *Annual Survey of American Law, 59,* 439-458.

Kan. Stat. Ann. § 72-1906 (c)(13)(Supp. 1996).

Lacireno-Paquet, N. (2004, June 15). Do EMO-operated charter schools serve disadvantaged students? The influence of state policies. *Education Policy Analysis Archives, 12*(26). Available at http://epaa.asu.edu/epaa/v12n26.

Lacireno-Paquet, N., Holyoke, T. T., Moser, M., & Henig, J. R. (2002). Creaming versus cropping: Charter school enrollment practices in response to market incentives. *Educational Evaluation and Policy Analysis, 24*(2), 145-158.

Lane, B. (1998). *A profile of the leadership needs of charter school founders.* Portland, OR: Northwest Regional Educational Laboratory. (ERIC Document Reproduction Service No. ED424671).

Legislative Office of Education Oversight. (2004, March). *The start-up costs of Ohio's eCommunity schools.* Columbus, OH: Author. Available at www.loeo.state.oh.us/reports/PreEleSec PDF/eCommunitySchoolsWeb.pdf.

The limits of choice: School choice reform and state constitutional guarantees of educational quality. (1996). *Harvard Law Review, 109,* 2002-2019.

McKinney, J. (1996). Charter schools: A new barrier for children with disabilities. *Educational Leadership, 54*(2), 22-25.

Mead, J. (2002). Determining charter schools' responsibilities of children with disabilities: A guide through the legal labyrinth. *The Boston Public Interest Law Journal, 11*(2&3), 167-189.

Mead, J. (2003). Devilish details: Exploring features of charter school statues that blur the public/private distinction. *Harvard Journal on Legislation, 40*(2), 349-379.

Metrolina Regional Scholars' Academy. (n.d.). *Why MRSA?* Available at www.scholarsacademy.org.

Metzger, G. E. (2003). Privatization as delegation. *The Columbia Law Review, 103,* 1367-1502.

Minnesota Charter School Law, Minn. Stat. 124D.10 (1991).

Mintrom, M., & Vergari, S. (1997). Education reform and accountability issues in an intergovernmental context. *Publius: The Journal of Federalism, 27*(2), 143-166.

Muholland, L. A. (1999). *Arizona charter school progress evaluation.* Tempe, AZ: Arizona State University, Morrison Institute for Public Policy. Available at www.ade.az.gov/charter schools/info/CharterSchoolStatusMainReport3-15-99.pdf.

Nathan, J. (1996). *Charter schools: Creating hope and opportunity for American education.* San Francisco: Jossey-Bass.

National Center for Education Statistics. (2002). *The condition of education 2002* (NCES 2002-025). Washington, DC: U.S. Government Printing Office. Available at http://nces.ed.gov/pubs2002/2002025.pdf.

Nelson, F. H., Rosenberg, B., & Van Meter, N. (2004, August). *Charter school achievement on the 2003 National Assessment of Educational Progress.* Washington, DC: American Federation of Teachers, AFL-CIO.

Paige, R. (2004). *Paige issues statement regarding New York Times article on charter schools.* U.S. Department of Education Press Release. Available at www.ed.gov/news/pressreleases/2004/08/08172004.html.

Parker, W. (2001). The color of choice: Race and charter schools. *Tulane Law Review, 75*(3), 563-626.

Peterson, P. E. (1998). School choice: A report card. *Virginia Journal of Social Policy and Law, 6,* 47-80.

Plank, D. N., Arsen, D., & Sykes, G. (2000). Charter schools and private profits. *School Administrator, 57*(5), 12-18.

Reid, K. S., & Johnson, R. C. (2001). Public debates, private choices. *Education Week, 21*(14).

Reinhard, J. R., & Lee, J. F., Jr. (1991). *American education and the dynamics of choice.* New York: Praeger.

Rich, W. (2002). Putting black kids into a trick bag: Anatomizing the inner-city public school reform. *Michigan Journal of Race and Law, 8*(1), 159-190.

RPP International. (1999). *The state of charter schools, third year report: National Study of Charter Schools.* Washington, DC: U.S. Department of Education, Office of Educational Research and Improvement.

RPP International. (2000). *The state of charter schools, fourth year report: National Study of Charter Schools.* Washington, DC: U.S. Department of Education, Office of Educational Research and Improvement.

RPP International. (2001). *Challenge and opportunity: The impact of charter schools on school districts.* Washington, DC: U.S. Department of Education, Office of Educational Research and Improvement.

RPP International and the University of Minnesota. (1997). *A study of charter schools: First-year report.* Washington, DC: U.S. Department of Education, Office of Educational Research and Improvement.

Ryan, J., & Heise, M. (2002). The political economy of school choice. *Yale Law Journal, 111*(8), 2043-2136.

Saporito, S., & Lareau, A. (1999). School selection as a process: The multiple dimensions of race in framing educational choice. *Social Problems, 46*(3), 418-439.

Sarason, S. (1999). Leadership and charter schools. *International Journal of Leadership in Education, 2*(4), 379-381.

Schemo, D. J. (2004, August 17). Charter schools trail in results, U.S. data reveals. *The New York Times,* A1.

School District of Kansas City v. Williamson, 141 S.W.3d 418 (Mo. Ct. App. 2004).

Smith, K., & Willcox, J. (2004). A building need. *Education Next, 4*(2), 44-51. Available at www. educationnext.org/20042/44.html.

SRI International. (2002). *A decade of public charter schools* (SRI Project No. P03615). Washington, DC: Author. Available at www.sri.com/policy/cep/choice/yr2.pdf.

Stargate School. (n.d.). *The Stargate Solution.* Available at www.stargateschool.org/brochure.html.

Sykes, L., Jr. (2004, March 14). In seeking best education, some choose segregation. *Milwaukee Journal Sentinel,* A1.

Townley, A. (2000). Charter schools. In W. Camp, M. J. Connelly, K. Lane, & J. Mead (Eds.), *The principal's legal handbook* (2nd ed.) (pp. 351-357). Dayton, OH: Education Law Association.

U.S. Charter Schools. (n.d.). *Overview.* Available at www.uscharterschools.org/pub/uscs_docs/o/index. htm#national.

U.S. Department of Education. (1998). *Charter schools and students with disabilities.* Review of existing data. Washington, DC: Office of Educational Research and Improvement.

U.S. Department of Education. (2000). *Charter schools and students with disabilities: A national study.* Washington, DC: Office of Educational Research and Improvement.

U.S. Department of Education. (2004a). *Evaluation of the public charter schools program: Final report.* Washington, DC: Office of the Deputy Secretary. Available at www.ed.gov/ rschstat/eval/choice/pcsp-final/index.html.

U.S. Department of Education. (2004b). *Innovations in education: Successful charter schools.* Washington, DC: Office of Innovation and Improvement. Available at www.ed.gov/admins/ comm/choice/charter.

Vergari, S. (2001). Charter school authorizers: Public agents for holding charter schools accountable. *Education and Urban Society, 33*(2), 129-140.

Vergari, S. (2003). Charter schools: A significant precedent in public education. *New York University Annual Survey of American Law, 59*(3), 495-512.

Walk, D. (2003). How educational management companies serve charter schools and their students. *Journal of Law & Education, 32*(2), 241-254.

Wall, J. (1998). The establishment of charter schools: A guide to legal issues for legislatures. *Brigham Young University Education and Law Journal, 1998*(1), 69-102.

Wamba, N., & Ascher, C. (2003). An examination of charter school equity. *Education and Urban Society, 35*(4), 462-476.

Wells, A. S. (Ed.). (2002). *Where charter school policy fails: The problems of accountability and equity.* New York: Teachers College Press.

Wells, A. S., Holme, J. J., Lopez, A., & Cooper, C. W. (2000). Charter schools and racial and social class segregation: Yet another sorting machine? In R. Kahlenberg (Ed.), *A nation at risk: Preserving education as an engine for social mobility* (pp. 169-222). New York: Century Foundation Press.

Westport Community Secondary Schools v. School District of Kansas City, Missouri, Case No. 04CV212292 (Div. No. 11, 2004).

Zollers, N. J., & Ramanathan, A. K. (1998). For-profit charter schools and students with disabilities: The sordid side of the business of schooling. *Phi Delta Kappan, 80*(4), 297-304.

CHAPTER 2

ENHANCING OR DESTROYING EQUITY? AN EXAMINATION OF EDUCATIONAL VOUCHERS

Kim K. Metcalf and Kelli M. Paul

Research on educational programs often focuses on their impacts on measurable student outcomes, usually students' academic achievement. This emphasis on what might be considered traditional academic goals is both reinforced by and reinforces policy trends that similarly use academic achievement as the primary measure of efficacy. Research and policy on vouchers is no exception to this pattern and, in many ways, may represent the prime example, as this factor tends to be highlighted more than any other by both advocates and opponents.

Students' learning of academic content is, undeniably, an important purpose of public education. As such, it is a legitimate goal and point of focus for researchers and for policy makers. However, academic learning is not the only product of public education or voucher programs, and it is only one of several factors that families cite as important to them when they choose their children's schools. In fact, we have hypothesized that these factors, including but not limited to academic achievement, may reflect low-income parents' desire to leverage their limited social capital to obtain greater social capital for their children by using a voucher (Metcalf & Legan, 2005; Metcalf, Legan, & Paul, 2003). Whether or not this and similar hypotheses are true, those on both sides of the voucher issue agree that such programs are likely to influence, perhaps substantially, differences between and among groups of different economic means, education, race, and ethnicity.

In the remainder of this work, we examine what is known about school voucher programs in the U.S., with emphasis on describing our own research on the publicly funded voucher program in Cleveland, Ohio. We begin not with an exhaustive review of literature, but with a discussion of the structure and operation of several of the more substantive voucher programs operating in the U.S. This is followed by a brief synthesis of research drawn from across these programs. We then turn to a summary of our longitudinal work in Cleveland, including an overview of findings from across the seven years of the project. We close with an examination of potential implications for current and future school voucher programs.

Publicly Funded Voucher Programs

Five publicly funded voucher programs currently exist in the United States: the Milwaukee Parental Choice Program, the Cleveland Scholarship and Tutoring Program, the Opportunity Scholarship Program and the McKay Scholarship Program in Florida, and the federally funded Opportunity Scholarship Program in Washington, DC. Though the programs share many similarities, each is unique in its own right. Each program is described below, and when applicable, information is given on evaluations conducted of the programs.

The Milwaukee Parental Choice Program

The oldest and largest publicly funded voucher program, the Milwaukee Parental Choice Program (MPCP) targets low-income students residing in Milwaukee, Wisconsin. Designed as an experimental program, a random selection process was employed to select students applying for enrollment in oversubscribed schools (Witte, 2000). In its first year of operation (1990-1991), the program served 341 students in 7 schools (Witte, 1998). By the 2004-2005 academic year, however, the program had grown and currently serves over 15,000 students in approximately 117 schools (MPCP, 2004). Since its inception in 1990, the program has undergone two expansions, the first of which occurred in 1993 when the program increased the percentage of choice students allowed per school, the total number of students who could participate, and the maximum amount of the voucher. The second expansion occurred in 1995 when the MPCP allowed religious private schools to participate for the first time and once again increased the maximum amount of the voucher, to $4,600 (Witte, 2000).

Conducted by a research team led by John Witte, the evaluation of the MPCP began in 1990 and continued for four years. During the evaluation, various data were collected on the students, families, and schools that participated in the MPCP. Specifically, data on various outcomes (e.g., achievement, attendance, parental attitudes, etc.) were collected using parent surveys, achievement tests, and case studies (Witte, 2000). The most attention—and consequently the most debate—has focused on the impact of using a voucher on the outcome of student achievement.

Over time and due to the application and selection process, multiple groups of students were available for study (e.g., selected choice students, nonselected choice students, choice students who left the program, students in the control group in the Milwaukee Public Schools [MPS] who never applied to the program). In order to determine the impacts of using a voucher on student achievement, Witte argued that the most appropriate comparison was between choice students and the random sample of low-income students enrolled in the MPS (as opposed to the full control group of MPS students). The low-income control group was composed of students within the Milwaukee Public Schools that qualified for free and reduced-price lunch (1.35 times and 1.85 times the poverty line, respectively), and since the majority of the low-income control group qualified for free lunch, they would have been eligible for the choice program (Witte, 1998, 2000). Though not the primary focus of the evaluation, Witte compared choice students and the full MPS control group as well as nonselected choice applicants (Witte, 1998, 2000).

The Cleveland Scholarship and Tutoring Program
Until 1996, the MPCP was the only publicly funded voucher program in the United States. However, the Cleveland Scholarship and Tutoring Program (CSTP) in Cleveland, Ohio, became the second such program when it was enacted in 1995 and began enrolling students during the 1996-1997 school year. Unlike the MPCP, the CSTP included parochial schools from the beginning. Initially, students in kindergarten through third grade were eligible for a scholarship, with an expected expansion by one grade per year. Over 30,000 students within Cleveland were eligible to apply for a scholarship in the program's first year, with just over 6,000 applications being received. In 1996-1997, approximately 1,800 students used a scholarship to attend one of 41 participating private schools (Metcalf, Boone, Stage, Chilton, Muller, & Tait, 1998). By the 2004-2005 academic year, over 5,000 students in 45 private schools enrolled in kindergarten through tenth grade participated in the program (www.schoolchoiceinfo.org/facts; www.ode.state.oh.us/school_options).

In the nine years of the program's existence, few changes have been made to the CSTP. The first major programmatic changes since its inception in 1996 occurred during the summer of 2003. While the program remains focused on providing private school choice to low-income families residing within the enrollment boundaries of the Cleveland Municipal School District, two changes served to expand the program. First, the program was expanded into high school, as previously students were able to use a scholarship only through eighth grade. However, beginning in the 2003-2004 academic year, students who had used a scholarship to attend a private school in eighth grade during the previous year were eligible for a scholarship for enrollment in ninth grade. Similarly, during the following academic year (2004-

2005), students who used a scholarship in ninth grade were eligible for a scholarship for tenth grade. The second change increased the amount of tuition that could be covered by the scholarship and differentiated between the amount that could be used for scholarships for students enrolled in grades K-8 and in grades 9-12 (Metcalf, Legan, Paul, & Boone, 2004).

Evaluation of the CSTP was conducted by Kim Metcalf and a research team from Indiana University. Details of the evaluation methodology and its findings are presented later in this chapter.

Florida's Opportunity Scholarship Program and the McKay Scholarship Program
In 1999, Florida passed and implemented two scholarship programs aimed at improving the performance of students and schools. Unlike other voucher programs in the United States, the programs in Florida do not just target low-income families. Rather, the Opportunity Scholarship Program targets schools, not individual students per se, and the McKay Scholarship Program targets special education students. Both programs, however, expand the range of educational choices available to students and their families by providing vouchers for students to attend private or parochial schools.

The Opportunity Scholarship Program. The Opportunity Scholarship Program was created under the Bush/Brogan A+ Plan in 1999, and despite being the state's most well-known school choice option, it is the least often utilized (Richard, 2004). The program, also known as Florida's A+ Program, combines two of the most contentious education reform policies: vouchers and high stakes testing. Students in all Florida public schools take the state's accountability test, the Florida Comprehensive Assessment Test (FCAT), and based on their students' scores on the FCAT, all public schools receive a grade (A through F). If a school receives a failing grade of F for any two years during a four-year period, the school is considered to be a chronically failing school, and parents whose children attend that school are allowed the choice to move their child to a higher performing public school or to receive state funding (a voucher) to enroll their child in a private school. The theory behind the program is that the provision of scholarships will help failing schools improve by motivating the schools to improve their performance in order to avoid the embarrassment of receiving a failing grade and possibly losing revenue due to students receiving vouchers to attend other schools (Greene, 2001; Greene & Winters, 2003).

During 1999-2000, the Opportunity Scholarship Program's first year of implementation, two schools were labeled as failing. Vouchers were offered to students in these two schools, and parents of 52 children chose to enroll their children in a private school using a voucher, and parents of 78 children chose to enroll their children in a public school other than their assigned school (Greene, 2001). No new scholarships were awarded in 2000-2001 or in 2001-2002 since no Florida school received a second failing grade. However, in 2002-2003 ten new schools received a second failing grade, and in 2003-2004 twenty-one schools in nine counties were designated as receiving two Fs, making students at these schools eligible for an Opportunity Scholarship (Greene & Winters, 2003). By the 2004-2005 academic year, student enrollment in the program had increased to over 690 students (Sack, 2004).

Currently, the future of the Opportunity Scholarship Program is uncertain as legal battles over its constitutionality continue to be debated in the Florida Supreme Court. Florida District Courts of Appeals have struck down the program three times since 2002, with the most recent ruling on November 12, 2004, calling the program unconstitutional since it allows students to attend religious schools using funds from taxpayers, which is a violation of the state's constitution (Richard, 2004; Sack, 2004).

The McKay Scholarship Program. The McKay Scholarship Program for Students with Disabilities was created by the Florida legislature in 1999. This program is the only school choice program in the U.S. specifically designed for special education students. The McKay Program provides vouchers to any special education student enrolled in Florida public schools for at least one year. The program was fully implemented in the 2000-2001 academic year after a one-year demonstration period. With over 374,000 special education students in Florida public schools in 2001-2002 alone, the McKay Program has the largest pool of potential participants of any choice program in existence in the country. Currently just over 9,000 students use McKay vouchers to attend private schools. Unlike the programs in Milwaukee and Cleveland, students who use McKay vouchers are not randomly selected or assigned to use or not use a voucher; rather, all special education students are eligible to use a voucher (Greene & Forster, 2003).

The Opportunity Scholarship Program in Washington, DC

The Opportunity Scholarship Program in Washington, DC, not only is the newest publicly funded voucher program but also is the first federally funded voucher program in the United States. Operated by the Washington Scholarship Fund, the program targets low-income families residing within the District of Columbia and provides them with the opportunity to enroll their children in private schools using a voucher. Scholarships cover costs associated with tuition, fees, and transportation expenses up to a maximum value of $7,500. Eligible families must have students who are entering grades K-12 and have a family income at or below 185 percent of the poverty level. Prior to the first year of the scholarship program, over 2,700 applications were accepted, with over 1,800 applicants being eligible for the program. A two-phase lottery system is utilized to award scholarships to students, with the first lottery awarding scholarships to students conditionally upon being accepted into a private school. The second phase of the lottery is used only if the school and grade to which a student applies for enrollment is oversubscribed. Of the eligible applicants in 2004-2005, over 1,000 enrolled in 53 private schools (Washington Scholarship Fund, 2004a, 2004b).

Privately Funded Voucher Programs

In addition to the publicly funded voucher programs described above, there are numerous privately funded voucher programs in operation in the United States. Four of the most researched programs are described below. Specifically, the four programs are located in New York City, Washington, DC, Dayton, Ohio, and San Antonio, Texas.

Programs in New York City, Washington, DC, and Dayton, Ohio
Privately funded voucher programs were created in New York City, Washington, DC, and Dayton, Ohio. All three were designed as randomized field trials, and separate evaluations were conducted of each program using similar methodologies (Howell & Peterson, 2002). These three voucher programs shared many similarities. Specifically, all three programs gave participants a full choice of private schools; all three held lotteries for selection and awarding of vouchers; all three provided vouchers of relatively small size; and most importantly, as mentioned above, all three were designed as randomized field trials.

In 1997, the School Choice Scholarship Foundation (SCSF) initiated a program whereby 1,300 scholarships would be provided to low-income families with students in grades K-4 in New York City public schools so that students could transfer from public to private schools. Vouchers were worth up to $1,400 and could be used for up to four years at a religious or secular school. The evaluation of the program was conducted between spring 1997 and June 2000. The program in Washington, DC, served students in kindergarten through eighth grade and was funded by the Washington Scholarship Fund. Evaluation of this program was conducted between spring 1998 and May 2001. Finally, Parents Advancing Choice in Education funded the voucher program in Dayton, Ohio. Similar to the program in Washington, DC, Dayton's program served students enrolled in kindergarten through eighth grade. The evaluation of the Dayton program was conducted between spring 1998 and May 2000.

Similar methodology was used in all three cities, enabling comparisons to be made between the three programs. In each city, baseline data were collected prior to the lottery to assign vouchers randomly to students, the lottery was then held, and subsequent data were collected from participants. Because lotteries were used, students were either assigned to the treatment group (awarded a voucher) or to the control group (did not receive a voucher). The evaluation sought to examine the effect of changing from a public to a private school; therefore, comparisons were made between students who used a voucher to switch from a public to a private school and students who remained in public schools but who would have used a voucher had it been offered to them (Howell & Peterson, 2002).

The Children's Educational Opportunity Program in San Antonio, Texas

The Children's Educational Opportunity (CEO) Program provides partial tuition scholarships to low-income families so that they may enroll their children in private schools in San Antonio or in public schools outside of the San Antonio Independent School District (SAISD). The scholarships cover half of the tuition at a private school, with a maximum value of $750. Unlike voucher programs that use a lottery to award vouchers, the CEO Program awards scholarships on a first-come, first-served basis, and as a result students are not randomly selected to receive a scholarship. To be eligible for a scholarship, students must reside in the San Antonio metropolitan area and must qualify for free or reduced-price lunch. Scholarships are given to families of students whose children were enrolled in public schools as well as to families whose children already are enrolled in private schools, so as not to penalize low-income families who have made necessary sacrifices to send their children to private schools. During the 1992-1993 academic year, the program's first year of operation, 936 students were provided with scholarships to attend private schools. Two years later, the program continued to be oversubscribed with over

1,800 names on the waiting list (Martinez, Godwin, & Kemerer, 1995).

Findings from Publicly and Privately Funded Voucher Programs

Evaluations have been conducted on most if not all of the previously described programs. Typically, the evaluations have focused on student outcomes such as student achievement, but factors related to the characteristics of students and families who participated in the programs also have been examined. While some findings have been consistent across programs, other findings have yielded discrepancies. The major findings from these studies are presented below.[1]

Student Characteristics

The majority of both publicly and privately funded voucher programs target low-income students and families so as to provide the opportunity to attend private school to students who, without a voucher, would not otherwise have the option of enrolling in these schools. Research suggests that these programs are successful in attracting and awarding vouchers to the students and families that they target.

---

[1] Findings from the Opportunity Scholarship Program in Washington, DC, and the McKay Scholarship and Opportunity Scholarship Programs in Florida are not included in this discussion due to reasons specific to each program. The evaluation of the DC program is still in its infancy, so little data is currently available. The McKay program targets special education students, and results from this program have limited generalizability beyond special education populations. However, specific findings from the program can be found in Greene and Forster (2003). Finally, the Opportunity Scholarship Program in Florida examines the impact of the program on public schools (e.g., whether the increased choice provided by the program causes schools to improve) rather than individual student achievement. Results from evaluations of this program can be found in Greene (2001) and Greene and Winters (2003).

Families of choice students (both students who applied for but were not awarded a voucher and students who were awarded a voucher) in Milwaukee were found to be similar to one another and to the low-income public school control group. However, each of these groups differed from the overall public school control group that included students representing families of all income levels, indicating that the program was serving the low-income families that it specifically targeted (Witte, 2000). Similar results were obtained in Dayton, Washington, DC, and New York City, where students using a voucher and those who declined an offered voucher were from low-income families (Howell & Peterson, 2002). The CEO program in San Antonio also targets low-income families. However, while the majority of families of voucher users reported incomes below $20,000 annually, these families were found to have slightly higher incomes than families who chose not to apply for a voucher (Martinez, Godwin, & Kemerer, 1995).

Choice students in Milwaukee were more likely to be African American and Hispanic, more often were from families headed by a single parent, had fewer children, had mothers who were more educated, were more religiously observant, and were less mobile than nonchoosing students in the public school control groups (Howell & Peterson, 2002; Witte, 2000). The CEO Program in San Antonio yielded similar findings, such that choice students came from smaller families with more educated parents than nonchoosing students (Martinez, Godwin, & Kemerer, 1995).

While there were similarities with the findings in Milwaukee and San Antonio, comparisons of students that used a voucher with students who declined an offered voucher revealed slight differences between programs in Dayton, Ohio, Washington, DC, and New York City. In both Dayton and Washington, DC, students who chose to use a voucher had mothers with more education than students who did not use a voucher. While there were no differences in mother's education between students who did and did not use a voucher in New York City, the level of education was similar to mothers in Dayton and Washington, DC (approximately 12 to 13 years of education). Additionally, in New York City, students using a voucher were more likely to be African American than were students who declined a voucher. However, it should be noted that the majority of students who used and declined a voucher in Dayton were White, but the opposite was found in Washington, DC, where the majority of students (over 90%) were African American. Similarly, in New York City, just over 40 percent of students who either used or declined a voucher were African American and 40 percent were Hispanic (Howell & Peterson, 2002).

Motivation for Participation in a Voucher Program
Families who choose to participate in voucher programs tend to be motivated to do so for similar reasons. Parents indicate that various factors are important in their decision to apply for a voucher, the most important of which are educational quality, teacher quality, teaching style and content, and school discipline. Religious instruction and the location of the school also are identified as important reasons for participating in voucher programs (Howell & Peterson, 2002; Witte, 2000). Contrary to popular belief, despite exercising choice by applying for a voucher, not all students offered a voucher to attend private school actually do so. The most common reason given by families for not using an offered voucher was that the family was unable to pay the remaining tuition and costs not covered by the voucher. So, while vouchers do provide financial assistance to families that otherwise might not be able to consider enrolling their child in a private school, sometimes the remaining costs beyond those covered by the voucher are too much for families to bear. Other reasons for not using a voucher include a lack of transportation, lack of space in a desired school, or the late notification of a voucher award (Howell & Peterson, 2002).

Parental Satisfaction
Satisfaction (or more accurately, dissatisfaction) also seems to be a motivating factor for families to participate in voucher

programs. Parents who apply for vouchers tend to be less satisfied with their child's public schools than parents of public school students who do not apply for a voucher. Additionally, parents of children enrolled in private schools using a voucher report higher levels of satisfaction with their children's private school than parents of public school children. Specifically, parents of private school students report greater satisfaction with their child's school overall as well as with various aspects of the school, including location, school safety, teaching, parental involvement, class size, school facilities, discipline, and academic quality—many of the same factors with which they were the most dissatisfied in their child's prior public school (Howell & Peterson, 2002; Mayer, Peterson, Myers, Tuttle, & Howell, 2002; Peterson, Howell, Wolf, & Campbell, 2003; Witte, 2002).

However, to gain a better understanding of parental satisfaction generally as well as the impacts of participation in a voucher program on satisfaction, an important question is whether satisfaction levels are maintained with continued participation in the program or whether the initially high satisfaction levels are due to other factors (e.g., simply being awarded a voucher or having the opportunity to choose one's child's school). While parents of students using vouchers tended to remain more satisfied than parents of public school children overall, there is some evidence of a decrease in satisfaction over time. Specifically, while satisfaction levels remained fairly stable in Washington, DC, and New York City, the satisfaction of parents in the Dayton program decreased between years one and two (Howell & Peterson, 2002).

Parental Involvement
One expectation of vouchers is that they will increase parents' involvement in their children's education. As a result of having the opportunity to select their children's school through the use of a voucher, it is believed that parents will become more engaged in their children's education. Across all student groups and prior to entering the program, families of students in New York City, Dayton, and Washington, DC, exhibited high levels of

parental involvement. Contrary to what was expected, after having used an awarded voucher, there seemed to be little additional impact on parental involvement (Howell & Peterson, 2002). Different results were found in Milwaukee, where findings were more consistent with expectations of parent involvement. Prior to entering the voucher program, parents of choice students were found to be more involved in their child's education than public school families. After having participated in the program, parental involvement increased significantly, indicating parents' increased engagement in their child's education (Witte, 2000).

Academic Achievement
        While evaluations of voucher programs have examined many factors, their primary focus has been on impacts of the program (e.g., using a voucher) on students' academic achievement. As a result, the findings regarding achievement typically receive the most attention and often are the most debated among researchers. For example, Witte's analyses regarding the effect of the Milwaukee Parental Choice Program (MPCP) on student achievement are some of the most contested of his findings from the evaluation (Powers & Cookson, 1999). Upon release of the annual evaluation reports and data, the data were reanalyzed by multiple researchers, each with differing results.
        Witte found inconsistent effects of the voucher program in Milwaukee on the achievement of choice and public school students. While some significant gains were found in reading and mathematics, most comparisons were not significant and negative for choice students. In reading, few effects were found, with the only significant finding actually favoring public school students, while in mathematics no differences were found between choice and public school students. As a result, Witte concluded that there were no differences in reading and mathematics between choice and public school students (Witte, 2000).
        Contrary to Witte's findings, reanalyses of the data by Greene, Peterson, Du, Boeger, and Frazier (1996) suggested a trend over time in student performance favoring choice students.

Greene et al. argued that Witte's focus on comparisons between choice students and public school control group students was not the most appropriate focus. Rather, they argued that it was more appropriate to focus on the comparison between choice and nonselected choice students, both groups being formed as a result of the experimental design of the MPCP. When comparisons were made between these two groups (and after correcting for errors found in the original data), Greene et al. reported advantages for choice students enrolled in the program for three or more years. Specifically, choice students enrolled in the program continuously for three or more years outperformed nonselected students in both reading (3-5 percentile points higher) and mathematics (5-12 percentile points higher).

Further reanalyses of the data were conducted by Rouse (1998), with her analyses building upon those of both Witte and Greene. Similar to Witte and Greene, she included both unsuccessful applicants (nonselected choice students) and a random sample of public school students as comparison groups. However, her analyses differ from Witte and Greene in that she controlled for individual fixed-effects. Once again, the analyses resulted in inconsistent results, such that her findings for reading achievement differed from the findings of Greene, while her findings for mathematics achievement differed from those of Witte. Specifically, Rouse found that scores for reading were inconsistent over the years and gains were not different from zero. However, in mathematics, achievement scores were found to increase by 1.5-2.3 percentile points for choice students per year (Rouse, 1998).

Similar to the results from Milwaukee, the findings from New York City, Dayton, and Washington, DC, have received much attention and debate. These achievement data also have been subjected to reanalysis by other researchers who question the findings obtained as part of the evaluations conducted of the programs. In the evaluations of each program, all achievement analyses controlled for students' baseline scores obtained prior to the lottery. As a result, all findings represent the value added to a student's achievement by having participated in the voucher program. No overall impact of switching from a public to a private school was found. However, when results were examined by ethnic group, positive impacts were found for African American students but not for students of other backgrounds. This finding is consistent with prior research which has shown positive impacts of attending a private versus a public school, especially for African American students (Howell & Peterson, 2002).

Overall, African American students using a voucher gained approximately 3.9 percentile points in year one, 6.3 percentile points in year two, and 6.6 percentile points in year three. However, findings differed slightly between cities, such that in Dayton and Washington, DC, significant impacts were found only in year two, while findings in New York City were significant all three years of the evaluation for African American students. The most dramatic effects were found in New York City, where students gained 5.4, 4.3, and 9.2 percentile points in years one, two, and three, respectively (Howell & Peterson, 2002; Mayer, Peterson, Myers, Tuttle, & Howell, 2002). Speculating on the differences observed between the three cities, the researchers suggested that the findings in New York City may be more consistent than in either Dayton or Washington, DC, for four reasons: (1) New York City had a higher response rate; (2) the voucher usage rate was higher in New York City; (3) the emergence of charter schools in Washington, DC, led to many students in both public and private schools switching to charter schools; and (4) the quality of private schools was higher in New York City, where Catholic schools were more established than in the other two cities (Howell & Peterson, 2002).

Krueger and Zhu reanalyzed the achievement data collected in New York City. The data from New York City, rather than that from either of the other two cities, was selected for reanalysis for three reasons: (1) the data was made available for reanalysis; (2) the program in New York City was the best documented program, and of the three programs it had the lowest attrition rate, the highest rate of voucher uptake, and the largest sample size; and (3)

New York City was the only city that showed statistically significant gains in test scores for voucher recipients as compared to nonrecipients for African Americans at the end of the three-year experiment (Krueger & Zhu, 2004).

The reanalyses by Krueger and Zhu differed from the analyses of Howell and Peterson in four ways. First, Krueger and Zhu included students with missing baseline scores in the majority of their analyses, whereas Howell and Peterson did not. Krueger and Zhu argued that including students without baseline scores was justified and appropriate because random assignment handled the issue of missing baseline scores, and including these students increased sample size and generalizability. Second, Krueger and Zhu defined race more inclusively because Howell and Peterson suggested that student race impacted achievement gain, since effects were found only for African American students. While Howell and Peterson classified a student's race according to the race of the child's mother, Krueger and Zhu defined a child's race symmetrically across both the child's mother and father, such that information on both parents was utilized in determining a child's race. Third, while Howell and Peterson focused on the impact of switching from a public to a private school using a voucher, Krueger and Zhu focused on the "intent to treat," or the impact of offering a voucher on student achievement. They argued that the intention of treatment was more relevant to policy than the effect of changing from a public to private school. Finally, the reanalyses corrected for errors in the initial baseline weights and included families, not students, as the unit of analysis since the family was assigned a voucher via the lottery, not the individual student (Krueger & Zhu, 2004).

The findings suggested that the positive effect of vouchers on the achievement of African American students in New York City was less robust than was presented by Howell and Peterson. As a result, Krueger and Zhu concluded that there was little evidence to suggest that vouchers affected the achievement of African Americans more than would be expected by chance (Krueger & Zhu, 2004). In response to these reanalyses, Peterson and Howell

(2004) argued that including students without baseline scores and employing a more inclusive definition for the classification of race did not eliminate the effects of participation in the voucher program on the achievement of African American students.

Conflicting Results and Calls for
Randomized Field Trials

The results described above suggest that methodological arguments about the most appropriate way to study voucher programs have been nearly as frequent and often as contentious as debate of the issue itself. For a variety of reasons, those who have engaged in research on voucher programs (and the even greater number who merely critique such research) have employed or advocated somewhat divergent designs in their work. Paul Peterson of Harvard has been among the strongest voices for the application of randomized field trials as a way both to improve the robustness of findings and to provide commonality across studies. By randomly assigning children from families who applied for a voucher to receive or not to receive a voucher, it is assumed that two groups result that are equivalent in all ways except the instrumental variable: use of a voucher.

However, even randomized designs present a number of complications when applied to the study of voluntary programs. For example, members assigned to the treatment group refuse treatment, members assigned to the control group find other ways to receive the treatment, or members of both groups are unavailable for collection of data. Each of these complications arose in the evaluations conducted of privately funded voucher programs in New York City, Dayton, and Washington, DC; and to some extent these complications were found in publicly funded programs in Milwaukee and Cleveland. Further, and despite these issues, Heckman (1997) has suggested that random assignment of subjects to a desired program introduces a nonrandom but idiosyncratic factor that enhances the positive effect of the treatment for those who are selected to participate. In combination, these factors present a set of challenges in the research of voucher programs that few studies have been able either to address adequately or to overcome.

Evaluation of the Cleveland
Scholarship and Tutoring Program

We believe that the "choice-rich" environment in Cleveland provides a particularly unique context in which to examine the various impacts on students and families of school choice generally and vouchers specifically. The publicly funded voucher program is certainly the most visible and contentious of the choice options available to families in Cleveland, but it is not the only option available to students. Nearly 20 charter schools operate within the boundaries of the Cleveland Municipal School District (CMSD). However, even within the traditional public school realm, there are a range of choices available. Families who desire additional assistance for their children but who want to remain in public schools have multiple alternatives, including enrollment in one of several magnet schools located throughout the city. Public school families may also take advantage of a limited interdistrict choice program that allows them to select from among a small number of public schools located comparatively near their home. Beyond this, for families wishing to continue their involvement in public schools, the same program that provides publicly funded vouchers also provides tutoring grants that allow public school families to access additional assistance for their children from among a pool of authorized tutors.

This range of publicly funded educational options provides the opportunity to study the operation and impact of particular choice programs, like vouchers, in a setting where the program is not the sole alternative for families to traditional public school enrollment. In the approach we have taken to evaluating the voucher program in Cleveland, we attempted to take advantage of this unique context in a number of ways. Underlying our approach has been a focus on continuing to collect data on students as they move to and from particular school settings (e.g., public and private schools). As a function of this ongoing process, we have been able to identify multiple comparison groups reflecting somewhat distinct patterns of choice.

As we noted earlier, there has been substantial debate about the most appropriate, generally single comparison group by which to judge voucher programs. Much of the debate centers on the importance of using a randomly assigned control group and fully experimental designs in choice research. We will not revisit the details of this issue, but we note that our own work (Metcalf, 2004; Metcalf, Beghetto, & Legan, 2001) and that of others (e.g., Carnoy, 2001; Heckman, 1997) provide some reason for caution in conducting research of voluntary social programs, like vouchers, in which program impacts are judged by comparing individuals who wanted and were allowed to participate in the program against individuals who sought but were denied participation. In an attempt to gain the advantages that result from use of such a randomly established group of interested individuals while also avoiding the potential problems associated with making only this comparison, we have included four unique comparison groups in our research. In addition to the primary "treatment" (i.e., voucher) group, the sample includes

- *Applicant nonrecipients:* children whose families applied for but did not receive a voucher through the lottery process and who attend public schools (this group represents what many would consider to be the primary control group).
- *Nonapplicants:* children whose families did not apply for a voucher and who attend public schools (this is often used in choice research as a "default" comparison group).
- *Recipient nonusers:* children whose families applied for and were awarded a voucher but who chose not to use the voucher and, instead, attend public schools (in many ways, this group reflects a level of choice that may make it

among the most useful comparison groups in voucher research).

- *Former recipient users:* children whose families had obtained and used a voucher to enroll them in private schools for one or more years but who elected to give up their voucher and now attend public schools (as with recipient nonusers, these families have had available to them a very wide range of options and have chosen from more than one of them).

We believe these multiple comparison groups provide the opportunity to examine the voucher program in Cleveland from a more complete perspective than often is possible in such studies. However, their inclusion has only been made possible as a result of the longitudinal nature of the research design and our ability to identify these children as their families make educational choices over several years. In the fall of 1998, voucher program records identified 883 first-grade children who were using a voucher to attend private schools in Cleveland. Program records also identified 480 first-grade children whose families had applied for a voucher but had not received one and who were attending public schools (recipient nonusers). In addition, 32 children were identified who had used a voucher to attend private schools in kindergarten, but who were attending first grade in public schools (former recipient users).

The group of children we refer to as nonapplicants was established in the autumn of the first year of the study as the research team conducted achievement testing in each public and participating private school in Cleveland. Students in this group were the public school classmates of applicant nonrecipients and former recipient users. They were not randomly selected; however, because they were enrolled across virtually all public elementary schools in Cleveland, they can be assumed to be representative of the broader population of public school students.[2] The final comparison group, recipient nonusers, was not anticipated at the outset of the study, and was not identified until the beginning of second grade. However, they have been included in all aspects of the study since that time.

Employing multiple methodologies, we have used these five groups to examine four aspects of the voucher program in Cleveland. These are (a) the characteristics of children who use vouchers to attend private schools; (b) the characteristics of the teachers with whom voucher students work; (c) the decision making of families who choose from among the range of educational options in Cleveland, including vouchers; and (d) the impact of using a voucher on students' academic achievement.

To address these issues, we began collecting data on student characteristics, teacher characteristics, and student achievement in the autumn of 1998—the beginning of first grade. At that time, and in each subsequent spring, we have continued to collect these data using existing school and program records, and through on-site collection of teacher and achievement data using a cadre of proctors trained and supervised by our research team. As a result, over the past six years we have developed a database that includes repeated measures of each of these factors for all or most of the children in the voucher program and in each of the four comparison groups from the beginning of first grade through the end of sixth grade.[3] Importantly, this approach to data collection has allowed us to continue to collect data on students as their families make choices at least from among the public and private schools.

In addition to the annual data collection activities described above, the study has included telephone interviews of randomly

---

[2] In fact, our own data suggest that these students are statistically equivalent to their public school peers in minority status, gender, and eligibility for free or reduced-price lunch.
[3] While data have been collected through sixth grade, analyses are complete only through fifth grade.

selected families who reflect the distinctions among each of the five research groups as well as families whose children are enrolled in charter schools in Cleveland. The most recent set of interviews, conducted in the spring of 2002, included 1,329 families who were asked a series of questions about their families, the factors they believed important in selecting a school, and their satisfaction with the choices they had made.

The complexity and length of the study have resulted in a tremendous number of specific findings, conclusions, and emergent questions. The details of these have been reported in a series of annual technical reports. We have chosen not to attempt to convey all of these in this chapter. Instead, we turn our attention now to a discussion of basic findings associated with each of the four areas of investigation over the period of the study. Those who wish more detailed and technical information about the study and our findings are encouraged to review one or more of the annual project reports.[4]

Findings from the Cleveland Scholarship and Tutoring Program

Student Characteristics

Students whose families use a scholarship for private school enrollment through fifth grade differ from public school students in ethnicity and family income. Across the years of the study, the demographic characteristics of students in the longitudinal cohort have changed in relation to those of students in the comparison groups. This appears to be a result of a number of factors, including student exit from the program over time and the administrative processes used in previous years to award unused vouchers. However, by fifth grade, students who had used a voucher to attend private school since first grade were much less likely to be of minority status than students in any of the public

---

[4] All reports are publicly available and may be accessed at www.crlt.indiana.edu/research/cstpe.html.

school groups. Only about one-third of voucher students were non-White, compared with nearly 80 percent of students in the public school groups. It is worth noting that, of minority students, those using a voucher were much more likely to be Hispanic (7.2%) or multiracial (4.2%) than students in the public school groups (5.2% and 1.7% respectively). Fifth-grade students who used a voucher and those who had applied for but had not received a voucher were also much less likely than students in the remaining public school groups to be eligible for free or reduced-price lunch.[5] Over 80 percent of students who had never applied for a voucher were eligible for free lunch compared with 64 percent for applicant nonrecipients and 43 percent of voucher users.

Students who choose to leave the voucher program over time are more likely to be of minority status and of lower income than those who remain. Students who exit the program, particularly those who exit after kindergarten or first grade (i.e., after only one or two years in the program) are much more likely to be of minority status (87.4%) and eligible for free lunch (71.6%) than students who continue using a voucher. As we will discuss later, the financial burden of even the minimal required tuition often is too great for very low-income families and forces them to leave the program.

Students who enter the program over time are more likely to be White and are of higher income than those who entered in kindergarten and first grade. In general, the proportion of new students to the longitudinal cohort who are of minority status has decreased each year since kindergarten (from 68% to 53%). The pattern for income is similar but much less consistent, with new students consisting of proportionally more minority students than continuing voucher students only in fourth grade (65%). This

---

[5] Because private school students are not classified according to eligibility for free lunch, we have computed an estimated meal code for these students using family income data provided to the voucher program and federal guidelines.

gradual shift in demographics seems largely dependent upon whether students enter the program from public or private schools, however. Separate analyses indicate that students who enter the program from public schools are virtually identical to their public school classmates in terms of minority status and family income. In contrast, students who enter the voucher program from private schools are much more likely to be nonminority and of comparatively higher income. It was this pattern that prompted the voucher program to revise the process by which it awarded unused vouchers, a process that unexpectedly gave an advantage to students already enrolled in private schools. The impact of this procedural change on the demographic makeup of the voucher cohort in coming years remains to be seen.

Voucher students are somewhat less mobile than their public school peers. The average number of school changes made by students in each of the groups was less than one between first and fifth grade. However, whereas about two-thirds of students who had used a voucher from first to fifth grade had never changed schools, only slightly more than half of public school students had remained in the same school throughout the period. It is interesting to note, however, that even voucher students tended to have been more mobile than their nonvoucher private school classmates. Ninety-three percent of these nonvoucher students had attended the same school from kindergarten through fifth grade.

Teacher Characteristics

Early in our work, we were influenced by a debate that arose among members of the independent advisory group that was established to assist us. There was general agreement among the members of this group that data should be collected on at least some classroom level factors. However, while several members argued that this was necessary in order to account for these differences before comparing public and private school students' achievement, an equal number felt that these factors were an integral part of the potential impact of the program itself and should be examined independently of student achievement. In the end, we have chosen to collect and analyze data on the characteristics of teachers and on class size each year in order to understand better what may be different experiences for voucher and public school students. But we have not attempted to establish whether apparent differences are best viewed as interrelated to or independent from the efficacy of the voucher program.

In many ways, the basic classroom characteristics experienced by public school students and voucher students in private schools are surprisingly similar. Students in both settings work in classrooms of about 22 students. They work with teachers who have worked in the same school for comparable periods of time (slightly more than six years). They also tend to work overwhelmingly with teachers who are fully certified, although a greater percentage of private school teachers have provisional certification (10%) than do public school teachers (3%).

However, public and private school teachers of students in our sample differed significantly in terms of their highest degree earned and overall years of experience. Public school teachers were much more likely to have pursued coursework beyond their baccalaureate degree (78%) than were private school teachers (37%). In fact, nearly 55 percent of public school teachers had completed at least a master's degree in contrast to only 6.1 percent of private school teachers. Perhaps relatedly, public school teachers had somewhat more years of teaching experience (14 years) than did private school teachers (11 years), although teachers in both groups could be considered relatively well experienced.

Minority students, particularly those in public schools, tend to experience smaller classes than nonminority students. The teachers experienced by minority and nonminority students in the present sample differ very little between public and private schools. In terms of teacher education level, teacher certification, and teacher experience, there is no evidence that minority students in either school type are exposed to differentially prepared or experienced teachers. However, we have found across years that nonminority students in public schools have generally worked in classes that were roughly 10 percent larger than their minority peers enrolled in these same public schools. This appears to hold true only for students in public schools, however. Class size for both minority and nonminority students enrolled in private schools was generally equivalent.

Families' Educational Decisions

One of the interesting but largely unexplored issues surrounding the viability and desirability of school choice programs is how or why families make the educational decisions that they do. In order to design programs and policies that are likely to lead families to make wise educational choices for their children, understanding the factors that influence their decisions, the reasons for their decisions, and their satisfaction with these decisions is of great importance. Through telephone interviews with families who have made distinctly different choices from among the myriad of options available to them in Cleveland, some interesting patterns emerge.

The safety of their children is the most important school factor to families, regardless of the educational option they may choose, but it is followed closely by the basic quality of the education their children receive. Among the most striking findings across the groups of families we interviewed is the consistency with which parents rate the relative importance of particular school factors or attributes. In fact, across public school, private school, and charter school families, the relative priority given to each of ten school factors was virtually identical. In every case and for every subgroup of families, safety was rated as the most important factor in choosing their children's schools. The importance attached to this factor is further reinforced by the fact that safety was the second most frequently cited reason for parents' intention to change schools in the next academic year.

In addition to safety, families also attach great importance to the quality of the education their children receive. Though never rated as highly as safety, the quality of teachers in a school and the academic quality of the school were rated as the second and third most important factors to families across groups. The relative unimportance of several factors also is noteworthy and consistent. The size of classes in a school was never rated higher than sixth out of ten factors by any subgroup of families, and the diversity of the school population was never rated higher than ninth out of ten factors, with no differences in these responses found between families of differing minority status and income. The single factor that was found to differ notably across groups was the importance of extracurricular activities and programs. This factor was considered much more important to families who had chosen public schools for their children than it was to families whose children used a voucher to attend private schools or whose children attended charter schools.

There are identifiable groups of families who desire and seek educational settings that meet their children's needs, but who have been unable to do so. Former voucher users are the clearest example of families in an ongoing search for appropriate educational settings for their children. These families have used a voucher in the past for private school enrollment, but have chosen to give up the voucher and return to public schools. They report having been moderately unsatisfied with their children's former (private) schools and are only slightly more satisfied with their children's current (public) schools. While they are about equally as likely as other public school families to have considered charter schools for their children, they are nearly twice as likely to have enrolled their children in charter schools for one or more previous years.

This ongoing search is difficult to explain from the data available in our work. With the exception of families who applied for but did not receive a voucher, former users are about as likely to be minority and are of roughly similar income as voucher and other public school families. They are slightly less religious than are current voucher users (about 34% consider themselves very religious compared with 38% of voucher families) but about equally as religious as other public school families. Of note is that the mothers of former voucher users are similar to both voucher mothers and charter school mothers in that a majority have attended at least some college. These families, it may be assumed, have a strong appreciation for education and they are knowledgeable of the options available to them. Perhaps their expectations of their children's schools are sufficiently high that they cannot be met, or at least have not been met, by the options they have tried.

The cost to families and the limited range of participating private schools discourages many families from pursuing a voucher. For many families, the financial burden of paying even the relatively small portion of their children's private school tuition is more than they can bear. While the voucher covers as much as 90 percent of the total cost of tuition up to $2,750, families must bear the balance. For families of very low income, as the majority of voucher families are, the minimum of $275 that they must pay is a substantial problem and forces many families to leave the program, even though they were happy with their children's private schools. Further, many families have more than one child who is eligible to use a voucher, thus multiplying their financial burden. Nearly half of former voucher families indicated the financial burden as the primary reason for their departure from the program. The second most commonly cited reason either for leaving the voucher program or for not accepting an awarded voucher was the limited range of school types (predominantly religiously affiliated) and school services (e.g., capacity to serve students with special needs). About one-third of former users and recipient nonusers indicated that this had led them to their decision about participation in the voucher program.

Academic Achievement

The most closely watched and hotly debated findings of any study on vouchers are those associated with the impact of the program on students' academic achievement. As we have described above, highly public conflicts between researchers who examine data drawn from the same study (e.g., Howell & Peterson vs. Krueger & Zhu; Witte vs. Greene, Peterson, & Du [1998]) have arisen in nearly every study to date. The same is true of our own findings in the early years of the project (see Greene, Howell, & Peterson, 1997; Metcalf, Boone, Stage, Chilton, Muller, & Tait, 1998). However, by examining the comparative academic achievement of the students in our sample from first through fifth grade, we believe that some sense can be gained not only of the impact of the voucher program in Cleveland at any particular point in time, but also of the variation in comparative achievement that occurs over time.

Early in our cohort's first-grade year, we began administering the Terra Nova, a standardized achievement test produced by CTB/McGraw-Hill. In first through third grades the test assesses students' achievement in the areas of reading, language arts, and mathematics; and these three scores are aggregated into what is called the overall score. In third grade, the test adds assessment of social studies and science, but these are not aggregated into the overall score. Thus, for students in our longitudinal sample, we have measures in the first three subject areas obtained on six occasions (fall first grade and each spring from first through fifth grade), and we have measures of students' achievement in social studies and science from spring of third grade through spring of fifth grade. The results that we discuss below are drawn directly from these data and represent achievement levels after adjusting (covarying) for students' minority status. For brevity, we do not present, either graphically or descriptively, all of the data for each individual achievement area (reading, language arts, mathematics, science, and social studies). However, Figure 1 graphically presents data on students' overall achievement scores (an aggregation of reading, language arts, and mathematics scores) by way of example. Similar patterns were found across achievement areas.

Figure 1. Adjusted Overall Achievement: 1998-2003.

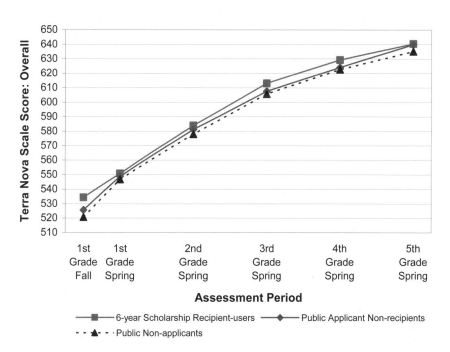

The cumulative impact of participation in the voucher program on students' academic achievement from first through fifth grade remains unclear. As can be seen in Figure 1, there is substantial variation in the comparative achievement of students over the five years for which data have been analyzed. Though not depicted in Figure 1, the performance of voucher students is consistently higher than that of recipient nonusers and former recipient users in each of the achievement areas and at each testing point. Students who elect to leave the voucher program are generally achieving at lower levels prior to returning to public schools than students who remain in the program. The achievement of the students who leave the voucher program tends to drop slightly in their first year in public schools when compared with other students in the sample. For some of these students, particularly those who left the program in their first or second grade years, achievement growth in subsequent years nearly parallels that of voucher students, but their comparative performance remains lower than that of continuing voucher students. For students who exited the voucher program in upper elementary grades, achievement growth does not appear to rebound from the initial impact of moving from private to public schools. For many of these students, the level of achievement growth they experience remains less than that of voucher students and that of both applicant nonrecipients and nonapplicants.

The pattern of comparative performance between voucher students and public school students who applied for but did not receive a voucher and those who never applied for a voucher varies somewhat across years. Clearly, voucher students entered first grade achieving at significantly higher levels than did both groups of public school students. In all areas except language these differences were significant even after adjusting for students' minority status. However, while the performance of voucher students was never found to be lower than that of students in these two public school groups, their achievement advantage fluctuated in each of the subsequent years. Table 1 presents the results of post hoc comparisons between and among the three groups of students in each achievement area and at each testing point.

In general, voucher students tended to achieve at consistently higher levels in most areas than did students whose families had never applied for a voucher. Language is an area in which this trend does not appear, and the trend is somewhat less apparent in overall score. In contrast, achievement of voucher students is significantly higher than that of applicant nonrecipients at some points and in some areas, but not in all areas or at all times. The substantial differences between these two groups at the beginning of first grade are nearly eliminated by the end of first grade and no longer exist in any of the achievement areas by the end of second grade. In third grade, voucher students achieve at higher levels in overall score and reading, but not in any of the four other achievement areas. This pattern continues through fourth grade, with voucher students also coming to achieve at higher levels in social studies. In another change in comparative performance, by the end of fifth grade, the only area in which voucher students achieve at higher levels than students whose families applied unsuccessfully for a voucher is in social studies.

Table 1. Subjects of Significant Pairwise Differences Favoring Scholarship Students over (a) Applicant Nonrecipients (ANR) and (b) Nonapplicants (NA) by Testing Episode[a]						
Subject	**Testing Episode**					
	Fall 1st Grade	Spring 1st Grade	Spring 2nd Grade	Spring 3rd Grade	Spring 4th Grade	Spring 5th Grade
Overall	ANR			ANR	ANR	
	NA*	NA	NA*	NA	NA	NA*
Reading	ANR			ANR	ANR	
	NA*		NA*	NA	NA	NA*
Language	No significant differences indicated					
Mathematics	ANR	ANR				
	NA	NA		NA		
Science	Not assessed			No significant differences indicated		
Social Studies	Not assessed				ANR	ANR
				NA*	NA	NA*
* Indicates comparisons in which nonapplicants were found to obtain significantly lower scores than applicant nonrecipients. [a] Empty cells indicate no significant difference between scholarship students and the particular comparison group.						

Across grades and subjects, it is clear that students who elect to leave the voucher program and enter public schools (former recipient users) tend to be of lower achievement levels than those who remain. Further, students who receive a voucher but choose not to use it and, instead, remain in public schools (recipient nonusers) also tend to be lower achieving students. Much less clear is whether voucher students do better than they might have been expected to do had they remained in public schools. They never achieve at lower levels than comparable students in public schools and, at some points and in some subjects, they perform significantly better. In addition, voucher students' pattern of achievement and achievement growth is generally higher than that of students whose families never applied for a voucher. Thus, there is some evidence to suggest that using a voucher may provide some academic benefit. However, there is substantial reason for caution in making this claim. There is no instance, either in time or in any achievement area, wherein voucher students consistently achieve at higher levels than students who applied for but did not receive a voucher—what many would consider the principal comparison group.

Conclusion

And so, we return to the issues that opponents and advocates raise and debate. Do voucher programs serve to diminish or to increase segregation among families on the basis of ethnicity or income? Do they promote greater academic achievement for students from low-income families, or would these students be as well or better served by remaining in their public schools? Some who have examined the literature and research on voucher programs have concluded that we still do not know. Gill, Timpane, Ross, and Brewer (2002) conclude, "Many of the important empirical questions about vouchers . . . have not yet been answered" (pp. 202-203). We are, perhaps not surprisingly, less cynical about the value of the collective findings of voucher research. We believe that there are, in fact, a number of things that can be drawn from this body of work, although there are certainly many things that remain to be known or understood.

The voucher programs to date have, without exception, attempted to target families for whom private school enrollment is unlikely or impossible without the assistance that such programs provide. Our own research and that of others suggests that vouchers can be and generally are successful in this regard. Families who are awarded a voucher tend to be of low income and of racial or ethnic minorities. On the surface, our own work in Cleveland seems to contradict this in that our voucher sample has, over time, come to include proportionally fewer low-income and minority students. However, this appears to be a result of particular programmatic and procedural factors that can be changed if desired. In fact, on the basis of our findings in earlier years, the admission process has already been revised to give greater priority to low-income families.

Lower-income families appear to be much less likely to take advantage of an awarded voucher or to continue using a voucher than families of comparatively higher income. There may be a number of reasons for this, but economics must be considered among them. In our own work, even the minimal percentage of tuition that families must pay (10% or up to $275) is prohibitive for families of extremely low income. This is an instance in which a seemingly rational policy that was intended to ensure some commitment and ownership on the part of voucher recipients may, in practice, diminish participation in the program by the very families it intends to serve. In any event, the financial impediments to participation can be eliminated or further diminished if desired.

In virtually every study, voucher families indicate that the school factors they value are nearly identical to those valued by families who make very different educational decisions for their children. Safety, academic quality, quality of teachers, and classroom discipline are of greatest importance. Conversely, many of the factors that policy makers and educators believe important (e.g., class size and a diverse student population) are of much less importance to families. The implications of this are not necessarily clear and there is much about parents' educational decision making that we do not know. However, knowing what families value in their children's schools should allow us to develop and support school policies and reforms that integrate these characteristics.

Further, and notably, despite the commonality in families' educational values, their perceptions of these values lead them to choose distinctly different educational options for their children. We have hypothesized elsewhere that voucher families may seek to use the opportunity provided by a voucher to leverage greater social capital for their children (Metcalf & Legan, 2005; Metcalf, Legan, & Paul, 2003). To the extent this is true, academic and behavioral outcomes associated with safety and classroom discipline are only particular elements of a much broader set of social and interpersonal values these families desire that their children obtain. Our work to date does not allow us to draw conclusions about the validity or accuracy of this hypothesis, but we believe it to be an extremely important question for further research.

Thus, while we believe the research on vouchers does provide us with some defensible and useful findings, we must concur with Gill et al. and others that we do not know whether voucher programs lead to higher student achievement, particularly among students in the populations they target. Data from across multiple studies do not offer any clear pattern either supporting or refuting the academic benefits of using a voucher to attend private school. On the basis of our own data and that of others, there is no reason to believe that students' academic achievement is diminished through use of vouchers. The academic achievement of voucher students, even after adjusting for demographic factors and prior levels of achievement, has been at least as high as that of students attending public schools.

It is much more difficult, however, to draw conclusions about whether use of vouchers leads to greater academic performance than students would have attained had they attended public schools. Several researchers, including our team, have reported such effects for specific groups of students, in particular subjects, and at particular points in time. Unfortunately, these studies generally do not provide evidence about the impacts of vouchers on students' academic achievement over an extended period of time. The longitudinal nature of our study in Cleveland suggests that, at least through fifth grade, the benefits of using a voucher to attend private schools vary from year to year, with voucher students sometimes seeming to gain more than their public school peers and sometimes gaining at roughly the same rate. We reiterate, however, that even our own study has examined this issue for only five years of students' education.

The long-term academic value of vouchers for students of low income and with otherwise limited educational options is unknown. Nonetheless, it seems reasonable to conclude that, if positive effects result from such programs, the magnitude of these effects in the early grades is comparatively small, probably not exceeding .2 standard deviations. We urge restraint on the part of those who would be quick to claim that such an effect size is too small to justify public funding of voucher programs. This is an effect of approximately the same magnitude associated with the landmark Tennessee STAR study, which has been used to support the expenditure of millions of dollars to reduce class size in schools throughout the country (Finn & Achilles, 1999).

Do vouchers represent a potentially viable tool for enhancing the education and thus the lives of children whom we often consider to be "at-risk"? If we mean by this only whether or not they will result in higher academic achievement for these students, then any answer must be equivocal. However, if we recognize, as do a sizeable number of the families who have chosen to take advantage of vouchers in the small number of cities where they are available, that academic achievement is only one part of the benefits their children can derive from a good education, then we must acknowledge that vouchers may, in fact, be a very useful tool. They are, however, only a tool. Like any tool, this will be effective only to the extent that it is thoughtfully designed and carefully applied in ways that are directly aligned with its intended purposes. And, to continue this simile, we must take the time to patiently use, study, revise, and refine the tool and our uses of it.

References

Carnoy, M. (2001). *Do school vouchers improve student performance?* Washington: Economic Policy Institute.

Finn, J. D., & Achilles, C. M. (1999). Tennessee's class size study: Findings, implications, and misconceptions. *Educational Evaluation and Policy Analysis, 21,* 97-109.

Gill, B. P., Timpane, P. M., Ross, K. E., & Brewer, D. J. (2002). *Rhetoric versus reality: What we know and what we need to know about vouchers and charter schools.* Santa Monica, CA: Rand Corporation.

Greene, J. P. (2001). *An evaluation of the Florida A-Plus Accountability and School Choice Program.* Florida State University, the Manhattan Institute, and the Harvard Program on Education Policy and Governance. Available at www.manhattan-institute.org/html/cr_aplus.htm.

Greene, J. P., & Forster, G. (2003). Vouchers for special education students: An evaluation of Florida's McKay Scholarship Program. The Manhattan Institute. Available at www.manhattan-institute.org/html/cr_38.htm.

Greene, J., Howell, W., & Peterson, P. (1997). *Lessons from the Cleveland Scholarship and Tutoring Program.* Paper presented at the Annual Meeting of the Association of Public Policy and Management. Washington, DC, November 1997.

Greene, J. P., Peterson, P. E., & Du, J. (1998). School choice in Milwaukee: A randomized experiment. In P. Peterson & B. Hassel (Eds.), *Learning from school choice.* Washington, DC: The Brookings Institution.

Greene, J. P., Peterson, P. E., Du, J., Boeger, L., & Frazier, C. L. (1996). *The effectiveness of school choice in Milwaukee: A secondary analysis of data from the program's evaluation.* Paper given at the American Political Science Association Annual Meeting. San Francisco, CA, August 29 to September 1.

Greene, J. P., & Winters, M. A. (2003). *When schools compete: The effects of vouchers on Florida public school achievement.* The Manhattan Institute. Available at www. manhattan-institute.org/html/ewp_02.htm.

Heckman, J. (1997). Instrumental variables: A study of implicit behavioral assumptions used in making program evaluations. *Journal of Human Resources, 32*(3), 441-462.

Howell, W. G., & Peterson, P. E. (2002). *The education gap: Vouchers and urban schools.* Washington, DC: Brookings Institution Press.

Krueger, A. B., & Zhu, P. (2004). Another look at the New York City school voucher experiment. *American Behavioral Scientist, 47,* 658-698.

Martinez, V., Godwin, K., & Kemerer, F. R. (1995). Private vouchers in San Antonio: The CEO Program. In T. M. Moe (Ed.), *Private vouchers.* Stanford: Hoover Institution Press.

Mayer, D. P., Peterson, P. E., Myers, D. E, Tuttle, C. C., & Howell, W. G. (2002). *School choice in New York City after three years: An evaluation of the School Choice Scholarships Program. Final Report.* Washington, DC: Mathematica Policy Research, Inc.

Metcalf, K. K. (2004). A review of *The education gap: Vouchers and urban schools. Journal of Education for Students Placed at Risk, 8,* 371-376.

Metcalf, K. K., Beghetto, R. A., & Legan, N. A. (2001). *School voucher research: The use and misuse of comparison groups.* Paper presented at the annual meeting of the American Educational Research Association, New Orleans.

Metcalf, K. K., Boone, W., Stage, F., Chilton, T., Muller, P., & Tait, P. (1998). *A comparative evaluation of the Cleveland Scholarship and Tutoring Grant Program, year one: 1996-97.* Columbus, OH: Ohio Department of Education, Division of Policy Analysis and Research.

Metcalf, K. K., & Legan, N. (2005). *Do school vouchers leverage social capital for low-income families?* Paper presented at the Hawaii International Conference on Education, Honolulu.

Metcalf, K. K., Legan, N., & Paul, K. (2003). *Families in search of social capital via school vouchers.* Paper presented at the 7th Oxford International Conference on Education and Development, Oxford, UK.

Metcalf, K. K., Legan, N., Paul, K., & Boone, W. (2004). *Longitudinal evaluation of the Cleveland Scholarship and Tutoring Program: 1998-2003.* Technical and Summary Reports. Bloomington, IN: Indiana University, School of Education.

Milwaukee Parental Choice Program (2004). MPCP Facts and Figures for 2004-2005. Available at www.dpi.state.wi.us/dpi/dfm/sms/choice.html.

Peterson, P. E., & Howell, W. G. (2004). Efficiency, bias, and classification schemes. *The American Behavioral Scientist, 47,* 699-717.

Peterson, P. E., Howell, W. G., Wolf, P. J., & Campbell, D. E. (2003). School vouchers: Results from randomized experiments. In C. M. Hoxby (Ed.), *The economics of school choice.* Chicago: The University of Chicago Press.

Powers, J. M., & Cookson, Jr., P. W. (1999). The politics of school choice research: Fact, fiction, and statistics. *Educational Policy, 13,* 104-122.

Richard, A. (2004). Florida weighs impact of ruling against voucher program. *Education Week.* Available at www.edweek.org/ew/articles/2004/09/01/01vouch.h24.html?querystring=Florida%20Vouchers.

Rouse, C. E. (1998). Private school vouchers and student achievement: An evaluation of the Milwaukee Parental Choice Program. *Quarterly Journal of Economics, 113,* 553-602.

Sack, J. (2004). Florida vouchers dealt another legal blow. *Education Week.* Available at www.edweek.org/ew/articles/2004/11/24/13fla.h24.html.

Washington Scholarship Fund. (2004a). *DC K-12 Scholarship Program: Frequently asked questions about private school participation.* Available at www.aisgw.org/documents/042804_wsf_faq.pdf.

Washington Scholarship Fund. (2004b). More than 1,000 DC Opportunity Scholars enroll in private elementary, middle, and high schools. *WSF News*. Available at www.washington scholarshipfund.org/PDF/wsfNewsfall-04Final.pdf.

Witte, J. F. (1998). The Milwaukee voucher experiment. *Educational Evaluation and Policy Analysis, 20,* 229-251.

Witte, J. F. (2000). *The market approach to education.* Princeton, NJ: Princeton University Press.

CHAPTER 3

ACCOUNTABILITY v. ADEQUATE FUNDING: WHICH POLICIES INFLUENCE ADEQUATE PREPARATION FOR COLLEGE?[1]

Glenda Droogsma Musoba

Introduction

While most young people aspire to attain a college degree, the percentage of students who actually pursue a higher education is much lower. Data from Stanford University's Bridge Project (Venezia, Kirst, & Antonio, 2003) showed that 88 percent of all U.S. eighth grade students plan to attend some form of postsecondary education. Yet in 2002 only 38 percent of 19-year-olds were enrolled in college as degree-seeking students (Mortenson, 2004). Participation is also disproportionately White and upper income. With many more students needing a college education to support economic growth and to maximize

[1] The Indiana Commission for Higher Education and the College Board provided data used in these analyses, and Edward St. John provided guidance in the writing. This support is sincerely appreciated. The opinions expressed in this chapter are the author's and do not represent official policies or positions of those organizations and individuals that supported the project.

employment rates (Reich, 1991), this gap is disturbing. There are several factors that appear to contribute to this gap between aspirations and participation. Two main explanations are given: financial access and academic access (Hearn 1991; St. John & Musoba, 2002).

Researchers and policy advocates on the academic access side of the debate maintain that students, particularly low-income students, are underrepresented in college enrollments because they are not academically prepared to be successful in college and therefore would not fully benefit from a college education until they are better prepared. Concerns in the K-12 literature about the poor performance of American school children in international comparisons parallel the apprehension about students' weak academic preparation in the college access literature. In the last two decades, school reform has been the key recommended solution to inadequate academic preparation (Finn, 1990). The logic is straightforward: reforming schools will raise student achievement (National Commission on Excellence in Education, 1983), thus academically preparing students for college. Once the academic barriers are removed, students will enroll (Choy, 2002; Choy, Horn, Nuæz, & Chen, 2000; Horn & Chen, 1998; NCES, 2001). Schools and students are responsible for the students' academic preparation for college.

The opposing argument is that low-income students who are academically prepared do not participate at similar rates to high-income students; therefore the participation gap is a financial access issue, as students cannot financially afford to attend (Advisory Committee on Student Financial Assistance, 2002). There is a substantial body of research evidence to corroborate this affordability argument (see Heller, 1997; Jackson, 1978; St. John, 2002). Both financial and academic factors appear to influence college access.

If one accepts the premise that academic preparation is important to college access (Hearn, 1991), then the unequal distribution of preparation in society becomes problematic. Those who argue for improving academic preparation maintain that students must be ready to benefit from a college education and have the necessary skills and knowledge. Within the academic preparation position, the discussion moves from the question of why some students are less prepared for college to how to rectify the situation.

The gaps in readiness for college are well documented but the assumptions, causes, and solutions proposed to address the disparity are not well substantiated or researched. As a result of this lack of certainty, conflicting evidence, and political expediency, there is debate on what is the best way to educate students at all levels of education, from early childhood through graduation.

There are two main philosophical approaches to improving education. During the 1970s and earlier the focus was on policies for equalizing or providing supplemental school funding for schools with more underprepared students; for example, Title I was concerned with the schools' responsibility for raising student achievement. These policies focused on equalizing school resources between high- and low-funded schools and providing supplemental services and resources for students who were less advanced. At the core of these reforms was an understanding of society's role in creating the disparities between income groups or, at minimum, society's responsibility to redress these inequalities. Current positions that are in line with this philosophy include arguments for greater equity in school funding.

In the last two decades, school reform has been the key recommended solution for inadequate academic preparation (Finn, 1990; 2002). With a change in philosophy, educators and policy makers abandoned the idea of parity of resources and equal opportunity for parity of outcomes focusing on achievement at all schools, and school productivity and efficiency became important considerations (Finn, 1990; 2002). The emphasis is on measuring student outcomes, usually through standardized tests, rather than measuring school resources or inputs. High stakes high school exit exams are a clear example of this approach. This position maintains that outcomes are the most appropriate way to define school success, and how students or schools get to that point is less relevant. The recent federal education legislation, the No Child Left Behind Act of 2001 (NCLB), has many features that are in line with this philosophy. To comply with NCLB, states must engage in standardized outcomes testing, and schools will be held accountable if student test scores do not show improvement over time. Yet there are no provisions in NCLB for equalization of school resources in ways that would level the playing field between schools. Reform of this kind is based on the assumption that students and their families, rather than their school system, are responsible for students' performance. This is particularly true of the high stakes high school exit exams that withhold student diplomas without addressing the broad disparity in the pass rates between high schools, suggesting differences between schools in opportunities to learn. As yet there is limited evidence that teachers and administrators at identified schools need fear for their jobs from state accountability systems (Finn, 2002).

An assumption of these policies that has not been tested is the principle that policy can affect student outcomes without adding any new money. Many districts claim that the new requirements for testing in NCLB exceed the additional resources allocated; therefore any reforms or changes schools make to respond to the new policy are implemented with no additional funds. While it is easier to test the ensuing policies associated with these assumptions than the assumptions themselves, it is important to keep these assumptions in mind when doing the research.

While there is substantial policy implementation that aligns with these assumptions, the assumptions and implemented policies have not been adequately tested. The number of states instituting high stakes high school exit exams is growing even though the research evidence for high stakes exams is inconclusive at best. Considering the substantial cost of such programs, the effectiveness of these reform policies has important implications for taxpayers as well as the students who are living and learning under these policies. Several policies are being implemented on a large scale with limited or inconclusive research.

Research Question and School Reforms

The key question in this research came from an interest in learning whether state education reforms have made a difference in higher education. *Do state school reform policies improve higher education access by improving students' academic readiness for college?* Given that these proposed policy solutions had not been tested, further research was needed. Of particular need was research that takes into account that often several policies are implemented simultaneously in the same state. At issue in this study was not what individual schools or districts can do but what states can do at a policy level to improve education. Because of the variability between states in school reform policies, the state was also a useful unit of analysis for examining the impact of policies.

Specifically this study tested the relationship between the proposed school reform policy solutions and students' abilities for college as measured by the SAT. The policies that were examined here were mathematics graduation curriculum requirements, availability of advanced placement courses, state implementation of standards-based reform, high stakes high school exit exams, and average K-12 school funding (Table 1). A brief examination of the prior research on these policies is useful before looking at research on the SAT.

Mathematics Graduation Curriculum Requirements

Numerous studies in the 1980s and 1990s, some supported by the National Center for Educational Statistics (NCES), found a strong relationship between course taking, particularly in mathematics, and achievement or college enrollment (Lee, Burkam, Chow-Hoy, Smerdon, & Goverdt, 1998; Mullis, Dossey, Owen, & Phillips, 1991; NCES, 1997a, 1997b; Pallas & Alexander, 1983; Pelavin & Kane, 1990). Later NCES studies went a step further, suggesting that it was course taking beyond algebra that was most significant for college enrollment and persistence (Adelman, 1999). Earlier the National Commission on

			Table 1. School Reform Policy Implementation in 2000			
State	**High Stakes Exit Exam**	**Honors Diploma Policy**	**Minimum Math Credits Required for Graduation**	**Percentage High Schools Offering AP**	**Standards-based Activity**[c]	**K-12 Funding per FTE**[d]
Alabama	Yes	Yes	4	36.3	79	2,963
Alaska	Developing[a]	No	2	12.6	61	4,711
Arizona	Developing	No	2	51	77	2,657
Arkansas	No	No	3	33	66	2,985
California	Developing	Yes	2	74.7	85	3,452
Colorado	No	No	Local	49.9	86	3,271
Connecticut	No	No	3	85.2	81	5,664
Delaware	No	No	3	64.4	85	4,593
Florida	Yes	No	3	64.8	84	3,269
Georgia	Yes	Yes	3	65	78	3,513
Hawaii	Yes	Yes	3	72.7	60	3,750
Idaho	No	No	4	42	67	2,936
Illinois	Developing	No	2	54.1	80	3,788
Indiana	Yes	Yes	4	59.1	81	3,949
Iowa	No	No	Local	33.3	31	3,677
Kansas	No	No	2	24.4	83	3,300
Kentucky	No	Yes	3	66.4	91	3,188
Louisiana	Yes	Yes	3	24.6	85	3,109
Maine	Developing	No	2	63.3	76	4,536
Maryland	Yes	Yes	3	79.3	98	4,407
Massachusetts	Developing	No	Local	86.4	89	5,163
Michigan	No	No	Local	56.7	86	4,137
Minnesota	Yes	No	1[b]	44.6	57	4,011
Mississippi	Yes	No	3	38.7	62	2,630
Missouri	No	Yes	2	32.6	78	3,413
Montana	No	No	2	34.3	40	3,578
Nebraska	N	No	Local	21.7	61	3,746
Nevada	Yes	Yes	3	38.7	80	3,185
New Hampshire	No	No	2	79.5	76	4,018

			Table 1. School Reform Policy Implementation in 2000 (cont.)			
State	High Stakes Exit Exam	Honors Diploma Policy	Minimum Math Credits Required for Graduation	Percentage High Schools Offering AP	Standards-based Activity[c]	K-12 Funding per FTE[d]
New Jersey	Yes	No	3	87.8	68	5,833
New Mexico	Yes	No	3	50	91	2,863
New York	Yes	Yes	2	76.7	94	6,017
North Carolina	Yes	No	3	67.7	87	3,295
North Dakota	No	No	3	8.8	50	3,096
Ohio	Yes	Yes	2	63.1	83	3,656
Oklahoma	Developing	Yes	2	42	83	2,984
Oregon	Developing	No	2	50.2	86	3,829
Pennsylvania	No	No	3	63.4	63	4,594
Rhode Island	No	Yes	2	70.1	57	5,321
South Carolina	Yes	No	4	74	87	3,166
South Dakota	No	No	2	19.2	61	2,873
Tennessee	Yes	Yes	3	53.1	59	3,210
Texas	Yes	Yes	3	63.1	84	3,344
Utah	Developing	No	2	78.6	73	2,620
Vermont	No	No	2.5	72.2	65	4,587
Virginia	Yes	Yes	3	74.7	86	3,699
Washington	No	No	2	58.1	67	3,552
West Virginia	No	No	3	55.2	69	3,921
Wisconsin	No	No	2	65.3	65	4,499
Wyoming	No	No	3	33.3	60	3,775

[a]Those listed as developing were considered not to have an exam for this analysis because an exam under development could not be expected to affect current student achievement.

[b]Data missing for 2000; MN teacher reported 1 credit (personal communication), but the state has shifted the focus to meeting standards and the teacher's own school has higher requirements.

[c] Degree of implementation of standards-based reform.

[d] Unadjusted dollars for the Cost of Education Index.

Excellence in Education (1983) had recommended new graduation requirements, known as the "new basics," and most states raised their requirements, particularly in math and science (Clune, White, & Patterson, 1989). One policy conclusion was rather simple: raising graduation requirements would increase the amount of mathematics courses students take, which would subsequently raise student achievement and the number of students going to college.

Yet these more recent research studies were correlational and ignored the fact that many students already chose to take more courses than was required of them. Therefore, policies were given credit for student choice beyond the policy. Chaney, Burgdorf, and Atash (1997), who also found increases in test scores related to course taking, expressed this concern about the bias from students' self selection into higher mathematics courses. Their research ascertained that many students took more than the minimum requirements, and therefore probably were not affected by the requirements. Yet when examined separately, academically marginal students still benefited from additional coursework, particularly if it was a more rigorous course in the math hierarchy rather than simply more time in a similar course. While the relationship between graduation requirements and test scores was weaker for this marginal group, it was still significant. Hoffer (1997), using NELS:88 data, found no effects on graduation rates or achievement gains for raising mathematics graduation requirements and found raising requirements did not narrow the socioeconomic gap.

More recently Dee (2002) tested the impact of higher curriculum requirements and minimum competency testing on high school graduation rates, college enrollment, and employment. Although higher graduation curriculum requirements were associated with more academic course taking, they were also associated with lower high school graduation rates, particularly for African American students, and were not significantly associated with college enrollment. Dee did not test an achievement outcome.

These findings suggested that the present study was needed to test the ability gains associated with raising graduation requirements. Students who take more than the minimum coursework are overrepresented in SAT test takers; therefore individual course taking must be a control variable. Research that separates out the influence of policy from student behavior is important in assessing the impact of raising curriculum standards. In this study, states that required three or more courses in mathematics for graduation were compared to states with lower or no requirements.

Advanced Placement Courses

Advanced Placement (AP) coursework is almost necessary for admission to an elite college today. AP scores offer the only national benchmark other than the SAT on which students can be evaluated. Yet AP courses are less available in Hispanic and African American schools and in racially mixed schools. Further, enrollment in AP and honors classes is divided along racial lines (Tierney & Hagedorn, 2002).

A total of 747,922 students took an Advanced Placement exam in 2000 (College Board, 2000). If considering only those students who enrolled in college, this study would be expected to confirm the positive effects of AP courses (Willingham & Morris, 1986). However, not all students who take the SAT enroll in college, and not all AP courses are created equal. While research is rather conclusive that AP classes benefit those students who take them, research is contradictory whether other students in the school benefit, are not affected, or are harmed (Gamoran, 1992; Willingham & Morris). It is established that the teachers of AP classes are more experienced and better prepared (Gamoran).

This study is a test of state policy regarding AP coursework; therefore, it tests the prevalence of AP courses or percentage of schools in a state participating in the AP program in 1998 rather than individual student AP courses. Every state had some schools that offered AP classes; therefore, the variability is in the percentage of schools that participate.

Standards-Based Reform

In theory, standards-based reforms are designed to change the classroom practices of teachers by clearly defining rigorous academic content and teaching practices that emphasize active student learning. The National Council of Teachers of Mathematics (NCTM) took the lead in standards-based reform when it released the NCTM *Curriculum and Evaluation Standards for School Mathematics* (1989). The standards were designed to change the focus and methods of mathematics instruction to develop higher-order skills such as problem solving and reasoning. In theory, states followed this model, and standards-based reform was an important aspect of school reform in the 1990s. There are four key parts to the standards-based reform agenda: content standards, performance standards, aligned assessments, and professional standards.

While almost every state is engaged in standards-based reform at some level, there is wide variability in the depth and form of implementation at the state level. According to *Education Weeks' Quality Counts 2001*, in 2000, 47 states had academic content standards in four core subjects (Orlofsky & Olson, 2001). All 50 states do some student assessment of learning but the link between those assessments and standards-based reform and content standards varies widely. Only seven states use essay questions in any subject other than English, and only two states use portfolios or compilations of students' work as part of their assessments (Orlofsky & Olson, 2001). Only 27 states have some public form of school accountability. *Education Week* gives Maryland the highest grade of A for almost full implementation of standards and Iowa F for the least implementation. The relationship between assessments and standards has come under strong criticism. In general, the level of state policy activity declines with each of the four aspects of reform and the difficulty of implementation.

Swanson and Stevenson (2002) tested the relationship between the variability in state policy activity related to standards-based reform and changes in classroom instructional practice by math teachers. They found a significant relationship between state policy sophistication and teacher practice, yet only 3 percent of the variability in math teachers' instructional practice was associated with state-level variables. They also showed a school-level effect indicating more resource-rich schools already engaged in standards-based instructional practices before reform was initiated. However, the state policy effect was no longer significantly related to math teacher practice when classroom-level innovation factors were added to the model; this nonsignificance, they suggested, may be related to teacher receptivity or resistance to reform, teacher knowledge about the reform and reform practices, and teacher professional development.

They did not model student achievement and recommended large scale modeling of the relationship between state standards policy and student achievement as a next step. Overall, while standards-based reform is highly touted in education policy circles, little research has been done at the policy level on the effects of standards-based reform. There is skepticism whether the state standard will "trickle down" all the way to student performance.

High School Exit Exams

High stakes testing is generally defined as occurring "when significant educational paths or choices of an individual are directly affected by test performance" (Brennan, Kim, Wenz-Gross, & Siperstein, 2001) or when there are consequences from testing for schools or staff. Proponents of high stakes testing argue that exit exams will provide meaningful incentives to motivate students and schools to raise achievement. They argue that diplomas were being awarded for attendance and compliance rather than for documented achievement or subject mastery; therefore, exams were needed to assure quality and return credibility to the high school diploma.

Those who argue against high stakes testing suggest assessments may not challenge disparities but may instead reinforce or worsen inequalities. One study found the often touted score increases on the Texas Assessment of Academic Skills

(TAAS) were not matched by proportionate increases in National Assessment of Educational Progress (NAEP) scores for Texas students (Klein, Hamilton, McCaffrey, & Stecher, 2000). The authors suggested the TAAS progress may represent a better alignment between teaching and the exam or test preparation. McNeil (2000), also looking at the Texas TAAS, concluded that teachers and administrators in low-performing schools who were pressured to raise test scores often respond by replacing a substantive academic curriculum with test preparation materials. High stakes testing has also been shown to disproportionately impact African American and Hispanic students, who are more likely to fail to meet cutoff scores (Berger & Coelen, 2002; Brennan et al., 2001; Kornhaber, Orfield, & Kurlaender, 2001).

However, several other studies provided evidence of positive outcomes associated with testing in school (Winfield, 1990), state (Carnoy & Loeb, 2002; Winfield), and international comparisons (Bishop, 1998). On the other hand, Jacob (2001) established a relationship between exit exams and increased chances of student withdrawal from school for students with low academic achievement, contradicting the Carnoy and Loeb conclusion that testing does not hurt graduation rates. Jacob also found no significant relationship between state graduation tests and 12th-grade math and reading achievement as measured by the National Educational Longitudinal Survey assessments, suggesting testing was not raising achievement. However, this merits further examination because he was using 1992 data, and there have been policy changes.

Berger and Coelen (2002) found little relationship between one high stakes test and SAT score and concluded the negative impact of high stakes testing would be greater for underrepresented minorities. In Dee's (2002) analysis of minimum competency testing and curriculum graduation requirements, testing was not significantly related to high school graduation or college enrollment in general. However, when ethnicity was considered, testing was negatively associated with graduation rates among African American males.

In 2000, 19 states had implemented graduation exit exams and 9 states were in the process of developing them. For purposes of this study, those states that were developing exams were counted as not having exams because exams in development could not be expected to impact current student achievement. It was speculated that the minimum competencies measured in high school exit exams only affect students at the margin of graduation and, therefore, would not affect the preparation of students considering college. States with a high stakes exam policy were compared to states without an exam as a dichotomous variable.

K-12 School Funding

Common sense would suggest that when you pay more, you get more. Yet researchers on school funding radically disagree on this topic. From the Coleman Report (National Commission on Excellence in Education, 1983) forward, some make the argument that the discrepancies in achievement are explained by student demographics and student choices rather than school characteristics or quality as measured by expenditures per student (Finn, 1990; Paige, 2003). According to one study, once the differences in initial inputs such as students' ethnicity and socioeconomic status are accounted for, the significance of school funding on student achievement disappears (Hanushek, 1996). Ludwig and Bassi (1999) argue that these studies are flawed and underestimate the real impact of school funding. Stressing that value-added models are misspecified and underestimate the benefits of school funding, Ludwig and Bassi assert that models that use instrumental variables methods are more correct. They reviewed seven studies that used instrumental variables methods, all of which found significant relationships between school resources and student outcomes, including one that demonstrated positive effects of school resources on SAT scores (Card & Payne, 1998). Similarly, Payne and Biddle (1999), controlling for curriculum, poverty, and race, found significant net effects of school funding on student achievement. The research suggests the relationship between school resources and student achievement is sufficient to warrant further policy consideration. In this study, state average per-pupil K-12 school funding in 1998 was left as a continuous variable of instructional expenditures after adjusting with a cost-of-education index and rescaling.

All of these policies merit consideration either in their own right or as context variables that must be controlled for in the consideration of other policies. While there are other policies that would also have been interesting to consider, either the data is not currently available or the nature of hierarchical models limited the number of policy variables.

Research Approach

One way to measure readiness for college is through SAT scores. While the SAT was not designed as a measure of school outcomes, it is a measure of students' academic ability to do college work. While some would argue this is measuring schools and policies against the wrong yardstick, it could also be argued that readiness for college is precisely the purpose of high school education today. If the majority of the current generation will need some postsecondary education (Reich, 1991), then preparing students for college is an appropriate standard against which K-12 education policy should be measured.

A brief examination of prior research using the SAT will situate this study. Several studies examined the relationship between individual coursework and SAT score. Morgan (1989), using a 1987 cohort, found high school coursework in mathematics, science, and foreign languages was related to SAT score, controlling for students' prior academic achievement. In a study of gifted students, Brody and Benbow (1990) concluded that long-term exposure to a rigorous academic curriculum was related to SAT score, particularly in mathematics and science for the SAT math scores; and coursework in verbal subjects, particularly foreign languages, was related to SAT verbal scores. These studies further supported the conclusion that SAT scores were related to opportunities to learn and were therefore susceptible to state policy adjustments. In addition, they suggested that in future studies of the SAT, it is important to control for individual student coursework.

Studies that examined the relationship between state SAT participation rates, state-level educational and demographic variables, and state average SAT score concluded that when a higher percentage of students from a state take the exam, then a broader range of academic abilities are represented in that state's testing population. Participation rate accounts for some of the variance in state average SAT score (Powell & Steelman, 1996; Taube & Linden, 1989). Taube and Linden also established that state per-pupil expenditures (+), adult college completion rate (+), percentage of urban population (+), percentage of minority students (-), teachers' mean salary (-), and high school graduation rate (+) were significant predictors of state mean SAT score beyond the effects of participation rate.

St. John, Musoba, and Chung (2003) focused on education policy and demographic characteristics using state aggregated data from 1991-2000 in a fixed effects regression analysis of state mean SAT scores and state high school graduation rates. The SAT regression showed mathematics guidelines consistent with NCTM recommended standards (high curriculum requirements in mathematics in high schools); and the percentage of high schools in the state that participate in the AP program positively predicted state mean SAT score, while honors diploma policies had a negative relationship with state average SAT score. Equally important were the school reform variables that were not significant in the state data, such as exit exams, local board control of mathematics curriculum requirements, and K-12 instructional expenditures per student. When they examined high school graduation rates, high curriculum requirements in mathematics were negatively associated with graduation rates as was having state guidelines consistent with NCTM standards and the percentage of schools participating in the AP program. Instructional expenditures and having a policy for high school exit exams were positively related to high school graduation rates.

This study built on these analyses and examined the impact of education policy variables on student achievement using both state- and individual-level cross-sectional data rather than aggregated data. Individual-level characteristics and state-level policies were used to predict combined verbal and math individual SAT score. Second, the relationship (slope) between individual math course taking and SAT score was modeled by the state-level policy variable mathematics graduation curriculum requirements. The following student-level independent variables were included:

- Gender: Males were compared to females.
- Ethnicity: African American, Hispanic, Asian American, Native American/Other, and no response were compared to Whites.
- Language: Students whose primary home language was a language other than English were compared to students from primarily English speaking homes.
- Parent education: The highest education level of either parent was used. Students whose parent(s) did not finish high school, had two-year degrees, had bachelor's degrees, had graduate degrees, and students who did not respond were compared to students whose parent(s) had high school diplomas.
- Family income: Student income was collapsed into four groups: students from low-income families (less than $30,000), students from high-income families (over $70,000), and students who did not report their parents' income were compared to middle-income students (between $30,000 and $70,000).
- Educational aspirations: This categorical variable was dummy-coded into six groups. Students who aspired to an associate's, master's, or doctoral degree and students who were undecided or did not respond were compared to students who aspired to a bachelor's degree.
- High school coursework: Students whose most advanced math course was precalculus or trigonometry and students

who took calculus were compared to students whose highest math course was algebra II or lower. Students who had taken physics in high school were compared to students who had not.[2]

- High school grade point average: Students' self-reported grades were collapsed into four groups: grades 3.7 or higher were classified as As, grades between 2.7 and 3.3 were classified as Bs, and grades 2.3 or below were classified as C or lower. Students in the A, C or lower, and no response groups were compared to students in the B group.
- Class rank: Students who were ranked in the top 10 percent of their high school class were compared to students who reported class ranks in the lower 90 percent.
- Prior testing experience with the PSAT: Students who had taken the PSAT exam before taking the SAT were compared to students who had not taken the PSAT.
- School type: Students who attended independent schools (usually private) and students who were home schooled, attended charter schools, or other classifications were compared to students who attended public schools.
- School locale: Students who attended schools that were located in the center of large or medium-sized cities and students attending schools in rural areas were compared to students who attended schools in suburban communities, small cities or towns, or who did not respond. Locale was based on the census classifications for the schools' zip code rather than the students' addresses.

State policy and control variables were entered at the second level. Recent studies of achievement suggest the importance of

---

[2] The majority of students (about 80%) had taken biology and chemistry; therefore, physics appeared to be the best course to distinguish a more rigorous science curriculum.

considering the context in which student individual achievement should be measured (Raudenbush, Fotiu, & Cheong 1998). Controlling for the SAT participation rate accounted for variations between states in the academic ability of students taking the exam. SAT participation rate was entered as a continuous variable in the HLM (hierarchical linear modeling) models.

State-level policy variables were the key measures of the regression models. In the hierarchical model, state policy variables were used to predict the intercept of the model and the slope of the mathematics course taking level one coefficients. In other words, the model estimated the state-level variables' influence on between-state differences in the outcome, and the difference within states was estimated by the level one independent variables. Further, the models analyzed whether state mathematics graduation requirements influenced the relationship between student mathematics course taking and SAT score.

As identified earlier, the state-level policy variables were

- Mathematics graduation curriculum requirements (2000)[3]
- Percentage of schools offering Advanced Placement courses as a continuous variable[4]
- Academic standards policy implementation (2000), a continuous variable, was the state ranking for degree of standards-based reform policy implementation[5]

---

[3] Graduation curriculum requirements in mathematics were reported in NCES's *Condition of Education* and collected by the Council of Chief State School Officers in the *State Policies and Practices Survey, 2000*.

[4] The percentage of schools in the state participating in the AP program was published on the Web site of the College Board.

[5] Published in *Education Week's Quality Counts 2001*, the scale selected here scores or ranks states on their degree of implementation of standards-based reform, with criteria weighted as follows: adoption of standards, 15%; clarity and specificity of standards, 25%; types of assessments, 30%; and state practices for school (not student) accountability, 30%.

- High stakes high school exit exams (2000)[6]
- Adjusted, per-pupil K-12 school funding (1998)[7]

As noted, data on implementation of policy variables that were tied to a high school class, such as exit exams, were used from the year this cohort of students graduated (2000). Policy variables that help make up the students' education context, such as the prevalence of AP courses and school funding, were taken from the year prior to the year most students took the SAT (i.e., 1998, two years before graduation). One exception is noted. While standards-based reform was part of the school context, data from 2000 were used because of changes in the scoring criteria. In years prior to 2000, high school exit exams accounted for part of the standards reform score and, therefore, would have been included twice in these analyses if 1998 data had been used.

Statistical Model

These analyses used hierarchical linear modeling (HLM), a multilevel regression procedure. Multilevel analysis was most appropriate for these data because individual students were nested within states, violating the assumption of independence of cases. Multilevel modeling can also handle differences in group size

---

[6] High stakes high school exit exams were part of the State Student Assessment Database from NCES. This was cross-referenced with survey data published in the *Digest of Education Statistics.*

[7] School funding was adjusted for the variability in the cost of education between states to account for the differences in purchasing power. Chambers' (1998) Geographic Cost of Education Index (GCEI) (similar to a general cost-of-living index) was selected because it considers the cost of employing comparable teachers (experience and training) as well as other educational inputs like administrators, noncertified personnel, and nonpersonnel inputs. State mean K-12 school instructional expenditures and enrollments from two years prior to graduation were downloaded from the NCES Web site. K-12 instructional expenditures were divided by enrollment and rescaled by dividing by 100.

(number of students in each state). In individual-level disaggregated models, states like California or Texas would dominate. While HLM was the preferred method for this study, the small number of level two variables was methodologically problematic. In these analyses, it was important to consider simultaneously multiple policy variables and one level two control variable. Prior analyses which only considered one or two of the policies were criticized for not simultaneously considering variables outside the model (Dee, 2002). However, the small number of level two cases limits the number of level two policy variables that could be included in this model.

Level one variables were grand mean centered. Schreiber (in press) and Kreft, de Leeuw, and Aiken (1995) argue that the decision regarding centering should be theoretical rather than mathematical and based on the research question asked rather than on efforts to stabilize the model. Grand mean centering and raw score models are mathematically equivalent because it is a linear transformation to the variables; while they may partition the variance differently, they are considered equivalent (Kreft, de Leeuw, & Aiken). For this study, grand mean centering best portions out the variance among individual-level variables (which may vary between and within states) and group-level variables. With grand mean centering, the intercept was the adjusted mean for the sample or the expected value of the outcome (combined SAT score) for the average student in the whole sample, nationally. When categorical or dummy variables are centered, the resulting variable in effect represents the percentage of cases with each value, one or zero. The centered variable represents the average outcome for that variable (i.e., average between males and females) and the coefficient can be interpreted as the coefficient for the difference between values of one or zero. Level two variables were not centered, therefore a level two coefficient represents the change in the level one intercept associated with a one unit change in the level two variable.

Data Sources

Educational Testing Service provided a national random sample of 100,000 SAT scores and questionnaires from the SAT test takers who graduated from high school in the spring of 2000. Of those, 91,095 legitimate cases were available for the state policy analyses[8] and were merged with a number of state demographic and policy variables collected from federal and association sources. Most individual-level variables were self-reported, taken from the student descriptive questionnaire of the SAT.

Limitations

Several key limitations should be noted. This study did not challenge the flaws in standardized testing and the SAT in particular. There are socioeconomic and racial biases in all standardized testing (Stricker, Rock, Pollack, & Wenglinsky, 2002), and using one instrument to measure the complexity of factors associated with success in college is illogical. Further, using a standardized test did not challenge the definition of merit inherent in the SAT, a definition that is biased toward abilities valued by the elite (Rothstein, 2002). Acknowledging these flaws that are present in large-scale standardized assessments and the narrowness of using one standardized assessment, the SAT is a legitimate measure of readiness for college. While high school grades are a better predictor of college grades, the SAT does add to the predictability of success in college and is a national yardstick across secondary education institutions.

Second, not all high school students take the SAT, therefore, the SAT and this study were limited by a self-selection limitation. The sample did not include those students who withdrew from school before reaching their junior year and those students who for

---

[8] Of the 100,000 cases, 5,497 elected not to complete the student descriptive questionnaire, and 3,408 cases did not have an identified state of residence

any number of reasons did not take the SAT. However, many students that plan to go to college do take the SAT; therefore, it is a reasonable measure of academic aptitude related to college access, and the self-selection factor is constant across all state policy contexts. The inclusion of the state SAT participation rate controlled for differences among states.

There are dangers in using extant data. For example, students' self-reporting of family income in the student descriptive questionnaire of the SAT may be inaccurate in some cases. The collapsing of income into three categories controlled for minor errors in student self-reports, but uncertainty remains regarding the final accuracy. State policy variables were less suspect, although they also came from extant data. When possible, the variables and values of state education policies were compared to a second data source for accuracy and completeness. This was not possible with all variables, but when comparisons were made, there was very little variation.

Finally, it would have been useful to consider more policies simultaneously and to consider school level as an intermediate level in a three-level HLM model to measure the degree of local implementation of the reforms. Both of these alternatives were not available with the current data.

Findings

Multilevel models provide findings regarding the influence of individual- and group-level variables. While the state policies were the primary concern, the individual-level variables revealed some interesting findings and will be discussed first.

Descriptive Statistics for the Full Sample

Individual Level. As is typical for a sample of SAT test takers, more than half were female (54.4%) and the majority were White (61%) (Table 2). While the vast majority of students came from homes where English was the primary language, 7 percent came from homes where another language was the primary

Table 2. Descriptive Statistics for Variables in the HLM Regression Models	
Individual-Level Variable	Percentage
Gender	
Female	54.4
Male	45.6
Ethnicity	
African American	10.1
Hispanic	8.2
Asian American	7.4
Native American	0.7
"Other" race	3.0
No response on race	9.8
White	61.0
Primary Language in the Home	
Other than English	7.0
English	93.0
Parents' Education	
Did not finish high school	3.5
High school graduate/No response	23.3
Two-year degree	25.6
Bachelor's degree	20.3
Graduate degree	27.3
Family Income	
Low income (< $30,000)	17.9
Middle income (between $30,000 and $70,000)	33.5
High income (> $70,000)	27.2
No response	21.5
Students' Educational Aspirations	
Associates/Certificate/Other	3.1
Bachelor's degree	22.7
Master's degree	27.3
Doctoral degree	19.1
Undecided	11.0
No response	16.8

Table 2. Descriptive Statistics for Variables in the HLM Regression Models (cont.)	
Individual-Level Variable	**Percentage**
High School Coursework	
Highest math is algebra II	38.3
Took precalc/trig	40.4
Took calculus	21.3
Did not take physics	54.9
Took physics	45.1
High School GPA	
A grades	36.3
B grades	43.8
C or lower grades	11.5
No response	8.4
Top 10% Class Rank	17.3
Lower 90% class rank	82.7
Prior Experience with PSAT	72.9
Did not take the PSAT	27.1
School Type	
Public high school/no response	84.7
Independent	14.7
Home/correspondence/charter	0.6
School Locale	
Large/medium-sized city	34.6
Rural areas	10.5
Suburbs/towns/no response	54.9
State-Level Variables	
High school exit exams	38.0
No exam	62.0
High math graduation curriculum requirements (3+)	50.0
Low requirements/local board control of math	50.0
	Mean
Percentage of schools w/AP	54.3
Standards implementation score	74.0
SAT participation rate	36.4
K-12 school funding per pupil (unadjusted dollars)	3,767
Outcome Variable	
Mean combined SAT score	1,020
Number of cases	90,910

spoken language. A small percentage (3.5%) of the students had parents who did not finish high school, while 23 percent had parents who had finished high school or were students who did not answer the question. About 26 percent had parents with an associate's degree. Another 29 percent of parents had bachelor's degrees and 27 percent had graduate degrees. The percentage of students with parents who had at least a four-year degree was higher than in the general young adult population, but was more typical of an SAT test-taking sample. Only 18 percent of the sample was students that were classified as low-income, with incomes below $30,000, while 27 percent were identified as high-income. The largest group was middle-income students (33%), and the remainder was students who had not answered the family income question (22%).

The majority of test takers aspired to at least a bachelor's degree and many to higher degrees. In the sample, 27 percent aspired to a bachelor's degree, 19 percent aspired to doctoral degrees, and 27 percent aspired to master's degrees, while only 3 percent aspired to an associate's degree or certificate. Eleven percent of the sample was undecided about their educational plans, and 17 percent did not answer the question.

Examination of students' high school experiences revealed that for 38 percent of the students, their most advanced math course was algebra II or lower. The largest group (40%) was students who finished precalculus or trigonometry while 21 percent of test takers had taken calculus. Less than half (45%) of the students took high school physics. Only 36 percent of students reported their high school grade point average was A, while the largest group of students (44%) reported their cumulative grade point average was B. Only 11.5 percent of test takers reported grades of C or lower. A full 17 percent of test-takers reported they were in the top 10 percent of their high school class, and 73 percent of SAT test takers had taken the PSAT exam prior to taking the SAT. The majority (85%) of students attended public high schools or did not respond to the question. While less than 1 percent of students were home schooled, took correspondence courses, or attended charter schools, 15 percent of students attended independent high schools. The majority of students (55%) attended high schools in suburban areas (urban fringe), small or large towns, or did not respond to this question. A substantial portion, 35 percent, lived in the center of large or medium-sized cities, while 11 percent attended rural high schools.

State Policy Level. Only 38 percent of states had high school exit exams with consequences for students or schools. Half of states required students to take three or more mathematics courses for graduation, while the other half required two or less courses or allowed local school boards to set curriculum graduation requirements.[9]

While nationally about 69 percent of high schools offered Advanced Placement courses, the mean of the state percentages was 54 percent. The average standards implementation score for states was 74. The average of the state K-12 school funding per pupil was $3,767 before adjusting for the cost of education index. The mean combined SAT score was 1020 in this sample.

HLM Analysis. The HLM regression model showed individual-level variables had a greater influence on ability than state-level factors. The interclass correlation from the unconditional (null) model showed that only about 9 percent of the variance in SAT score can be attributed to state-level factors (see Table 3). While the majority of the variance was attributable to individual differences, level two variables did offer an independent influence on the outcome. The decrease in the deviance between the prior and final model shows that the final model was an improvement over the prior model. The significant individual-

---

[9] Preliminary analyses also tested the effects of local board control of mathematics requirements because it was significant in a study of high school graduation rates (St. John, Musoba, & Chung, 2003). However, in the preliminary analyses of this study, local board control was not significantly different from low mathematics requirements, and in subsequent analyses local control was part of the reference group.

Model	Null/ Uncondit.	Final Model
Table 3. Variance and Model Fit Estimates for HLM Models for the All-Student Sample and the Low-Income Sample		
Variance Estimates		
τLevel 2 variance/intercept variance	3819.90	181.71
τ_{10} Level 2 slope variance precalc/trig		168.47
τ_{11}Level 2 slope variance calc		323.57
σ^2Level 1 variance	40739.15	21027.70
P Interclass correlation	0.086	
Model Fit Estimates		
Deviance for prior model^^		1163365.31
# of parameters in prior model		1
Deviance		1162900.17
# of parameters		7
Significance of change in deviance		***
Reliability of intercept	0.964	0.761[10]
Reliability of precalc/trig slope		0.485
Reliability of calc slope		0.554
^^Prior model is model with level one and level two variables, but level two variance and covariance fixed.		

level variables are discussed first, and then the state-level policy variables are reviewed (see Table 4).

Individual-level Variables. Consistent with other research on the SAT, the gender gap in SAT scores was significant, an average

---

[10] The reliability of the intercept—the ratio of the parameter variance to the parameter variance plus the error variance—in the full model was high, at .761. While the reliabilities of the slope coefficients were lower, they were still very high.

41-point gap advantaging males over females on the combined score. Prior research (Pallas & Alexander, 1983) suggested that advanced coursework by males explained some of this differential, yet this gap persisted in this analysis in spite of the inclusion of mathematics and science coursework.

Similarly the racial score gaps continued to persist in spite of the inclusion of parent education, family income, prior achievement and some high school coursework. The coefficient for the differential between African American and White students was most substantial, at 105, while the gap between Hispanic and White students had a coefficient of 56. Students from homes where English was not the primary language spoken were also disadvantaged. As the SAT's administrator, Educational Testing Service (ETS), maintains, ethnicity appears to continue to represent some factor which may include variables not considered in the model, such as opportunities to learn, cultural capital, and school contexts, rather than simply racial differences.

There appeared to be a rather linear relationship between parents' education and SAT score. The differential between students whose parents did not graduate from high school and those whose did graduate had a coefficient of -30. The gap between no college and a two-year degree or higher was also significant and as expected. Students whose parents had four-year college degrees on average scored significantly higher (coefficient of 46) than students whose parents only finished high school.

Family income was also associated with SAT scores in significant ways. The score differential between low- and middle-income students was about -25 points, advantaging middle-income students. Similarly the gap between middle- and high-income students was associated with a 19-point score difference.

Students' educational aspirations were also positively associated with SAT scores. Higher student aspirations were associated with higher SAT scores. Comparing students who aspired to less than a bachelor's degree and students who aspired to a bachelor's degree, the gap was associated with a -33 coefficient. Comparing students who aspired to a bachelor's degree and those who aspired to graduate degrees, the coefficients followed a similar pattern: master's degree compared to bachelor's had a coefficient of 26, and doctoral degrees had a coefficient of 52. Undecided students who take the SAT do not appear to be uninformed students; instead they appear to be students choosing between degree options. Students who were undecided compared to students who aspired to a bachelor's was associated with a coefficient of 32, suggesting undecided students were more like students who aspired to graduate degrees.

High school mathematics coursework showed a strong relationship with SAT score. The difference between students who took calculus and students whose highest mathematics course was algebra II was associated with a coefficient of 122. While smaller, the coefficient (52) for the gap between students who took precalculus or trigonometry and students who finished with algebra II was still substantial. Taking physics in high school was also associated with higher SAT scores (32 point differential).

The relationship between high school grades and SAT score was as expected. Students with higher grades tended to score higher on the SAT. The differential between students who reported A grades and B grades had a positive coefficient of 71. The differential between B and C or lower students was associated with a -60 point score gap.

Similarly, class rank was positively associated with SAT score. Students who had taken the PSAT exam generally scored higher than students who had not taken the PSAT. Taking the PSAT may represent a practice effect and comfort with testing or earlier college aspirations and sophistication with the college preparation process.

While the coefficient comparing independent and public schools was not large (20), independent high schools appeared to advantage students, controlling for the other variables in the model. The small percentage of students who participated in home schooling, charter schools, and correspondence education and the diversity of options within this group mean the positive coefficients for this group should be interpreted as preliminary.

These findings appear to add to the weight of evidence pointing to problems in public schools. Alternatively, parents of these students take a more active interest in their children's education. Finally, the self-selection of more affluent students who opt to attend well-resourced private schools may explain these differences. The findings suggest that further examination, more narrowly targeted on these educational experiences, is needed before interpreting these differences.

Students attending high schools in urban and rural areas were disadvantaged compared to students attending high schools in suburbs or towns. The gap in achievement was larger for rural students who may not have had the same opportunities for a rigorous high school curriculum but also important for urban students who were similarly disadvantaged.

State-Level Variables. Among the state-level variables, some policies were significant, but several appeared to have no relationship with the achievement they were designed to raise (see Table 4). The percentage of schools in the state offering Advanced Placement courses appeared to have no relationship with individual student achievement. Likewise, the degree of implementation of educational standards and the presence of high school exit exams were not significantly related to student achievement. Several state-level variables were significantly associated with SAT score. High requirements in math for high school graduation were negatively associated with SAT score.

Analyses examining the impact of the high math requirements policy on the coefficient or slope of the relationship between math course taking and SAT score showed a positive relationship between math policy and the coefficient for advanced math courses for both levels, but the relationship was only significant for precalculus or trigonometry. States with high math requirements have steeper slopes than do states with low math requirements. In other words, states with high math requirements have a stronger relationship between advanced coursework or precalculus and SAT score than states with low requirements. Not only does math course taking affect SAT score, but policies that

Table 4. Achievement Analysis: HLM Model of Intercepts and Slopes as Outcome for SAT Score			
Fixed Effects			
Individual Variable	**Coeff.**	**SE**	**Sig.**
Intercept/Mean SAT Score	1027.23	16.90	***
Gender: Male	40.52	0.99	***
Race			
African American	-105.22	1.79	***
Hispanic	-55.95	2.04	***
Asian American	-10.38	2.15	***
Native American	-43.36	6.02	***
"Other" race	-18.20	2.90	***
No response on race	46.09	2.64	***
Primary Language			
Other than English	-40.29	2.19	***
Parents' Education			
Did not finish high school	-29.97	3.00	***
Two-year degree	20.43	1.57	***
Bachelor's degree	46.60	1.69	***
Graduate degree	73.28	1.66	***
Family Income			
Low income (<$30,000)	-24.74	1.51	***
High income (>$70,000)	18.63	1.32	***
No response	19.84	1.60	***
St's Educational Aspirations			
Associates/Certificate/Other	-33.30	2.93	***
Master's degree	25.75	1.39	***
Doctoral degree	51.54	1.58	***
No response	25.10	2.32	***
Undecided	32.49	1.56	***

Table 4. Achievement Analysis: HLM Model of Intercepts and Slopes as Outcome for SAT Score (cont.)			
Fixed Effects			
Individual Variable	**Coeff.**	**SE**	**Sig.**
High School Coursework			
Took precalc/trig	51.84	3.83	***
Took calculus	121.92	4.97	***
Took physics	32.29	1.13	***
High School GPA			
C or lower grades	-59.88	1.66	***
A grades	70.91	1.31	***
No response	68.62	2.36	***
Top 10% Class Rank	74.06	1.55	***
Prior Experience with PSAT	42.38	1.28	***
School Governance Type			
Independent	20.19	1.43	***
Home/correspond/charter	46.60	6.49	***
School Locale			
Large/medium-sized city	-12.58	1.12	***
Rural areas	-28.88	1.67	***
State-Level Variables	**Coeff.**	**SE**	**Sig.**
% Schools w/ AP	0.11	0.17	N/S
Standards implementation rank	-0.21	0.18	N/S
High school exit exams	3.79	5.20	N/S
High math grad requirements (3+)	-14.36	5.39	*
K-12 school funding	0.92	0.26	***
SAT participation rate	-0.47	0.13	***
Math policy/math course			
Slope/Highest math is precalc	13.09	5.20	*
Slope/Highest math is calc	10.20	6.78	N/S
Number of cases			90910

require additional coursework are strengthening that relationship, making taking advanced courses more important in those states with the policy. This suggests that the policy may be moving some students who might have stopped at algebra II to take the next level of courses, bringing the desired effect from the policy. However, this interaction was not influential in relation to taking calculus. It appears students who take calculus are probably self-motivated and not significantly affected by the policy. It may also be true that because the SAT does not cover calculus, the relationship between policy, student behavior, and the abilities measured by the SAT may not be significant.

In their reanalysis of NELS:88 data, St. John and associates (in review) found math graduation policy did influence course taking in advanced math. They found a positive relationship between high math requirements and taking calculus. Students in states that required three or more math courses had a higher chance of taking calculus (1.543 odds ratio). It was hypothesized in this instance as well that the graduation requirements policy has a positive effect on course taking. This hypothesized indirect effect of the education reform policies on SAT score through affecting student course taking in mathematics was tested in a separate analysis (Appendix A). In that analysis, the outcome compared students taking calculus and students taking precalculus or trigonometry to students whose most advanced course was algebra II, in a multinomial regression model. There was no significant relationship between math graduation requirements and the likelihood students would take calculus or precalculus. Therefore, the relationship between math requirements and SAT score does not appear to be mitigated by student course taking behavior, as hypothesized.

Adjusted average K-12 school funding was significantly and positively associated with students' college readiness. School funding was the only policy variable positively associated with SAT score. While this finding adds another study to the school funding debate, some of the additional controls in this model (including individual differences in students and other state policies) make this an important contribution, confirming the importance of adequate funding for education.

Consistent with prior research, the percentage of students in a state taking the SAT exam was negatively associated with SAT score, though the coefficient was small here. Participation rate also helped control for nonpolicy differences between states.

Discussion

Individual Variables

Several significant demographic variables are disturbing, considering the number of other variables or controls in this model. While these findings are not new, they merit a brief discussion. ETS maintains that the SAT measures individual developed abilities and that, therefore, differences in scores are attributable to students' developed abilities, rather than group demographic differences. Yet there are group differences in SAT scores based on race, gender, and family income, after controlling for prior academic performance and high school curriculum. In this study, much of the variation in individual student SAT scores was attributed to individual-level variation between students. Because most of the variance was at level one, to some degree this confirms ETS's claim that variance is a measure of individual ability. Yet the significant relationship of SAT score with gender, race, parent education, and family income raise the question whether it is just a measure of abilities. Either there are remaining test biases, or there are genuine differences across demographic groups in ability, or there are other explanations for these differences beyond ability. Other variables not considered in this model may be correlated with these demographic variables and may be the real explanation of these differences. It is probable that the SAT measures both natural ability and some other factor or factors. Rothstein (2002) offered that the SAT functions as "affirmative action for high-SES children" (p. 3), measuring school-level demographics and opportunities to learn in addition to individual differences. Clearly, further research is needed.

The benefits of taking rigorous high school courses were also confirmed in this study. Students, who self-select to take calculus, on average, would be expected to score over 100 points higher than students who do not, and there was about a 30-point difference associated with physics. The value of *encouraging* all students to self-select into a rigorous curriculum is clear and consistent with other recent reports (ACT, 2004).

State Policies

Advanced Placement Courses

The state percentage of schools offering Advanced Placement courses was not statistically related to student SAT score. This finding was somewhat surprising considering prior research and the importance institutions place on Advanced Placement coursework in the admissions process. St. John, Musoba, and Chung (2003) showed the percentage of schools participating in the AP program was positively associated with state average SAT score. In a subsequent study, St. John and associates (in review) found the percentage of schools offering Advanced Placement courses was positively associated with taking calculus. Because taking calculus was associated with the SAT at the individual level in this study, it was hypothesized that the relationship between school involvement in Advanced Placement and SAT is indirect, via encouraging students to take more rigorous coursework. Yet in a supplemental analysis (Appendix A) there was no significant relationship between the percentage of schools offering AP courses and students' advanced math course taking. This study suggests that statewide participation in Advanced Placement has little to do with SAT score or with influencing student course taking, yet further research should be done before making policy decisions.

Standards-Based Reform

In this study, standards-based reform implementation was not significantly associated with students' abilities for college work. While standards-based reform appeared hopeful when it was introduced because of its emphasis on higher-order thinking skills, particularly when math standards were modeled after the NCTM standards, standards-based reform has not met expectations, or it is not being implemented at the local level. Standards established at the state level may be too removed from students to make a difference. With the appropriate controls, Swanson and Stevenson (2002) found no relationship between teacher practice and state standards-based activity, and the results of this study are consistent with their findings that state standards-based reforms are having less impact than envisioned. It is also important to note that states active in standards-based reform may also be states with more centralized policy structures. Iowa, with the lowest standards-based implementation ranking, is a state with a philosophy of local control for education policy, which may be related to more teacher receptivity toward and ownership of reform.

St. John, Musoba, and Chung (2003) showed the degree of agreement between state math standards and NCTM standards was positively associated with state average SAT score. However, they only examined math content standards, while this study looked across academic subject areas and also looked at assessments and institutional accountability, a much broader measure. Math standards may be the furthest developed and may be qualitatively different from other content standards focusing on process outcomes and higher-order skills. Interestingly, the math standards came from the National Council of Teachers of Mathematics, a teachers' association, not a state governing agency. It may be that teachers were more receptive to standards developed by their professional peers rather than imposed by the state hierarchy.

Finally, it should be noted that most states have not fully implemented all four components of standards-based reform and it may be too early to reject it on the basis of implementation results. Yet this study compared states on a continuum of development and implementation of standards, therefore standards would have been expected to be significant if there was a difference between states with high and low implementation.

High School Exit Exams

High stakes school exit exams were not significantly related to SAT score, confirming studies that found no relationship between exit exams and achievement (Berger & Coelen, 2002; Jacob, 2001; St. John, Musoba, & Chung, 2003). While Winfield (1990) found state exams in New York were associated with higher SAT scores, controlling for SES, the present study appears to have had more extensive controls.

Several features of testing may explain this nonsignficance. First, exit exams are designed to measure the minimum skills needed to earn a high school diploma, while the SAT is intended to measure the abilities necessary to do college-level work successfully. It was hypothesized that these two types of exams measure different ability sets. This study tested whether exam policies were an incentive or in some other way influenced students' college academic readiness, and they did not.

However, this analysis included individual student course taking, which some might suggest accounted for the influence of exit exams at the individual level. A supplementary analysis (Appendix A) showed that there was not a significant relationship between exit exams and advanced coursework in mathematics. Individual course taking variables did not account for the positive effect of exams.

A third possible reason for the nonsignificance of exams may be related to school-level adjustments to state exams. Several studies have suggested that in low-performing schools, teachers may adjust for testing by narrowing the curriculum and focusing on test preparation rather than on higher-order thinking skills and varied knowledge (Klein, Hamilton, McCaffrey, & Stecher, 2000; McNeil, 2000). Therefore, the exit tests may be reducing overall achievement as much as or more than inspiring it. When the consequence of the high school exit exam is refusal of an academic diploma, exit exams appear to follow a deficit theory and emphasize individual agency, holding students and their families responsible for their poor performance rather than systemic factors or school quality. Yet when exam pass rates are not evenly distributed across schools, the exams are measuring something in addition to individual ability, challenging the assumptions of individual agency.

Finally, it should be noted that the implementation of testing has been much weaker than the initial rhetoric. Moreover, those students considering college (the population who take the SAT) would probably have skills that are more advanced than required to pass exit exams and, therefore, would not be influenced by those exams in a substantial way.

It is clear that, while exit exams might affect students at the margin by increasing drop-out rates (St. John, Musoba, & Chung, 2003) or by slightly boosting achievement among low-performing students, they are not raising overall college readiness. Based on this and other analyses, it is important to question the continued use of high stakes exit exams. Why suffer the negative consequences of drop outs for little or no aptitude gains? If the goal is to assure more students are ready for college, it appears that this approach is not a good public investment.

Mathematics Curriculum Graduation Requirements
Math graduation requirements were negatively associated with SAT scores in this study. This policy may be a disincentive for some students, or it may be that in states with lower requirements students were more likely to self-select into harder courses. It is important to note that the states with low requirements also included states with local board control of requirements, where parents may take a more active role, and states where the ACT is emphasized over the SAT exam.

The relationship between high math requirements and aptitude in this study differs from some prior research. In their fixed effects analysis of state average SAT scores, St. John, Musoba, and Chung (2003) found a positive relationship between high math requirements and average SAT scores. However, several distinctions between the studies make the differences in their findings less contentious.

It was hypothesized that individual course taking accounted for some of the variance attributed to the graduation policy in prior studies, but the supplementary analysis (Appendix A) showed that math requirements were not significantly related to student course taking behavior in math. There may be a subtly different explanation. Dee (2002) found that high curriculum requirements led to more course taking by students but that growth in achievement was more related to the level of courses rather than to the number of courses. At the individual level, this study measures the level of courses, not the quantity of courses. Therefore, state policies that encourage more advanced courses may have a stronger influence on readiness for college than numeric course requirements.

Math Requirements and the Slope of Course Taking and SAT Score. The second test of the influence of math graduation requirements examined the influence of high requirements on the relationship between students' math course taking and SAT scores. Math graduation policy positively influenced the slope of the relationship between course taking and SAT score. This is not simply a measure of whether graduation requirements raise SAT scores through student course taking behavior but whether high graduation requirements made for a stronger relationship between SAT score and advanced course taking. States with high requirements had a stronger relationship between course taking and SAT score than states with low requirements or with local board control. This suggests that it may not be just the number of courses taken in those states, where that number was more standardized, but the rigor or level of those courses that was important. It may be that the three-course requirement helped students understand the importance of math and, therefore, led them to select a more rigorous track. This corresponds with Chaney, Burgdorf, and Atash's (1997) finding that it was more rigorous courses on the academic hierarchy rather than more time in the same courses that was important. The significance for precalculus but not calculus in this study was also consistent with their conclusion that it was students on the margin who were influenced by the policy and not students who self-selected into more rigorous courses.

Substantial time has passed since the changes in math requirements such that these findings are based on fuller implementation than is the case for some of the other policies that states implemented later. Considering the negative relationship between high math requirements and aptitude for college in this study and the mixed reviews regarding graduation rates (Dee, 2002; St. John, Musoba, & Chung, 2003), it is important to reconsider the value of requiring a set number of courses versus encouraging students to take more advanced courses, while assuring that all students in all schools have access to rigorous courses.

K-12 School Funding

The only state policy that showed a positive relationship in this study with student abilities measured by the SAT was state average per-pupil K-12 school funding. Higher average K-12 funding was associated with higher SAT scores. This was consistent with several prior studies that found school resources positively influenced SAT score or another measure of student achievement (Card & Payne, 1998; Payne & Biddle, 1999; Taube & Linden, 1989). While instructional expenditures were not significant in the St. John, Musoba, and Chung (2003) study of achievement, there were several differences here, including the use of HLM methodology, the use of individual SAT score rather than state average SAT score, and the use of the cost-of-education index adjustment.

Funding was also the only policy that showed positive effects when controlling for individual-level variables and examining several policies simultaneously. As a reform policy, funding is not highly debated right now. Considering the positive influence of funding and the lack of significance or negative effect of the other state policies, K-12 funding should move to the policy forefront again. Moreover, with funding's positive association with graduation rates (St. John, Musoba, & Chung, 2003), its slight positive association with students taking calculus, and its positive association with SAT score, funding is a well-substantiated policy investment with no observed negative consequences.

Arguments for adequate funding for K-12 schools fit with an academic preparation model consistent with social reproduction theory. This theory argues that those in power tend to protect the structures that support their own position (Oakes, 1985). Equalizing funding for K-12 schools between and within states would reduce the privilege of students and families in wealthier school districts. Equitable school funding is more consistent with the school reform arguments from several decades ago, when equity of opportunity was the goal, rather than with the current focus on quality for all and accountability outcomes. The shift away from equal opportunity and funding began with the conclusions drawn from the Coleman report—conclusions that focused on the responsibilities of the family rather than the responsibilities of the school or system. Recent reexaminations of these conclusions (Applebome, 1997; Bracey, 2002) question their validity; therefore, the policies that follow from those beliefs should also be questioned. The results of this study as well as other studies (Oakes, 1985; Oakes, Rogers, Lipton, & Morrell, 2002) challenge the wisdom and justice of these financial inequalities among schools. Yet some privileged parents and educators see democratizing access to high status curriculum eroding the advantages of their own children (Oakes et al., 2002).

It is also possible that funding has a greater impact on the availability of core advanced courses like calculus and physics. Therefore, some of the influence of funding may have been accounted for in the individual-level variables, suppressing an even larger positive effect. The slight positive relationship between school funding and the probability a student takes calculus supports this proposition (Appendix A).

Future analyses must address the inequity in funding within states and could include both an equity ratio between the richest and poorest schools within a state and state average funding in the same model. This would test both the questions of adequacy and equity. Alternatively, a three-level model including the school level could more precisely measure the impact of funding by having actual school funding at the individual students' schools rather than state average funding, which would control for both the equity and dollar amount issues. While these future analyses would be valuable, the current study, which does control for a number of individual- and state-level variables simultaneously, should not be discounted.

SAT Participation Rate

The SAT participation rate in this study was included as a state-level control variable because of the large variation between states in the percentage of students who take the SAT. As expected, SAT participation rate was negatively related to SAT score. However, the effect was smaller in this model than in the Powell and Steelman study (1996) because of the inclusion of policy variables they did not consider, the inclusion of individual-level variables, or the difference in modeling—a hierarchical versus an aggregated OLS model.

Conclusions

In this study, several state policies made little difference on SAT scores, and only one policy was positively associated with SAT scores. Several possible reasons for this discrepancy and the overall ineffectiveness of these policies should be discussed.

One possible reason may be that the reforms may not be benefiting the schools that most need change. Schools with greater resources may be more able to implement change. Alternatively, reforms like high stakes testing and graduation requirements do not challenge the social reproduction structures in the school system. Instead, they legitimize blaming the student and family. These policies do not challenge the definition of merit inherent in the exams and the methods of instruction and opportunities for instruction which advantage White upper- and middle-class students. As long as large variances in pass rates among schools exist, exams will punish students simply for living in the wrong school district. Better policy would assure that a rigorous college preparatory curriculum is available in every school within and across states and would assure that students are encouraged and prepared to enroll regardless of income or ethnicity. Lemann (1999) recommends that any measuring of merit and the sorting and selection of those who merit should take place after schooling. He councils that government and public schools should be in the business of guaranteeing a quality education to all students, not the business of sorting students.

The nominal or negative effects of reform policies may also be related to limited implementation. Organizational theorists suggest the loose coupling between states and classroom teachers may limit implementation. Pressman and Wildavsky (1984, as cited in Swanson & Stevenson, 2002) suggest the greater the number of intervening levels of organization, the less likely the goals will be attained. In addition to the loose coupling, teacher resistance to change (Fuhrman, Clune, & Elmore, 1991) can stymie education reform. These characteristics are true of any efforts at the state level for top-down mandated change or reform. It may be more appropriate for states to invest their energies in facilitating locally directed reform rather than state mandates that are distantly or negatively related to student outcomes.

Alternatively, state policies that raise students' preparedness for college might be better understood in a longitudinal rather than an immediate way. Therefore, to examine the state's role in college access through policy formation, it might be better to take a cross-generational focus. Not all variables at the individual level are outside the control of state policy if considered across generations, and some policies may take longer to realize their benefits. Several examples may illustrate this point.

Parent education and family income positively predicted student SAT score in this study. Current parent education levels are a consequence of K-12 policies and higher education access and finance policies during the 1970s. Considering that college participation between ethnic groups was relatively equal at that time, current parent education and income levels are a result of factors including greater access to financial aid, civil rights actions in the 1960s, equal education rights court decisions such as *Brown vs. Board of Education,* equalizing legislation such as Title I, and the overall growth in understanding of the value of advanced education for men and women. Education reform during that era was more focused on equalizing input and funding in education rather than on accountability and assessment. Government policies for adequate student aid and institutional subsidies that helped keep tuition lower may be indirectly related to student SAT score today via the influence of parent education at the individual student level. Similarly, course taking in high school is related to parent education and income, and advanced coursework in math, science, and foreign language was shown to affect SAT score.

In summary, in this study, the academic impact of the currently promoted accountability-based education reform policies was negative or insignificant, which brings us back to the question: accountability versus adequate funding—which policies influence adequate preparation for college? In striking contrast to accountability policies, adjusted average K-12 funding was positively associated with SAT score. While there are many problems related to funding policies including the wide disparity in funding between schools and districts within a state, funding was the only state policy examined that had a significant positive impact on academic readiness for college. During the 1960s and 1970s adequate funding was a prominent governmental policy, and there was a narrowing of the gaps in college participation between income and ethnic groups. Yet the political domain shifted, in part with the publication of *A Nation At Risk* (National Commission on Excellence in Education, 1983). The arguments for accountability rose from a sense that the school systems needed to be fixed from the outside. Nonetheless, the rise in accountability-based reforms and the simultaneous neglect of adequate funding has coincided with the widening in college participation gaps between ethnic groups and low- and high-income students. While most would agree that the education system needs reform, definitions of the problem and recommended solutions are not widely agreed upon. However, this study suggests the currently recommended accountability-based reform solutions should be called into question because these reforms are not raising students' readiness for college, in contrast to K-12 funding which was significantly associated with readiness. An appropriate battle cry in the policy arena might echo the words of Rod Tidwell in the movie *Jerry Maguire*: "Show me the money."

Appendix A

A secondary analysis was conducted examining the effects of state education policy on students' high school course taking in mathematics. This was done to examine the potential indirect effect of education policy on student readiness for college by influencing student course taking that would affect SAT score. The multinomial model looked at the probability of students taking calculus or precalculus/trigonometry compared to taking algebra II as the most advanced high school math course. All variables were left in the model to parallel the analysis in the primary text.

Table A.1 shows the results for the mathematics course taking model. High math requirements had no relationship with taking calculus, which is consistent with the other analyses that suggest students who take more courses than the minimum requirements are not affected by the policy. There was also no significant relationship between high math requirements and taking precalculus or trigonometry, which was somewhat unexpected.

There was no relationship between Advanced Placement participation, standards implementation and high school exit exams and student coursework in mathematics. The SAT participation rate was negatively associated with the probability of enrolling in precalculus or calculus in high school.

Table A.1. Mathematics Course Taking: HGLM Model of Effects of Individual Variables and State Education Policy on Student Course Taking in Mathematics

Individual Variable	Calculus			Precalculus or Trigonometry		
	Coeff.	SE	Sig.	Coeff.	SE	Sig.
Intercept	-1.58	0.49	**	-0.11	0.37	
Gender: Male	0.37	0.02	***	0.11	0.02	***
Race						
African American	-0.40	0.05	***	-0.19	0.03	***
Hispanic	-0.09	0.05	N/S	-0.02	0.03	N/S
Asian American	0.79	0.05	***	0.38	0.04	***
Native American	-0.35	0.15	*	-0.24	0.10	*
"Other" race	0.05	0.07	N/S	-0.02	0.05	N/S
No response on race	-0.25	0.07	***	-0.28	0.05	***
Primary Language						
Other than English	0.43	0.05	***	0.25	0.04	***
Parents' Education						
Did not finish high school	-0.01	0.07	N/S	-0.01	0.05	N/S
Two-year degree	0.12	0.04	**	0.09	0.03	***
Bachelor's degree	0.41	0.04	***	0.27	0.03	***
Graduate degree	0.52	0.04	***	0.29	0.03	***
Family Income						
Low income (< \$30,000)	-0.19	0.04	***	-0.12	0.03	***
High income (> \$70,000)	0.13	0.03	***	0.10	0.02	***
No response	-0.06	0.04	N/S	-0.04	0.03	***
St's Educational Aspirations						
Associate's certificate/Other	-0.38	0.08	***	-0.44	0.05	***
Master's degree	0.54	0.03	***	0.28	0.02	***
Doctoral degree	0.91	0.04	***	0.37	0.03	***
No response	-0.03	0.06	N/S	-0.24	0.04	***
Undecided	0.34	0.04	***	0.06	0.03	*
High School Coursework						
Took physics	2.41	0.03	***	1.23	0.02	***

Table A.1. Mathematics Course Taking: HGLM Model of Effects of Individual Variables and State Education Policy on Student Course Taking in Mathematics (cont.)						
	Calculus			Precalculus or Trigonometry		
	Coeff.	SE	Sig.	Coeff.	SE	Sig.
High School GPA						
C or lower grades	-1.32	0.06	***	-0.76	0.03	***
A grades	1.45	0.03	***	0.66	0.02	***
No response	-0.41	0.07	***	-0.83	0.04	***
Top 10% Class Rank	1.21	0.04	***	0.39	0.03	***
Prior Experience with PSAT	0.83	0.03	***	0.53	0.02	***
School Governance Type						
Independent	0.05	0.03	N/S	0.15	0.03	***
Home/correspond/charter	-1.23	0.17	***	-0.73	0.11	***
School Locale						
Large/medium-sized city	0.05	0.03	N/S	0.04	0.02	0.06
Rural areas	-0.06	0.04	N/S	-0.03	0.03	N/S
State-Level Variables	**Coeff.**	**SE**	**Sig.**	**Coeff.**	**SE**	**Sig.**
% Schools w/ AP	0.01	0.01	N/S	0.01	0.00	N/S
Standards implementation rank	0.00	0.01	N/S	0.00	0.00	N/S
High school exit exams	-0.02	0.17	N/S	0.13	0.13	N/S
High math grad requirements (3+)	-0.09	0.16	N/S	-0.23	0.13	N/S
K-12 school funding	0.02	0.01	*	0.01	0.01	N/S
SAT participation rate	-0.02	0.00	***	-0.01	0.00	**
Number of cases						90,910
*** $p<.001$, ** $p<.01$, * $p<.05$						

The only policy variable that showed a positive relationship with course taking was K-12 school funding. While K-12 funding was positively associated with taking calculus compared to finishing high school with algebra II, it was not significantly associated with taking precalculus or trigonometry.

References

ACT. (2004). *Crisis at the core: Preparing all students for college and work.* Available at www.act.org/ path/policy/pdf/crisis _report.pdf.

Adelman, C. (1999). *Answers in the tool box: Academic intensity, attendance patterns, and bachelor's degree attainment.* Washington, DC: Office of Research and Improvement, US Department of Education.

Advisory Committee on Student Financial Assistance. (2002). *Empty promises: The myth of college access in America.* Washington, DC: Author.

Applebome, P. (1997, June 11). A prophecy both false and successful. *The New York Times,* B9.

Berger, J. B., & Coelen, S. P. (2002). *Bridges and barriers: The impact of high stakes testing on college access.* Paper presented at the annual meeting of the Association for the Study of Higher Education, Sacramento, CA.

Bishop, J. (1998). *Do curriculum-based external exit exam systems enhance student achievement?* (CPRE Research Report Series RR-40). Philadelphia: Consortium for Policy Research in Education, University of Pennsylvania, Graduate School of Education.

Bracey, G. W. (2002). Test scores, creativity, and global competitiveness. *Phi Delta Kappan, 83*(10), 738-739.

Brennan, R. T., Kim, J., Wentz-Gross, M., & Siperstein, G. N. (2001). The relative equitability of high stakes testing versus teacher-assigned grades: An analysis of the Massachusetts Comprehensive Assessment System. *Harvard Educational Review, 71*(2), 173-216.

Brody, L. E., & Benbow, C. P. (1990). Effects of high school coursework and time on SAT scores. *Journal of Educational Psychology, 82*(4), 866-876.

Camara, W. J., & Schmidt, A. E. (1999). *Group differences in standardized testing and social stratification* (Report No. 99-5). New York: College Entrance Examination Board.

Card, D., & Payne, A. A. (1998). *School finance reform, the distribution of school spending and the distribution of SAT scores.* [Unpublished manuscript]. Cambridge, MA.

Carnoy, M., & Loeb, S. (2002). Does external accountability affect student outcomes? A cross-state analysis. *Education Evaluation and Policy Analysis, 24*(4), 305-331.

Chaney, B., Burgdorf, K., & Atash, N. (1997). Influencing achievement through high school graduation requirements. *Educational Evaluation and Policy Analysis, 19*(3), 229-244.

Choy, S. (2002). *Access and persistence: Findings from 10 years of longitudinal research on students.* Washington, DC: American Council on Education.

Choy, S. P., Horn, L. J., Nuæz, A.-M., & Chen, X. (2000). Transition to college: What helps at-risk students and students whose parents did not attend college? In A. F. Cabrera & S. M. La Nasa (Eds.), *New directions for institutional research: Vol. 107. Understanding the college choice of disadvantaged students* (pp. 45-63). San Francisco: Jossey-Bass.

Clune, W. H., White, P., & Patterson, J. (1989). *The implementation and effects of high school graduation requirements: First steps toward curricular reform* (No. RR-011). New Brunswick, NJ: Center for Policy Research in Education.

Cogan, L. S., Schmidt, W. H., & Wiley, D. E. (2001). Who takes what math and in which track? Using TIMSS to characterize US students' eighth-grade mathematics learning opportunities. *Educational Evaluation and Policy Analysis, 23*(4), 323-341.

College Entrance Examination Board. (2000). *AP national summary report 2000.* Available at www.collegeboard.com/ap/2000/ national_2000.pdf.

Dee, T. S. (2002, June 11). *Standards and student outcomes: Lessons from the "first wave" of education reform.* Paper presented at the conference Taking Account of Accountability: Assessing Politics and Policy, Kennedy School of Government, Harvard University.

Finn, C. E., Jr. (1990). The biggest reform of all. *Phi Delta Kappan, 71*(8), 584-592.

Finn, C. E., Jr. (2002). Making school reform work. *Public Interest, 148*, 85-96.

Fuhrman, S., Clune, W. H., & Elmore, R. (1991). Research on education reform: Lessons on the implementation of policy. In A. R. Odden (Ed.), *Education policy implementation* (pp. 197-218). Albany, NY: State University of New York Press.

Gamoran, A. (1992). Is ability grouping equitable? *Educational Leadership, 50*(2), 11-18.

Hanushek, E. A. (1996). School resources and student performance. In G. Burtless (Ed.), *Does money matter? The effect of school resources on student achievement and adult success* (pp. 44-73). Washington, DC: The Brookings Institution.

Hearn, J. C. (1991). Academic and nonacademic influences on the college destinations of 1980 high school graduates. *Sociology of Education, 64*(3), 158-171.

Heller, D. E. (1997). Student price response in higher education: An update to Leslie and Brinkman. *Journal of Higher Education, 68*(6), 624-659.

Hoffer, T. B. (1997). High school graduation requirements: Effects on dropping out and student achievement. *Teachers College Record, 98*(4), 584-607.

Jackson, G. A. (1978). Financial aid and student enrollment. *Journal of Higher Education, 49*(6), 548-574.

Jacob, B. A. (2001). Getting tough? The impact of high school graduation exams. *Educational Evaluation and Policy Analysis, 23*(2), 99-121.

Klein, S. P., Hamilton, L. S., McCaffrey, D. F., & Stecher, B. M. (2000). What do test scores in Texas tell us? *Education Policy Analysis Archives, 8*(49), 17.

Kornhaber, M., Orfield, G., & Kurlaender, M. (2001). *Raising standards or raising barriers? Inequality and high stakes testing in public education.* New York: Century Foundation Press.

Kreft, I. G. G., de Leeuw, J., & Aiken, L. (1995). The effect of different forms of centering in hierarchical linear models. *Multivariate Behavioral Research, 30,* 1-22.

Lee, V. E., Burkam, D. T., Chow-Hoy, T., Smerdon, B. A., & Goverdt, D. (1998). *High school curriculum structure: Effects on course taking and achievement in mathematics for high school graduates.* NCES-WP-98-09. ERIC ED 431 629. Washington, DC: National Center for Education Statistics.

Lemann, N. (1999). *The big test: The secret history of the American meritocracy.* New York: Farrar, Straus, and Giroux.

Ludwig, J., & Bassi, L. J. (1999). The puzzling case of school resources and student achievement. *Educational Evaluation and Policy Analysis, 21*(4), 385-403.

McNeil, L. M. (2000). Creating new inequalities: Contradictions of reform. *Phi Delta Kappan, 81*(10), 728-734.

Morgan, R. (1989). *An examination of the relationships of academic coursework with admissions test performance* (College Board Report No. 89-6). New York: College Entrance Examination Board.

Mortenson, T. (2004, November). Chance for college by age 19 by state 1986 to 2002. *Postsecondary Education OPPORTUNITY, 149,* 1-16.

Mullis, I. V. S., Dossey, J. A., Owen, E. H., & Phillips, G. W. (1991). *The state of mathematics achievement.* Washington, DC: National Center for Educational Statistics, U.S. Government Printing Office.

National Center for Education Statistics. (1997a). *Access to higher postsecondary education for the 1992 high school graduates.* NCES 98-105. By L. Berkner & L. Chavez. Project Officer: C. D. Carroll. Washington, DC: Author.

National Center for Education Statistics. (1997b). *Confronting the odds: Students at risk and the pipeline to higher education.*

NCES 98-094. By L. J. Horn. Project officer: C. D. Carroll. Washington, DC: Author.

National Center for Education Statistics. (2001). *Students whose parents did not go to college: Postsecondary access, persistence, and attainment.* By S. Choy. Washington, DC: Author.

National Commission on Excellence in Education. (1983). *A nation at risk: The imperative for educational reform.* Washington, DC: U.S. Government Printing Office.

National Council of Teachers of Mathematics. (1989). *Curriculum and evaluation standards for school mathematics.* Reston, VA: Author.

No Child Left Behind Act of 2001. Public Law 107-110.

Oakes, J. (1985). *Keeping track: How schools structure inequality.* New Haven, CT: Yale University Press.

Oakes, J., Rogers, J., Lipton, M., & Morrell, E. (2002). The social construction of college access: Confronting the technical, cultural, and political barriers to low-income students of color. In W. G. Tierney & L. S. Hagedorn (Eds.), *Increasing access to college: Extending possibilities for all students* (pp. 105-121). Albany, NY: State University of New York Press.

Orlofsky, G. F., & Olson, L. (2001). Quality counts 2001: A better balance. *Education Week, 20*(17), 8-193.

Paige, R. (2003, January 10). More spending is not the answer. Opposing view: Improving quality of schools calls for high standards, accountability. *USA Today,* 11A.

Pallas, A. M., & Alexander, K. L. (1983). Sex differences in quantitative SAT performance: New evidence on the differential coursework hypotheses. *American Educational Research Journal, 20*(2), 165-182.

Payne, K. J., & Biddle, B. J. (1999). Poor school funding, child poverty, and mathematics achievement. *Educational Researcher, 28*(6), 4-13.

Pelavin, S. H., & Kane, M. B. (1990). *Changing the odds: Factors increasing access to college.* New York: College Board.

Powell, B., & Steelman, L. C. (1996). Bewitched, bothered, and bewildering: The use and misuse of state SAT and ACT scores. *Harvard Educational Review, 66*(1), 27-59.

Raudenbush, S. W., Fotiu, R. P., & Cheong, Y. F. (1998). Inequality of access to educational resources: A national report card for eighth-grade math. *Educational Evaluation and Policy Analysis, 20,* 253-267.

Reich, R. B. (1991). *The work of nations: Preparing ourselves for 21st-century capitalism.* New York: A. A. Knopf.

Rothstein, J. M. (2002). *College performance predictions and the SAT.* Berkeley, CA: Center for Labor Economics, University of California.

St. John, E. P. (2002). *The access challenge: Rethinking the causes of the new inequality* (Policy Issue Report No. 2002-01). Bloomington, IN: Indiana University.

St. John, E. P., & Associates. (in press). *Education and the public interest: School reform, public finance, and access to higher education.* Dordrecht, The Netherlands: Springer.

St. John, E. P., & Musoba, G. D. (2002). Academic access and equal opportunity: Rethinking the foundations of policy on diversity. In M. C. Brown, II, & C. Freeman (Eds.), *Readings on equal education: Vol. 18. Equity and access in higher education: Changing the definition of educational opportunity* (pp. 171-192). New York: AMS Press, Inc.

St. John, E. P., Musoba, G. D., & Chung, C.-G. (2003). *Academic access to higher education: Evaluating the impact of state education policies.* Bloomington, IN: Indiana Education Policy Center.

Schreiber, J. B. (in press). Multilevel modeling in *The Journal of Educational Research*: Recommendations and review. *Journal of Educational Research.*

Stricker, L. J., Rock, D. A., Pollack, J. M., & Wenglinsky, H. H. (2002). *Measuring educational disadvantage of SAT candidates.* ETS RR-02-01. New York: College Entrance Examination Board.

Swanson, C. B., & Stevenson, D. L. (2002). Standard-based reform in practice: Evidence on state policy and classroom instruction from the NAEP state assessments. *Educational Evaluation and Policy Analysis, 24*(1), 1-27.

Taube, K. T., & Linden, K. W. (1989). State mean SAT score as a function of participation rate and other educational and demographic variables. *Applied Measurement in Education, 2*(2), 143-159.

Tierney, W. G., & Hagedorn, L. S. (Eds.). (2002). *Increasing access to college: Extending possibilities for all students.* Albany, NY: State University of New York.

Venezia, A., Kirst, M. W., & Antonio, A. L. (2003, March 4). *Betraying the college dream: How disconnected K-12 and postsecondary education systems undermine student aspirations.* Available at http://bridgeproject.stanford.edu.

Weaver, R. (2003, June 11). *The problem we all live with.* Available at www.nea.org/columns/rw030611.html.

Willingham, W., & Morris, M. (1986). *Four years later: A longitudinal study of Advanced Placement students in college* Report No. 86-2. Princeton, New Jersey: College Entrance Examination Board.

Winfield, L. F. (1990). School competency testing reforms and student achievement: Exploring a national perspective. *Educational Evaluation and Policy Analysis, 12*(2), 157-173.

CHAPTER 4

COMPREHENSIVE SCHOOL REFORM: INTERVENTION DESIGNS, TEACHER PRACTICES, AND CLASSROOM OUTCOMES[1]

Edward P. St. John, Carol-Anne Hossler, Glenda Droogsma Musoba, Choong-Geun Chung, and Ada B. Simmons

Comprehensive School Reform (CSR) funding through states and the U.S. Department of Education provides multiyear funding for schools implementing reform models. Funding includes support for training by model providers, proposals must address nine features outlined in federal regulations, and proposal development has become a political process in many school systems (Datnow, 2000). In the process of creating a large-scale and systematic process, it is possible that the focus has shifted to implementation and monitoring of systemic change without providing adequate attention to the ways the CSR reforms influence classrooms and students. Given federal regulations, state officials and school administrators might be tempted to view CSR as a systematic process involving implementation of research-based design, rather than as a complex intervention that involves

---

[1] The research reported in this chapter was completed with the support of the North Central Regional Educational Laboratory and the Michigan Department of Education. The interpretations are the authors' and do not necessary represent policies, positions, or views of the funding agencies.

133

teachers in changing their classroom practices in ways that can have an impact on student learning.

Most research to date examines the impact of CSR models on schoolwide test scores, but there has been relatively less research on the impact on teachers. Since these models require teachers to adopt new methods that often take substantial time for implementation on top of preparation and teaching, it is important to consider how these reforms involve teachers and influence classroom outcomes. This chapter examines the CSR reform process from the vantage point of teachers in an attempt to build an understanding of the relationship between the reform process, professional development, and student outcomes. First, a brief background on the evolution of CSR is presented, followed by discussions of the study approach, the findings, and the implications for integrating a greater emphasis on teachers and teaching into the reform process.

Comprehensive School Reform

Comprehensive School Reform (CSR) became a widely studied method of school improvement in the late 1990s. The U.S. Department of Education even funded a National Clearinghouse for Comprehensive School Reform to facilitate communication about reform methods. The clearinghouse provides access to research on reform models that is disseminated through electronic and other media to schools planning reform models. This is an important step because schools are expected to develop proposals for long-term funding that are based on research. Yet, if one were to look at the array of studies on CSR, it would be evident that most have been conducted by model providers. Most evaluation studies focus on implementation processes and lack a systematic approach for assessing how classrooms change as a result of these models. Few studies have compared the effects of different models on classrooms or on any student outcomes other than standardized test results. To build an understanding of why it is essential to develop a more explicit focus on teachers and student outcomes, it is necessary to reconsider how CSR came about in the first place.

The Evolution of Comprehensive Reform

To understand how CSR came about, it is necessary to turn the clock back to the early 1980s. In 1983, *A Nation At Risk* (National Commission on Excellence in Education, 1983) called national attention to a seemingly new set of problems in America's schools. Since the 1960s, federal education policy had focused on expanding and equalizing educational opportunity. The new report focused attention on the competitive position of America's schools and emphasized testing and standards. Policy analysts argued that the focus of federal policy should shift from providing funding to equalize opportunity to promoting strategies to improve student achievement (e.g., Finn, 1990). In response to the shift in the national discourse, many reformers began to experiment with new approaches to school reform.

There were diverse responses to the new challenge. Some reformers began to focus their efforts on schools that served populations considered to be educationally at risk. The most notable early models included Accelerated Schools (Hopfenberg, Levin, & Associates, 1993), Success for All (Slavin, Madden, Karweit, Donald, & Wasik, 1992; Slavin, Madden, Karweit, Livermon, & Dolan, 1990), and the School Development Process (Comer, Ben-Avie, Haynes, & Joyner, 1999). The early pilot schools for these models were situated in large urban areas, and the reformers argued that greater attention should be paid to urban schools. Over time, these models were generalized and tried out in large numbers of schools, not just schools with large low-income populations. Other reformers focused on creating "excellent" schools, including the Coalition for Essential Schools. By 1990, Title I of the Elementary-Secondary Education Act was modified to include a "school-wide" option that allowed states to fund some of these comprehensive reforms. In addition, several states developed cooperative strategies to work with the providers of these early models, often mixing funds from different state and federal programs in ways that enabled thousands of schools to try out these new methods.

In the early 1990s, the federal government also funded a set of model providers to design new models, such as Modern Red School House. Other projects funded through this legislation included some of the older models, such as Coalition for Essential Schools and Success for All. These new reforms expanded the range of options available to schools, school districts, and states. However, the 1997 legislation for funding these reforms was still tied to Title I, targeting schools with high percentages of low-income students. Thus new models of reforms became available for schools, while traditional approaches to providing supplemental services to students with special needs had fallen out of favor.

However, when educators consider the various reform models, they find that most of the research on the reform models has been conducted by the model providers. A number of reviews have been written (e.g., North Central Regional Educational Laboratory, 2000; Northwest Regional Educational Library, 2000b) that provide information to educators to help them choose models. However, if local change advocates read these reviews they find that, while most reform models are designed based on research, only a few models have much confirmatory research (e.g., Success for All). And most of the research has been conducted and published by the model providers and/or researchers who work directly with the model providers. This means that schools choosing a comprehensive model are choosing a reform that is based largely on a design concept without field testing other than a few widely reported "controlled experiments." The research reports on the interventions seem to have evolved in ways that suggest a general method of evaluation. Typically, the reports focus on analysis effect sizes, which are the differences in the average test scores for schools with the interventions compared to the differences in the test scores for comparison schools, an approach that has been praised in federal reports (e.g., Snow, Burns, & Griffin, 1998).

However, this method has a few important limitations. First, the tests used by the model evaluators may differ from the criterion-referenced tests used by states. Thus, these analyses may or may not be related to the achievement standards being used in states, depending on the alignment of various tests. Second, this approach—comparing schools with the model to matched schools—ignores important issues related to classroom practice. The CSR models may not have been fully implemented, these models may or may not include an emphasis on classroom practices (curriculum, organization, and instruction), and the comparison schools may or may not have some of the same classroom practices that are included in the reform models.

Thus, a complicated situation has evolved with respect to the issues facing educators choosing models and the education administrators who develop and manage reform strategies. The current approach to comprehensive school reform focuses on the selection of research-based models, but the research does not consider the actual elements of designs. The pattern of focusing on the design of reforms as a whole without explicitly considering the ways reforms affect classrooms has been carried forward into the organization of the CSR process—the application, award, implementation, and monitoring process used in the program.

The Focus on Reform as a Systemic Process

The Obey-Porter legislation (P.L. 103-382), promising financial support to schools that adopt comprehensive school reform, identified nine components of the reform process required for funding:

1. Effective, replicable research-based methods and strategies
2. Comprehensive design
3. Professional development

4. Measurable goals and benchmarks
5. Support within the school
6. Parental and community involvement
7. External technical support and assistance
8. Evaluation strategies
9. Coordination of resources

The processes used to implement CSR within states typically focused on these components. States hosted "fairs" to which they invited model providers included on different lists. The schools shopped around, reviewing the different models. They had to address the nine components in their proposals, and the reviews of their proposals were based on how well they addressed these components.

Viewing this process with an understanding of the evolution of CSR models, it is apparent that educators make choices about reform models at the design level, considering the model as a whole and the evaluation results that focus on the entire design. Typically, there are not measurable outcomes, at least in the early stages of the reform process, so school officials often rationalize their choice of reform models based on what the model designers say about how research has informed their designs. Further, for the models for which there is a history of research, such as Success for All, the research has focused on the model as a whole—on comparisons of test scores at schools with the model to those at schools without the model. Whether or not confirmatory research exists, educators are making choices about design concepts.

While the CSR evaluations are not yet complete, a few complexities have surfaced from the early implementation research. First, it is apparent that state and district preferences exert a great deal of influence in the choices that local educators make about model designs (Datnow, 2000). Further, it is also apparent that in the implementation process, teachers must confront fairly basic issues about their teaching. For example, one set of case studies found an apparent conflict between state standards and the requirements of CSR models in many instances (Manset-Williamson, St. John, Musoba, Gordon, Klingerman, & Simmons, 2001). Another qualitative study found that teachers experienced the process of implementing reform as stressful, given the emphasis on standardized testing (Skinner, 2001). This means that the process of selecting and implementing models takes place in a political environment influenced by district preferences and constrained by state standards.

Further, the recent research on outcomes indicates that not all models have the same effects on achievement tests and other student outcomes, nor do all models have their intended effects. For example, an Indiana study of the impact of reform models on early reading found that Success for All was actually negatively associated with higher reading scores (St. John, Manset-Williamson, Chung, & Worthington, 2001). In contrast, Literacy Collaborative, a reform based on design concepts from Reading Recovery, was positively associated with higher scores. Further, Success for All was associated with reduction in special education referrals, but Reading Recovery and Literacy Collaborative were associated with reductions in grade-level retention. Thus, none of the reforms appears to have uniform effects on student outcomes.

While the research on implementation is limited, these studies suggest greater attention should be paid to the impact of school reforms on classrooms, on both teaching and student learning. This requires a rethinking of the relationship between the features included in reform models and teachers' classroom practices.

Refocusing on Teachers and Students
Based on extensive reviews, we developed a research-based framework (see Figure 1) for the study of school reform (Musoba, St. John, & Simmons, 2001; St. John, Loescher, Jacob, Cekic, & Kupersmith, 2000). In this study, the Indiana Education Policy Center identified the following features:

Figure 1. Research-Based Framework for the Study of Comprehensive School Reform

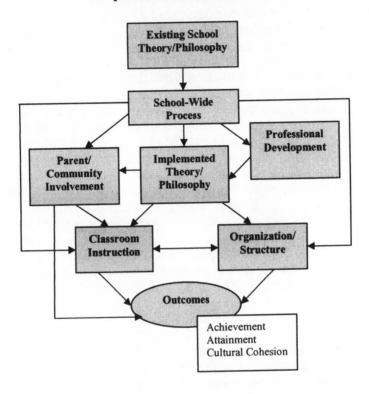

- *School-wide process* features involve the entire school faculty (rather than a single grade or subject area) and are designed to address school-wide needs. Examples are site-based management, school-within-a-school configurations and formative program evaluations addressing whole-school issues.
- *Implemented theory/philosophy* features are articulated beliefs about teaching and learning associated with the reform that are implemented through consistent practices. For instance, a curriculum focusing on multiple intelligences or multisensory approaches would be student centered, while a structured, grade-specific, prescribed curriculum would not.
- *Parent/community involvement* features are ways that the school engages parents and the community in the education of their students. Examples include programs that utilize parents as classroom volunteers or include them in the reform design team.
- *Professional development* features are those formal and informal methods used to instruct teachers about the reform and to develop their skills. Examples include in-services, networking, and teacher collaboration.
- *Organization/structure* features focus on the organization of learning and structures that guide it, such as a multi-age curriculum, student grouping practices, or diagnostic assessments for student placement.
- *Classroom instruction* features identify how instruction is delivered in the classroom and can include standard practices such as classroom lectures as well as project-based instruction, cooperative learning, or inquiry-based approaches.

Program features related to each of these components can influence the classroom practices (features related to instruction and organization/structure) that directly engage students and, thus, are linked to student outcomes. Parent and community involvement features that increase interaction between parents and students also have direct links to student outcomes. The framework also addresses the intended outcomes of school reform. While student learning as measured by achievement tests is a primary source of evaluation, it would be inappropriate to judge the full reform on one or two standardized state assessments. Therefore, the following three forms of outcomes are considered:

- *Achievement* outcome measures include standardized test scores (MEAP, ACT/SAT), pass rates on these tests, and grades or achievement-related observations by teachers, students, or parents.
- *Attainment* refers to indicators related to equal access to education, or the opportunity to learn by the lowest-achieving students. Attainment is an assessment of how effective the school is for those students who may face greater challenges. Teacher perceptions regarding the impact on struggling students or students with disabilities are indicators as well as the number of referrals for special education assessment, grade-level retentions, graduation rates, college-going rates, extent of inclusion, attrition and dropout rates, or the minimum competency of the lowest achieving students.
- *Cultural cohesion* within schools may be necessary for successful implementation. However, since we lack commonly accepted measures of cultural cohesion, this chapter explores how variables related to professional development can help us build a better understanding of collaboration.

The Indiana Education Policy Center study examined evidence related to attainment outcomes at the classroom level using teacher responses. Surveys asked questions about implementation and frequency of use of program features included in ten reform models. The surveys collected information about attainment and cultural outcomes. Prior research using this logical model had examined school-level outcomes related to early literacy, using school survey instruments completed by principals or their designees (St. John et al., 2003b; St. John, Manset-Williamson, Chung, & Michael, in press). This study was the first to use the teacher-level responses to examine classroom outcomes.

Research Approach

A wide range of reforms were funded through Michigan's CSR project. Our review of features of reform models indicated two generic types of reform designs: *process-based,* focusing on school-wide change strategies; and *classroom-based,* focusing on teaching practices. Most of the Michigan schools adopted one of the nine models identified in Table 1. Four of the models—including Different Ways of Knowing, Lightspan, Success for All, and Talent Development with Career Academies—emphasized specific forms of classroom practice. The designs of these models were based on instructional philosophies. In contrast, five other models focused on school-wide change strategies and are appropriately characterized as process based. The process-based reforms included ATLAS, Coalition of Essential Schools, Co-nect, Middle Start, and School Development Program. These reforms encouraged teachers to develop methods that met teachers' needs and engaged teachers more directly in change processes.

Given these underlying differences in intent, the Michigan CSR study asked a range of questions related to both classroom practices and professional development. The questions on professional development distinguished between involvement in school-wide change processes and engagement in instructional change practices. These distinctions permitted us to design a study that focused on the relationship between forms of professional practice and models of school reform.

Table 1. Typology of CSR Models		
CSR Model	**Classroom Based**	**Process Based**
ATLAS		X
Coalition of Essential Schools		X
Co-nect		X
Different Ways of Knowing	X	
Lightspan	X	
Middle Start		X
School Development Program		X
Success for All	X	
Talent Development with Career Academies	X	
Other Models		

Survey Design and Procedure

Teacher and principal surveys were sent to all 88 Michigan schools receiving Comprehensive School Reform funds. The principals' survey focused on school-level outcomes (such as grade retention rates, special education referral rates, and the principal's assessment of reform progress), school demographics (such as the percentage of students who have limited English proficiency and class size), school-wide reform features (such as site-based management, schools-within-a-school, visioning, and reform teams), school-wide parent features (such as health care assistance and parent instructional training), and district support. Of the 88 principals' surveys distributed, 47 principals responded, for a principal response rate of 53 percent (Table 2).

Table 2. Survey Response Rate				
Survey	**Number Distributed**	**Number Returned**	**Response Rate**	**Number Usable**
Principal Survey	88	47	53%	46
Teacher Survey	2,467	998	40%	983

The teachers' survey was distributed to all full-time teachers who spent their full day at the CSR school (thus, it did not include teachers who had joint appointments or who worked part time). The teachers' survey questions focused on teachers' perceptions regarding classroom-level outcomes (such as the percentage of students performing at grade level, the number of students referred for special education assessment, and the number of students the teacher anticipated would be retained at grade level), frequency of teachers' use of various classroom structures (such as ability grouping, individualized instruction, peer tutoring, and diagnostic procedures), classroom-level parent involvement (such as parent volunteers or learning contracts), frequency of use of various instructional practices (such as inquiry learning, multisensory activities, manipulatives, collaborative teams, and project-based instruction), frequency of professional development opportunities (such as collaboration and networking), extent of CSR implementation (such as personal involvement and attribution regarding change), and school community outcomes (such as support for leadership and a shared vision among employees). A total of 2,467 surveys were mailed to schools for distribution to teachers. A total of 998 surveys were returned, for a teacher response rate of 40 percent. A number of surveys were not complete; the responses on uncompleted surveys were not used in the analysis. One principal survey and 15 teacher surveys were fully removed from the data set.

Surveys were distributed via the school office with individual business reply envelopes addressed directly to the researchers to protect teacher confidentiality of responses. A letter from the

Michigan Department of Education encouraging participation accompanied the surveys. Principals were mailed reminder postcards to distribute to teachers to increase participation; however, teacher participation was voluntary. If a sufficient sample of teachers responded (more than 80%), schools were sent a school-level report of their data for use in their own formative evaluation.

Statistical Methods

The analyses used four multivariate methods to explore the relationships between the types of CSR models implemented, classroom practices, and classroom outcomes, controlling for school characteristics. Two sets of factor analyses were used to examine the relationships among classroom practices. The first set of factors related to classroom activities and the second to professional development. The factor analyses provided visibility into patterns of classroom practice and collaboration that were used by teachers.

We conducted correlations between the two sets of factors and the program models using point biserial correlation. By comparing reform models and patterns of practice, as measured by the factors, we hoped to build an understanding of the relationships between reform models and classroom practices.

Sequential models were used to examine the changes in special education referral and grade-level retention compared to no change, with reduction (less referral or retention) and increase (more referral or retention) compared to no change using teacher self-report survey results. The first model examined only school characteristics (percentage minority, percentage poverty, and large city locale [compared to other]). The second model added school-level variables, comparing process models to models that emphasize classroom practices. The third model added the classroom factors. This three-step approach allowed us to explore relationships among the three sets of variables included in our logical model: school context, school characteristics, and teacher practices. School context variables in this model are the percentage of students in the high school who are ethnic minorities, the percentage of the students who are low-income (eligible for free or reduced-price lunch), and the urbanicity of the school. School characteristics are the type of CSR model implemented, i.e., whether the reform is a process-based model or a classroom-based model. Teacher practices are the eight approaches to classroom teaching and the three factors of professional development, discussed in the section on classroom practices below.

Study Limitations

The survey relies on the responses of teachers and principals to make judgments about the extent of implementation. While it used a cohesive framework for analyzing the implementation of reform models, self-reported responses are not necessarily the best indicator of implementation. To contend with this limitation, this chapter also uses insights gained from site visits (Musoba, St. John, & Simmons, 2001) to complement survey responses, providing a more complete view of implementation.

The survey response rate was only 53 percent for principals and 40 percent for teachers. While this is disappointing, response was sufficient to build an understanding of the implementation process. Ideally the response rate for the teacher surveys should be over 50 percent to generalize to the population. We are certain that the analyses are representative of the nearly one thousand teachers who responded to the survey, but we use caution when generalizing to teachers in Michigan CSR schools because of variability in responses across different schools and the overall response rate. Since we treat the study findings as exploratory rather than confirmatory, we believe the low response rate is not especially problematic. Nevertheless, readers are cautioned about generalizing these findings.

Not all respondents supplied answers to all items on the surveys. The logistic regression analyses included about 200 fewer cases than did the analyses of descriptive statistics. This reduction in cases further limits the generalizability of the findings but does not undermine the exploratory aim of this study.

While the conceptual model suggests a causal framework, this chapter uses multivariate models but does not fully examine the implied causal linkages in the model. The sequential modeling used in this study implies a temporal relationship between the three sets of variables. However, since the outcomes are self-reported by the teachers, the notion of causality has limited meeting. The study does explore relationships between the self-reported practices of school teachers and the outcomes they expect in their classrooms.

Finally, it was not possible to survey comparison schools as part of the current study. Therefore, as part of the analyses, the study compares different types of reform models but could not compare schools with different types of reforms to schools that did not have CSR-funded reform models in place.

Findings

Classroom Practices

Eight approaches to classroom teaching practice were evident in the factor analysis of structural/organizational features and instructional features, illustrating the diversity of teaching strategies used in K-12 schools (see Table 3). While all of the approaches included in the various reform models and on the teacher survey are associated with reforms, they are also associated with normal practices in some areas of curriculum and instruction. Many of the classroom-based reforms include general methods for implementation across the curriculum.

Writing-based approaches are instructional practices including essays/creative writing, journals, meaning context/ predicting, metacognitive strategies, writing mechanics, and studying/test-taking skills. Most of these are associated with meaning-oriented approaches to literacy instruction which seem appropriate also in classrooms that emphasize engaged learning, including middle school and high school humanities courses.

Targeted approaches include ability groups, individualized instruction, one-on-one tutoring, ongoing written observation, and remedial methods. With the exception of remedial methods, these approaches are classified as organizational/structural practices, related to targeting students' specific learning needs. While these practices are included in many comprehensive reform models, they are also aligned with historic practice in special education, which provides a logical basis for the factor label. It is important to note that some reform methods, especially classroom-based reform, are consonant with historic practices in special education classrooms, which could mean that these models would be more compatible with mainstreaming special-needs students.

Creative arts approaches combine both structural/ organizational practices and instructional practices that are logically aligned with teaching in the arts. The structural/ organization practices include cross-year portfolios, student-initiated learning centers, and heterogeneous groups. The instructional practices include creative arts, meaning/context predicting, multisensory activity, and manipulatives/hands-on learning. Reforms that emphasize these practices can be viewed as integrating artistic methods across the curriculum.

Student-centered approaches are structural/organizational practices and include cooperative learning, interactive learning, peer tutoring, flexible grouping, and heterogeneous groups. These practices represent a distinctive philosophy of education that emphasizes actively engaging students in the teaching and learning process and can be used across subject areas.

Table 3. Loadings for Factors of Structural/Organizational and Instructional Features

Structural/Organizational Features	Writing-Based Approaches	Targeted Approaches	Creative Arts Approaches	Student-Centered Approaches	Project Inquiry Approaches	Performance-Based Approaches	Computer-Based Approaches	Scripted Lesson Approaches
Ability grouping		0.6336						
Cooperative learning				0.6762				
Cross-year portfolios			0.4646					
Diagnostic procedure		0.5979						
Individualized instruction		0.6750						
Interactive learning				0.6229				
One-on-one tutoring		0.5196						
Ongoing written observation		0.4918						
Peer tutoring				0.5721				
Pull-out instruction								
Student-initiated learning Centers			0.5460					
Supplemental learning								
Flexible grouping				0.5916				
Heterogeneous groups				0.6957				
Thematic units			0.5084					

Table 3. Loadings for Factors of Structural/Organizational and Instructional Features (cont.)

Instructional Features	Writing-Based	Targeted	Creative Arts	Student-Centered	Project Inquiry	Performance-Based	Computer-Based	Scripted Lesson
Authentic instruction					0.4658			
Calculator or computer as tool							0.7731	
Collaborative teams					0.6179			
Essays/creative writing	0.6552							
Computer-assisted instruction							0.6835	
Creative arts			0.6921					
Highly scripted lessons								0.5568
Inquiry learning					0.6453			
Interpreting/discussion								
Journals	0.6292							
Learning contract/student								
Meaning context/predicting	0.6589		0.4353					
Metacognitive strategies	0.4843					0.4090		
Multisensory activity			0.6562					
Performance assessment						0.5924		
Project-based instruction					0.6703			
Remedial methodologies		0.4674				0.4227		
Scaffolding						0.5803		
Worksheets/workbooks								0.6619
Writing mechanics	0.7928							
Manipulatives/hands-on learning			0.4462					
Studying/test-taking skills	0.5001							
Teacher lecturing								0.7121

Project-based approaches, which are instructional practices, use projects in instruction and also include authentic instruction, collaborative teams, and inquiry learning. These could also be student-centered practices, but they naturally align with project-based classrooms and teaching.

The final three approaches were named after the practices to which they had the strongest association. Performance assessment had the strongest loading score on the factor labeled *performance-based approaches.* Other instructional practices in this factor include metacognitive strategies, remedial strategies, and scaffolding. *Computer-based approaches* include two practices, one using calculators as a tool, the other using computer-based instruction. This factor is compatible with instruction in math and with reforms that use computer-assisted models. *Highly scripted lesson approaches* included three variables associated with traditional teaching: scripted lessons, worksheets, and lecturing.

When we used point biserial correlation to examine the relationships between these eight approaches and the reform models (Table 4), we found a very complex pattern. Neither the classroom-based nor the process-based models showed a clear set of associations with classroom-practice factors.

Only a few of the reforms seemed distinctive with respect to a particular pattern of classroom practice. Both ATLAS and Talent Development/Career Academies were positively associated with project-based approaches but were either negatively or not significantly associated with other approaches. These process-based reforms involved teachers in project-centered activities in their classrooms. It should also be noted that Success for All was the only reform model that was positively associated with highly scripted lesson approaches.

Three of the reforms were positively associated with the use of writing-based methods and three had a negative association. Co-nect, a process-oriented reform, and two classroom-based reforms, Different Ways of Knowing and Lightspan, were positively associated with writing-related methods. Two process-based reforms (Middle Start and School Development Program) and one classroom-based reform (Talent Development with Career Academies) were negatively associated with writing-based approaches.

Similarly, student-centered approaches, creative arts approaches, and computer-based approaches varied substantially across reform models and were significantly associated with many of the reform models. It is abundantly evident that the choice of reform models has implications for classroom practices, but the differences are evident at the level of specific reform rather than the type of reform.

Professional Development

A three-factor solution was evident in the factor analysis of professional development practices (Table 5): *collaboration on curriculum and instruction*, a factor related to collaboration in practices for teaching and learning; *school-wide collaboration,* a factor related to collaboration in organizational and governance issues; and *special needs,* a factor related to skills and teacher confidence in working with students with special learning needs. These factors loaded essentially as blocks of questions.

Collaboration on curriculum and instruction included all of the variables related to collaborating on teaching, subject matter, and co-curricular processes. This factor captures collaboration among teachers in their practice as teachers. The factor differs from the classroom practice factor since the practices included in those factors focused on the teacher's own classroom. In contrast, this factor focuses on collaboration among teachers on practices related to teaching.

School-wide collaboration had a strong association with six practices related to collaboration across the school and a modest loading of two variables related to curriculum and instruction. Teacher inquiry and portfolio, networking, teaching collaboration

	Writing-Based Approaches	Targeted Approaches	Creative Arts Approaches	Student-Centered Approaches	Project Inquiry Approaches	Performance-Based Approaches	Computer-Based Approaches	Scripted Lesson Approaches
ATLAS (P)			-	-	+			
Coalition of Essential Schools (P)	+	+	+		-		+	
Co-nect (P)	+	+			-		+	
Different Ways of Knowing (C)	+	-	+	+	-			
Lightspan (C)	+		+	-			+	
Middle Start (P)	-	-	-	+			-	-
School Development Program (P)	-	+	-	-			-	
Success for All (C)		+	+	+				+
Talent Development with Career Academies (C)	-	-	-	-	+		-	
Others *		+	+				+	

Table 4. Correlation Between CSR Reforms and Structural/Organizational and Instructional Feature Factors

(P) Process-based model
(C) Classroom-based model
+ Significant (p≤.1) and positive point biserial correlation.
- Significant (p≤.1) and negative point biserial correlation.
* Others = Breakthrough/Soar, Core Knowledge, Institute for Education Reform, Integrated Thematic Instruction, Koalaty Kids.

Table 5. Loadings for Factors of Professional Development Features			
	Collaboration on Curriculum & Instruction	School-Wide Collaboration	Special Needs
Professional Development Features			
Teacher inquiry/portfolio		0.6722	
Networking		0.6589	
Teachers collaborate within grade level		0.7073	
Teachers collaborate across grade levels		0.7737	
Teachers collaborate within subject		0.7632	
I have skills to teach at-risk students			0.7755
I have skills to teach students with disabilities			0.8464
I have skills to teach ESL students			0.7570
Teachers collaborate on student achievement and needs	0.7052		
Teachers collaborate on district/state/school initiatives	0.6984		
Teachers collaborate on pedagogy	0.6972	0.4524	
Teachers collaborate on curriculum/subject matter	0.7142	0.4163	
Teachers collaborate on reform/school improvement	0.7319		
Teachers collaborate on lives outside school	0.5887		
Teachers collaborate on school routines	0.8085		
Teachers collaborate on extracurricular events/PTO	0.7080		
Teachers collaborate on other	0.4628		

within and across grade levels, and teacher collaboration within subject loaded strongly on this factor. In addition, collaboration on curriculum/subject matter and on pedagogy also weakly correlated with *school-wide collaboration.* This is appropriate because all of the school-wide variables are also related to curriculum and pedagogy. Not only do reform models vary in the extent to which they emphasize school-wide involvement, but there is variability among teachers in school-wide involvement within models that have this emphasis. Therefore, it is appropriate to consider *school-wide collaboration* as a teacher-level variable.

In addition, the three variables related to skills loaded on the *special needs* factor: skills in teaching at-risk students, skills in teaching students with disabilities, and skills with ESL students. All teachers in diverse schools that focus on mainstreaming students would logically emphasize this skill set in their reform efforts. Therefore, this variable should cut across the two types of reform models.

Interestingly, the correlations of reform models and professional development factors (Table 6) did not neatly align with the two types of reform but, instead, seemed related to the specific reform models. Two process models (Coalition of Essential Schools and Co-nect) and one classroom model (Success for All) were positively correlated with *collaboration on curriculum and instruction.* In addition, one process model (School Development Program) and one classroom model (Talent Development/Career Academies) were negatively associated with this factor. In addition, one process model (ATLAS), one classroom model (Success for All), and other (infrequently chosen) models were positively associated with *school-wide collaboration,* while two process models (School Development Program and Middle Start) were negatively associated with this factor. Finally, *special needs* was positively associated with only one model, Different Ways of Knowing, while one process model (ATLAS) and one classroom model (Talent Development/Career Academies) were negatively associated with this factor.

Table 6. Correlation Between CSR Reforms and Professional Development Feature Factors			
	Collaboration on Curriculum & Instruction	School-Wide Collaboration	Special Needs
ATLAS (P)		+	-
Coalition of Essential Schools (P)	+		
Co-nect (P)	+		+
Different Ways of Knowing (C)			
Lightspan (C)			
Middle Start (P)		-	
School Development Program (P)	-	-	
Success for All (C)	+	+	
Talent Development/Career Academies (C)	-		-
Others*		+	

(P) Process-based model
(C) Classroom-based model
+ Significant ($p \leq .1$) and positive point biserial correlation
- Significant ($p \leq .1$) and negative point biserial correlation
* Others = Breakthrough/Soar, Core Knowledge, Institute for Education Reform, Integrated Thematic Instruction, Koalaty Kids

The descriptive statistics of the teachers responding to the survey indicated substantial diversity in school contexts and reform models (Table 7). The teachers from Michigan CSR schools responding to the surveys were from schools with high percentages of minority students (65%) and poverty (61%). This is expected, given the historic focus on poverty in Title I and CSR (Wong, 2003). More than one-third of the teachers were from urban schools (38%) and one-quarter (25%) were from high schools.

There was substantial variation in reform models represented among the teacher responses. More than one-quarter of the respondents were from schools that chose Middle Start (27%), a reform method widely used in middle schools in Michigan. More than one-tenth of the teachers were from Different Ways of Knowing (12%), the School Development Program (15%), and Talent Development/Career Academies (11%). All of the other models had fewer respondents.

Student Outcomes Findings

There was not an overall pattern in special education referrals after one or two years of the reform. Most teachers (68%) reported no change in the number of students referred for special education in the year of the study compared to prior to reform implementation, while 15 percent indicated reduced referrals and 17 percent indicated increased referrals. The multinomial analyses examined variables and factors associated with lower or higher referral rates, compared to no change (Table 8). The first model considered contextual variables, while the second added CSR type and school grade level factors, and the third added the instructional approaches and professional development factors.

Only one of the three variables related to school characteristics was significant in the final analyses of referrals. However, all three variables merit attention.

First, poverty was positively associated with both reduced and increased referrals in the first model, indicating that changes in teachers' special education referrals were more evident among teachers in schools with higher percentages of poverty. Interestingly, the positive association between poverty and higher referral rates was evident across the three models, while

Table 7. Descriptive Statistics of the Teacher Survey Sample		
	Mean	**Std. Dev.**
Outcome Variables		
Referral		
Lower	14.8%	
Higher	17.3%	
Same	68.0%	
Retention		
Lower	18.4%	
Higher	24.2%	
Same	57.4%	
School Characteristics		
% Minority	65.0%	32.0%
% Poverty	61.0%	15.0%
Large City**	38.0%	
CSR Model		
ATLAS (P)	9.2%	
Coalition of Essential Schools (P)	7.3%	
Co-nect (P)	4.8%	
Different Ways of Knowing (C)	12.0%	
Lightspan (C)	4.7%	
Middle Start (P)	27.1%	
School Development Program (P)	15.1%	
Success for All (C)	1.9%	
Talent Development w/ Career Academies (C)	10.9%	
Others	6.9%	
Teaching Grades		
High School***	24.8%	

Percentages only are reported for categorical variables. Average percentages and standard deviations are reported when percentages are used as continuous variables.
** Non-large city is the reference group.
*** Teachers from elementary and middle grades are the reference group.

Table 8. Multinomial Logit Regression on Teacher-Reported Change in Referrals for Special Education †

	Model 1				Model 2				Model 3			
	Lower		Higher		Lower		Higher		Lower		Higher	
	Coeff.	Sig.	Coeff.	Sig.	Coeff.	Sig.	Coeff.	Sig.	Coeff.	Sig.	Coeff.	Sig.
School Context												
% Minority	-0.0007		-0.0054		0.0026		-0.0039		0.0031		-0.0031	
% Poverty	2.4580	***	3.5070	***	0.7133		3.2750	***	0.6092		3.1363	***
Large City	0.5612	*	0.5728	*	0.4392		0.5504	*	0.2732		0.4791	
CSR Model and Teaching Grades												
Model ††					-0.4197	*	0.0792		-0.3169		0.1732	
High School					-1.0379	***	-0.1394		-0.9225	***	-0.1301	
Structural/Organizational and Instructional Feature Factors												
Writing-Based Approach									0.1034		-0.0629	
Special Needs Approach									-0.0189		-0.0032	
Creative Arts Approach									0.2481	**	0.2186	**
Student-Centered Approach									0.0988		-0.1060	
Project Inquiry Approach									0.1193		0.1243	
Performance-Based Approach									0.2720	**	0.0532	
Computer-Based Approach									0.0699		0.1647	
Scripted Lesson Approach									-0.0393		-0.0476	
Professional Development Factors												
Collaboration on Curr. & Instr.									-0.1760		-0.0006	
School-Wide Collaboration									-0.1980	*	-0.0569	
Special Needs									-0.1952	*	-0.0746	
N	764				764				764			
-2 Log Likelihood	374.6 (p =.000)				386.8 (p =.000)				1222.9 (p =.000)			
% Correctly Predicted	68.2				68.2				68.1			

† Reference category is "The same as last year."
†† Model is a dichotomous CSR model indicator; Process-based v. Classroom-based model. Classroom-based model is the reference group in this regression analysis. Process-based models: ATLAS, Coalition of Essential Schools, Co-nect, Middle Start, School Development Program. Classroom-based models: Different Ways of Knowing, Lightspan, Success for All, Talent Dev./Career Acad.

* $p \leq .1$, ** $p \leq .05$, *** $p \leq .01$

the association with lower referral rates ceased to be significant once the model variables entered the equation. These findings suggest that poverty plays a major role in special education referral, which could be stimulated by being involved in CSR and which is relatively immune to distinctions among reforms. Ironically, this finding may be related to pressure to raise test scores, given the consistent pattern of association between test scores and referrals in research on school reform (St. John, Manset-Williamson, Chung, & Michael, in press).

Second, urban schools were modestly more resistant to change, a finding related to characteristics of reform models. Teaching in a large urban area was modestly negatively associated (.1 alpha) with both higher and lower referral rates in the first model and was modestly associated with higher referrals in the second model but not the third. Since this is only a modest association, readers should be cautious about attributing too much meaning to this finding, but the pattern is interesting. It is conceivable that the choice of a reform model along with the resulting patterns of professional practice have implications for overcoming resistance to change in urban schools.

The categorization of reforms was significantly associated with lower referral rates. Teachers in schools with process-based models were modestly less likely to have lower referral rates (.1 alpha) in the second model, but not in the third. It is possible that process models include features (accounted for in the third model by the factors) that reduce special education referrals, an issue that merits further exploration. In addition, teachers in high schools were significantly less likely to report reductions in special education referrals in both the second and third models, another finding that merits attention in future studies of school reform.

Four of the factors were significant in the third model. All four were associated with lower referral rates, and one of these was also associated with higher referral rates. Each of these factors merits attention.

Creative arts approaches were associated with both higher and lower referral rates. These findings indicate that introducing the creative activity may improve teachers' ability to understand special learning needs. On the one hand, creative activities provide teachers with a capacity to reduce referrals, while on the other hand these approaches may enable teachers to see special needs and seek help.

Performance-based approaches were significantly and positively associated with lower referral rates. It appears that the introduction of performance-based methods as part of some of these reform models enabled larger numbers of teachers to meet the needs of diverse learners in their classrooms.

School-wide collaboration was negatively and modestly (.1 alpha) associated with lower referral rates. It is possible that diverting teacher attention to school-wide reform activities reduces rather than improves teachers' capacity to address the needs of students with diverse learning needs, at least in the short term. This relationship also merits attention in other studies of school reform.

Special needs skills were also negatively and modestly (.1 alpha) associated with lower special education referral rates. This means that having the skills to teach special needs children does not make teachers less likely to refer identified students. Apparently, teachers skilled in teaching special needs and high risk students are more likely to refer students for special education so the students can get the help they need to make educational progress—an intermediate hypothesis that merits further exploration.

Retention at Grade Level

Slightly more teachers reported increases in retention rates (24%) than reported reductions (18%) (Table 7), raising questions about the short-term benefits of comprehensive reform. This provides a further indication of the difficulty of improving classroom outcomes during the first two years of reform initiatives. There is reason for concern about this pattern, given that CSR and other reforms are implemented to raise low test scores. This means that, rather than enabling more children to achieve at grade level, schools may be finding quick ways to improve scores by retaining more children at grade level.

The logistic regression analyses (Table 9) indicate a complex pattern of change in CSR classrooms. Variables included in all three models were significant when they entered the equations, but the significance of school context and grade level changed across models.

Poverty rates were modestly (.1 alpha) and positively associated with lower grade retention rates and were significantly and positively associated with higher retention rates when considering school context. This indicates that poverty rates were related to the incentives to increase retention, and teachers in high-poverty schools may be expected to change teaching practice. In addition, teachers in large city schools were more likely to have lower retention rates after reform implementation, indicating that teachers in city schools may have made more substantial efforts to reduce retention. However, since neither of these variables was significant in the final two models (although *large city* had a modest association in the second model), it is apparent that there was a relationship between the school context and the choice of reform models.

Interestingly, teachers in high schools were significantly less likely to raise or lower retention rates, indicating more resistance to change. The *high schools* variable was also negatively associated with higher referral rates in the final model, but not with lower referral rates.

Four of the factors related to professional practice were significant in the final model. First, *writing-based approaches* were positively and significantly associated with lower retention rates and modestly (.1 alpha) associated with higher retention rates. This indicates that integration of writing in classroom activities represents a compelling and important reform strategy. Second, *creative arts approaches* had a modest (.1 alpha) negative association with higher retention rates, suggesting integration of the creative arts enables more students to make normal academic progress. Third, *collaboration on curriculum and instruction* was positively and significantly associated with lower retention rates, illustrating that involving teachers in professional development related to teaching has the potential to improve classroom outcomes. Finally, having skills with *special needs* was significantly and negatively associated with higher retention rates, indicating that improving teachers' skills in working with diverse students enables them to keep more students at grade level.

These findings suggest that classroom practices had a more substantial influence on educational improvement at the classroom level than did other variables related to reform models and school contexts. In the final model, only one variable other than factors related to classroom practices was significant (high schools' strong negative associations with higher retention rates), while four of the factors were significant. In addition, the third model is the best of the three, given the higher -2 Log likelihood and higher percentage correctly predicted.

Discussion

Comprehensive School Reform has become an important part of the school improvement arsenal used by state and the federal governments in their efforts to improve educational outcomes (Wong, 2003; St. John et al., 2003a, 2003b). CSR provides a viable alternative to charters and vouchers for motivating change in public schools that appear to be failing their students. However, the challenges facing schools in their efforts to implement comprehensive reforms are complex, given that the overall pattern of implementation may indicate resistance to change. Yet there may be reason for some optimism about the potential of CSR, especially if we focus on the implications for teaching practice.

Table 9. Multinomial Logistic Regression on Teacher-Reported Change in Grade-Level Retention †

	Model 1				Model 2				Model 3			
	Lower		Higher		Lower		Higher		Lower		Higher	
	Coeff.	Sig.	Coeff.	Sig.	Coeff.	Sig.	Coeff.	Sig.	Coeff.	Sig.	Coeff.	Sig.
School Context												
% Minority	0.0027		0.0000		0.0052		0.0057		0.0069		0.0048	
% Poverty	1.3759	*	1.7475	***	0.2708		0.5840		-0.0309		0.8828	
Large City	0.6824	**	0.2671		0.6127	*	0.2391		0.5363		0.1685	
CSR Model and Teaching Grades												
Model ††					-0.2241		0.2935		-0.2252		0.2172	
High School					-0.5917	**	-0.7456	***	-0.3413		-0.7616	***
Structural/Organizational and Instructional Feature Factors												
Writing-Based Approach									0.3687	***	0.1525	*
Special Needs Approach									-0.0198		-0.0938	
Creative Arts Approach									0.0203		-0.1804	*
Student-Centered Approach									0.1461		0.1459	
Project Inquiry Approach									-0.0138		0.1260	
Performance-Based Approach									0.0527		0.0311	
Computer-Based Approach									0.1257		-0.0574	
Scripted Lesson Approach									-0.1168		0.0287	

† Reference category is "The same as last year."
†† Model is a dichotomous CSR model indicator; Process-based model v. Classroom-based model. Classroom-based model is the reference group in this regression analysis. Process-based models include ATLAS, Coalition of Essential Schools, Co-nect, Middle Start, and School Development Program. Classroom-based models include Different Ways of Knowing, Lightspan, Success for All, and Talent Development with Career Academies.
* $p \leq .1$, ** $p \leq .05$, *** $p \leq .01$

Table 9. Multinomial Logistic Regression on Teacher-Reported Change in Grade-Level Retention (cont.) †

	Model 1				Model 2				Model 3			
	Lower		Higher		Lower		Higher		Lower		Higher	
	Coeff.	Sig.	Coeff.	Sig.	Coeff.	Sig.	Coeff.	Sig.	Coeff.	Sig.	Coeff.	Sig.
Professional Development Factors												
Collaboration on Curriculum & Instruction									0.2107	**	-0.1410	
School-wide Collaboration									0.0594		0.0598	
Special Needs									-0.0953		-0.1862	**
N	783				783				783			
-2 Log Likelihood	437.9 (p=.002)				460.4 (p=.000)				1448.1 (p=.000)			
% Correctly Predicted	57.0				57.0				58.4			

† Reference category is "The same as last year."

†† Model is a dichotomous CSR model indicator; Process-based model vs. Classroom-based model. Classroom-based model is the reference group in this regression analysis. Process-based models include ATLAS, Coalition of Essential Schools, Co-nect, Middle Start, and School Development Program. Classroom-based models include Different Ways of Knowing, Lightspan, Success for All, and Talent Development with Career Academies.

* p≤.1, ** p≤.05, *** p≤.01

First, teachers' classroom practices are crucial elements of the school reform process. In this study we found that factors related to classroom activities not only emerged from the factor analyses, but showed complex relationships with student outcomes. Given that this finding is confirmatory of the pattern found in prior studies (e.g., St. John et al., in press), it merits consideration in the design and selection of reform models. This finding also extends understanding of this relationship by showing that classroom practices were related to both increases and decreases in retention and referral, as reported by teachers.

Two of the factors related to classroom practices—*performance-based approaches* and *creative arts approaches*—were associated with reductions in special education referrals, indicating teachers using these methods enabled more students to achieve without special assistance. The first of these factors, *performance-based approaches*, combines performance assessment with metacognitive strategies, remedial strategies, and scaffolding—a combination of approaches that apparently enables teachers to engage more students. This is compelling evidence that reforms that emphasize performance-based strategies merit consideration by schools considering school reform options. *Creative arts approaches* can also make more engaging learning environments. Therefore, since this factor was associated with increases as well as reductions in special education referrals, it might be appropriate to combine creative arts approaches with performance-based approaches. However, since this study looked at a broad range of school reforms, considering all types of K-12 schools, the factors may oversimplify the challenges facing educators, suggesting a need to be cautious about the application of these findings.

In addition, it is noteworthy that *writing-based approaches* was associated with reduction in grade retention. This was also the strongest factor, indicating that the related practices—especially journals, essays/creative writing, context/meaning predicting, and writing mechanics—were strongly associated with each other as well. One of the apparent benefits of some reform models seems to be that they engage more teachers in the integration of writing into their classroom practices. However, the present emphasis in schools on content standards and testing may encourage teachers to de-emphasize writing.

Second, professional development practices also appear important in school improvement. This study extended prior research by adding a set of questions related to teachers' professional development activities. Distinct patterns emerged with three factors: *collaboration on curriculum and instruction*, *school-wide collaboration*, and *special needs. Collaboration on curriculum and instruction* was significantly associated with reductions in grade retention, suggesting that involving teachers in collaboration on teaching, pedagogy, and curriculum can create more engaging learning environments for students. This finding is consistent with a large, emerging body of research demonstrating that school reform efforts that enhance teacher discourse focused on curriculum and instruction result in improved teaching practice and teacher learning (Achinstein, 2002; Grossman, Wineburg, & Woolworth, 2001; Hossler & Musoba, in preparation; Little, 2003). Although the relationship of strong professional communities to student performance is documented in research (Louis & Kruse, 1995; Newmann & Wehlage, 1995), the linkages between teacher discourse and student achievement to date are more tenuous. Many studies call for more research in this area. Lewis (2002) states that "in Chicago, wherever schools had created strong professional communities with frequent teacher collaboration, reflective dialogue, [and] shared norms, their schools were four times more likely to be improving academically than schools with weaker professional communities" (p. 489). Teachers who believed they had the skills to teach students with special needs were also less likely to increase grade retentions under the pressures of reforms to increase test scores.

Third, while some reform models emphasize the change process and engaging teachers in the development of curriculum, while others emphasize specific classroom practices, the types of reforms were not significantly associated with changes in outcomes. In addition, the correlation of factors with reform models indicated that each reform was associated with distinct patterns of practice. This suggests that teachers and administrators should assess the program features of reforms (St. John, Loescher, & Bardzell, 2004) when choosing a reform model.

Conclusions and Implications

Comprehensive School Reform has been promoted as school-wide efforts aimed at transforming schools with records of low performance. At CSR schools, teachers and administrators reviewed possible reform models, selected one (or developed their own), wrote a proposal, and, if selected, engaged in a multiyear reform effort. Our analyses of Michigan CSR schools indicate that during the first two years of the reform process there was not a substantial improvement in the percentage of students who maintained normal academic progress. Instead, more teachers reported increasing retention at grade level and special education referral than reported decreasing these classroom outcomes. It is possible that CSR schools fall into the more general pattern now evident in schools: improving test scores by retaining and referring more students (St. John et al., in press). There is reason to question whether the CSR approach to reform will address the critical challenge of enabling more students to achieve at grade level.

Evidence in this study builds on other research examining program features of reforms (St. John, Loescher, & Bardzell, 2003; St. John et al., in press), specifically in the association of classroom practices and professional development in these schools with reductions in referral and retention. And, at least in this Michigan study, *performance-based approaches* and *writing-based approaches*, two sets of engaging classroom practices, were particularly associated with keeping more students in the educational mainstream. In addition, *collaboration on curriculum and instruction* was a pattern of professional development associated with enabling more students to make educational progress.

This study supports the argument that both state officials and school personnel should consider the features of school reforms when selecting reform designs (St. John, Loescher, & Bardzell, 2003). Perhaps the most crucial issue facing reform efforts is the need to select reform models that will enable more students to perform at grade level. Paying closer attention to the teacher practices associated with reform models seems crucial in future efforts to refine and improve school reform.

References

Achinstein, B. (2002). *Community, diversity, and conflict among schoolteachers: The ties that blind.* New York: Teachers College Press.

Comer, J. P., Ben-Avie, M., Haynes, N. M., & Joyner, E. T. (Eds.). (1999). *Child by child: The Comer process for change in education.* New York: Teachers College Press.

Datnow, A. (2000). Power and politics in adoption of school reform models. *Education Evaluation and Policy Analysis, 22,* 357-374.

Finn, C. E., Jr. (1990, April). The biggest reform of all. *Phi Delta Kappan, 71*(8), 584-592.

Grossman, P., Wineburg, S., & Woolworth, S. (2001) Toward a theory of teacher community, *Teacher College Record, 103*(6), 942-1012.

Hopfenberg, W. S., Levin, H. M., & associates. (1993). *The Accelerated Schools.* San Francisco: Jossey-Bass.

Hossler, D., & Musoba, G. D. (in preparation). *Transcending traditional boundaries: Teacher collaboration in the midst of Comprehensive School Reform.* Indiana University, Bloomington.

Lewis, A. C. (2002, March). Washington commentary: School reform and professional development. *Phi Delta Kappan, 83*(7), 488-489.

Little, J. W. (2003, August). Inside teacher community: Representations of classroom practice. *Teacher College Record, 105*(6), 913-945.

Louis, K., & Kruse, S., (Eds.). (1995). *Professionalism and community.* Thousand Oaks, CA: Corwin Press.

Manset-Williamson, G., St. John, E. P., Musoba, G. D., Gordon, D., Klingerman, K., & Simmons, A. B. (2001). *Comprehensive school reform: Promising practices and concerns for the inclusion of students with high-incidence disabilities.* Policy Research Report 01-04. Bloomington, IN: Indiana Education Policy Center.

Musoba, G. D., St. John, E. P., & Simmons, A. B. (2001). *Case studies in school reform: Comprehensive school reform in Michigan.* Bloomington, IN: Indiana Education Policy Center.

National Commission on Excellence in Education. (1983). *A nation at risk: The imperative for educational reform.* Washington, DC: U.S. Government Printing Office.

Newmann, F., & Wehlage, G. (1995). *Successful school restructuring.* Madison WI: Center on Organization and Restructuring Schools, Wisconsin Center for Education Research.

North Central Regional Educational Laboratory. (2000). *Comprehensive school reform: Making good choices.* Oak Brook, IL: Author.

Northwest Regional Educational Laboratory. (2000). *Catalog of school reform models.* Available at www.nwrel.org/scpd/natspec/catalog/talentdevhs.htm.

St. John, E. P., Loescher, S. A., & Bardzell, J. S. (2003). *Improving reading and literacy in grades 1-5: A resource guide to research-based programs.* Thousand Oaks, CA: Corwin.

St. John, E. P., Loescher, S., Jacob, S., Cekic, O., & Kupersmith, D. L. (2000). *Comprehensive school reform models: A study guide for comparing CSR models (and how well they meet Minnesota's learning standards).* Bloomington, IN: Indiana Education Policy Center. Naperville, IL: North Central Regional Educational Laboratory.

St. John, E. P., Manset-Williamson, G. M., Chung, C. G., & Michael, R. (2005, August). Assessing the rationales for educational reforms: An examination of policy claims about professional development, comprehensive reform, and direct instruction. *Education Administration Quarterly,* 42(3), 480-519.

St. John, E. P., Manset-Williamson, G. M., Chung, C. G., Musoba, G. D., Loescher, S., Simmons, A. B., Gordon, D., & Hossler, C. A. (2003a). Comprehensive school reform: An exploratory study. In L. F. Mir☐n & E. P. St. John (Eds.), *Reinterpreting urban school reform: Have urban schools failed, or has the reform movement failed urban schools?* (pp. 155-175). Albany, NY: SUNY Press.

St. John, E. P., Manset-Williamson, G., Chung, C. G., Simmons, A. B., Musoba, G. D., Manoil, K., & Worthington, K. (2003b). Research-based reading reform: The impact of state-funded intervention on educational outcome in urban elementary schools. In L. F. Mir☐n & E. P. St. John (Eds.), *Reinterpreting urban school reform: Have urban schools failed, or has the reform movement failed urban schools?* (pp. 129-153). Albany, NY: SUNY Press.

St. John, E. P., Manset-Williamson, G. M., Chung, C. G., & Worthington, K. (2001). *Assessing rationales for education reforms: A test of the professional development, comprehensive reform, and direct instruction hypotheses.* Policy Research Report 01-03. Bloomington, IN: Indiana Education Policy Center.

Skinner, B. (2001, August). Teachers and reforms: Results from interviews conducted in two elementary schools. In L. Hansel, B. Skinner, & I. C. Rotberg (Ed.), *The changing teaching environment* (pp. 7-22). Washington, DC: Institute for Education Policy, George Washington University.

Slavin, R. E. (1996). *Education for all: Contexts of learning.* Lisse, The Netherlands: Swets & Zeitlinger.

Slavin, R. E. (2002). Evidence-based education policy: Transforming education practice and research. *Educational Researcher, 31*(7), 15-21.

Slavin, R. E., Madden, N. A., Karweit, N. L., Donald, L. J., & Wasik, B. A. (1992). *Success for all: A relentless approach to prevention and early intervention in elementary schools.* Arlington, VA: Educational Research Service.

Slavin, R., Madden, N. A., Karweit, N. L., Livermon, B. J., & Dolan, L. (1990). Success for all: First outcomes of a comprehensive plan for reforming urban education. *American Educational Research Journal, 27,* 255-278.

Snow, C. E., Burns, M. S., & Griffin, P. (Eds.). (1998). *Preventing reading difficulties in young children.* Washington, DC: National Academy Press.

Wong, K. K. (2003). Federal Title I as a reform strategy in urban schools. In L. F. Mirʰn & E. P. St. John (Eds.), *Reinterpreting urban school reform: Have urban schools failed, or has the reform movement failed urban schools?* (pp. 55-76). Albany, NY: SUNY Press.

SECTION II

Postsecondary Encouragement

CHAPTER 5

WHO APPLIES FOR AND WHO IS SELECTED FOR WASHINGTON STATE ACHIEVERS SCHOLARSHIPS? A PRELIMINARY ASSESSMENT[1]

Amon Emeka and Charles Hirschman

An important debate in academic and public policy arenas has revolved around the relative importance of financial considerations, ability, and ambitions in shaping opportunities for higher education in the United States, especially among disadvantaged youth. On one side it is argued that no amount of money can make up for the social and intellectual deficits accrued in the formative years of childhood. On the other side, there is the belief that anyone can "make it" in American society if given the right opportunities.[2] Most youth, even those from poor families,

[1] This research was supported by grants from the Andrew C. Mellon Foundation and the Bill & Melinda Gates Foundation. We are grateful to Steven Thorndill and Patty Glynn for their support of this research. The authors are solely responsible for any errors of data analysis or interpretation. Direct all correspondence to Amon Emeka at emeka@usc.edu.
[2] This a fundamental premise of sociology. Whatever deficits we accrue in our early formative years, they are no match for the lifelong socialization process.

will rise to the occasion and become highly motivated students if they think that going to college is a real possibility for them.

School reformers, along with many influential institutions and foundations, subscribe to the latter view. Students of low socioeconomic status, it is believed, are more constrained by lack of opportunity than by lack of ability. This belief has given life to innovative policy initiatives, including the Washington State Achievers (WSA) program. Among the goals of the WSA program is to increase college enrollment among students from disadvantaged backgrounds at low-income high schools in Washington State. The foundation's program of support includes a scholarship program, mentoring services, and, ultimately, major school reforms.

The primary objective of this analysis is to examine the processes involved with the first of these three interventions— application to and selection for a Washington State Achievers scholarship. Our analysis is based on a survey of all high school seniors in five Achievers High Schools in 2002 and 2003. In particular, we measure (1) the association between background characteristics and application for the WSA scholarship and (2) the impact of background characteristics on the likelihood of being awarded the WSA scholarship.

The Washington State Achievers Program

Sixteen high schools in Washington State with large low-income populations are participants in the Washington State Achievers program. The generous scholarships program studied here is an important aspect of the WSA program, which will also include a profound restructuring of the participating schools. Each of the schools with students receiving WSA scholarships will, in time, be systematically transformed from a large comprehensive format to a more personalized, small-school format—with a handful of small, semiautonomous schools sharing a single physical plant. The combination of the scholarships and the school redesign, it is hoped, will create school environments that better encourage and facilitate college preparation and encouragement for all students.

Because the redesign program has gone into effect only very recently, we are unable to assess its impact. However, the Washington State Achievers scholarships have been made available to students in the WSA schools, beginning in 2001. By chance, three of the selected WSA schools are part of an ongoing longitudinal study of high school seniors in several high schools in Washington State—the University of Washington Beyond High School (UWBHS) project. The fortuitous overlap between our survey and the Washington State Achievers initiative allows us to compare scholarship recipients and nonrecipients in the Achievers High Schools and also to compare WSA schools with traditional high schools. In this chapter, we combine surveys of high school seniors in 2002 and 2003 who were the second and third cohorts to graduate from high school under the WSA program. In the coming years, we will be able to track these students with follow-up surveys.

There are good reasons to think that the scholarships alone will make a significant difference in the lives of students who receive them. Previous research has demonstrated the significant positive effects of financial aid on college enrollment, particularly among minority students (Jackson, 1990; St. John & Noell, 1989). Capable students from low-income households often find themselves unable to afford college education. Most often the affordability of college is thought of in terms of the direct costs of the education—for tuition, books, and room and board—and indeed these costs are often prohibitive. Less obvious are the "opportunity costs" associated with college attendance—that is, wages forgone by remaining a student rather than working. Both the "direct" and the lost "opportunity" costs are likely to be major concerns of young people and their families as they make their very important decisions regarding whether and when to attend college (Manski & Wise, 1983; Perna, 2000).

The Washington State Achievers scholarships alleviate and in some cases totally eliminate the direct costs associated with college attendance. Successful applicants for the scholarships may receive up to $8,400 per year for four years of college leading to a bachelor's degree, and they are expected to work to defray any educational expenses in excess of this amount. The opportunity to work part time while holding a WSA scholarship means that scholarship recipients may be able to contribute positively to the economics of their households while attending college, thus alleviating part of the opportunity costs of attending college. This may be a crucial factor in educational planning—particularly, among low-income students and families.

In seeking to reach students who may not have applied for college scholarships in the past, the Washington State Achievers program focuses on economic need and employs a broad definition of academic potential. The WSA scholarship program eligibility criteria are as follows:

- Candidates must attend and graduate from one of the 16 Achievers High Schools.
- Candidates must be actively working to prepare academically for college and must demonstrate academic potential through their commitment to classroom work and assignments.
- Candidates must plan to obtain a four-year college degree.
- Candidates must plan to attend an eligible public or independent Washington college or university for at least the first two years of college.
- Candidates must come from families who have and will continue to have an annual income that is in the lowest 35 percent of the State of Washington family incomes and have low or modest family assets.

Rather than simply choosing the best and the brightest students (based on GPA) from poor families around the state, this program focuses on selected low-income schools where it might be possible to create an institutional as well as an individual effect.[3] WSA scholarships are awarded to applicants on the basis of academic promise and noncognitive skills that are predictive of academic success among students from low-income families (see Arbona & Novy, 1990). By providing scholarships to relatively large numbers of students in the selected schools, the aim is to create among low-income students "a culture of college attendance" similar to that which is typical among middle- and upper-class families. Once the expectation of going to college is normative among *all* students in the high school regardless of family income, then students should increasingly see college attendance and completion as *realistic* goals and begin to exhibit behaviors in line with those goals. However, this may only happen if students in the participating schools are aware of the scholarships and believe they have a reasonable chance of getting one.

The Application and Selection Process for WSA Awards

As the title of this chapter suggests, this analysis seeks to answer the question: Who gets the Washington State Achievers awards? The process of selection has two stages. First, all eligible students are invited to apply in the fall of their junior year. In the five high schools in the University of Washington Beyond High School (UWBHS) senior surveys in 2002 and 2003, nearly a third (31%) of all seniors applied for Achievers scholarships. The application process reflects both eligibility to apply and motivation on the part of students (and/or their families) to attend college. Although we do not have direct measures of eligibility, we suspect

---

[3] This approach may be informed by the knowledge that the disadvantages of students from low-income backgrounds have as much to do with contextual effects as with direct effects. These students are disadvantaged not only because their parents have little in the way of financial resources but also because they are often surrounded by similarly challenged students, and this fact may further diminish their educational aspirations and expectations (Alwin & Otto, 1977; Coleman, 1990; Roscigno, 1998).

that there are many more students in these five high schools who could have applied but did not.

The second stage is the selection process among those who apply. The selection process is conducted by the Washington Education Foundation (WEF), which has gone to great lengths to identify alternative ways to assess academic potential among disadvantaged students—beyond grades and test scores (see Arbona & Novy, 1990; Pfeifer & Sedlacek, 1974). The WEF conducts interviews with all applicants in addition to carefully reviewing school records, letters of recommendation, and evidence of student engagement. The awards are limited to 500 scholarships for all 16 Achievers High Schools in the state. In the five high schools in the UWBHS senior survey, nearly two-thirds (64%) of all applicants were awarded Achievers scholarships. This high rate of selection may be partly attributable to the fact that this study is based on the early years of the program. The selection rate was much higher for the 2002 cohort (83%) than for the 2003 cohort (54%). As the number of applicants increases in subsequent years, the process may become more competitive, leading to a lower rate of selection. This increased competition will, however, not decrease the number of WSA scholarship recipients, often more than 30, in each high school.

The result of these two processes—application and selection—determines the number and composition of students who receive Achievers scholarships. Whatever the composition, the fact that one in five seniors receives an Achievers scholarship may quite possibly transform the culture of these low-income high schools such that college attendance becomes a norm rather than an exception.

The UWBHS Senior Survey

Beginning in 2000, the UWBHS project conducted surveys of all seniors in the five comprehensive high schools in a metropolitan district in Washington State. Two additional public school districts comprised of two schools each were included in the 2003 survey—for a total of nine comprehensive public high schools. The year 2001 marked the inception of the Washington State Achievers Program in five of these schools. The current analysis is based on the 2002 and 2003 senior surveys administered in these five high schools. In 2002, this meant three schools in a single district, and, in 2003, it meant five schools in three districts.

All told, 1,674 seniors in these high schools completed the survey. Although our aim was to include the universe of all seniors, we estimate that 75 to 80 percent completed the survey. Refusals were very few; less than 2 percent of seniors (or their parents) declined to take the survey. The majority of students that the survey missed simply were not in regular classrooms on the day of the senior survey and did not respond to four follow-up mailings to their homes. Many of the missed students were taking courses at local community colleges for part or all of the day, while others were in special education classes or had chronic attendance problems.

The UWBHS senior survey asked each senior if he or she had applied for a Washington State Achievers Scholarship and whether he or she had received one. We matched the survey data with WEF administrative records and found a high degree of validity of the survey measures. Of the survey respondents, 330 reported receiving a scholarship, and 326 of them had received one according to WEF records. The survey counted 534 students who applied for an Achievers scholarship, and 514 were confirmed in the WEF data. In all the subsequent analysis, we relied on the WEF-confirmed number of applicants and recipients.

Factors Influencing WSA Application and Selection

Tables 1a through 1e provide some preliminary answers to who applies for and who receives WSA awards, with a bivariate analysis of individual characteristics and the two outcome variables: application and selection. The relationships between receipt of the awards and various background characteristics[4] provide a sketch of these processes. In the final part of the chapter, we combine all of the background variables in a multivariate analysis to assess the relative importance of the various background characteristics. The analysis begins with simple comparisons to see how likely it is that members of different groups will receive the Washington State Achievers Awards. As was mentioned earlier, this means looking at probabilities of application and probabilities of receipt among those who apply.

The first row in Table 1a reveals that a fifth (20%) of all seniors in the five high schools studied here received a WSA scholarship. More than a quarter (31%) of all students applied, and nearly two-thirds of all applicants (64%) were awarded the scholarship. The single most important predictor of who receives a scholarship may be *application*, but there are many other factors that influence the probability of students' selection.

Ascribed Characteristics

Among the factors relevant in the application and selection of WSA awards are ascribed characteristics, which students themselves have no control over. *Gender* is one such factor that influences the probability of selection for WSA awards (Table 1a). Girls appear to have been more likely than boys to receive the awards (23% and 16%, respectively). This is partly explained by different rates of application between boys and girls. Nevertheless, girls were also more likely to be selected—better than two-thirds (68%) were granted awards while 57 percent of male applicants received a scholarship.

---

[4] In the social sciences we refer to such relationships as "bivariate" since we look at the relationship between one variable and another, ignoring other variables which may influence the relationship. In other words, we simply ask does x influence y?

We might expect *race or ethnicity* to play an important role in selection for WSA scholarships as well. Statistics in the third column of Table 1a indicate that nearly half of the 59 Vietnamese seniors in the Achievers High Schools received awards. They were more than twice as likely as nearly all other groups to receive the awards. A quarter (or more) of African American and Cambodian students received the awards. These differences in the receipt of WSA scholarships are largely explained by differential rates of application across racial or ethnic categories. Overall, 31 percent of all students applied, but 73 percent of Vietnamese students did so. While they were more than twice as likely as other students to apply, however, this fact did not help them once they were in the applicant pool; 63 percent of Vietnamese applicants received the awards—a figure not significantly different from that for all students (64%). African American applicants seem to have fared best in the selection process, while Filipino and "other Asian" students were considerably less likely to be selected than students of all other groups. All of this said, it is important to point out that the racial and ethnic differentials in selection were very modest. Even among Filipinos and other Asians, who were least likely to get the scholarships, better than 4 of 10 were successful. What little role race and ethnicity did play in determining scholarship receipt seems to reside primarily in application rates. Once students applied, race appears to have been immaterial.

Nativity and home language are also relevant background factors that may influence scholarship receipt (Table 1a). On one hand, foreign-born students who speak English as a second language might be marginal students in some schools—more isolated from teachers, counselors, and administrators and less familiar with the American educational system. Such students might be less likely to hear about and less encouraged to apply for the scholarship. On the other hand, first- and second-generation students may be highly motivated to "achieve the American dream" and, thus, more likely to seek out any and all opportunities for postsecondary education (Kao & Tienda, 1995; Portes &

	% of All Who Apply	X	% Recipients of Applicants	=	% Recipients of All Students	All Students (N)	All Students %
All Seniors	31		64		20	1674	100
Gender							
Males	28		57		16	770	47
Females	34		68		23	880	53
Race/Ethnicity							
Hispanic	26		64		17	202	12
African American	35		72		25	320	19
East Asian	35		62		22	133	8
Cambodian	51		57		29	69	4
Vietnamese	73		63		46	59	4
Filipino & other Asian	34		42		14	77	5
Am Indian & Pac Islander	28		60		17	90	5
White	24		63		15	724	43
Immigrant Generation							
First (foreign born)	41		54		22	322	19
Second	35		68		24	296	18
Third or higher	27		66		18	1056	63
Home Language							
English	27		69		19	1045	66
Another language	39		56		22	533	34

Table 1a. Percentage of Students Who Applied For and Who Received Achiever Scholarships, by Gender, Race/Ethnicity, Immigrant Generation, and Home Language, in Three High Schools in the Pacific Northwest

Data Source: UWBHS Senior Survey, 2002 & 2003

Rumbaut, 2001). Results presented here are more in accordance with the second hypothesis. Table 1a shows that foreign-born students (first-generation) and American-born students of foreign-born parents (second-generation) were more likely to receive the scholarships than American-born students of American-born parents (third-generation or higher). Further, students from non-English speaking homes were more likely to receive the awards than native English speakers, but these outcomes can largely be explained by the fact that first- and second-generation students (many of whom come from non-English speaking homes) were more often eligible and, thus, more likely to apply than other students. First-generation students and students from non-English speaking homes were, however, slightly less successful in being selected once they were in the applicant pool.

Socioeconomic Background
Because the Washington State Achievers program is specifically designed to ameliorate the effects of poverty and/or economic disadvantage on educational opportunities, we might guess that students from low socioeconomic status (SES) backgrounds are more likely to receive awards. Although we do not have direct measures of household or family income, *parental education* and *homeownership* provide good proxy measures for SES. Our results show that students with highly educated parents were less likely to receive the awards because they were less likely to apply, presumably because they were not eligible (Table 1b). For example, about a fifth of students whose fathers had a high school education or less were scholarship recipients, while only 12 percent of those with college-educated fathers were. Similarly, we found that students whose families owned their homes were less likely to receive the awards than students from families who were (presumably) renting. Higher SES students were less likely to be granted awards because they were less likely to apply. This should come as no surprise, given the eligibility criteria outlined earlier.

Table 1b. Percentage of Students Who Applied For and Received Achiever Scholarships, by Socioeconomic Background and Family Structure, in Three High Schools in the Pacific Northwest

	% of All Who Apply	x	% Recipients of Applicants	=	% Recipients of All Students	All Students (N)	All Students %
All Seniors	31		64		20	1674	100
Father's Education							
No father figure	40		69		27	210	13
Less than 12th grade	36		57		21	263	16
HS graduate	30		66		20	413	25
Some college	30		64		20	506	30
College grad+	21		58		12	282	17
Mother's Education							
No mother figure	30		54		16	138	8
Less than 12th grade	35		61		21	318	19
HS graduate	30		66		20	437	26
Some college	32		62		20	524	31
College grad+	24		72		17	257	15
Homeownership							
Live in owner-occupied home	27		62		17	940	58
Live in rented home	36		66		24	613	38
Don't know	31		64		20	70	4
Family Structure							
Lives with both parents	28		56		15	861	54
Does not live with both parents	35		71		25	729	46

Data Source: UWBHS Senior Survey, 2002 & 2003

Family structure has historically been associated with SES. We considered its effects in terms of family "intactness," defining an intact family as one in which the student resides with two married parents. Previous studies have shown that children from single-parent families are less likely to receive higher education (Krein & Beller, 1988; McLanahan & Sandefur, 1994). The WSA award may provide partial compensation for this disadvantage, as students from single-parent families were more likely to apply for and receive scholarships (Table 1b). In short, the WSA awards—in principle and in practice—are for students from disadvantaged home environments.

Parents and Significant Others
It makes sense that what goes on in the home—irrespective of household structure—will have an impact on students' chances for success (Coleman, 1990; Lareau, 2000). With this in mind, we examined the effects of *parental support, supervision, and control* on the probabilities that students would apply for and receive a WSA award. Parental support is a scale measure meant to capture the quality of communication between students and their parents as well as the perception of parental support. Our measure of parental supervision is based on two items that ask students how familiar their parents are with their friends and their friends' parents. The parental control measure is based on the extent to which parents limit school-night activities and/or check to see that their children have completed their homework assignments each night. There are good reasons to believe that such parental influences would shape patterns of scholarship application and receipt, but we found only modest relationships between these factors and the probability of applying for and/or receiving a WSA scholarship (Table 1c). This is not to say that a student's home and community life do not make a difference.

Parents are not the only agents of socialization that matter. With this in mind, we included an *encouragement* index, which is the sum of all individuals in the student's life who believe that college is the most important thing for the student to do after he or she graduates from high school. Mother, father, other

Table 1c. Percentage of Students Who Applied For and Received Achiever Scholarships, by Parenting Style and Degree of Encouragement, in Three High Schools in the Pacific Northwest							
	% of All Who Apply	X	% Recipients of Applicants	=	% Recipients of All Students	All Students	
						(N)	%
All Seniors	31		64		20	1674	100
Parental Influences:							
Communication & Support							
0 low	33		67		22	9	1
0.5	42		55		23	48	3
1	35		69		24	136	8
1.5	32		50		16	323	19
2	31		62		19	589	35
2.5	28		76		21	427	26
3 high	29		63		18	142	8
Supervision (Knows Friends)							
0 low	41		79		33	82	5
0.5	37		64		24	105	6
1	31		57		18	334	20
1.5	32		64		20	362	22
2	29		63		18	460	27
2.5	23		54		12	172	10
3 high	30		73		22	159	9
Control/Checking							
0 low	38		73		28	219	13
0.5	23		58		13	189	11
1	28		61		17	253	15
1.5	30		65		19	361	22
2	31		58		18	275	16
2.5	30		63		19	243	15
3 high	38		63		24	134	8
Encouragement Index							
0	12		33		4	123	7
1	14		25		4	84	5
2	19		35		7	90	5
3	23		54		12	123	7
4	28		59		17	224	13
5	34		71		24	381	23
6	39		68		26	649	39

Data Source: UWBHS Senior Survey, 2002 & 2003

adults, siblings, friends, and favorite teacher were among the possible sources of encouragement that registered in the UWBHS survey

The bottom panel of Table 1c demonstrates clearly that encouragement was positively related to students' chances of receiving a scholarship. Highly encouraged students were more likely to receive the award—mainly because they were more likely to apply than other students.

Student Behaviors

Thus far, we have considered only one behavioral factor—application; the rest have been factors that students themselves cannot control. *Grades,* on the other hand, are at least in part reflective of the decisions, efforts, and talents of the students themselves. They may be taken as measures of "academic potential," which is one of the eligibility criteria for the WSA program. Not surprisingly, students with better grades were more likely to apply and more likely to be granted the award (Table 1d). However, the most important finding is that *applying was the key* to getting the scholarship. Among those who did not apply, the chance of receiving a scholarship was zero. Among those with relatively poor grades (mostly Cs and lower) the chance of receiving a scholarship was 45 percent. Even among C students, nearly half of those who applied did receive a scholarship.

Patterns of attendance and preparedness did not have clear relationships with the measured outcomes. There were some incipient patterns, but none was consistent across the range of these variables. Due to low application rates, students who are often in trouble are less likely to receive the scholarship than others. However, "troublemakers" who do apply have a better than average chance of receiving it. It appears that the Achievers Scholarships provide a second chance for many students who have not had the best records for attendance, preparation in class, and completion of homework. The only clear behavioral influence on scholarship receipt is *contact with counselors.* Those students who frequented their counselor's office were more likely to have received the awards because they were more likely to have applied for and more likely to have received an award once in the applicant pool (Table 1d). Their success in the applicant pool may reflect their relatively close relationships with counselors who may have been more likely to write them strong letters of recommendation. Furthermore, the Washington State Achievers program stays in close touch with high school counselors, reminding them of various programs and deadlines. This being true, it is not surprising that those students who have the most contact with counselors would have the highest rates of application. The most important behavior, then, in determining scholarship receipt may be application, and application, in turn, partly depends on contact with counselors.

Personality

Personality traits such as *self-esteem* and *self-efficacy,* often referred to in school achievement literature as "locus of control" or "internalized locus of control," might also have some bearing on the behaviors and outcomes of students. It is easy to imagine that students who think highly of themselves and their abilities to effect change in their own lives would be most likely to take action to improve their life chances (Coleman, 1990). Such action might include applying for scholarships like the Washington State Achievers award. Indeed, Table 1e suggests that this is at least partly true. While self-esteem did not seem to affect scholarship application or receipt, self-efficacy appears to have had strong effects on both processes. The relationship between self-efficacy and receipt of the scholarship was particularly striking. Forty-three percent (43%) of those low on this measure received the award while 74 percent of those high on this measure won the award. Perhaps students who have confidence in themselves and a strong internal sense of direction are seen as particularly able candidates by raters. They may also be better able to deal with adversity, leaders rather than followers, and popular among their peers.

Table 1d. Percentage of Students Who Applied For and Received Achiever Scholarships, by Behaviors, in Three High Schools in the Pacific Northwest					
	% of All Who Apply	x % Recipients of Applicants	= % Recipients of All Students	All Students	
				(N)	%
All Seniors	31	64	20	1674	100
Self-Reported Grades					
Mostly As	37	80	30	306	19
Half As and half Bs	38	62	23	450	27
Mostly Bs	36	64	23	303	18
Half Bs and half Cs	19	54	10	392	24
Mostly Cs and lower	21	45	9	202	12
Student Behaviors:					
Truant/Tardy/Absent					
Never	31	69	21	52	3
1 or 2 times	31	62	19	404	24
3 to 6 times	29	65	19	775	46
7 to 9 times	32	61	19	339	20
10 or more times	38	64	24	104	6
Unprepared for Class					
Never	29	59	17	151	9
1 or 2 times	31	64	20	704	42
3 to 6 times	30	62	19	620	37
7 to 9 times	31	71	22	124	7
10 or more times	35	69	24	75	4
In Trouble/Punished					
Never	33	65	21	1193	71
1 or 2 times	27	59	16	413	25
3 times or more	19	69	13	68	4
Hours Spent on Homework/Week					
None	25	68	17	185	12
less than 1 hr	26	44	11	368	23
1 to 2 hrs	26	71	19	430	27
3 to 4 hrs	33	67	22	304	19
5 to 6 hrs	40	58	24	119	7
7 to 9 hrs	43	65	28	87	5
over 10 hrs	49	80	39	114	7
Contact with Counselor(s)					
Hardly ever	19	52	10	370	22
Sometimes	29	59	17	892	54
Frequently	45	74	33	395	24
Data Source: UWBHS Senior Survey, 2002 & 2003					

Numerous studies have attempted to measure *popularity,* and most often they have relied on subjective measures (see Ainsworth-Darnall & Downey, 1998). The UWBHS senior survey included an objective measure of popularity and/or leadership by counting the number of times each student was nominated by another as one of his or her best friends. We might expect that students with high counts would be more successful than others. Table 1e hints that there may be some truth to this. Students with high counts (more nominations) on this measure seem to have had better chances of receiving the scholarships, both because they were more likely to apply and because they were more likely to be selected. This may reflect the importance placed on leadership ability and/or other intangible qualities by the Washington State Achievers program.

An overview of the bivariate statistics suggests that students' chances of receiving the WSA award have depended on a combination of individual and household characteristics including gender, race/ethnicity, parents' education, homeownership, family intactness, nativity, home language, encouragement, grades, contact with counselors, self-efficacy, and popularity. Some of these are important because they affect the probability of application, and others are important because they affect the probability of selection among those who apply. Some may not be important in and of themselves, but only insofar as they influence or are influenced by some other covariate or unobserved factor. These possibilities are addressed in the following multivariate analysis.

A Multivariate Analysis of Factors Influencing WSA Application and Selection

Thus far, we have looked at scholarship receipt at the bivariate level. This type of analysis yields results that are interesting but that do not take into account the overlapping effects of the independent variables. To further our inquiry, we undertook

Table 1e. Percentage of Students Who Applied For and Received Achiever Scholarships, by Self Image and Popularity						
	% of All Who Apply	x	% Recipients of Applicants	=	% Recipients of All Students	All Students
						(N)	%
All Seniors	31		64		20	1674	100
Self-Image/Popularity:							
Self Esteem							
low	34		59		20	202	12
medium	31		57		18	616	37
high	30		69		21	856	51
Self-Efficacy/Locus of Control							
low	29		43		13	229	14
medium	30		56		17	656	39
high	32		74		24	789	47
Popularity/Nominations as Friend							
0	26		56		14	497	30
1	29		63		18	448	27
2	33		63		21	324	19
3	31		67		21	224	13
4	37		76		28	103	6
5	57		79		45	42	3
6 or more	44		63		28	36	2
Data Source: UWBHS Senior Survey, 2002 & 2003							

a multivariate analysis which assessed whether each variable had a significant net influence on scholarship receipt, all else being equal. For example, if everyone were the same in all respects except gender, would gender make a difference? Logistic regression was employed since it is the most appropriate multivariate statistical technique for dichotomous outcome variables (Long, 1997) such as those examined here.

Table 2 provides results from the estimation of three regression equations. The first predicts the odds of applying for the scholarship among all students; the second, the odds of receiving the scholarship among students who applied; and the third, the overall odds of receiving the scholarship among all students. Numbers in each column represent the odds of scholarship application or receipt relative to those of the omitted category for each independent variable. Exp(B)s[5] less than 1 suggest that the odds of scholarship application or receipt diminish as values on the corresponding independent variable increase. Conversely, Exp(B)s greater than 1 suggest that the odds of scholarship application or receipt improve as values on the independent variable increase.[6] Statistical significance is indicated by asterisks located next to the numbers in each column.

Who Applies?

Looking first at column one in Table 2, we see that there are twelve factors which significantly influenced the odds of applying for the Washington State Achievers award—eight positively and four negatively, net of all relevant background variables. Vietnamese students were more likely to apply than other students, and this finding is not a function of any other measured covariate. Encouragement, as captured by the number of significant others (father, mother, favorite teacher, etc.) who think that college is the most important thing to do after high school, had

---

[5] Exponentiated beta coefficients from logistic regression.

[6] For dichotomous variables such as homeownership, where homeowners get a "1" and nonhomeowners get a "0," a coefficient greater than 1 reflects the benefit of being a homeowner. For a continuous variable such as parents' years of schooling a coefficient greater than 1 reflects the average benefit respondents receive for every additional year of education their parents have attained.

Table 2. Logistic Regression Models of Application and Receipt of Achiever Scholarship Among Senior Students in Three High Schools in the Pacific Northwest

	Application Among All Students	Sig.	Receipt Among Applicants	Sig.	Receipt Among All Students	Sig.
Gender	Exp(B)		Exp(B)		Exp(B)	
Female	1.01		0.82		1.07	
Male	Omitted		Omitted		Omitted	
Race/Ethnicity						
Hispanic	0.98		1.14		1.10	
African American	1.47	*	1.68		1.65	*
East Asian	1.24		1.30		1.24	
Cambodian	1.99	*	1.52		2.07	
Vietnamese	6.01	***	1.92		4.27	***
Filipino/other Asian	1.36		0.41		0.73	
American Indian	1.21		1.09		1.26	
White	Omitted		Omitted		Omitted	
Family Structure						
Student lives with both parents	0.62	***	0.49	**	0.49	***
Not intact	Omitted		Omitted		Omitted	
Mother's Education	0.99		1.03		1.01	
Father's Education	0.94	*	0.93		0.92	**
Homeownership						
Own	0.83		1.03		0.81	
Rent	Omitted		Omitted		Omitted	
Nativity						
First generation	1.07		0.89		1.06	
Second generation	1.08		1.85		1.38	
Third generation or more	Omitted		Omitted		Omitted	
Home Language						
English	0.90		1.63		1.23	
Other language	Omitted		Omitted		Omitted	

Table 2. Logistic Regression Models of Application and Receipt of Achiever Scholarship Among Senior Students in Three High Schools in the Pacific Northwest (cont.)

	Application Among All Students	Sig.	Receipt Among Applicants	Sig.	Receipt Among All Students	Sig.
Parental Influences						
Support	0.69	**	1.05		0.74	
Supervision	0.82	*	0.75		0.75	**
Control/checking	1.07		0.85		0.96	
Encouragement	1.26	***	1.26	**	1.41	***
Student Behaviors						
Frequency of truancy/absence	1.03		1.00		1.01	
Frequency of unpreparedness	1.07	*	1.14	**	1.11	**
Frequency of trouble/punishment	0.89		1.09		0.90	
Hours spent on homework	1.09	***	1.07		1.08	**
Contact with counselor(s)	1.05	***	1.06	***	1.07	***
Self-reported grades	1.57	***	2.19	***	1.81	***
Self-Image/Popularity						
Self-esteem	1.11		0.72		0.95	
Self-efficacy/locus of control	0.91		3.47	***	1.66	*
Nominations as friend	1.09	*	1.08		1.12	*
McFadden's R Square	15.2%		20.4%		20.6%	
N=	1650		510		1650	
*p<.05 **p<.01 ***p<.001						
Data Source: UWBHS Senior Survey, 2002 & 2003						

a strong positive effect as well.[7] Along the same lines, hours spent on homework, contact with school counselors, and grades all had strong positive net effects. Popularity also had a significant positive effect on application rates. With 64 percent of applicants selected for a scholarship, the determinants of application are very consequential.

On the other hand, students living in households headed by married couples who were highly educated and supportive parents were significantly less likely to be in the applicant pool—probably because such families typically earn more income than allowable for children to qualify for the WSA scholarship. This is not surprising, given that the Gates Foundation has targeted for the scholarships students who would not likely attend college without external assistance. Less obvious, however, are the reasons that students with parents who know their friends and the parents of their friends (supervision) were underrepresented in the applicant pool, as we found. We might expect that such community cohesion or "social capital" (Coleman, 1990) would have increased the likelihood of application, but this expectation found no empirical support here.

Who Among the Applicants Receives the Awards?

As noted earlier, the relatively small size of the applicant pool limits our ability to answer the question of which applicants receive the awards with great certainty. Moreover, the limitation of our analysis to the first two years of the program may obscure our

---

[7] Other research using the UWBHS data has demonstrated that encouragement effects sometimes overwhelm the effects of race and ethnicity (Hirschman, Lee, & Emeka 2004). This does not happen in the case of Vietnamese students, who are significantly more likely to receive these scholarships because they are significantly more likely to apply. Why they are more likely to apply is a question that cannot be answered here.

view of patterns and relationships that may change as the program evolves.[8]

Column 2 of Table 2 provides Exp(B)s from a logistic regression equation predicting the odds of receiving the Washington State Achievers award among those who apply. Four of the factors that significantly influenced application also influenced selection. Among applicants, those with highly educated fathers and two married parents living in their homes were less likely to be selected. Such students may include borderline cases—in terms of the income requirement—who were ultimately declined because their family incomes were too high.

All other things being equal, applicants who had good grades, who did their homework, and who had more contact with counselors were more likely to have been selected to receive scholarships. These students may be thought of as "safer bets" than other applicants. Second-generation (American-born children of immigrant parents) students appear to have better odds of selection than others as well.

There are some anomalies in the results as well. Mother's educational attainment had a positive and significant impact on the odds of receiving the award, while father's educational attainment had a significant negative effect. The unexpected positive effect of mother's education may reflect the fact that we are dealing with mothers who are divorced, have never been married, or are married to men with low levels of education—any of which circumstances might lower the family income into the bottom third of Washington's family income distribution. Students from low-income families with relatively highly educated mothers may have been advantaged in the selection process due to patterns of language, speech, and comportment, which may be taken as signs

---

[8] Several rather large coefficients are not statistically significant. The fact that particularly large or small odds ratios are not found to be statistically significant probably reflects that they are based on a small number of cases.

of "academic potential"[9] acquired through lifelong interactions with an educated mother. Such mothers might also be particularly involved in the education of their children (Lareau, 2000). It was also found, contrary to expectation, that self-esteem appears to have a negative effect on selection—another fact that eludes easy explanation.

Who Among All Students Receives the Awards?

The chance of getting a Washington State Achievers scholarship may be understood as a product of application rates among all students and selection rates among those who apply. Column 3 of Table 2 provides clues as to which students (among the total student body) were most likely to receive the awards. By looking at coefficients in all three columns we may determine what factors were important and why. For the sake of clarity these factors are classified on two dimensions: the valence of their influence and the vehicle of their influence. On the first dimension, some factors impacted the odds of scholarship receipt negatively and others positively. On the second dimension, some factors acted on scholarship receipt by way of their influence on application rates, others by way of their influence on selection once the student was in the applicant pool, and still others influenced both application and selection rates.

We begin with the factors negatively associated with scholarship receipt. The third column in Table 2 indicates that there were three factors which were negatively and statistically significant in shaping one's odds of scholarship receipt: residence with both parents, fathers' educational attainment, and parental supervision. Living with both parents reduced both the odds that one would apply for the WSA scholarship and the odds that one would receive the scholarship once in the applicant pool. The more educated one's father, the lower were one's chances for receiving a WSA scholarship, but there is no statistically

---

[9] Pierre Bourdieu (1974, 1973) referred to these patterns as "cultural capital."

convincing evidence that this was because such students were disfavored in the selection process. Rather, high educational attainments among fathers significantly reduced the chance that students would apply. Both of these findings make sense given that the aim of the WSA program is to offset the disadvantages faced by students from lower class families—many of which are headed by lesser educated single adults. More vexing is the finding that parental supervision was negatively related with application and, thus, receipt of the WSA award.

There are nine variables in the third column of Table 2 that were positively associated with scholarship receipt and were statistically significant. Of these, four influenced WSA scholarship receipt primarily by way of application rates. Race and/or ethnicity seemed to play a part. African American and Vietnamese students applied more and, thus, received the scholarships more often, though there is no statistically sound evidence that they were favored in the selection process. The same is true of students who did lots of homework and students who had lots of friends. The diligence associated with engagement in more than trivial amounts of homework, it makes sense, might also lead such students to apply for the scholarships in disproportionate numbers. Those with large friendship networks might be more likely to hear of the award and, therefore, more likely to apply than their less well-connected classmates. There is no obvious explanation as to why African American and Vietnamese students were more likely to apply, all else being equal.

Interestingly, there is only one factor—negative or positive—whose influence on WSA scholarship receipt was wholly a function of favor in the selection process, and that was self-efficacy, or locus of control. Students who scored high on this measure were no more likely to apply for the scholarship than other students but were significantly more likely to be granted the award once in the applicant pool. Perhaps this belief in the self and in the mastery of one's own fate is the prime "intangible" that impresses selection committee members and, maybe, foretells bright futures for those who possess it.

Encouragement from significant others, contact with counselors, and good grades were all positively associated with scholarship receipt. Highly encouraged students who frequented their counselor's office and earned high grades were more likely to apply and more likely to be selected than others for the WSA award once in the applicant pool. Perhaps the most counterintuitive finding of this study is that students' unpreparedness (showing up to class without pen/pencil, books, paper, homework) was positively associated with both application and selection for the scholarships. In any case, this suggests as strongly as any other finding in this study that WSA scholarships are not being granted solely on the basis of conventional measures of academic success and/or potential. Rather, the program casts a much broader net and may effectively grant dozens of disadvantaged students a new lease on life.

Conclusions

This chapter began by framing the Washington State Achievers program in a larger debate over how we can best ameliorate the effects of poverty in our society. The Washington State Achievers program falls clearly on the side of those who argue that what the poor need most is *opportunity*—educational opportunity in particular. It is too early in the life of the program to ask whether the Washington State Achievers program will create a "culture of college attendance" in low-income schools. However, the program is moving forward quickly and the baseline objectives of the program are being met: (1) students who receive Achievers awards attend high schools with large numbers of low-income students; (2) students who apply are, themselves, from low socioeconomic status backgrounds; and (3) the majority (64%) of those who applied in 2002 and 2003 received the scholarships.

Among eligible students, those who are highly encouraged by parents and peers, who have frequent contact with school counselors, who get good grades, who are popular among their peers, and who have a heightened sense of self-efficacy are likely to be awarded the scholarships.[10] Some of these findings may seem unexceptional; we would expect students with good grades to get scholarships. However, other positive influences listed above may not be as obvious or intuitive. This is perhaps because a goal of the WSA program has been to identify students of great potential but whose promise may not be evident via conventional measures. Our measure of internalized locus of control (self-efficacy) captures students' tendency or ability to "take the bull by the horns"—to instigate change for the better in their own lives. Such ability may not always show up in GPAs or standardized test scores but may be no less predictive of success later in the lives of these or any group of students. The above findings hold up in our multivariate analysis and are the patterns of behavior consistent with the culture of college attendance that the Washington State Achievers program is trying to encourage.

Directions for future research in this area involve questions whose answers may be central to educational policy debates and to reform efforts in the future. As data on the recipients and nonrecipients stream in over the coming years, we will be able to see how successful the students are and, ultimately, how effective the Washington State Achievers program is. Data on these students may inform broader debates regarding the roles of financial constraints and financial aid in shaping patterns of college attendance, college completion, and life chances. The continued study of Achievers schools will provide us the opportunity to see the effects of scholarship programs and alumni successes on the culture of the schools and, in turn, the lives of

---

[10] However, it is important to note that these are not the only low-income students who win the awards. Receipt rates are high at all levels of encouragement, grades, popularity, etc. Thus, highly visible opportunities for college attendance are now widespread among low-income students in the Achievers schools. This fact may have a dramatic effect on the culture of these schools and their students.

future generations of students—for these schools may become places where students of all backgrounds not only *hope* to go to college but *expect* to and *believe* they can. For now, suffice it to say that the Washington State Achievers program is doing what it set out to do. It has made college attendance a real possibility for large numbers of low-income students, potentially altering the courses of their lives and their alma maters for the better.

References

Ainsworth-Darnall, J. W., & Downey, D. B. (1998). Assessing the oppositional culture explanation for racial/ethnic differences in school performance. *American Sociological Review, 63,* 536-553.

Alwin, D. F., & Otto, L. B. (1977). High school context effects on aspirations. *Sociology of Education, 50,* 259-273.

Arbona, C., & Novy, D. M. (1990). Noncognitive dimensions as predictors of college success among Black, Mexican-American, and White students. *Journal of College Student Development, 31,* 415-422.

Bourdieu, P. (1973). Cultural reproduction and social reproduction. In R. Brown (Ed.), *Knowledge, education, and cultural change.* London: Tavistock.

Bourdieu, P. (1974). The school as a conservative force: Scholastic and cultural inequalities. In J. Eggleston (Ed.), *Contemporary research in the sociology of education.* London: Metheun.

Coleman, J. S. (1990). *Equality and achievement in education.* San Francisco: Westview.

Hirschman, C., Lee, J. C., & Emeka, A. (2004). *Explaining race and ethnic disparity in educational ambitions.* Paper presented at the annual meeting of the Population Association of America, Boston, MA, April 2004.

Jackson, G. A. (1990). Financial aid, college entry, and affirmative action. *American Journal of Education, 98,* 523-550.

Kao, G., & Tienda, M. (1995). Optimism and achievement: The educational performance of immigrant youth. *Social Science Quarterly, 76,* 1-19.

Krein, S. F., & Beller, A. H. (1988). Educational attainment of children from single-parent families: Differences by exposure, gender, and race. *Demography, 25,* 221-234.

Lareau, A. (2000). *Home advantage: Social class and parental intervention in elementary education.* New York: Rowman & Littlefield.

Long, J. S. (1997). *Regression models for categorical and limited dependent variables.* Thousand Oaks, CA: Sage Publications.

Manski, C. F., & Wise, D. A. (1983). *College choice in America.* Cambridge, MA: Harvard University Press.

McLanahan, S., & Sandefur, G. (1994). *Growing up with a single parent: What hurts, what helps.* Cambridge, MA: Harvard University Press.

Perna, L. W. (2000). Differences in the decision to attend college among African Americans, Hispanics, and Whites. *Journal of Higher Education, 71*(2), 117-141.

Pfeifer, C. M., Jr., & Sedlacek, W. E. (1974). Predicting Black student grades with nonintellectual measures. *The Journal of Negro Education, 43,* 67-76.

Portes, A., & Rumbaut, R. G. (2001). *Legacies: The story of the immigrant second generation.* Los Angeles: University of California Press.

Roscigno, V. J. (1998). Race and the reproduction of educational disadvantage. *Social Forces, 76,* 1033-1061.

St. John, E. P., & Noell, J. (1989). The effects of student financial aid on access to higher education: An analysis of progress with special consideration of minority enrollments. *Review of Educational Research, 64,* 531-555.

CHAPTER 6

EARLY ACADEMIC BEHAVIORS OF WASHINGTON STATE ACHIEVERS

William E. Sedlacek and Hung-Bin Sheu

Introduction

The Washington State Achievers (WSA) scholarship program provides funding for students from Washington to attend most colleges or universities in the state to obtain a four-year degree. It is funded by the Bill & Melinda Gates Foundation and managed by the Washington Education Foundation (WEF). The scholarship is available to students attending one of 16 WSA high schools in the state of Washington with family incomes less than 35 percent of the median family income in the state. The WEF began selecting scholars in April 2001 and will make 500 awards per year for 13 years.

Unique aspects of the program include the intention to give awards to students with high potential, not just high grades, and to provide mentors while they are in college. Applicants are evaluated on their creativity, their concern for their community, and how they have overcome any difficult circumstances.

Alternatives to standardized tests and prior grades as predictors of success have been studied for many years (Sedlacek, 1998a, 1998b, 2004, 2005). A system of noncognitive variables that measures a wider range of attributes than more traditional methods—and is more equitable for students with other than an upper-middle-class, suburban background—has been developed. The noncognitive variables are self-concept, realistic self-appraisal, negotiating the system/racism, long-range goals, support person, leadership, community, and nontraditional knowledge.

The noncognitive variables noted above were used to select the Washington State Achievers, along with other assessments. The goals of the selection process are to judge the academic potential of students who show their abilities in ways other than in the more traditional standardized tests and prior grades. In a study of the 1,142 high school students who applied for WSA scholarships in 2004, Cronbach's alpha reliability estimates of ratings by judges of each of the variables ranged from .78 to .80 and was .83 for the overall noncognitive score.

Understanding the success in college of the Washington State Achievers is critical to the success of the entire program. The Achievers were chosen for their academic potential, but that potential was likely shown in ways other than test scores and grades, ways which were investigated in this study. Since the program is relatively new it may be premature to examine all aspects of the academic success of Achievers. However, studying their early academic performance may provide valuable information to those concerned with the program and to others interested in similar students in other states.

Results of this study will help us choose future Achievers in the best way possible. Results will also allow educators to plan better for retention and student service programs while Achievers are in school and to maximize their chances of having a positive experience leading to graduation.

Method

Procedure

The National Opinion Research Center (NORC) mailed a paper-and-pencil survey to 500 Achievers in April 2002 who had been selected as Achievers in 2001. The items on the survey were developed from previous surveys conducted by NORC with input from the WEF staff and the Research Advisory Committee.

Participants

For this study, 372 recipients of WSA funding who were enrolled in higher education at the time they responded to the survey were included. Participants were 69 percent female, 31 percent male, 41 percent White, 26 percent Asian American/Pacific Islander, 13 percent Hispanic, 11 percent African American, 2 percent Native American, 5 percent individuals with multiethnic backgrounds, and 2 percent individuals who indicated other racial/ethnic backgrounds. Among these participants, 47 percent attended two-year colleges, 40 percent attended four-year public schools, and 13 percent attended four-year private schools.

Results

To describe the early academic behaviors of WSA recipients who were enrolled in college, the results section consists of (a) credits taken/academic major/experiences as a WSA recipient, (b) academic engagement, (c) community engagement, (d) leadership/extracurricular activities, and (e) educational aspirations. A short paragraph follows to describe WSA recipients who were not receiving funding when the survey was administered.

Because of unequal cell sizes, several General Linear Models (GLMs) were conducted to detect group differences for continuous outcome variables. For noncontinuous variables, χ^2 tests were performed. The significance (alpha) level for all statistical analyses was set at the .05 level. In addition to statistical significance level, effect size indices of η^2 and d are also reported to explain clinical meaningfulness of these statistical tests. According to Cohen (1988), the effect sizes of an η^2 that is larger than .0099 and a d that is larger than .2 are considered small, an η^2 larger than .0588 and a d larger than .5 are considered medium, and an η^2 larger than .1379 and a *d* larger than .8 are considered large. The η^2 index was derived directly from the SPSS (v.11.5) output, while the formulas from Cortina and Nouri (2000, p. 13) were used to compute the *d* index.

Credits Taken/Academic Major/Experiences as a WSA Recipient
    As of April 2002, when the survey was administered, there were significant differences on credits taken among WSA recipients who were enrolled in two-year colleges, four-year private colleges/universities, and four-year public colleges/ universities (F = 3.20, p = .042, η^2 = .018), while gender difference (F = .17, p = .679, η^2 < .0001) and the gender by type of school interaction (F = 1.54, p = .215, η^2 = .009) were not present. Type of school differences on credits taken was both statistically significant and clinically meaningful, with a small effect size. Specifically, LSD Post Hoc analyses suggested that those who attended four-year schools had taken more credits than those who attended four-year private schools (36 credits versus 26 credits).
    For credits taken in April 2002, the interaction of gender and type of school was significant (F = 4.04, p = .018, η^2 = .022). Results of simple main effects indicated that males (14.67 credits) in two-year colleges took more credits than their female counterparts (13.69 credits) with the effect size (*d*) of .279, whereas males (12.50 credits) in four-year private schools took fewer credits than their female counterparts (14.87 credits) with the effect size (*d*) of .638. There was no gender difference on credits taken for those who attended four-year public schools. See Figure 1 for the interaction.
    Results of χ^2 analysis (χ^2 = 5.00, p = .025) indicated that females (64%) were more likely than males (51%) to have decided on their academic majors. There was no relationship between type of school and decision on major (χ^2 = 3.86, p = .145).
    There were no significant effects by gender or type of school or gender by type of school interactions on participants' perceived importance of the WSA funding (see Table 1). On a 1 (strongly

Figure 1.
Gender, by Type of School Interaction on
Credits Taken in April 2002

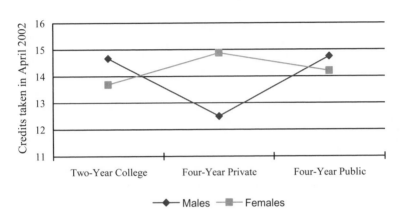

Table 1. Means* of Participants' Perceived Importance of WSA Funding								
	Two-Year College			**Four-Year Private**			**Four-Year Public**		
	M	F	T	M	F	T	M	F	T
N	45	128	173	15	30	45	53	96	149
Critical to attending this college	3.24	3.14	3.17	3.60	3.33	3.42	3.30	3.33	3.32
Provided me with a network of friends	2.84	2.62	2.68	2.33	2.43	2.40	2.79	2.46	2.58
A strong affinity with other WSAs	2.71	2.51	2.56	2.33	2.50	2.44	2.66	2.45	2.52

Note: M = males; F = females; T = total for the corresponding type of school.
*1 = strongly disagree; 4 = strongly agree

disagree) to 4 (strongly agree) scale, participants seemed more to agree that WSA funding was important for attending college (3.26) but less to agree that being a WSA recipient provided a network of friends (2.60) or that they felt a strong affinity with other WSA recipients (2.53).

There was no relationship between gender and whether or not participants were assigned a WSA college mentor ($\chi^2 = .249$, $p = .883$). A majority of male (82%) and female (84%) Achievers knew they were assigned a mentor while 8 percent of male Achievers and 8 percent of female Achievers responded that they were not assigned a mentor, and 10 percent of male Achievers and 8 percent of female Achievers did not know whether they were assigned a mentor. Type of school was also not related to assignment of a WSA college mentor ($\chi^2 = 4.089$, $p = .394$). Most participants in two-year (81%), four-year private (89%), and four-year public (86%) schools were assigned a mentor. Moreover, there was no gender main effect ($F = .07$, $p = .790$, $\eta^2 < .0001$), type of school main effect ($F = 2.09$, $p = .125$, $\eta^2 = .011$), or gender by type of school interaction ($F = 1.87$, $p = .155$, $\eta^2 = .010$) on participants' frequencies of meeting with a WSA college mentor. On a 1 (not at all) to 5 (four or more times) scale, male participants had met with their mentors 3.91 times on average, whereas females had met with mentors 3.73 times on average. On the other hand, four-year private school students (4.29 times) seemed to meet more frequently than four-year public school students (3.89 times) and two-year college students (3.57 times); however, these differences were not statistically significant. Finally, in terms of importance on participants' experiences with WSA college mentors, there was no gender main effect ($F = .16$, $p = .685$, $\eta^2 < .0001$), type of school main effect ($F = .68$, $p = .508$, $\eta^2 = .004$), or gender by type of school interaction ($F = 1.24$, $p = .291$, $\eta^2 = .007$). On a 1 (not important) to 3 (very important) scale, male (2.30) and female (2.18) participants as well as those who attended two-year (2.13), four-year private (2.38), and four-year public (2.26) schools perceived their experiences with WSA mentors as somewhat important to very important.

Academic Engagement

Using a 1 (never) to 5 (four or more times a week) scale, five items were included in the survey to assess participants' frequencies of (a) working with students on schoolwork outside of class, (b) discussing ideas from readings/class with students outside of class, (c) discussing ideas from readings/class with faculty outside of class, (d) working harder than you thought you could to meet instructors' expectations, and (e) working on creative projects. The assumption of homogeneity of variance was supported by the Box's M test ($F = 1.04, p = .387$). The result of a Multivariate GLM on these five items indicated that the type of school main effect was present (Wilks' $\Lambda = .930$, $p = .004$, $\eta^2 = .036$) with a small effect size, whereas there was no gender main effect (Wilks' $\Lambda = .983$, $p = .292$, $\eta^2 = .017$) or gender by type of school interaction (Wilks' $\Lambda = .971$, $p = .391$, $\eta^2 = .015$). Although the gender main effect and the gender by type of school interaction were not statistically significant, they reached the level of a small effect size.

Students attending different types of schools showed different frequencies of working with students on schoolwork outside of class ($F = 9.35$, $p < .0001$, $\eta^2 = .049$) and discussing ideas from readings/class with students outside of class ($F = 4.61$, $p = .011$, $\eta^2 = .025$) (see Table 2). LSD Post Hoc analyses indicated that WSA recipients who attended four-year public (3.28) and private (3.18) schools were engaged more frequently than those who attended two-year schools (2.75) in working with students on schoolwork, with the effect sizes (d) of .490 and .403 respectively. Four-year public (3.40) and private (3.43) school students were also more involved than two-year college students (3.01) in discussing ideas from readings/class outside of class, with the effect size (d) of .364 and .376 respectively. There were no main effects or interactions for the other three items.

Table 2. **Frequencies* of Working with Other Students on Schoolwork and Discussing Ideas from Readings/Class with Other Students Among Participants Attending Three Types of Schools**

	Two-Year College n = 173		Four-Year Private n = 44		Four-Year Public n = 149		LSD Post Hoc
	M	SD	M	SD	M	SD	
Work w/ students on schoolwork	2.75	1.11	3.18	.90	3.28	1.05	4-year public > 2-year 4-year private > 2-year
Discuss ideas w/ students	3.01	1.11	3.43	1.15	3.40	1.03	4-year public > 2-year 4-year private > 2-year
* 1 = never; 5 = very often							

Results of GLM indicated that females (16.53 hrs/week) spent more time than males (14.55 hrs/week) on studying ($F = 4.24, p = .040, \eta^2 = .012$). Also, the type of school main effect was significant on study time ($F = 4.85, p = .008, \eta^2 = .026$). The gender by type of school interaction was not present ($F = .49, p = .612, \eta^2 = .003$). Specifically, four-year public school students (17.85 hrs/week) spent more time than two-year college students (14.08/week) studying with the effect size (d) of .331.

Community Engagement
    Using a 1 (never) to 5 (very often) scale, six items were included in the survey to assess participants' frequencies of engaging in community activities, including (a) events sponsored by fraternity/sorority, (b) residence hall activities, (c) activities sponsored by groups reflecting the student's cultural heritage, (d) tutoring sessions for specific courses, (e) community service activities, and (f) religious/spiritual activities. Results of a Multivariate GLM indicated that the gender by type of school interaction was significant on these items (Wilks' $\Lambda = .924$, $p = .005, \eta^2 = .039$). However, because the Box's M test did not support the assumption of homogeneity of variance ($F = 2.24$, $p < .0001$), the Multivariate GLM findings should be interpreted

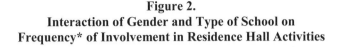

Figure 2.
Interaction of Gender and Type of School on
Frequency* of Involvement in Residence Hall Activities

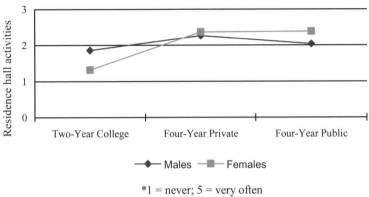

*1 = never; 5 = very often

with caution. Findings of univariate analyses suggested that the gender by type of school interaction was significant on participants' frequencies of involvement in residence hall activities ($F = 6.64$, $p = .001$, $\eta^2 = .035$) and community service activities ($F = 4.50$, $p = .012$, $\eta^2 = .024$) (see Table 3 for more information).

For involvement in residence hall activities (see Figure 2 and Table 3), analyses of univariate simple main effects indicated that two-year male college students (1.86) were more engaged than their female counterparts (1.32) in these activities ($F = 30.46$, $p < .0001$, $d = .709$). However, for those who attended four-year public schools, females (2.36) were more involved than males (2.04) in residence hall activities ($F = 9.05$, $p = .003$, $d = .292$). There was no gender difference for those who attended four-year private schools ($F = 1.38$, $p = .241$, $d = .085$).

Table 3. Frequencies* of Community Engagement					
	Two-Year College n = 174		Four-Year Private n = 45		Four-Year Public n = 150	
Types of Activities	Male n = 44	Female n = 130	Male n = 15	Female n = 30	Male n = 54	Female n = 96
Fraternity/ sorority	1.41/.82	1.28/.74	1.60/1.18	1.20/.55	1.98/1.31	1.78/1.22
Residence hall	1.86/.91	1.32/.71	2.27/1.03	2.37/1.25	2.04/1.08	2.36/1.26
Cultural group	2.16/1.18	1.88/1.19	1.80/1.15	2.20/1.50	2.74/1.49	2.39/1.48
Tutoring sessions	2.73/1.23	2.35/1.23	2.27/1.53	2.17/.99	3.22/1.37	2.57/1.29
Community service	2.59/1.21	2.26/1.20	2.13/.99	3.03/1.33	2.44/1.19	2.66/1.16
Religious/ spiritual	2.41/1.42	2.25/1.52	2.40/1.45	2.43/1.33	2.39/1.34	2.28/1.39

Note: Numbers before the stroke are means, and numbers after the stroke are corresponding standard deviations.
* 1 = never; 5 = very often.

The interaction of gender and type of school showed a slightly different pattern for participants' engagement in community service activities (see Table 3 and Figure 3) than on the other engagement items. Those male students (2.59) who attended two-year colleges were more involved than their female counterparts (2.26) in community service activities ($F = 5.18$, $p = .023$, $d = .274$). This gender difference was reversed for four-year private college students; in other words, females (3.03) participated more frequently than males (2.13) in community service activities ($F = 7.37$, $p = .007$, $d = .734$). The gender difference on frequency of involvement in community service activities was absent for four-year public college students ($F = 1.62, p = .204, d = .188$).

Figure 3.
Interaction of Gender and Type of School on
Frequency* of Involvement in Community Service Activities

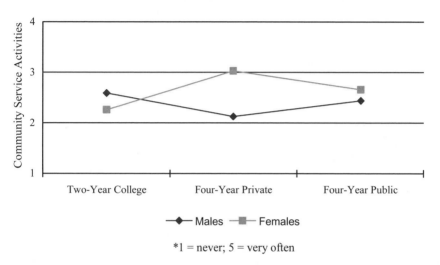

*1 = never; 5 = very often

Leadership/Extracurricular Activities

There was no gender difference (13% for both males and females) on holding campus leadership positions ($\chi^2 = .031$, $p = .861$). However, those who attended four-year private (24%) and public (18%) schools tended to be more likely than those who attended two-year colleges (5%) to hold campus leadership positions ($\chi^2 = 18.41, p < .0001$).

There was a gender main effect ($F = 4.56$, $p = .033$, $\eta^2 = .012$) and a type of school main effect ($F = 12.70, p < .0001$, $\eta^2 = .066$) on hours per week spent on extracurricular activities, whereas its interaction was not significant ($F = 1.84$, $p = .161$, $\eta^2 = .010$). Specifically, males spent more hours per week (3.71) than females (2.61) on extracurricular activities. LSD Post Hoc analyses indicated that those who attended four-year private (3.87 hrs) and public (4.41 hrs) schools spent more time on extracurricular activities than those who attended two-year colleges (1.46 hrs) with effect sizes (*d*) of .588 and .666, respectively. In terms of hours spent relaxing/socializing, the type of school main effect was significant ($F = 3.74$, $p = .025$, $\eta^2 = .021$), whereas both the gender main effect ($F = .43$, $p = .510$, $\eta^2 = .001$) and the gender by type of school interaction ($F = 2.13$, $p = .121$, $\eta^2 = .012$) were absent. LSD Post Hoc analyses suggested that four-year public school students (18.63 hrs/week) spent more time than four-year private school students (13.69 hrs/week) and two-year college students (13.16 hrs/week) relaxing/socializing with effect sizes (*d*) of .318 and .398, respectively.

Educational Aspirations

There was no gender difference on the highest degree expected ($\chi^2 = 2.01$, $p = .919$). However, the relationship between type of school and the highest degree expected was significant ($\chi^2 = 27.03$, $p = .008$). Specifically, there tended to be more four-year private and public school students than two-year college students who expected to receive higher degrees (e.g., master's degree and above). For more information on expected highest degree, see Table 4. On a 1 (very likely) to 4 (very unlikely) scale, the type of school main effect ($F = 5.65$, $p = .0004$, $\eta^2 = .030$) was significant on how likely participants would drop out of school, whereas the gender main effect ($F = 2.91$, $p = .089$, $\eta^2 = .008$) and the gender by type of school interaction ($F = .63$, $p = .533$, $\eta^2 = .003$) were not significant. LSD Post Hoc analyses indicated that students in four-year public schools felt they were less likely to drop out of school than were those in two-year colleges ($d = .348$).

Unfunded Washington State Achievers

There were 42 participants who identified themselves as Washington State Achievers but who were not receiving funding when the data were collected in April 2002. One-third of this group of participants were male, and most were White (n = 13, 31%) and Hispanic (n = 13, 31%), followed by Asian

Table 4. Percentage of Highest Degree Expected								
	Two-Year College			Four-Year Private			Four-Year Public		
	M	F	T	M	F	T	M	F	T
Two-year college	5.7	3.1	3.9	0.0	0.0	0.0	1.7	0.0	0.6
Four-year college	49.1	36.5	39.6	31.3	23.3	26.1	27.1	32.4	30.4
Post-BA certificate	7.5	6.9	7.1	12.5	0.0	4.3	5.1	4.9	5.0
Master's degree	26.4	28.3	27.8	18.8	33.3	28.3	30.5	30.4	30.4
Professional degree	0.0	4.4	3.3	25.0	23.3	23.9	8.5	10.8	9.9
Doctoral degree	5.7	8.2	7.5	12.5	6.7	8.7	13.6	12.7	13.0
Not sure	5.7	12.6	10.8	0.0	13.3	8.7	13.6	8.8	10.6
Total	100	100	100	100	100	100	100	100	100

Note: Numbers in cells represent percentage (%) in the corresponding column.
M = males; F = females; T = total for the corresponding type of school.

Americans/Pacific Islanders (n = 7, 17%), African Americans (n = 6, 14%), and people with multiethnic backgrounds (n = 3, 7%). Although not receiving WSA funding, 55 percent (n = 23) of them were enrolled in higher education, while 45 percent (n = 19) were not. For those who were enrolled in a college/university, the average credits taken as of April 2002 were 23.14, with a standard deviation of 28.39.

Discussion

A number of interesting patterns among WSA recipients emerged in the study. While participants felt that receiving WSA funding helped their decision to go to school, they were less likely to feel that it provided a network of friends or to feel an affinity with other WSA recipients. Thus, it appears that the WSA program funding is meeting its goal of helping students go to a college or university, but recipients may not see the benefits of a network that can help them build a community or negotiate the system of higher education. Having a community and learning to work through the system are important correlates of success in higher education (Sedlacek, 1998a, 1998b, 2004, 2005). The WSA program can provide help for many students in these areas and ways could be explored to help recipients see the benefits of receiving a WSA award for their postmatriculation activities.

The great majority of WSA recipients were aware they were assigned mentors and were having contact with them. This is an important part of the WSA program in that developing a supporting relationship has been shown to be critical for student retention and graduation and was one of the noncognitive variables used in the selection of Achievers (Sedlacek, 2004).

Other findings related to developing a community came from student responses to community engagement activities. While females were more likely than males to engage in community service or residence hall activities in four-year schools, males were more active than females in two-year colleges. This finding should be explored further. While the literature suggests that involvement is correlated with success in higher education, generally, females tend to get more involved than males. Something may be occurring in two-year colleges to make it more difficult for females to become involved due to child-care, family, or other issues. On the other hand, males may be less likely to work if they receive funding. The role that WSA funding plays in this process should be studied further.

Many of the findings describing differences between two-year and four-year schools might be expected, such as four-year school students spending more time on extracurricular activities and relaxing/socializing than two-year school students. This was true even though two-year college students were carrying course loads equal to or greater than those in four-year schools. Also, students in four-year schools expected to achieve higher degrees, were less likely to feel they would drop out of school, and were more likely to be involved in leadership positions than those in two-year schools. Additionally, four-year school students tended to study more and to discuss ideas and do schoolwork with students outside of class than did two-year college students.

While these results may be expected, studies indicate that students with higher degree aspirations, who are involved in leadership, who feel they will stay in school, who study more and discuss and study with their peers are more likely to be successful students, regardless of the type of institution attended (Noonan, Sedlacek, & Veerasamy, 2005; Sedlacek, 1998a, 1998b, 2004, 2005; Sedlacek & Sheu, 2004). Thus, the processes of attending two-year or four-year schools appear different and those differences should continue to be studied.

There were many differences by gender that could have important implications for work with the program mentors. Females were more likely than males to have decided on a major and to spend more time studying, both of which correlate with academic success. Also, females were more likely to be engaged in community service activities, while males were more likely to be engaged in extracurricular activities. All such activities are potentially valuable for academic success but further studies should concentrate on how students are learning or otherwise benefiting developmentally from these activities. Also, males in private four-year schools tended to take fewer college credits on average than males or females attending two-year or four-year public schools. While this pattern may be realistic, depending on the difficulty of the courses taken, males in private schools may take a longer time to complete their degrees if the trend continues.

The people who were identified as Washington State Achievers but were not receiving funding in the program are an interesting group that should be studied more directly. While we know that 55 percent were enrolled in higher education, we do not know why they were not receiving funding through the WSA program. Whether they were funded from other sources or other issues were involved should be investigated further. Also, it would be useful to find out the plans and concerns of those who were not in school. Such studies would likely help the WSA program administrators address any changes that would seem useful.

In conclusion, the Washington State Achievers seem to be doing well overall. While their grades were not studied here,

Achievers were engaged in a number of activities associated with their ultimate success in school. The differences found by gender and type of school attended should continue to be explored and program implications determined from those studies.

References

Cohen, J. (1988). *Statistical power analysis for the behavioral sciences* (2nd ed.). Hillsdale, NJ: L. Earlbaum Associates.

Cortina, J. M., & Nouri, H. (2000). *Effect size for ANOVA designs*. Thousand Oaks, CA: Sage.

Noonan, B. M., Sedlacek, W. E., & Veerasamy, S. (2005). Employing noncognitive variables in admitting and advising community college students. *Community College Journal of Research and Practice, 29,* 1-7.

Sedlacek, W. E. (1998a). Admissions in higher education: Measuring cognitive and noncognitive variables. In D. J. Wilds & R. Wilson, *Minorities in higher education, 1997-98* (pp. 47-71). Sixteenth Annual Status Report. Washington, DC: American Council on Education.

Sedlacek, W. E. (1998b). Multiple choices for standardized tests. *Priorities, 10,* 1-16.

Sedlacek, W. E. (2004). *Beyond the big test: Noncognitive assessment in higher education.* San Francisco: Jossey-Bass.

Sedlacek, W. E. (2005). The case for noncognitive measures. In W. J. Camara & E. W. Kimmel (Eds.), *Choosing students: Higher education admission tools for the 21st century* (pp. 177-193). Mahwah, NJ: L. Erlbaum Associates.

Sedlacek, W. E., & Sheu, H. B. (2004). Academic success of Gates Millennium Scholars. In E. P. St. John (Ed.), *Readings on equal education: Vol. 20. Improving access and college success for diverse students: Studies of the Gates Millennium Scholars Program* (pp. 181-198). New York: AMS Press, Inc.

CHAPTER 7

THE IMPACT OF GUARANTEES OF FINANCIAL AID ON COLLEGE ENROLLMENT: AN EVALUATION OF THE WASHINGTON STATE ACHIEVERS PROGRAM[1]

Edward P. St. John and Shouping Hu

The Washington State Achievers (WSA) program, funded by the Bill & Melinda Gates Foundation and administered by the Washington Education Foundation, is a comprehensive intervention program that involves both school reform and financial assistance. It was the nation's first program to provide financial support both for school reforms aimed at improving academic preparation by students attending high-poverty schools and for guarantees of financial assistance for some students attending those high schools. This study evaluates the impact of guarantees of financial aid on the educational aspirations of high

[1] This chapter was prepared with support from the Bill & Melinda Gates Foundation. The opinions expressed are the authors' and do not necessarily reflect policies or positions of the foundation. An earlier version of this chapter was presented at the annual meeting of the American Educational Research Association, San Diego, CA. We thank Laura Perna for her review of the earlier draft of this chapter and for her recommendations for revisions.

school seniors and college enrollment by students in the 2002 class who had received a promise of financial assistance in the 11th grade. This cohort did not have the benefit of the school reforms initiated as a consequence of the WSA program. Therefore, the study focuses on the impact of the guarantee of financial assistance on educational aspirations and on whether and where students enrolled in colleges.

The WSA program provides a guaranteed grant award amount of $6,400 for enrollment in independent colleges and universities, $5,400 for public four-year colleges and universities, and $3,600 for community colleges. As a last-dollar grant, the award meets need after other scholarships and grants, plus expected family contribution, up to the minimum award amount. The Washington Education Foundation committed to topping off the grants and scholarships the students were awarded from other sources. To be eligible, students had to be enrolled in one of the 15 WSA high schools and meet income requirements. The selection process used noncognitive criteria related to student background and goals.

This chapter examines the direct and indirect effects of the guarantee of a WSA scholarship on aspirations and enrollment. First, we provide background on the conceptual approach of the study. Next, we summarize our research approach, providing information on the survey and the statistical methods used for the study. Then, the study findings are presented, providing a comprehensive set of multivariate analyses of the impact of the program on aspirations and enrollment. Finally, we provide a few conclusions and consider policy implications.

Background

The importance of WSA to the policy debates on college access is best understood if the program is situated in the context of that discourse. Below, we examine the WSA in relation to this policy discourse, introduce the "balanced access model" used as a framework for the study, and, finally, discuss how we used this model in the study.

WSA in the Context of Education Policy on Access
    While there was substantial growth in the rate of college enrollment by high school graduates in the last two decades of the twentieth century, the opportunity to enroll in college became more unequal, both for minorities compared to majority students and for low-income students compared to upper- and middle-income students (St. John, 2003b). These new inequalities were especially substantial with respect to enrollment in four-year colleges (Ellwood & Kane, 2000; St. John, 2003b). To some extent, the growth in the rate of enrollment by high school graduates—and especially the fact that enrollment was higher than the National Center for Education Statistics (NCES, 1980, 1990) had projected (St. John, 2003b)—obfuscated the causes of the increased inequality. Many recent policy studies have simply assumed that inequalities have always existed—without testing their assumption or considering the causes for the growth in unequal opportunity to enroll (e.g., Adelman, 1999; Greene & Forster, 2003; NCES, 1997a, 2001; Pennington, 2003). To untangle the reasons why so many analysts failed to consider the growing inequality and to show how research on the WSA program can help answer basic questions about the roots of unequal education opportunity, we need to consider three strands of the education discourse and how they relate to arguments about college access.

Early Arguments about Net Price and College Access
    The net price argument is that low-income students respond to the net price of the attended college (tuition minus grants) and that reductions in net price can improve enrollment rates. Economists have long argued that the amount of financial assistance low-income students receive influences their ability to pay for college (Becker, G. S., 1975; Becker, W. E., 2004; Hansen

& Weisbrod, 1969). Many policy analysts have also attempted to review economic research and to develop standardized measures of price elasticity and/or a price response coefficient (Heller, 1997; Jackson & Weathersby, 1975; Leslie & Brinkman, 1988; McPherson, 1978; National Commission on the Financing of Postsecondary Education [NCFPE], 1973). These standardized measures have provided an empirical basis for the net price argument, making it possible to predict the enrollment effects of funding student aid programs (NCFPE, 1973).

The logic of net price was also used to build rationales for funding student aid programs in the 1960s and 1970s (e.g., Hansen & Weisbrod, 1969; NCFPE, 1973), and equality in access improved until the late 1970s (St. John, 2003a). However, in the 1980s, this rationale broke down when college enrollment rates of high school graduates continued to increase even after the net price of college grew due to steadily increasing tuition charges and reductions in grant aid (St. John, 2003b). The growing financial inequality was less visible because of the growth in overall enrollment rates.

Thus, while economic thinking about net prices was once widely espoused in policy research, the arguments for funding need-based student grant programs ceased to receive serious consideration in the 1980s, especially at the federal level. Federal funding for grant programs—generally available (need-based) plus specifically directed (e.g., social security survivors benefits)—declined by more than 50 percent on a per student basis between 1980 and 1999 (St. John, 2003b). Some states continued to invest in need-based grants, but there was much more growth in state spending on specifically directed grants—particularly merit grants (Heller & Marin, 2002; St. John, Chung, Musoba, Simmons, Wooden, & Mendez, 2004).

The WSA program has features of a need-based grant program, given that students must meet a need threshold to be eligible for funding. However, decisions about whether to offer awards to applicants are based on other criteria, a set of noncognitive indicators. Thus, the older logic from economics simply does not apply to the evaluation of the impact of WSA. Not only would the net-price logic misspecify the problem because this logic overlooks the role of the award criteria but also because it would not fully consider the other reasons why this aid was given in the first place. The WSA program is actually a hybrid program with features related to both need-based and non-need grants. The merit criteria, however, are noncognitive.

Arguments about the Role of Academic Preparation
Another argument that has been made widely about college access is that improvements in high school preparation can increase the number of students who enroll. This logic evolved from early studies conducted by the U.S. Department of Education in response to concerns that reductions in federal student financial aid could be the cause for the downturn in college participation rates for African Americans that became evident in the early 1980s (Wilson, 1986). Those studies (Chaikind, 1987; Pelavin & Kane, 1988) did not consider the direct effects of student aid, but instead focused on correlations between math courses taken in middle school and high school and eventual college enrollment.

This academic preparation rationale was integrated into NCES studies of college access and persistence (Choy, 2002; NCES, 1997a, 1997b, 2001) which examined a sequence of steps—aspirations, academic preparation, taking entrance exams, and applying for college—as a "pipeline" to college. However, these studies ignored the influence of family finances—and the prospect of paying for college—on whether students prepared for college. The critical error, however, was to integrate into the eligibility index (Becker, 2004) both taking entrance exams and applying for college during high school—steps typically taken only by a subset of the population: prepared students who apply in advance to colleges that require advance application. Open admissions colleges and even some moderately selective colleges allow students to apply at or near the time of enrollment (St. John, 2003).

The NCES (1997a) analyses indicated fewer people prepared for college than actually attended (St. John, 2002), but this does not mean all students who were prepared had the opportunity to enroll. Reanalyses clearly demonstrate that when only courses, grades, and test scores are used as criteria, more prepared low-income students do not have the opportunity to enroll in college (Fitzgerald, 2004; Lee, 2004). One of these analyses estimated that four-million qualified low- and middle-income students would be denied the opportunity to enroll in four-year colleges during the first decade of this century (Fitzgerald, 2004).

Because the WSA program provided the guarantee of grant aid, we have the opportunity to examine the impact of this guarantee on whether prepared students actually enrolled. In addition to examining how the guarantee of this award influenced enrollment behavior, it is important to consider whether the guarantee had any impact on preparation. However, it is necessary to use a balanced approach in this task.

In their studies of college access, NCES (1997a, 1997b, 2001) used the model of an academic pipeline that focused on aspirations, preparation (high school courses), taking college entrance exams, applying for college (i.e., filling out applications the prior spring), and enrolling in college. They argued that if students took all of the steps, including application to college (as measured in response to a question asked in the spring of high school), that all "eligible" students attended college. They ignored the influence of family finances (and expectations about student aid) on preparation, the direct effects of financial aid on enrollment, and the fact that more students enrolled in college than applied in advance (Becker, 2004; Heller, 2003; St. John, 2002, 2003b). Using the NCES logic, we would not consider the impact of WSA on preparation during the first year of the program, before the effects of school reform could be measured.

The Balanced Access Model

The balanced access model, developed as a means of addressing these oversights (St. John, 2002, 2003b), brings a focus on the role of finances to the pipeline model used by NCES, as illustrated in Figure 1. The balanced access model carries forward the key components of the preparation process from the NCES logical model—from aspirations to application, enrollment, and persistence. It introduces two ways in which finances can influence the process:

- Concerns about college costs and student aid can influence whether students take the steps to prepare, and
- Student financial aid can influence whether students who prepare (or apply) actually enroll in college.

Initially this logical model was used to reexamine the NCES reports (St. John, 2002, 2003b) to illuminate the ways in which the NCES interpretations of their own reported statistics had overlooked the role of financial aid. Then, a study of Indiana's Twenty-First Century Scholars Program revealed that providing a commitment for aid to low-income students during middle school influenced academic preparation as well as enrollment (St. John, Musoba, Simmons, Chung, Schmit, & Peng, 2004). The analyses of financial access further confirm the logic of the model, indicating that merit aid and high tuition charges discourage preparation, as measured by high school graduation.

The balanced access model provides an appropriate logical basis for assessing the impact of being selected for WSA scholarships in 11th grade on aspirations in 12th grade, as well as for examining the effects of the award on enrollment.[2] The

---

[2] Unfortunately it is not appropriate to examine the impact of WSA on high school courses (e.g., taking AP courses) using this study's survey data. Since the awards were given in the junior year, the recipients had mostly prepared for college prior to receiving the award.

Figure 1. The Balanced Access Model

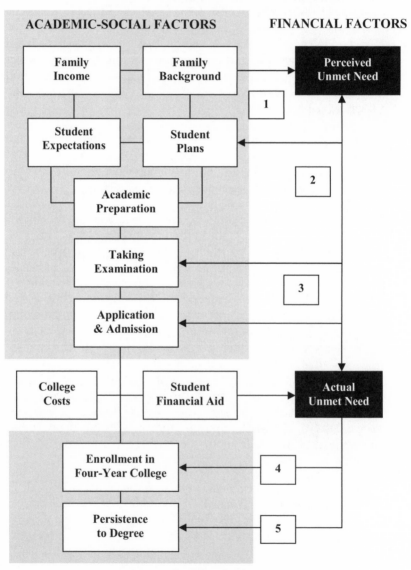

Source: St. John, 2003.

surveys collected by Emeka and Hirschman (Chapter 5) provided a database we could use to examine these linkages. The balanced access model can also be adapted to examine the impact of high school reforms on preparation during high school.

In addition, the balanced access model provides a basis for rethinking the role of social capital. Family support comes down through the pipeline process—from parents to children— influencing aspirations and preparation. In contrast, the support of mentors would provide an external influence on preparation. In this test of the balanced access model, we explore the role of family support as a form of social capital.

Framing this Evaluation Study
    In this study the statistical models were developed based on the logic of the balanced access model. Two sets of analyses were developed: one set focusing on the effects of receiving the guarantee (being selected for WSA) on aspirations to attain a college degree and the other set focusing on the effects on enrollment decisions. The variables in both sets of models are depicted in Table 1 and are discussed briefly below.

Analyses of Preparation
    The analyses consider four specific outcomes related to aspirations and preparation from the senior survey:

- *Aspiring to attain a four-year degree*: Students who aspired to attain a four-year degree were compared to students who did not. Students may aspire to attain a degree even if they plan to delay enrollment for financial or other reasons.
- *Educational expectations*: Students who expected to attain a four-year degree were compared to students who did not. Some students who aspire to attain a degree might not *expect* to attain this goal for financial or other reasons.

- *Gap between aspirations and expectations*: If students have expectations that are lower than their aspirations, there will be a gap, or difference. Students who had an expectations gap were compared to students who did not. If students are ensured of having adequate financial aid, then they may be more likely not to have an expectations gap.
- *Applied for student financial aid*: Students who applied for student financial aid were compared to students who did not. This is a general indicator of whether students completed the steps of preparing for college. However, some high-income students do not apply for financial aid, so some students who do not apply for aid enroll in college.

Fortunately, the Hirschman database included information on the students who attended high schools that had the WSA program along with students from high schools that did not have this funding. The WSA high schools had higher poverty rates than the non-WSA high schools, which suggests that students from the higher poverty schools would have had lower odds of enrolling in college under normal conditions. The first step in our analyses compared three groups of students in WSA high schools to students in non-WSA high schools: students who did not apply for a WSA scholarship, students who applied for but were not awarded WSA, and students who were awarded WSA. The first step in the analyses of preparation compared these groups of students in a simple logistic regression model. However, given that other factors, in addition to student aid, can influence aspirations and preparation, we also needed to analyze the same outcome using an appropriate set of statistical controls.

| Table 1. Variable Description for Analyses of Financial Access ||
Variable	Description
Educational Aspiration	
Aspiring to attain a four-year degree	A dummy variable (Yes=1, No=0)
Educational Expectation	
Expecting to attain a four-year degree	A dummy variable (Yes=1, No=0)
Gap Between Aspiration & Expectation	
Lost aspiration (Expectation below aspiration)	A dummy variable (Yes=1, No=0)
Applying for Financial Aid	
Applying for financial aid	A dummy variable (Yes=1, No=0)
College Enrollment	
Access	
Attending any type of college	A dummy variable (Yes=1, No=0)
(Not attending/Undecided)	Reference group
Institutional Type I	
Attending a four-year college	A dummy variable (Yes=1, No=0)
(All others)	Reference group
Institutional Control I	
Attending a private college	A dummy variable (Yes=1, No=0)
(All others)	Reference group
Institutional Location I	
Attending an in-state college	A dummy variable (Yes=1, No=0)
(All others)	Reference group
Institutional Type II	
Not attending/Undecided	A dummy variable (Yes=1, No=0)
Attending a four-year college	A dummy variable (Yes=1, No=0)
(Attending a two-year college)	Reference group
Institutional Control II	
Not attending/Undecided	A dummy variable (Yes=1, No=0)
Attending a private college	A dummy variable (Yes=1, No=0)
(Attending a public college)	Reference group
WSA	
Nonapplicants in WSA schools	A dummy variable (Yes=1, No=0)
Aid applicants but non-awardees in WSA schools	A dummy variable (Yes=1, No=0)
Aid awardees in WSA schools	A dummy variable (Yes=1, No=0)
(Students in non-WSA schools)	Reference group
Gender	
Males	A dummy variable (Yes=1, No=0)
(Females)	Reference group
Ethnicity	
African American	A dummy variable (Yes=1, No=0)
Hispanic	A dummy variable (Yes=1, No=0)
Asian American	A dummy variable (Yes=1, No=0)
American Indian	A dummy variable (Yes=1, No=0)
(White)	Reference group
Parents' Education	
Father's education	College grad or above (Yes=1, No=0)
Mother's education	College grad or above (Yes=1, No=0)

Table 1. Variable Description for Analyses of Financial Access (cont.)	
Variable	Description
Family Support	
Family support	Sum of family expectation and
Family Structure	
Living with both parents	A dummy variable (Yes=1, No=0)
Home Language	
Other than English	A dummy variable (Yes=1, No=0)
Missing report	A dummy variable (Yes=1, No=0)
(English)	Reference group
Cumulative Grade	
Mostly As	A dummy variable (Yes=1, No=0)
Mostly Cs	A dummy variable (Yes=1, No=0)
Mostly Ds	A dummy variable (Yes=1, No=0)
(Mostly Bs)	Reference group
Educational Aspiration	
High school or less	A dummy variable (Yes=1, No=0)
Less than two-year college	A dummy variable (Yes=1, No=0)
Two-year college	A dummy variable (Yes=1, No=0)
(Four-year or above)	Reference group
AP Course	
Taken or taking	A dummy variable (Yes=1, No=0)

Consistent with the logic of the balanced access model (St. John, 2002, 2003b) and related research on student choice (St. John, Asker, & Hu, 2001), we examined the influence of the following variables on each of the preparation-related outcomes:

- *Gender*: Males were compared to females.
- *Race/ethnicity*: African Americans, Hispanics, Asian Americans, and American Indians were compared to Whites.
- *Parents' education*: Students whose fathers had a college degree were compared to students whose fathers did not have a college degree. In addition, students whose mothers had a college degree were compared to those who did not.

- *Family support*: Sum of responses (rated 1 for low to 4 for high) to questions on (a) family expectations of college enrollment and (b) discussion of college with parents. Responses ranged from 2 for low on both responses to 8 for high on both. This composite variable provided a measure of social capital.
- *Family structure*: Students who lived with both parents were compared to students with other family structures.
- *Home language*: Students who spoke a language other than English at home and students who did not respond to this question were compared to students who spoke English at home.
- *Cumulative GPA (self-reported)*: Students with mostly A grades, mostly C grades, or mostly D grades were compared to students with mostly B grades.
- *Educational aspirations*: Aspirations to attain any of three levels of education lower than a four-year college degree—high school or less, less than two years of college, and completion of two-year college—were compared to aspirations to attain a four-year degree.
- *AP courses*: Students who had taken or planned to take at least one advanced placement (AP) course were compared to students who had not taken or did not plan to take an AP course.

Analyses of Enrollment Behavior

The second set of logistic regression analyses of enrollment behavior also used this two-step approach, considering only the treatment variables in the first step, then adding the other control variables. In addition to the variables set noted above, the analyses also considered variables related to *postsecondary aspirations*: students who expected to complete high school or less, students who expected less than a two-year degree, and students who aspired to attain a two-year degree were compared to students who aspired to attain a four-year degree. The analyses of enrollment behavior considered the following outcomes:

- *Enrollment in any college (access)*: Students attending any type of college were compared to students who did not attend. Selected students who enrolled in two-year colleges received WSA awards.
- *Enrollment in four-year colleges*: Students attending four-year colleges were compared to students who did not (inclusive of students in two-year colleges). WSA encouraged preparation for and enrollment in four-year colleges. Awards were given to selected students who enrolled in four-year colleges.
- *Enrollment in private colleges*: Students who enrolled in private colleges were compared to students who did not (including students who enrolled in public colleges). WSA provided a last-dollar grant sufficient to ensure enrollment in private colleges in the state.
- *Enrollment in in-state colleges*: Students who enrolled in colleges in the state of Washington were compared to students who did not (including students who enrolled out of state). WSA did not provide financial support for WSA students who enrolled out of state.

The first three outcomes represent successively more expensive enrollment options. The maximum award under WSA was higher for four-year colleges than for two-year colleges and higher for independent colleges than for public campuses. However, the program did not fund students if they enrolled out of state. By examining this successive set of outcomes, we were able to provide a comprehensive assessment of the direct effects of WSA on enrollment behavior. Enrollment in an in-state college represents the explicit goal of the program, but is not a precise indicator of college access.

Analyses of Enrollment Destinations

In the analyses of enrollment, we compared a series of dichotomous outcomes. To further verify the relationships between WSA and other independent variables and college enrollments, we completed two analyses that compared multiple outcomes:

- *Type of institution*: Students who did not enroll and students who enrolled in four-year colleges were compared to students who enrolled in two-year colleges.
- *Control of institution*: Students who did not enroll and students who enrolled in private colleges were compared to students who enrolled in public colleges.

These analyses provide further insight into the relationships between receiving a guarantee of aid and college enrollment decisions. In combination, these analyses provide a comprehensive examination of the relationship between WSA and college choices.

Research Approach

To respond to concerns about minority enrollments in the state of Washington after the demise of affirmative action, based on voter preferences, Charles Hirschman (Hirschman, Lee, & Emeka, 2003), a professor of sociology at the University of Washington, surveyed schools in Tacoma, Washington, an area with a relatively high percentage of minority students. The schools were selected without consideration of the WSA program, however, the database developed as a result of this study was ideal for the purpose of evaluating the direct and indirect effects of WSA on financial access.

The Database

Hirschman surveyed seniors in Tacoma area high schools in spring 2002. The response rate was 80 percent (Hirschman, Lee, & Emeka, 2003). The database was used for analyses of students' educational aspirations (Hirschman et al., 2003) and other issues. The urban community had high schools that were part of WSA and high schools that were not part of the program. Members of the research team examined the factors that influenced application for WSA and selection to the program within the WSA schools (Emeka & Hirschman, Chapter 5), finding that family support had an influence on the decision to apply for the program and that student diversity had an influence on selection. As a follow-up to the survey, the University of Washington researchers telephoned respondents to determine whether they were enrolled in college and which colleges they were enrolled in. A total of 1,097 students responded with sufficient data for the analyses in this evaluation study.

The survey instrument asked questions about student background, family support, and educational aspirations. The questions provided sufficient detail for a comprehensive analysis of the impact of WSA using the model specified above. Given the timing of the survey and the general nature of the questions asked about AP courses, it was not possible to assess the impact of the program on whether selected students were influenced to take these courses, since information on the timing of AP courses would have been needed for this purpose. However, there was an unexpected confluence of events that enabled us to use the University of Washington survey for this chapter, as a secondary analysis.

Statistical Methods

The analyses in this chapter present descriptive statistics for the sample, along with logistic regression analyses using the methods noted above. Logistic regression is an appropriate method for statistical analyses of dichotomous outcomes such as those examined above, and this approach is now frequently used in research on college access (Peng, So, Stage, & St. John, 2002).

The logistic regression analyses in this chapter provide the beta coefficients for predictor variables, the standard errors, and odds ratios—a comprehensive set of statistics widely recommended in the research methods literature in higher education (Cabrera, 1994; Peng et al., 2002). Three levels of statistical significance are also reported for independent variables (.001, .01, and .05). In addition, two forms of logistic models were used. Logistic models examining dichotomous outcomes were used from the analyses of preparation and college enrollment. Then, multinomial logistic models, an approach appropriate for comparison of multiple outcomes, were used for the destinations analyses used to further confirm the findings.

In addition, our analyses present three model indicators: -2 log likelihood, chi square, and the Cox & Snell R^2 (a pseudo R^2). The first two measures provide indicators of the quality of the model. Although not widely understood in educational research, they are presented here for informed readers without discussion. Our discussion of model quality focuses instead on the Cox & Snell R^2, a conservative estimate of the amount of variance explained by the model. Since logistic regression analyses do not provide a real R^2, we use this measure as a general indicator of model quality because the R^2 (or pseudo R^2) is generally understood in the educational research community.

Limitations

This study uses generally accepted research procedures, appropriate statistical methods, and sound logical models. However, the study does have a few limitations that merit note.

First, we did not have data on some desirable variables related to family background. For example, we lacked questions about family income, a variable that would be crucial if we were assessing the effects of need-based grant aid (St. John, 1991). However, as noted above, the WSA is a directed award, given to low- and lower-middle-income students based on noncognitive criteria. Further, an effort was made to control for the characteristics of students and the types of schools they attended. In addition, the parents' education variables provided measures directly related to social class. Using these measures, we have workable controls for socioeconomic status (SES), especially given the nature of this program. However, it is important to note that this is not an economic study of student demand. Instead, the study design provides an evaluation of the effects of the WSA program on preparation and enrollment, controlling for selection status, schools, and student characteristics.

Second, this evaluation does not consider the effects of high school reform on academic preparation. Instead, it considers the direct effects of WSA on financial access (i.e., whether students who prepared have the opportunity to enroll) and the indirect effects on enrollment through aspirations, using the logic of the balanced access model. It would be possible to refine the logic of the balanced access model further to consider the effects of the school reform features of the program on academic access.

Third, logistic regression analyses provide measures of the influence of predictor variables, but do not provide causal analyses. Some researchers recommend making a Heckman adjustment (Becker, 2004) to factor in the probability of selection for student aid programs. It may be possible in the future to make this type of selection adjustment, but we did not take this additional step in the current study. Nevertheless, the current study provides a generally accepted method of measuring the impact of financial aid on student enrollment.

Findings

When evaluating the impact of early interventions on financial access to higher education it is important to consider the indirect effects that the commitment of aid can have on preparation and aspirations, along with the direct effects on enrollment behavior. Both the direct and indirect effects of the Washington State Achievers program are examined below, after a discussion of the sample characteristics.

Sample Characteristics
The descriptive statistics for the sample (all schools) and for WSA schools compared to non-WSA schools are presented in Table 2. The numbers of students from each type of school were relatively equal, with 529 from two non-WSA schools and 568 from three WSA schools. The WSA sample included 143 students who had been awarded WSA scholarships, 36 who had applied for but were not awarded WSA, and 389 who had not applied for WSA. The summary breakdown of preparation and aspirations, enrollment behaviors, and independent variables follows.

Aspirations and Preparation
    The percentages of students aspiring to attain four-year degrees were similar (within 3 percentage points) for the two groups: 74 percent in non-WSA schools and 71 percent in WSA schools. The expectation of receiving a four-year degree was 8 percentage points higher in the non-WSA schools (67%) than in the WSA schools (59%). Consequently the gap between expectations and aspirations were substantially greater in WSA schools (13 percentage points) than in non-WSA schools (8 percentage points). The gap for WSA recipients was 8 percentage points, but students in the other groups in WSA schools had substantially larger gaps in expectations compared to students in the comparison schools. In addition, substantially higher percentages of WSA recipients than of students in non-WSA schools both aspired to attain a four-year degree and expected to do so.

Table 2. Descriptive Statistics for Variables Used in Analyses of Financial Access

Variable	All Schools	Non-WSA Schools	All WSA Schools	WSA Schools		
				Non-Applicants of WSA	Applicants but Non-Awardees of WSA	Awardees of WSA
Educational Aspiration						
Aspiring to attain a four-year degree	72.5%	74.3%	70.8%	64.5%	52.8%	92.3%
Educational Expectation						
Expecting to attain a four-year degree	63.1%	67.3%	59.2%	51.9%	36.1%	84.6%
Gap						
Lost aspiration	10.3%	7.9%	12.5%	13.9%	16.7%	7.7%
Applying for Financial Aid						
Applying for financial aid	47.1%	44.1%	50.0%	39.6%	38.9%	81.1%
College Enrollment						
Access						
Attending any type of college	64.1%	69.3%	59.3%	50.1%	50.0%	86.7%
Not attending/Undecided	35.9%	30.8%	40.7%	49.9%	50.0%	13.3%
Institutional Type I						
Attending a four-year college	30.3%	33.6%	27.1%	19.5%	13.9%	51.0%
All others	69.7%	66.4%	72.9%	80.5%	86.1%	49.0%
Institutional Control I						
Attending a private college	13.6%	12.7%	14.4%	12.1%	2.8%	23.8%
All others	86.4%	87.3%	85.6%	87.9%	97.2%	76.2%
Institutional Location I						
Attending an in-state college	53.1%	55.2%	51.1%	39.8%	50.0%	81.8%
All others	46.9%	44.8%	48.9%	60.2%	50.0%	18.2%
Institutional Type II						
Not attending/Undecided	35.9%	30.8%	40.7%	49.9%	50.0%	13.3%
Attending a four-year college	30.3%	33.6%	27.1%	19.5%	13.9%	51.0%
(Attending a two-year college)	33.8%	35.5%	32.2%	30.6%	36.1%	35.7%

Institutional Control II						
Not attending/Undecided	35.9%	30.8%	40.7%	49.9%	50.0%	13.3%
Attending a private college	13.6%	12.7%	14.4%	12.1%	2.8%	23.8%
(Attending a public college)	50.5%	56.5%	44.9%	38.0%	47.2%	62.9%
Gender						
Male	44.1%	44.8%	43.5%	46.0%	58.3%	32.9%
Ethnicity						
African American	17.0%	11.2%	22.4%	21.3%	16.7%	26.6%
Hispanic	9.8%	7.6%	11.8%	12.6%	13.9%	9.1%
Asian American	18.0%	13.8%	21.8%	17.8%	33.3%	29.4%
American Indian	4.6%	4.7%	4.4%	4.1%	8.3%	4.2%
Parents' Education						
Father's education	22.0%	28.7%	15.5%	19.3%	8.3%	7.0%
Mother's education	19.8%	25.5%	14.4%	17.0%	0.0%	11.2%
Family Support						
Family support	6.9	6.7	6.7	6.6	6.4	7.0
Family Structure						
Living with both parents	57.7%	61.4%	54.2%	57.1%	72.2%	42.0%
Home Language						
Other than English	26.2%	18.2%	33.6%	29.6%	55.6%	39.2%
Missing report	2.7%	3.0%	2.5%	3.1%	2.8%	7.0%
Cumulative Grade						
Mostly As	23.3%	26.5%	20.4%	19.3%	2.7%	28.0%
Mostly Cs	25.5%	22.1%	28.7%	31.4%	38.9%	18.9%
Mostly Ds	5.1%	4.9%	5.3%	6.7%	5.6%	1.4%
Educational Aspiration						
High school or less	2.5%	1.7%	3.2%	4.4%	2.8%	0.0%
Less than two-year college	5.6%	3.8%	7.2%	9.8%	8.3%	0.0%
Two-year college	19.5%	20.0%	18.8%	21.3%	36.1%	7.7%
AP Course						
Taken or taking	45.3%	49.3%	41.6%	37.0%	33.3%	55.9%
N	1,097	529	568	389	36	143

In addition, the WSA students applied for aid more frequently than other groups of students. In fact, 81 percent of the WSA recipients applied for student aid, compared to only 44 percent of the students in non-WSA high schools. Since aid applications were part of the commitment these students made when they were selected for WSA, their applications indicate a fulfillment of the preparation process. However, these students had financial need, a criterion for selection to the WSA program, which may not have been the case for students in non-WSA schools.

The majority of students in all groups actually planned to attend college, ranging from 93 percent for WSA recipients to 69 percent of non-WSA applicants in WSA schools. Seventy-nine percent of the students in non-WSA schools planned to attend. Thus, WSA recipients had more ambitious aspirations, expectations, and plans than other groups, including students in the comparison (non-WSA schools).

Enrollment Behavior

The high expectations evident among WSA students were also manifested in their enrollment behavior. Ninety-three percent of the WSA awardees enrolled in college, compared to 69 percent of students from the comparison schools and only 59 percent of the respondents in the WSA schools. Only 50 percent of the other WSA students (non-applicants and applicant nonrecipients) actually enrolled in college.

Further, 82 percent of WSA recipients attended colleges in the state of Washington, compared to 50 percent of the applicant nonrecipients and 40 percent of the non-applicants in WSA schools. Only 5 percent of the WSA recipients attended college out of state, compared to 14 percent of students from comparison (non-WSA) schools, 10 percent of non-applicants in WSA schools, and 0 percent of the WSA applicants. Here is where the real complexity of the program lies: low- and middle-income students who applied for WSA and were not awarded it had more limited opportunity. Thus, larger percentages of students from comparison schools and from the non-applicant group at WSA schools could afford to attend out of state. Students who applied for WSA were largely constrained to attend in-state colleges. However, students in WSA had greater opportunity to enroll in four-year colleges, including private colleges, than their high school peers.

Student Characteristics
Simple comparisons of aspirations and enrollment by students in the various groups do not reveal possible alternative explanations for differences in aspirations and enrollment behavior. Compared to students in non-WSA schools, the WSA recipients had a larger percentage of females, were more diverse ethnically and racially, and had parents with lower education levels. However, they enjoyed about the same level of parental support as the comparison students (7.0 on the 8 point scale for WSA recipients compared to non-WSA schools). The WSA schools were more diverse ethnically and had lower levels of parents' education than the non-WSA schools. A substantially higher percentage of students in WSA schools were also from families that spoke a language other than English at home (34% in WSA schools, compared to 18% of the respondents in non-WSA schools). In short, the WSA schools were in higher poverty areas of the city, consistent with the intent of WSA.

However, WSA students performed as well in high school as the typical student in non-WSA schools. Of the WSA recipients, 28 percent reported having A grades compared to 27 percent of the students in non-WSA schools. Further, 56 percent of the WSA recipients reported they had taken or planned to take AP courses, compared to 49 percent of the students in the non-WSA schools. In contrast, only about one-third of the other students in WSA schools had taken AP courses, and their grades were lower. In other words, WSA students had academic behavior similar to students in more elite high schools in their city, yet they were from low- and middle-income families.

What cannot fully be determined from these data, given the timing of the surveys, is how participation in WSA influenced academic preparation—AP courses and grades in high school. Did WSA select students who were prepared or did selection influence preparation? We can untangle this question a bit in the logistic regression analyses, but it is not possible to address this question fully. Nevertheless, the descriptive statistics on preparation illustrate why academic reform is a crucial issue in high schools that serve low-income urban students.

Analyses of Aspirations and Expectations
    The analyses of aspirations, expectations, and the gap between aspirations and expectations provide information on the indirect effects of WSA on access. In addition, the analysis of the effects of WSA on aid applications provides a specific measure of the impact of WSA on preparation for WSA awardees.
Aspirations. The association between being awardees of WSA in 11th grade and aspiration to attain a four-year degree, as measured in response to a question asked in the 12th grade, is examined in Table 3. When recipients and other students in WSA high schools are compared to students in comparison high schools without other controls (step 1), WSA awardees were substantially more likely to hold this aspiration (4.2 odds ratio), while other WSA applicants and others in these schools were less likely to have this aspiration. When the effects of background variables were also considered, then being selected as WSA awardees still had a positive association with this aspiration (3.4 odds ratio) while other WSA applicants did not differ significantly from students in the comparison schools or other students in WSA schools.

    In addition to WSA, eight of the background variables were significantly associated with aspiring to attain a four-year degree. African Americans were more likely to hold this aspiration, as were students whose fathers had a college education, students with

,

Table 3. Coefficient Estimates from Logistic Regression Model: Aspiring to Attain a Four-Year Degree

	Variable	Coefficients	S.E.	Odds Ratio	Sig.	Coefficients	S.E.	Odds Ratio	Sig.
WSA	Non-applicants in WSA schools	-.4630	.1454	.6294	**	-.3715	.2058	.6897	
	Aid applicants but non-awardees in WSA schools	-.9499	.3484	.3868	**	-.6353	.4000	.5298	
	Aid awardees in WSA schools	1.4237	.0995	4.1523	***	1.2202	.3717	3.3880	***
Gender	Male					-.1216	.1595	.8855	
Ethnicity	African American					.6261	.2282	1.8703	**
	Hispanic					.3714	.2806	1.4498	
	Asian American					.3223	.2716	1.3804	
	American Indian					-.1616	.3513	.8507	
Parents' Education	Father's education					.5275	.2542	1.6946	*
	Mother's education					.4191	.2679	1.5206	
Family Support	Family support					.2847	.0553	1.3294	***
Family Structure	Living with both parents					.1907	.1618	1.2101	
Home Language	Other than English					-.2989	.2262	.7416	
	Missing report					-1.0412	.4131	.3530	*
Cumulative Grade	Mostly As					.6834	.2541	1.9806	**
	Mostly Cs					-.3875	.1774	.6787	*
	Mostly Ds					-.8875	.3157	.4117	**
AP Course	Taken or taking					.9658	.1817	2.6269	***
-2 log likelihood		1236.370				1032.889			
Cox & Snell R²		.049				.210			
Chi square		54.702				258.183			

Note: *** p < 0.001, ** p < 0.01, * p < 0.05.

family support, students with A grades, and students who had taken AP courses. Having no reported information on language at home and having low grades (mostly Cs or mostly Ds) were negatively associated with this aspiration. Given the descriptive statistics (discussed above), it appears that improvements in access to AP courses help explain the decline in the direct effects of WSA between steps 1 and 2 (odds ratio dropping from 4.2 to 3.4).

Expectations. The association between being offered WSA award and having expectations to receive a four-year degree are examined in Table 4. Compared to students in other high schools, WSA recipients were more likely to expect to attain a college degree, while students who applied for but were not awarded WSA and other students in WSA schools were less likely to hold this expectation. These variables were significant in both steps although the strength of the effects (size of coefficients and significance) were more modest in the second step. Both steps in the expectations models (Table 4) explained more variance than the two steps in the aspirations analysis (Table 3), as is evident in a comparison of the R^2s for the two sets of models.

The analyses of the effects of background variables on expectations were similar for the first set of analyses. The variables had similar effects: being African American, having fathers with college degrees, having high family support, living with both parents, having A grades, and taking AP courses had positive associations with expectations, while missing information on expectations and getting low grades had negative associations.

The Gap Between Aspirations and Expectations

The descriptive statistics indicated a gap between aspirations and expectations was lower for WSA recipients than for the other groups in these schools (Table 2). The analyses of the impact of

Table 4. Coefficient Estimates from Logistic Regression Model: Expecting to Attain a Four-Year Degree

	Variable	Coefficients	S.E.	Odds Ratio	Sig.	Coefficients	S.E.	Odds Ratio	Sig.
WSA	Non-applicants in WSA schools	-.6445	.1374	.5249	***	-.4848	.2065	.6158	*
	Aid applicants but non-awardees in WSA schools	-1.2922	.3592	.2747	***	-.8942	.4207	.4089	*
	Aid awardees in WSA schools	.9828	.2496	2.6719	***	.9686	.3081	2.6343	**
Gender	Male					-.1379	.1575	.8712	
Ethnicity	African American					.5665	.2231	1.7620	*
	Hispanic					.4228	.2782	1.5262	
	Asian American					.2627	.2670	1.3004	
	American Indian					-.5053	.3481	.6033	
Parents' Education	Father's education					.7111	.2443	2.0362	**
	Mother's education					.2230	.2486	1.2498	
Family Support	Family support					.3357	.0572	1.3990	***
Family Structure	Living with both parents					.3809	.1596	1.4636	*
Home Language	Other than English					-.4219	.2249	.6558	
	Missing report					-1.0025	.4461	.3670	*
Cumulative Grade	Mostly As					.5079	.2277	1.6618	*
	Mostly Cs					-.7153	.1766	.4890	***
	Mostly Ds					-1.7724	.3934	.1699	***
AP Course	Taken or taking					1.1577	.1709	3.1826	***
-2 log likelihood		1377.284				1060.126			
Cox & Snell R²		.060				.296			
Chi square		67.514				384.672			

Note: *** $p < 0.001$, ** $p < 0.01$, * $p < 0.05$.

WSA on the gap in expectations (Table 5) indicated that non-WSA applicants in the WSA schools were more likely than students in non-WSA schools to have a gap between aspirations and expectations before other variables were considered (step 1), but not in the full model.

Three of the background variables were significantly associated with the gap in expectations. Students who had low grades—mostly Cs or Ds—were more likely than B students to have a gap between aspirations and expectations. In addition, taking AP courses substantially reduced the odds of having an expectations gap. Thus, AP courses played an important role in minimizing the gap in expectations for all students.

Applications for Student Financial Aid

WSA awardees were obligated to apply for financial aid in order to receive their actual WSA scholarship. Since most of these students were also eligible for federal and state financial aid, the WSA program provided a positive incentive to apply for aid. The analyses (Table 6) indicate a substantial positive association between being offered a WSA award and applying for aid, although the effects were more substantial before background variables were considered. In addition, the influence of background variables and aid applications was similar to the prior models. The background factors that influence aspirations and expectations were also associated with aid applications.

Looking across these models, it is apparent that the guarantee of WSA was positively associated with the behaviors related to preparation—e.g., high grades and AP courses—and this association helped explain why WSA had a stronger effect on aspirations and expectations in the first steps of these models. However, the measurable direct effect of WSA on aspirations, expectations, and financial aid applications was substantial. These findings indicate that WSA has a positive association with preparation, but given the timing of data collections, we cannot conclude this linkage is causal.

Table 5. Coefficient Estimates from Logistic Regression Model: Lost Aspiration—Whether Expectations Were Lower Than Aspirations

	Variable	Coefficients	S.E.	Odds Ratio	Sig.	Coefficients	S.E.	Odds Ratio	Sig.
WSA	Non-applicants in WSA schools	.6254	.2176	1.8689	**	.3025	.2797	1.3532	
	Aid applicants but non-awardees in WSA schools	.8411	.4752	2.3189		.4329	.5295	1.5418	
	Aid awardees in WSA schools	-.0343	.3526	.9663		-.1292	.4140	.8788	
Gender	Male					.0169	.2152	1.0170	
Ethnicity	African American					.0593	.2892	1.0610	
	Hispanic					-.2858	.3893	.7514	
	Asian American					-.0606	.3539	.9412	
	American Indian					.6082	.4280	1.8372	
Parents' Education	Father's education					-.6186	.3755	.5387	
	Mother's education					.2436	.3509	1.2758	
Family Support	Family support					-.0792	.0723	.9238	
Family Structure	Living with both parents					-.2778	.2174	.7574	
Home Language	Other than English					.4287	.2860	1.5353	
	Missing report					-.2107	.6430	.8100	
Cumulative Grade	Mostly As					.0111	.3480	1.0112	
	Mostly Cs					.6846	.2410	1.9830	**
	Mostly Ds					.9511	.3718	2.5884	**
AP Course	Taken or taking					-1.0207	.2790	.3603	***
-2 log likelihood		716.760				653.963			
Cox & Snell R^2		.010				.065			
Chi square		10.865				73.662			

Note: *** p < 0.001, ** p < 0.01, * p < 0.05.

Table 6. Coefficient Estimates from Logistic Regression Model: Applying for Financial Aid								
Variable	Coefficients	S.E.	Odds Ratio	Sig.	Coefficients	S.E.	Odds Ratio	Sig.
WSA Nonapplicants in WSA schools	-.1833	.1357	.8325		-.2070	.2027	.8130	
Aid applicants but non-awardees in WSA schools	-.2127	.3529	.8084		-.0996	.4150	.9052	
Aid awardees in WSA schools	1.6970	.2309	5.4577	***	1.2179	.2792	3.3799	***
Gender Male					.0292	.1489	1.0297	
Ethnicity African American					.7673	.2148	2.1540	***
Hispanic					.2620	.2635	1.2995	
Asian American					.1389	.2454	1.1490	
American Indian					-.6582	.3739	.5178	
Parents' Education Father's education					-.4604	.2088	.6310	*
Mother's education					-.1337	.2108	.8748	
Family Support Family support					.3054	.0602	1.3572	***
Family Structure Living with both parents					.0804	.1530	1.0837	
Home Language Other than English					.6005	.2142	1.8230	**
Missing report					-.4070	.4782	.6657	
Cumulative Grade Mostly As					.6571	.1862	1.9293	***
Mostly Cs					-.6473	.1860	.5235	***
Mostly Ds					-.7894	.3955	.4541	*
Educational Aspiration High school or less					-2.0971	1.0466	.1228	*
Less than two-year college					-1.0811	.3979	.3392	**
Two-year college					-.5884	.1926	.5552	**
AP Course Taken or taking					.7672	.1597	2.1537	***
-2 log likelihood	1434.787				1186.816			
Cox & Snell R²	.072				.260			
Chi square	82.358				330.329			

Note: *** p < 0.001, ** p < 0.01, * p < 0.05.

Enrollment Behavior

In addition to the intent of improving academic preparation, the WSA program aid aimed to improve enrollment of awardees. Therefore, it is important also to examine the impact of the guarantee of WSA awards on enrollment behavior.

Enrollment in Any College. The analysis of the impact of WSA on enrollment in any postsecondary institution (two-year or four-year) is presented in Table 7. WSA awards were positively associated with enrollment in both models, while not applying for WSA reduced the odds of enrolling in WSA schools. Students who applied for but were not awarded WSA were modestly less likely to enroll before background variables were considered (step 1) but not when these other factors were taken into account.

Ten background variables were significantly associated with enrollment. Asian Americans were more likely than Whites to enroll. Having A grades and taking AP courses were also positively associated with enrollment. Living in homes where English was not reported as the major language (missing or language other than English), receiving low grades (mostly C grades or mostly D grades) and having expectations to attain less than an four-year degree (high school or less, less than two years of college, and two-year degree) were negatively associated with college enrollment. In addition, the associations between background variables and enrollment were similar to the relationships with aspirations, expectations, and enrollment.

Enrollment in Four-Year Colleges. The effects of WSA on enrollment in four-year colleges were more substantial than for any of the other analyses (Table 8), indicating an intended effect on enrollment behavior. WSA students were more likely than students in comparison schools to enroll in four-year colleges, while other students in WSA schools were less likely to enroll in four-year colleges. These effects were even more substantial after the influences of background variables were considered. The odds ratios for WSA increased from 2.1 in the first model to 2.8 in the second, indicating that WSA students had 2.8 times the odds of students in comparison schools of enrolling in four-year colleges.

The background variables had similar associations with enrollment in four-year colleges (Table 8) as with enrollment in two-year colleges (Table 7). A comparison of the models indicates a greater influence of AP courses and a less substantial influence of aspirations, as indicated by changes in significance and size of odds ratios across these two tables. Thus, it is apparent that WSA had a substantial influence on enrollment in four-year colleges. In addition, given the increased size of the odds ratio for WSA, it appears that WSA also exerted an influence on intervening variables, especially taking or planning to take AP courses.

Enrollment in Private Colleges. The analyses of the association between WSA and enrollment in private colleges (Table 9) also indicate a substantial positive effect of the program. WSA recipients had 2.9 times the odds of enrolling in private colleges over students enrolled in comparison high schools. The effects of WSA were more substantial after the influence of background was considered, indicating a suppressed positive effect of the program most likely attributable to the impact of participation in the program on preparation.

Five variables had a substantial positive association with enrollment in private colleges: having a mother with a college degree, having family support, living with both parents, receiving mostly As, and taking (or planning to take) AP courses. This last variable increased the odds of enrolling in four-year colleges by 2.9 times compared to not having taken these advanced courses.

Enrollment in State Colleges. The WSA program limits the award of aid to students who attend in-state colleges, thus constraining the colleges that students might consider. However, this is a widespread practice. In most states, state grant awards are limited to students who enroll in in-state colleges.[3] The analyses presented in Table 10 showed that WSA had a substantial direct effect on enrollment in state, indicating—before background was considered—that the program increased the odds of enrolling in state by 3.7 times compared to students enrolled in comparison schools. Controlling for background, the effects were still substantial (3.1 odds ratio) but somewhat less than in step 1. The major differences between these analyses and the prior analyses of enrollment behavior were

- Asian Americans were substantially more likely than Whites in both sets of schools to enroll in in-state institutions.
- Having taken (or planning to take) AP courses was not significantly associated with enrollment in in-state colleges and universities.

---

[3] A few state programs, such as the Michigan merit grant programs (St. John & Chung, 2004), allow students to enroll out of state, but most state grant programs limit residents to enrolling in state (Heller, 2004).

	Variable	Coefficients	S.E.	Odds Ratio	Sig.	Coefficients	S.E.	Odds Ratio	Sig.
WSA	Non-applicants in WSA schools	-.8037	.1384	.4477	***	-.6709	.1661	.5113	***
	Aid applicants but non-awardees in WSA schools	-.8089	.3464	.4454	*	-.4648	.3976	.6283	
	Aid awardees in WSA schools	1.0660	.2637	2.9039	***	.8440	.2925	2.3257	**
Gender	Male					.0739	.1574	1.0767	
Ethnicity	African American					-.1811	.2142	.8343	
	Hispanic					.0380	.2712	1.0388	
	Asian American					.7613	.2729	2.1410	**
	American Indian					-.2903	.3522	.7481	
Parents' Education	Father's education					.2762	.2307	1.3181	
	Mother's education					-.1309	.2354	.8773	
Family Support	Family support					.3697	.0579	1.4473	***
Family Structure	Living with both parents					.3009	.1576	1.3510	
Home Language	Other than English					-.3696	.2213	.6910	
	Missing report								
Cumulative Grade	Mostly A					.5455	.2238	1.7254	*
	Mostly C					-.4981	.1789	.6077	**
	Mostly D					-.6808	.3404	.5062	*
Educational Aspiration	High school or less					-1.3657	.6060	.2552	*
	Less than two-year college					-1.1089	.3369	.3299	***
	Two-year college					-.5874	.1844	.5558	**
AP Course	Taken or taking					.6311	.1693	1.8797	***
-2 log likelihood				1357.843				1092.507	
Cox & Snell R²				.068				.268	
Chi square				76.994				342.330	

Table 7. Coefficient Estimates from Logistic Regression Model: Attending Any Type of College

Note: *** p < 0.001, ** p < 0.01, * p < 0.05.

	Variable	Coefficients	S.E.	Odds Ratio	Sig.	Coefficients	S.E.	Odds Ratio	Sig.
WSA	Non-applicants in WSA schools	-.7364	.1575	.4788	***	-.4348	.2065	.6474	*
	Aid applicants but non-awardees in WSA schools	-1.1449	.4905	.3183	*	.0546	.5971	1.0562	
	Aid awardees in WSA schools	.7210	.1909	2.0564	***	1.0342	.2566	2.8129	***
Gender	Male					-.0762	.1836	.9266	
Ethnicity	African American					.1064	.2653	1.1123	
	Hispanic					.1167	.3281	1.1238	
	Asian American					.1290	.2918	1.1377	
	American Indian					-.3283	.4739	.7202	
Parents' Education	Father's education					.4388	.2386	1.5509	
	Mother's education					.1681	.2420	1.1831	
Family Support	Family support					.3052	.0849	1.3569	***
Family Structure	Living with both parents					.6093	.1902	1.8391	**
Home Language	Other than English					-.6814	.2593	.5059	**
	Missing report					-.5059	.8267	.6030	
Cumulative Grade	Mostly As					.6835	.1962	1.9808	***
	Mostly Cs					-1.4878	.3133	.2259	***
	Mostly Ds					-2.1242	1.0620	.1195	*
Educational Aspiration	High school or less					-.8954	1.1330	.4084	
	Less than two-year college					-6.2600	7.0519	.0019	
	Two-year college					-2.4890	.4764	.0830	***
AP Course	Taken or taking					1.3063	.1889	3.6924	***
-2 log likelihood		1287.178				827.333			
Cox & Snell R²		.051				.376			
Chi square		57.936				517.781			

Table 8. Coefficient Estimates from Logistic Regression Model: Attending a Four-Year College

Note: *** p < 0.001, ** p < 0.01, * p < 0.05.

Table 9. Coefficient Estimates from Logistic Regression Model: Attending a Private College

Group	Variable	Coefficients	S.E.	Odds Ratio	Sig.	Coefficients	S.E.	Odds Ratio	Sig.
WSA	Non-applicants in WSA schools	-.0538	.2032	.9746		.3973	.2329	1.4879	
	Aid applicants but non-awardees in WSA schools	1.0134	1.0134	.2009		-.4860	1.0584	.6151	
	Aid awardees in WSA schools	.2360	.2360	2.1509	**	1.0814	.2848	2.9489	***
Gender	Male					-.1162	.2131	.8903	
Ethnicity	African American					.2518	.3009	1.2864	
	Hispanic					.2356	.3816	1.2657	
	Asian American					.2235	.3344	1.2505	
	American Indian					.4248	.5275	1.5293	
Parents' Education	Father's education					-.0952	.2671	.9092	
	Mother's education					.9576	.2564	2.6054	***
Family Support	Family support					.2077	.1041	1.2308	*
Family Structure	Living with both parents					.4514	.2232	1.5706	*
Home Language	Other than English					-.7134	.3029	.4900	*
	Missing report					.3053	.7897	1.3571	
Cumulative Grade	Mostly As					.7011	.2180	2.0161	**
	Mostly Cs					-.4500	.3526	.6377	
	Mostly Ds					-5.3933	7.4952	.0045	
Educational Aspiration	High school or less					.0902	1.0915	1.0944	
	Less than two-year college					-1.5032	1.0656	.2224	
	Two-year college					-.9960	.4480	.3693	*
AP Course	Taken or taking					1.0738	.2452	2.9266	***
-2 log likelihood		854.762				682.652			
Cox & Snell R²		.028				.158			
Chi square		16.940				189.049			

Note: *** p < 0.001, ** p < 0.01, * p < 0.05.

Table 10. Coefficient Estimates from Logistic Regression Model: Attending an In-State College

	Variable	Coefficients	S.E.	Odds Ratio	Sig.	Coefficients	S.E.	Odds Ratio	Sig.
WSA	Non-applicants in WSA schools	-.6206	.1335	.5376	***	-.5233	.1495	.5925	***
	Aid applicants but non-awardees in WSA schools	-.2087	.3446	.8116		-.1152	.3792	.8912	
	Aid awardees in WSA schools	1.2953	.2338	3.6521	***	1.1269	.2537	3.0862	***
Gender	Male					-.1019	.1398	.9031	
Ethnicity	African American					-.3092	.1998	.7341	
	Hispanic					-.1154	.2453	.8910	
	Asian American					.6362	.2360	1.8894	**
	American Indian					-.1529	.3308	.8582	
Parents' Education	Father's education					.0535	.1949	1.0549	
	Mother's education					-.2712	.1984	.7624	
Family Support	Family support					.2831	.0547	1.3272	***
Family Structure	Living with both parents					.1880	.1428	1.2069	
Home Language	Other than English					-.0519	.1973	.9495	
	Missing report					-1.4308	.5197	.2391	**
Cumulative Grade	Mostly As					-.1197	.1768	.8872	
	Mostly Cs					-.3700	.1718	.6907	*
	Mostly Ds					-.6252	.3392	.5352	
Educational Aspiration	High school or less					-1.0519	.5839	.3493	
	Less than two-year college					-.9909	.3429	.3712	**
	Two-year college					-.3062	.1786	.7362	
AP Course	Taken or taking					.0785	.1534	1.0817	
-2 log likelihood		1436.244				1308.487			
Cox & Snell R²		.071				.173			
Chi square		80.426				208.183			

Note: *** p < 0.001, ** p < 0.01, * p < 0.05.

The first of these findings—that Asian Americans were more likely to enroll in state—illustrates the role of finances in constraining choice sets. Asian American students in Washington are generally from lower income families than Whites. The higher probability of enrollment in state for Asian students is largely an artifact of financial constraints—all state grant programs in Washington constrain grant aid to in-state enrollment (St. John, 1999). So, low- and moderate-income students only receive state funding if they enroll in state.

The second finding—that AP courses were not significant— reveals the complexity of academic access in relation to financial access. Clearly, WSA generally expands opportunities to enroll in colleges, as substantiated by the findings on in-state enrollment. However, advanced preparation is more directly related to enrollment in four-year colleges than to enrollment in state.

College Destinations

Two supplemental analyses of college destinations are provided to further illustrate and verify the role of WSA in promoting college choice. These analyses compared multiple outcomes related to type (two-year, four-year) and control (public, private) of college chosen.

Type of Institution. The multinomial analyses of the type of college students chose further verify an association between WSA and enrollment in four-year colleges (Table 11). Controlling for other variables, WSA students were more likely to enroll in four-year than in two-year colleges, but there were not significant differences for enrollment in two-year colleges compared to not enrolling. In contrast, students in WSA schools who did not apply for WSA were significantly more likely not to enroll than to enroll in four-year colleges. In addition, there were positive associations for family support, A grades, and AP courses with enrollment in four-year colleges. These findings further verify the roles of academic preparation and family support in four-year colleges.

Control of Institution. In addition, the multinomial analyses of type of institution further verify that WSA awards influence ability to pay for enrollment in private colleges (Table 12). WSA students were less likely than students in comparison schools not to enroll and were more likely to enroll in private colleges than in public colleges. In contrast, non-WSA applicants in WSA schools were more likely not to enroll and to enroll in other colleges than were students in comparison schools.

In addition, mothers' education, A grades, and AP courses were positively associated with enrollment in private compared to public colleges. In contrast, family support—our social capital measure—was negatively associated with not enrolling compared to enrolling in two-year colleges but was not significant in relation to enrolling in private colleges. This suggests that, controlling for cultural and economic capital as measured by parents' education[4] and other factors, social capital improves the chances of enrollment but does not overcome barriers to enrollment in more expensive private colleges.

Conclusions and Implications

These analyses indicate a substantial positive effect of the WSA program on preparation for college—as measured by effects on aspirations, expectations, and applications for financial aid—as well as on enrollment behavior. In addition, the impact of WSA on enrollment in four-year colleges was even more substantial after the effects of background variables like high school courses and aspirations were considered. In combination, these findings

---

[4] Given the strong association between parents' education and family income (Becker, 2004; Heller, 2004), parents' education serves as a proxy for income when income is not included in models of this type.

Table 11. Coefficient Estimates from Multinomial Logistic Regression Model: Institutional Type

	Variable	No College v. Two-Year College				Four-Year v. Two-Year College			
		Coefficients	S.E.	Odds Ratio	Sig.	Coefficients	S.E.	Odds Ratio	Sig.
WSA	Nonapplicants in WSA schools	.616	.175	1.851	***	-.203	.219	.816	
	Aid applicants but non-awardees in WSA schools	.480	.412	1.617		.228	.624	1.256	
	Aid awardees in WSA schools	-.602	.311	.548		.852	.268	2.344	***
Gender	Male	-.009	.164	.916		-.105	.192	.900	
Ethnicity	African American	.219	.229	1.245		.196	.283	1.216	
	Hispanic	-.004	.284	.963		.010	.345	1.105	
	Asian American	-.802	.280	.449	**	-.102	.301	.903	
	American Indian	.137	.365	1.146		-.286	.497	.751	
Parents' Education	Father's education	-.101	.249	.904		.401	.254	1.494	
	Mother's education	.232	.256	1.260		.245	.259	1.278	
Family Support	Family support	-.315	.060	.730	***	.179	.090	1.196	*
Family Structure	Living with both parents	-.136	.165	.873		.565	.199	1.759	**
Home Language	Other than English	.246	.229	1.279		-.588	.271	.556	*
	Missing report	1.431	.526	4.183	**	-.334	.925	1.396	
Cumulative Grade	Mostly As	-.244	.248	.783		.607	.210	1.834	**
	Mostly Cs	.249	.183	1.283		-1.390	.323	.249	***
	Mostly Ds	.446	.340	1.562		-1.917	1.080	.147	
Educational Aspiration	High school or less	1.362	.656	3.905	*	.001	1.270	1.009	
	Less than two-year college	.783	.333	2.188	*			Empty cell [1]	
	Two-year college	.246	.185	1.278		-2.389	.483	.010	***
AP Course	Taken or taking	-.200	.181	.819		1.233	.200	3.431	***
-2 log likelihood						1588.800			
Cox & Snell R²						.450			
Chi square						656.408			

Note: *** p < 0.001, ** p < 0.01, * p < 0.05. [1] "Empty cell" indicates no students with "less than two-year college" aspiration in 4-year college.

Table 12. Coefficient Estimates from Multinomial Logistic Regression Model: Institutional Control

	Variable	No College v. Public College				Private v. Public College			
		Coefficients	S.E.	Odds Ratio	Sig.	Coefficients	S.E.	Odds Ratio	Sig.
WSA	Nonapplicants in WSA schools	.760	.170	2.138	***	.601	.238	1.824	*
	Aid applicants but non-awardees in WSA schools	.480	.399	1.616		-.365	1.067	.694	
	Aid awardees in WSA schools	-.704	.297	.495	*	.936	.287	2.551	***
Gender	Male	-.010	.160	.908		-.145	.217	.865	
Ethnicity	African American	.214	.220	1.238		.315	.309	1.370	
	Hispanic	-.002	.276	.980		.224	.389	1.251	
	Asian American	-.758	.275	.469	**	.010	.337	1.094	
	American Indian	.329	.362	1.389		.508	.544	1.661	
Parents' Education	Father's education	-.286	.235	.751		-.158	.272	.854	
	Mother's education	.328	.244	1.389		1.029	.263	2.797	***
Family Support	Family support	-.358	.059	.699	***	.010	.107	1.100	
Family Structure	Living with both parents	-.242	.160	.785		.391	.227	1.478	
Home Language	Other than English	.299	.224	1.348		-.639	.308	.528	*
	Missing report	1.683	.531	5.382	**	1.277	.896	3.584	
Cumulative Grade	Mostly As	-.401	.230	.670		.638	.222	1.893	**
	Mostly Cs	.475	.182	1.609	**	-.258	.360	.773	
	Mostly Ds	.557	.339	1.745				Empty cell[1]	
Educational Aspiration	High school or less	1.536	.666	4.648	*	1.217	1.240	3.378	
	Less than two-year college	1.055	.343	2.873	**	-.901	1.092	.406	
	Two-year college	.523	.187	1.686	**	-.797	.454	.451	
AP Course	Taken or taking	-.485	.173	.616	**	.934	.248	2.544	***
-2 log likelihood						1526.863			
Cox & Snell R²						.345			
Chi square						463.988			

Note: *** p < 0.001, ** p < 0.01, * p < 0.05. [1]"Empty cell" indicates no students with "mostly D" grades in private college.

indicate that the WSA program had substantial direct and indirect effects on improving educational opportunity. These findings are consistent with other recent studies of the effects of early preparation programs, including Indiana's Twenty-First Century Scholars Program (St. John, Musoba, Simmons, & Chung, 2002; St. John, Musoba, Simmons, Chung, Schmit, & Peng, 2004).

While these initial analyses of WSA did not examine the impact of the school restructuring portion of the program on improvements in academic preparation, it is evident that the financial guarantee provided by the program encouraged students to prepare within the existing curriculum. Thus, the financial guarantee of access provided by comprehensive encouragement programs like WSA and Twenty-First Century Scholars appears to be a critical element of efforts to expand access. It is still to be tested whether the current efforts to improve high school preparation, including the school restructuring component of WSA, actually improve preparation and academic access.

The finding that providing a guarantee of adequate grant aid improves preparation for college enrollment has implications for state policy on higher education finance. This guarantee of support has a substantial and direct effect on enabling students to enroll in in-state institutions, public and private. Low-income students who had the guarantee of future support had higher odds of enrolling in college than their peers at more affluent high schools, even after controlling for the influence of background and high school preparation. In addition, these awards enabled students to enroll in four-year colleges compared to two-year and in private colleges compared to public colleges.

On the other hand, these findings indicate that federal and state grants currently available in the state of Washington did not provide a sufficient financial guarantee of financial access for low-income students. Washington generally ranks about 10th among states in need-based grant aid. Prior research on the adequacy of aid in Washington indicates the efficacy of grant aid in promoting persistence, depending on the level of state funding for grants (St.

John, 1999). This study extends these earlier findings, indicating that one consequence of the unstable pattern of grant funding in the state of Washington is that some high school students fail to prepare for or to enroll in college as a consequence of not having adequate grant aid available. Students who applied for WSA grants but were not awarded these assurances were consistently less likely to enroll in college, at least before the influence of background and preparation were considered. These findings further illustrate how the instability of public funding for grant programs reduces student aspirations and preparation.

Finally, the study findings illustrate that guaranteeing adequate grant aid has a more substantial influence on retaining students in state than does providing the opportunity to take advanced courses in their high schools. Students who had taken advanced courses were more likely to enroll in college as well as to enroll in four-year colleges and private colleges, but they were not more likely to enroll in state. Many middle- and upper-income students who take advanced courses eventually decided to attend college out of state. In sharp contrast, students who were offered the WSA awards in 11th grade were about three times more likely than students in comparison high schools to enroll in state, even after controlling for the effects of background and preparation.

Since advanced courses were associated with enrollment in four-year colleges, these findings do not diminish the importance of state and federal efforts to extend opportunity for advanced high school courses. Yet they do illustrate that ensuring adequate grant aid had a more substantial effect on in-state college enrollment than did having the opportunity to take advanced high school courses. Clearly, both strategies are important in efforts to expand college access in the U.S. However, if states are concerned about retaining educated students in state, then providing a guarantee of adequate grant aid appears to have a better chance of success than would improvements in high school curriculum without such a guarantee.

Finally, this study illustrates the role of social capital through family support of preparation. The family support variable had an influence on preparation as well as on enrollment. In addition, controlling for preparation and other background variables, family support improved the odds of enrolling in two-year colleges while preparation influenced enrollment in four-year colleges and private colleges in our destinations analyses. Thus, there is evidence that family support has indirect effects on enrollment through preparation, as well as a direct influence on enrollment. In addition, financial aid guarantees had a substantial influence on both preparation and enrollment. While social capital increases the chances of enrollment, it does not replace the role of financial aid in college access.

References

Adelman, C. (1999). *Answers in the tool box: Academic intensity, attendance patterns, and bachelor's degree attainment.* Washington, DC: National Center for Education Statistics.

Becker, G. S. (1975). *Human capital: A theoretical and empirical analysis, with special consideration of education* (2nd ed.). New York: National Bureau of Economic Research.

Becker, W. E. (2004). Omitted variables and sample selection in studies of college-going decisions. In E. P. St. John (Ed.), *Readings on equal education: Vol. 19. Public policy and college access: Investigating the federal and state roles in equalizing postsecondary opportunity* (pp. 65-86). New York: AMS Press, Inc.

Cabrera, A. F. (1994). Logistic regression analysis in higher education: An applied perspective. In J. C. Smart (Ed.), *Higher education: Handbook of theory and research,* Vol. 10 (pp. 225-256). New York: Agathon.

Chaikind, S. (1987). *College enrollment by black and white students.* Prepared for the U.S. Department of Education. Washington, DC: D.R.C.

Choy, S. P. (2002). *Access & persistence: Findings from 10 years of longitudinal research on students.* Washington, DC: American Council on Education.

Ellwood, D., & Kane, T. J. (2000). Who is getting a college education? Family background and the growing gaps in enrollment. In S. Danziger & J. Waldfogel (Eds.), *Securing the future: Investing in children from birth to college* (pp. 264-282). New York: Russell Sage Foundation.

Emeka, A., & Hirschman, C. (2003). *Who applies for and who is selected for Washington State Achievers scholarships? A preliminary assessment.* Presented at the University of Washington workshop "The UW Project on Beyond High School in Washington State," August 4, 2003, Seattle, Washington.

Fitzgerald, B. (2004). Federal financial aid and college access. In E. P. St. John (Ed.), *Readings on equal education: Vol. 19. Public policy and college access: Investigating the federal and state roles in equalizing postsecondary opportunity* (pp. 1-28). New York: AMS Press, Inc.

Greene, J. P., & Forster, G. (2002). *Public high school graduation and college readiness rates in the United States.* Education Working Paper, No. 3. New York: Center for Civic Innovation at the Manhattan Institutes.

Hansen, W. L., & Weisbrod, B. A. (1969). *Benefits, costs, and finance of public higher education.* Chicago: Markham Publishing Co.

Heller, D. E. (1997). Student price response in higher education: An update to Leslie and Brinkman. *Journal of Higher Education, 68*(6), 624-659.

Heller, D. E. (2003). *Review of NCES research on financial aid and college participation.* Report prepared for the Advisory Committee on Student Financial Assistance, Washington, DC.

Heller, D. E., & Marin, P. (Eds.) (2002). *Who should we help? The negative social consequences of merit scholarships.* Cambridge, MA: The Civil Rights Project, Harvard University.

Hirschman, C., Lee, J. C., & Emeka, A. S. (2003). *Explaining race and ethnic disparities in educational ambitions.* Presented at the University of Washington workshop "The UW Study of Beyond High School in Washington State," August 4, 2003, Seattle, Washington.

Jackson, G. A., & Weathersby, G. B. (1975). Individual demand for higher education. *Journal of Higher Education, 46*(6), 623-652.

Lee, J. B. (2004). Access revisited: A preliminary reanalysis of NELS. In E. P. St. John (Ed.), *Readings on equal education: Vol. 19. Public policy and college access: Investigating the federal and state roles in equalizing postsecondary opportunity* (pp. 87-96). New York: AMS Press, Inc.

Leslie, L. L., & Brinkman, P. T. (1988). *The economic value of higher education.* New York: Macmillan.

McPherson, M. S. (1978). The demand for higher education. In D. W. Breneman & C. E. Finn, Jr. (Eds.), *Public policy and private higher education* (pp. 143-146). Washington, DC: Brookings Institution.

Mir☐n, L. F., & St. John, E. P. (Eds.). (2003). *Reinterpreting urban school reform: Have urban schools failed, or has the reform movement failed urban schools?* Albany, NY: SUNY Press.

National Center for Education Statistics. (1980). *Projections of education statistics to 1988-89.* By M. M. Frankel & D. E. Gerald. Washington, DC: Author.

National Center for Education Statistics. (1990). *Projections of education statistics to 2001: An update.* NCES 91-683. By D. E. Gerald & W. J. Hussar. Washington, DC: Author.

National Center for Education Statistics. (1997a). *Access to higher postsecondary education for the 1992 high school graduates.* NCES 98-105. By Lutz Berkner & Lisa Chavez. Project Officer: C. Dennis Carroll. Washington, DC: Author.

National Center for Education Statistics. (1997b). *Confronting the odds: Students at risk and the pipeline to higher education.* NCES 98-094. By Laura J. Horn. Project officer: C. Dennis Carroll. Washington, DC: Author.

National Center for Education Statistics. (2001). *Students whose parents did not go to college: Postsecondary access, persistence, and attainment.* By Susan Choy. Washington, DC: Author.

National Commission on the Financing of Postsecondary Education (NCFPE). (1973). *Financing postsecondary education in the United States.* Washington, DC: G.P.O.

Pelavin, S. H., & Kane, M. B. (1988). *Minority participation in higher education.* Prepared for the U.S. Department of Education, Office of Planning, Budget and Evaluation. Washington, DC: Pelavin Associates.

Peng, C. Y. J., So, T. S. H., Stage, F. K., & St. John, E. P. (2002). The use and interpretation of logistic regression in higher education journals: 1988-1999. *Research in Higher Education, 43*(3), 259-293.

Pennington, H. (2003). *The economic imperative for "Doubling the Numbers:" Release of research about the nation's need and will to improve postsecondary attainment.* Presented at "Double the Numbers: Postsecondary Attainment and Underrepresented Youth," October 23, Washington, DC.

St. John, E. P. (1991). What really influences minority student attendance? An analysis of the High School and Beyond sophomore cohort. *Research in Higher Education, 32*(2), 141-158.

St. John, E. P. (1999). Evaluating state grant programs: A case study of Washington's grant program. *Research in Higher Education, 40*(2), 149-170.

St. John, E. P. (2002). *The access challenge: Rethinking the causes of the new inequality.* Policy Issue Report No. 2002-1. Bloomington, IN: Indiana Education Policy Center.

St. John, E. P. (2003). *Refinancing the college dream: Access, equal opportunity, and justice for taxpayers.* Baltimore: Johns Hopkins University Press.

St. John, E. P., Asker, E. H., & Hu, S. (2001). College choice and student persistence behavior: The role of financial policies. In M. B. Paulsen & J. C. Smart (Eds.), *The finance of higher education: Theory, research, policy, and practice.* New York: Agathon.

St. John, E. P., & Chung, C. G. (2004). Merit and equity: Rethinking award criteria in the Michigan scholarship program. In E. P. St. John & M. D. Parsons (Eds.), *Public funding of higher education: Changing contexts and new rationales* (pp. 124-140). Baltimore: Johns Hopkins University Press.

St. John, E. P., Chung, C. G., Musoba, G. D., Simmons, A. D., Wooden, O. S., & Mendez, J. (2004). *Expanding college access: The impact of state finance strategies.* Indianapolis: Lumina Foundation for Education.

St. John, E. P., Musoba, G. D., Simmons, A. B., & Chung, C. G. (2002). *Meeting the access challenge: Indiana's Twenty-First Century Scholars Program.* New Agenda Series, Vol. 4, No. 4. Indianapolis: Lumina Foundation for Education.

St. John, E. P., Musoba, G. D., Simmons, A. B., Chung, C. G., Schmit, J., & Peng, C. J. (2004). Meeting the access challenge: An examination of Indiana's Twenty-First Century Scholars Program. *Research in Higher Education, 45*(8).

Stage, F. K., Carter, D. F., Hossler, D., & St. John, E. P. (Eds.) (2003) *Theoretical perspectives on college students.* ASHE Reader Series. Boston: Pearson.

Wilson, R. (1986). *Overview of the issue: Minority/poverty student enrollment problems.* Paper presented at the third annual NASSG/NCHELP Conference on Student Financial Aid Research, Chicago, IL.

CHAPTER 8

POSTSECONDARY ENCOURAGEMENT AND ACADEMIC SUCCESS: DEGREE ATTAINMENT BY INDIANA'S TWENTY-FIRST CENTURY SCHOLARS[1]

Edward P. St. John, Jacob P. K. Gross, Glenda Droogsma Musoba, and Anna S. Chung

Providing the guarantee of adequate student aid has a substantial, measurable influence on academic preparation in high school and college enrollment, at least as is evident from studies of Indiana's Twenty-First Century Scholars Program (Musoba, 2004; St. John, Musoba, Chung, Simmons, Schmit, & Peng, 2004) and the Washington State Achievers Program (St. John & Hu, Chapter 7). Both are comprehensive encouragement programs that provide academic support to students and encourage school reform, while providing aid guarantees. Relatively little is known about the effect these programs have on academic success in college, including attainment of degrees. The primary concern for foundations and state agencies that fund these programs should be both whether they enable more students to prepare for and enroll in colleges and whether the students who do enroll have the same chances of academic success as other college students.

[1] Lumina Foundation for Education provided financial support for the research reported in this paper. The analyses and interpretations are the authors' and do not reflect policies or positions of the funding agency.

271

This chapter provides the first study to examine the long-term effects of Indiana's Twenty-First Century Scholars Program. Following a description of the program, the research approach—including the database, statistical model and methods, and limitations—is presented. Then, the findings and implications are discussed.

The Program

Indiana's Twenty-First Century Scholars was the nation's first statewide comprehensive postsecondary encouragement and scholarship program (St. John, Musoba, Simmons, & Chung, 2002) and has been used as a model by other states. Middle school students who qualify for the free and reduced-price lunch program (a rough indicator of poverty) are eligible for the Twenty-First Century Scholars Program. Participation in the program requires students to take and keep a pledge in the seventh or eighth grade. The Scholars' pledge is to

- Graduate from an Indiana high school
- Maintain at least a 2.0 GPA
- Apply for admission to an Indiana college
- Apply for financial aid
- Refrain from using illegal drugs and alcohol
- Refrain from committing a crime
- Enroll full time at an Indiana college or university within two years after high school.

In return, the state of Indiana makes a commitment to the students who take this pledge. The state pledges to

- Pay in full the Scholars' tuition and fees at any public college in Indiana, or contribute a like portion of tuition at an independent college
- Provide support services for Scholars, including tutoring, mentoring, college visits, and activities for parents

- Disseminate information about higher education and encourage Scholars to pursue a college preparatory high school curriculum.

The pledge process encourages low-income students to take advantage of opportunities to prepare for college as well as to enroll in college. The additional financial aid costs to the state for students in the program are relatively modest. Indiana's grant programs currently provide high-need students with grants nearly equal the amount of aid they can receive through the Scholars program. The Twenty-First Century Scholars Program supplements the state grants Scholars receive due to their aid eligibility. Additional aid from the Scholars program may be relatively smaller for high-need students (students with large Pell and/or state grants) or relatively larger for low-need students. In short, Twenty-First Century Scholars provides last-dollar support.

One prior study has examined the impact of the Twenty-First Century Scholars Program on persistence within the first year of college by students enrolled in the public system of higher education in Indiana (St. John et al., 2002). Using logistic regression, the study found that Scholars had higher odds of early persistence than students who did not have aid but had similar odds to students who received other forms of student aid. No differences in persistence among low-income students were found. Scholars received more grant aid and less in loans than did other low-income students. This prior study provides a foundation to explore the impact of the Scholars program on degree attainment.

Research Approach

The statistical model used in the prior study was adapted for this study to examine degree attainment over four years—the 1999-2000 through 2002-2003 academic years. The database used here is described below, followed by discussion of the logical model, the statistical methods, and the study limitations.

Data Sources

Six data sources contributed information for the merged database for the 1999 cohort used in the analyses:

1. The Indiana Career and Postsecondary Advancement Center (ICPAC) (now the Learn More Resource Center, www.learnmoreindiana.org) conducts an annual survey of all Indiana ninth graders regarding their career and educational aspirations, collecting data on key predictor variables such as family living situation, current grades, etc. With about an 80 percent response rate, this survey provides a good representation of Indiana students as they enter high school. This data set had 65,975 observations.

2. ICPAC also provided accurate records of which Indiana students had applied for and enrolled in the Twenty-First Century Scholars Program in eighth grade. This data set contained 5,035 records of students who applied for the Scholars Program.

3. The Indiana Commission for Higher Education (ICHE) collects from public college and university records data regarding each student who attends an Indiana public institution. This database, the Student Information System (SIS), includes records of cumulative GPAs, high schools attended, degree plans, other campuses attended, credits earned, campus living situations, family incomes, demographic information, and financial aid information, including receipt of a Twenty-First Century Scholarship. The SIS data set had 275,130 observations, including all undergraduates in the 1999-2000 database.

4. The State Student Assistance Commission of Indiana (SSACI), which administers the state grants, provided access to students' Free Application for Federal Student Aid (FAFSA) records. The records indicated whether the student received a state grant or applied for aid for an out-of-state school. SSACI data contained records for all students from Indiana who applied for financial aid regardless of attendance. The data set had 106,097 observations, including

undergraduates born in 1980-1982 (students who could reasonably be expected to be in ninth grade at the time of the 1995 ICPAC survey).

5.   The Indiana Department of Education's Internet-based school data records provided high school information such as the percentage of students receiving free and reduced-price lunch, the percentage of graduates who earned honors diplomas, and other institutional variables.

6.   The ICHE SIS database for subsequent years was used to generate measures of attainment. The database for 2002-03 was used to provide indicators of whether students were enrolled in the state system in 2002-03 and the type of public college in which they were enrolled or from which they had graduated. In addition, the databases for intervening years were used to provide indicators of degree attainment during 2000-01 and 2001-02.

The SIS and FAFSA records were merged using student identification numbers. Because the ninth-grade surveys did not have identification numbers, a concatenation of the student's birth date, high school code, gender, ethnicity, and home zip code was used to match records. Progressive combinations of this concatenation from most restrictive (i.e., all the variables) to least restrictive were applied. In the first matches, variables from the SIS data were matched. When that was exhausted, a concatenation of first and last name, birth date, and gender was used to match remaining survey records with FAFSA records. A total of 21,615 observations were matched. All observations were retained in the file because students who did not match with the SIS or FAFSA file have no evidence of higher education enrollment and represented the reference group in the multinomial regression modeling. Finally, high school level variables were matched to the observations using the high school code, unique to each Indiana high school. This produced a database of 65,975 cases, of which 63,169 have no missing values and were used in the multinomial regression on college attainment. Of this data set, 25,823 students had attended public two- or four-year colleges in Indiana and were considered in the persistence analysis. Of those, 24,062 cases had no missing values that could not be categorically coded and were included in the regression on persistence.[2] Whenever possible, cases were retained in the model and the categorical coding of variables with missing values kept cases in the model.

Statistical Model and Population Characteristics
Multinomial logistic regression is the recommended statistical procedure for categorical outcome variables such as those in this study: earned degree(s), still enrolled, or withdrew. Multinomial models have not been widely used in research on higher education (Peng, So, Stage, & St. John, 2002), therefore when using the method it is important that appropriate comparisons be made. In this study, each of the attainment options is compared to dropping out, an appropriate specification for analyses of different types of attainment.

The logical model for the analysis assumed that attainment was related to family background, preparation, high school context, type of college, achievement in college, and student aid. The variables and coding are presented in Table 1, along with the descriptive statistics for variables in the model. Three types of variable coding were used: dichotomous, design sets, and continuous.

Two distinct multinomial analyses were conducted to examine the influence of the Scholars program. The first compared Scholars to all students in the 1999 first-year cohort, whereas the second analysis examined only low-income students. Because the Scholars program targets low-income students, it was appropriate to consider the program effects for those students who

---

[2] Cases dropped from the regression because of missing values were those with no high school corporation data from the Indiana Department of Education. Many of these students may have been home schooled. Therefore, no data were available with respect to variables such as percentage minority students or percentage free and reduced-price lunch.

received Scholars aid versus those low-income students who received other forms of aid. Those students whose families earned less than $30,621 and who received financial aid—Twenty-First Century Scholar Program aid or other aid—constituted this sample of 2,391 students. The model and method used in this second analysis were identical to those used for the full group. The reasons for the second analysis were concerns with selecting the appropriate group for comparison to Scholars and accounting for Scholar self-selection into the program. These concerns are outlined more fully in the limitations section.

The following discussion includes significant findings from the results of the full analysis. Descriptive statistics as well as regression results for the first model are provided. Results from analyses of low-income only students are discussed near the conclusion of the chapter, with descriptive statistics and findings from the regression model appended.

Most of the students in the sample either were still enrolled (42%) or had attained a bachelor's degree (18%) or a two-year degree (7%) or both (1%). Less than one-third had dropped out (32%). While this persistence rate may seem high (more than two-thirds of the sample), it is reasonably consistent with the eight-year rate reported in the reanalysis of the National Education Longitudinal Study (St. John & Chung, Chapter 9)

Individual Background. Background variables included gender (males and unknown gender were compared to females), ethnicity (design set with African Americans, other minorities, and students who did not answer the question compared to Whites), parents' education (college compared to fewer years of education), family structure (design set with alternatives compared to two-parent homes), language spoken at home (other languages compared to English/missing), and income (a design set with categories of income for aid applicants compared to no reported income [interpreted as not applicants for aid]). The profile of the Hoosier undergraduate in public college was predominantly White, high income (or not reported), living with both parents, and had one or more parents who completed college. The typical

Scholar would not fit this profile, especially with respect to parents' income, since eligibility was related to being in the free and reduced-price lunch program, an indictor of poverty. The preceding is a more complete set of background variables than is typically used in research on college attainment.

Academic Preparation. High school GPA (design set with B grades as comparison) and educational aspiration (design set compared categories of aspiring to attain a college degree or higher to lower aspirations) served as proxies for academic preparation. The typical Indiana ninth-grade student had B grades and aspired to complete college. Because we did not have individual variables related to high school courses, we also considered high school context variables related to preparation.

High School Context. Variables related to high school context included the percentage of students earning honors diplomas (high percentage compared to other), the locale (design set compared urban fringe, town, and missing to urban and rural), the concentration of low-income students (high percentage free and reduced-price lunch compared to other), and the concentration of minorities in the high school (high percentage compared to other). The typical Hoosier attended a high school with a low percentage of low-income students and minorities (Table 1). However, a relatively higher percentage of students in the Twenty-First Century Scholars Program were enrolled in urban and rural schools with higher percentages of low-income and minority students (St. John, Musoba, Chung, Simmons, Schmidt, & Peng, 2004).

College experience. Students in two-year colleges and in "other" four-year colleges were compared to students in research universities. Grades during the freshman year were coded into a design set with B grades compared to A grades, C grades, below C grades, and missing grades. The typical student attended an "other" four-year college (a branch campus or a state university) and received B grades as a freshman. Students who lived on campus their first year were compared to students in other living situations.

Table 1. Descriptive Statistics for Variables in the Multinomial Regression, Indiana's Public Colleges, 1999-2003			
Variable *(Type)*	**Values** *(Coding)*	**# Cases**	**%**
Gender *(dichotomous)*	Male and unknown	13,511	52.3
	Female	12,341	47.7
Ethnicity *(design set)*	Missing or prefer not to answer	3,691	14.3
	Other minority	1,330	5.1
	African American	1,448	5.6
	White *(comparison)*	19,383	75.0
Parental education level *(design set)*	Parent(s) went to college	16,187	62.6
	No college for parent(s) or unknown parent education *(comparison)*	9,665	37.4
Who the student lived with in ninth grade *(design set)*	Live with one parent *(comparison)*	4,088	15.8
	Do not live with parent	516	2.0
	Live with two parents or unknown living situation	21,248	82.2
Main language spoken in the home *(dichotomous)*	Spanish or other language	207	0.8
	English or unknown *(comparison)*	25,645	99.2
GPA in ninth grade *(design set)*	Missing/did not answer	1,285	5.0
	Mostly As	3,416	13.2
	Mixed Bs and Cs and mostly Cs	6,806	26.3
	Mixed Cs and Ds or lower	1,462	5.7
	Mixed As and Bs and mostly Bs *(comparison)*	12,883	49.8
Percentage graduates in the student's high school who earned an honors diploma *(dichotomous)*	Low percentage honors graduates *(comparison)*	17,571	72.3
	High percentage honors graduates (over 26%)	6,716	27.7
Locale of high school attended *(design set)*	Urban	3,675	14.2
	Rural	4,678	18.1
	Urban fringe, town and unknown *(comparison)*	17,499	67.7
Student's aspirations in ninth grade for education completion *(design set)*	Undecided/other/no response	3,579	13.8
	Aspire to a high school diploma or less	1,069	4.1
	Aspire to less than a two-year degree	871	3.4
	Aspire to a two-year degree	1,611	6.2
	Aspire to a four-year degree or higher *(comparison)*	18,722	72.4

Table 1. Descriptive Statistics for Variables in the Multinomial Regression, Indiana's Public Colleges, 1999-2003 (cont.)

Variable *(Type)*	Values *(Coding)*	# Cases	%
Percentage students in the student's high school who are minorities *(dichotomous)*	Relatively low minority concentration *(comparison)*	19,443	77.7
	Relatively high minority concentration (over 13.7%)	5,593	22.3
Percentage students in the student's school who receive free and reduced-price lunch *(dichotomous)*	Low percentage students *(comparison)*	20,269	80.6
	High percentage students (over 17.7%)	4,883	19.4
Family income quartiles *(design set)*	Low income (below $30,621)	3,544	13.7
	Lower-middle income (between $30,621 and $52,719)	3,716	14.4
	Upper-middle income (between $52,719 and $75,316)	3,774	14.6
	High income (above $75,316)	3,798	14.7
	No reported income (did not apply for financial aid)	11,020	42.6
Dependency status *(dichotomous)*	Self-supporting	423	1.6
	Dependent on parents or indeterminate	25,429	98.4
College cumulative GPA *(design set)*	A	3,057	11.8
	B *(comparison)*	10,896	42.1
	C	4,587	17.7
	Below C	6,562	25.4
	Missing	750	2.9
Living situation while in college *(dichotomous)*	On campus	12,242	47.4
	Live off campus, with parents or elsewhere *(comparison)*	13,610	52.6
Institutional type *(design set)*	Other four-year college	13,041	50.4
	Two-year college	4,019	15.5
	Research university *(comparison)*	8,792	34.0
Aid package, first year *(design set)*	21st Century Scholar with aid	855	3.3
	Other aid recipient	12,038	46.6
	No aid *(comparison)*	12,959	50.1
Attainment outcomes *(multinomial outcomes)*	Nonpersister, no degree *(comparison)*	8,336	32.2
	Persister, no degree	10,855	42.0
	Two-year degree	1,874	7.2
	Both two- and four-year degrees	190	0.7
	Four-year degree	4,597	17.8

Financial Aid. Students who received student aid and Twenty-First Century Scholars were compared to students who did not receive student aid. Self-supporting students were compared to students who were supported by their families. (Note: the percentage of traditional-age enrollees with this characteristic was only 1.6%). A very small percentage of students (3.3%) were in the Scholars program while over four-tenths received other forms of student aid.

Limitations

There are two key selection problems (the appropriate comparison group and endogenous variables) that cannot be fully resolved in research on the Twenty-First Century Scholars Program. First, it was difficult to determine the appropriate comparison group. The Scholars program is voluntary, so not all eligible students take the pledge, and the ninth-grade survey did not include information about whether individual students were in the free and reduced-price lunch program (key eligibility criteria). Therefore, we could not distinguish eligible students who did not enroll from ineligible (higher income) students. Prior research findings that wealthy students, nationally and in Indiana, are generally more likely to persist suggest that this limitation may make our findings regarding the program more tentative.

Simultaneously, there is also potential unobserved heterogeneity in the sample. There is the possibility that there are differences among students eligible for the Scholars program that are associated with enrolling in the program. Hypothetically, Scholar enrollees may be more able, better prepared, or just more driven students. If, in fact, this were true, the program effects may be overestimated. Prior research has examined high school characteristics in an enrollment analysis (St. John, Musoba, Chung, Simmons, Schmidt, & Peng, 2004) as a means of understanding the role of contexts (possible heterogeneity). That study concluded that the Twenty-First Century Scholars program does improve the odds of preparation for low-income students. These context variables were carried into the current study.

In order to address these limitations, two distinct regression analyses were conducted and both are presented for consideration. The findings regarding the Scholars program are subtly different between the analyses.

Findings

The multinomial model is presented in four parts: attainment of four-year degrees, attainment of two-year and four-year degrees, attainment of two-year degrees, and currently enrolled. Each analysis compared the preceding outcomes to dropping out. However, since the set of analyses was part of a single equation, it is also possible to compare across the groups. We examine each discrete analysis then take a look across the analyses.

The tables present four levels of statistical difference (.001, .01, .05, and .10). The first three of these levels are generally considered statistically significant and are discussed as such. The fourth (alpha .10) is not considered significantly different from zero and is referred to in the text as a "moderate" difference. Coefficients, standard error, and odds ratios are presented along with statistical significance for independent variables. A relatively high percentage of total variation in outcomes is explained (Nagelkerke $R^2 = 0.418$ and McFadden $R^2 = 0.160$) by the full equation (see model statistics in Table 2, Part A).

Attainment of Four-Year Degrees
The attainment analysis of four-year degrees indicates that most categories of variables included had statistically significant relationships between the specific variables (such as gender) and the likelihood of degree attainment[3] (Table 2, Part A). The high

---

[3] Multinomial logistic regression, like other regression models, considers a set of predictor variables simultaneously, therefore, separating the distinct influence of each in the context of the others. When interpreting significant regression coefficients, it is understood that they are the

school context variables, which were not statistically significant, were an exception. First, both parents' education and family income were strongly associated with persistence. Students whose parents attended college were more likely to persist than those whose parents did not. In addition, lower-middle-income students were less likely than students who did not have income reported (and did not apply for aid) to attain four-year degrees. Upper-middle- and high-income students had the same odds of persisting as students that did not apply for aid. Further, females were less likely than males to receive four-year degrees.

Second, student background variables related to academics were also found to be statistically significant. Specifically, having high grades in ninth grade was associated with an increased likelihood of attaining a four-year degree. Educational aspirations among ninth graders were also significant. Being undecided about college plans lowered the odds of receiving a four-year degree.

Third, college achievement variables were associated with an increased likelihood of degree attainment. Having high grades as a freshman improved the odds of attaining a bachelor's degree after four years, while low grades decreased the odds. Furthermore, compared to students who enrolled in four-year public research universities, students who started in other four-year institutions were less likely to obtain a four-year degree after four years.

Fourth, receipt of a Twenty-First Century Scholarship was insignificant compared to receiving no aid. Controlling for other variables, students in the Scholars program did not have significantly different odds of attaining four-year degrees than students who did not receive aid.

In summary, parents' education, higher high school and college grades, and student aid were positively associated with bachelor's degree attainment after four years. Being female, coming from a lower-middle-income family, and receiving low grades in college were negatively associated with the receipt of a

---

coefficient or influence of that particular variable, while holding all other variables constant.

bachelor's degree after four years. Because receiving the Twenty-First Century Scholar award was not statistically significant, recipients did not differ significantly in their persistence compared to students who did not receive aid.

Attainment of Both Two- and Four-Year Degrees. Students who attained both two-year and four-year degrees within four years had a different and smaller set of significant variables (Table 2, Part B). Once again, none of the high school context variables was significant.

First, females were more likely than males to attain both degrees. This is a different finding from the previous table, where being female was negatively associated with the four-year degree attainment. This might be explained by the fact that being female results in higher odds of attending a two-year college (St. John, Musoba, Simmons, & Chung, 2002). Students in the lower-middle income category were less likely to have attained both types of degrees. This finding may be explained by presupposing that students who have not applied for aid may be more likely to come from affluent backgrounds. Race/ethnicity, parents' education, and degree aspirations were not statistically significant.

Second, both college grades and the type of college attended during the freshman year were significantly associated with the likelihood of degree attainment. Students with A grades were more likely than students with B grades to attain both degrees, while student with C grades and lower were less likely to attain

Table 2. Part A. Multinomial Regression Analysis of Variables Associated with Completion of Four-Year Degree, Indiana's Public Colleges, 1999-2003				
Variables	Coefficient	Std.	Odds ratio	Sig.
Female compared to male and unknown (zsex3)	-0.190	0.047	0.827	****
Compared to White (zxsethn2)				
Missing or prefer not to answer	-0.022	0.077	0.978	
Other minorities	-0.201	0.111	0.818	*
African American	0.039	0.128	1.040	
Parents went to college compared to no or unknown parent higher education (zxfirst2)	0.191	0.050	1.211	****
Compared to living with two parents or unknown living situation (zxslive2)				
Live with one parent	-0.158	0.069	0.853	**
Do not live with parent	-0.167	0.179	0.846	
Spanish or other language spoken at home compared to English or unknown language spoken at home (zxlangu2)	-0.507	0.303	0.602	*
Compared to mixed As and Bs and mostly Bs in 9th grade (zxgpa2)				
Missing/did not answer	0.431	0.137	1.539	**
Mostly As	0.384	0.067	1.468	****
Mixed Bs and Cs and mostly Cs	-0.227	0.066	0.797	
Mixed Cs and Ds or lower	0.182	0.115	1.200	
Compared to families with no reported income (did not apply for financial aid) (zincome)				
Low income (below $30,621)	-0.170	0.111	0.844	
Lower-middle income ($30,621 – $52,719)	-0.205	0.097	0.814	**
Upper-middle income ($52,719 – $75,316)	0.022	0.088	1.022	
High income (above $75,316)	0.108	0.079	1.114	
Self-supporting students compared to students dependent on parents or indeterminate dependency status (depend2)	-0.384	0.285	0.681	
Compared to suburban/town/unknown (zlocale2)				
Urban school locale	0.019	0.076	1.019	
Rural school locale	0.027	0.061	1.027	
Low (compared to high) percentage students in the student's school who receive free and reduced-price lunch (zlunch)	0.057	0.075	1.059	

Table 2. Part A. Multinomial Regression Analysis of Variables Associated with Completion of Four-Year Degree, Indiana's Public Colleges, 1999-2003 (cont.)

Variables	Coefficient	Std. Err.	Odds ratio	Sig.
Low (compared to high) percentage minority students in high school (zminor)	0.055	0.070	1.057	
Low (compared to high) percentage honors diploma grads in high school (zhonor)	-0.087	0.051	0.917	
Compared to plans for a four-year degree or higher (zedexp2)				
Undecided/other/no response	-0.209	0.085	0.812	**
Aspire to a high school diploma or less	-0.122	0.130	0.885	
Aspire to less than a two-year degree	-0.111	0.140	0.895	
Aspire to a two-year degree	-0.188	0.112	0.829	*
Compared to students with a B cumulative college GPA (zcumgpa)				
A	0.634	0.065	1.886	****
C	-1.175	0.069	0.309	
Below C	-3.748	0.140	0.024	****
Missing††	-20.706	2227	0.000	
Students who lived on campus compared to students who lived off campus, with parents, or elsewhere (zhousing)	0.706	0.054	2.025	****
Compared to students who enrolled in a public research university (zenroll)				
Other four-year college	-0.921	0.056	0.398	****
Two-year college	-4.568	0.265	0.01	
Compared to students who received no financial aid (zaid2)				
21st Century Scholar with aid	0.014	0.163	1.014	
Other aid recipient	0.132	0.072	1.141	*
Dependent variable: enrollment outcome by 2003				
****p<0.001, ***p<0.01, **p<0.05, *p<0.10				
N of cases= 24,062; 1790 cases were excluded from the regression due to missing values.				
-2 Log likelihood= 37,1916.855				
Chi-square= 14.955**				
McFadden= 0.160				
Nagelkerke= 0.350				

††The standard error for the variable "missing grades" was substantial. This is largely an artifact of the practice of not reporting grades for students who dropped before the term was ended and grades were reported. Our aim in these analyses was to retain all cases and note all missing cases. Given this goal, this standard error term could not be avoided.

Variables	Coefficient	Std. Err.	Odds ratio	Sig.
Table 2. Part B. Multinomial Regression Analysis of Variables Associated with Completion of Both Two- and Four-Year Degrees, Indiana's Public Colleges, 1999-2003				
Female compared to male and unknown (zsex2)	0.607	0.17	1.835	****
Compared to White (zxsethn2)				
Missing or prefer not to answer	0.130	0.260	1.138	
Other minorities	-0.295	0.432	0.744	
African American	0.053	0.500	1.055	
Parents went to college compared to no or unknown parent higher education (zxfirst2)	0.212	0.180	1.236	
Compared to living with two parents or unknown living situation (zxslive2)				
Live with one parent	0.157	0.236	1.170	
Do not live with parent	-1.172	1.017	0.310	
Spanish or other language spoken at home compared to English or unknown language spoken at home (zxlangu2)	-0.358	1.029	0.699	
Compared to mixed As and Bs and mostly Bs GPA in the 9th grade (zxgpa2)				
Missing/did not answer	-0.010	0.475	0.990	
Mostly As	0.364	0.221	1.439	*
Mixed Bs and Cs and mostly Cs	-0.185	0.238	0.831	
Mixed Cs and Ds or lower	-0.102	0.392	0.903	
Compared to families with no reported income (did not apply for financial aid) (zincome)				
Low income (below $30,621)	-0.676	0.426	0.509	
Lower-middle income ($30,621 - $52,719)	-1.110	0.407	0.330	**
Upper-middle income ($52,719 - $75,316)	-0.655	0.340	0.519	*
High income (above $75,316)	-0.568	0.300	0.567	*
Self-supporting students compared to students dependent on parents or indeterminate dependency status (depend2)	0.628	0.789	1.873	
Compared to suburban/town/unknown (zlocale2)				
Urban school locale	0.087	0.282	1.091	
Rural school locale	0.386	0.202	1.471	*

Variables	Coefficient	Std. Err.	Odds ratio	Sig.
Table 2. Part B. Multinomial Regression Analysis of Variables Associated with Completion of Both Two- and Four-Year Degrees, Indiana's Public Colleges, 1999-2003 (cont.)				
Low (compared to high) percentage students in the student's school who receive free and reduced-price lunch (zlunch)	0.463	0.303	1.589	
Low (compared to high) percentage minority students in high school (zminor)	-0.171	0.247	0.843	
Low (compared to high) percentage honors diploma grads in high school (zhonor)	0.004	0.183	1.004	
Compared to plans for a four-year degree or higher (zedexp2)				
Undecided/other/no response	0.151	0.279	1.163	
Aspire to a high school diploma or less	0.121	0.439	1.128	
Aspire to less than a two-year degree	0.537	0.406	1.710	
Aspire to a two-year degree	0.097	0.370	1.102	
Compared to students with a B cumulative college GPA (zcumgpa)				
A	1.036	0.184	2.817	****
C	-1.117	0.284	0.327	****
Below C	-3.563	0.590	0.028	****
Missing††	-21.057	0	0.000	
Students who lived on campus compared to students who lived off campus, with parents or elsewhere (zhousing)	0.234	0.194	1.263	
Compared to students who enrolled in a public research university (zenroll)				
Other four-year college	-0.792	0.208	0.453	****
Two-year college	-1.662	0.347	0.19	****
Compared to students who received no financial aid (zaid2)				
21st Century Scholar with aid	0.125	0.662	1.133	
Other aid recipient	-0.009	0.267	0.991	
Comparison group for enrollment outcome is nonpersisters				
****p<0.001, ***p<0.01, **p<0.05, *p<0.10;				
N of cases= 24,062; 1790 cases were excluded from the regression due to missing values.				
-2 Log likelihood= 37,1916.855; Chi-square= 14.955**; McFadden= 0.160; Nagelkerke= 0.350				
††The standard error for the variable "missing grades" was substantial. This is largely an artifact of the practice of not reporting grades for students who dropped before the term was ended and grades were reported. Our aim in these analyses was to retain all cases and note all missing cases. Given this goal, this standard error term could not be avoided.				

both degrees.[4] Interestingly, compared to students in public research universities, students who began at other four-year institutions as well as at two-year colleges were less likely to attain both a two-year and a four-year degree. It should be noted that two of the four-year campuses also had two-year programs. Finally, neither receipt of Scholars aid nor receipt of any other form of aid was found to be statistically significant relative to attainment of both degrees. To summarize, being female, having high grades in college, having a reported income, and being enrolled in an Indiana public research university increased the odds of a student's receipt of multiple (two- and four-year) degrees after four years.

Attaining Two-Year Degrees
    Existing research suggests that the profile of students earning two-year degrees differs from those earning four-year degrees (Table 2, Part C). Hence, it was reasonable to expect that for this analysis we would obtain a different set of the significant variables.

---

[4] The odds ratio for the variable "missing grades" was unusually small (see Table 2, Parts A and B). This is largely an artifact of the practice of not reporting grades for students who dropped before the term was ended and grades were reported. Our aim in these analyses was to retain all cases and note all missing cases. Given this goal, this standard error term could not be avoided.

Table 2. Part C. Multinomial Regression Analysis of Variables Associated with Completion of Two-Year Degree, Indiana's Public Colleges, 1999-2003

Variables	Coefficient	Std. Err.	Odds ratio	Sig.
Female compared to male and unknown (zsex3)	-0.063	0.069	0.939	
Compared to White (zxsethn2)				
Missing or prefer not to answer	-0.148	0.114	0.862	
Other minorities	0.147	0.146	1.159	
African American	-0.194	0.203	0.824	
Parents went to college compared to no or unknown parent higher education (zxfirst2)	-0.030	0.077	0.970	
Compared to living with two parents or unknown living situation (zxslive2)				
Live with one parent	-0.031	0.098	0.970	
Do not live with parent	-0.425	0.285	0.654	
Spanish or other language spoken at home compared to English or unknown language spoken at home (zxlangu2)	0.477	0.315	1.612	
Compared to mixed As and Bs and mostly Bs GPA in the 9th Grade (zxgpa2)				
Missing/did not answer	-0.103	0.194	0.903	
Mostly As	0.038	0.118	1.038	
Mixed Bs and Cs and mostly Cs	-0.489	0.086	0.613	****
Mixed Cs and Ds or lower	-0.998	0.193	0.369	****
Compared to families with no reported income (did not apply for financial aid) (zincome)				
Low income (below $30,621)	-0.606	0.148	0.545	****
Lower-middle income ($30,621 - $52,719)	-0.597	0.134	0.550	****
Upper-middle income ($52,719 - $75,316)	-0.386	0.124	0.680	**
High income (above $75,316)	-0.399	0.127	0.671	**
Self-supporting students compared to students dependent on parents or indeterminate dependency status (depend2)	0.249	0.260	1.283	
Compared to suburban/town/unknown (zlocale2)				
Urban school locale	0.105	0.111	1.111	
Rural school locale	-0.021	0.086	0.979	
Low (compared to high) percentage students in the student's school who receive free and reduced-price lunch (zlunch)	-0.059	0.106	0.942	

Table 2. Part C. Multinomial Regression Analysis of Variables Associated with Completion of Two-Year Degree, Indiana's Public Colleges, 1999-2003 (cont.)				
Variables	Coefficient	Std. Err.	Odds ratio	Sig.
Low (compared to high) percentage minority students in high school (zminor)	0.242	0.111	1.274	**
Low (compared to high) percentage honors diploma grads in high school (zhonor)	0.293	0.083	1.340	****
Compared to plans for a four-year degree or higher (zedexp2)				
Undecided/other/no response	0.012	0.113	1.012	
Aspire to a high school diploma or less	0.046	0.176	1.047	
Aspire to less than a two-year degree	-0.122	0.194	0.885	
Aspire to a two-year degree	0.219	0.123	1.245	*
Compared to students with a B cumulative college GPA (zcumgpa)				
A	-0.067	0.109	0.935	
C	-0.507	0.093	0.602	****
Below C	-1.654	0.098	0.191	****
Missing	-2.342	0.298	0.096	****
Students who lived on campus compared to students who lived off campus, with parents or elsewhere (zhousing)	-0.222	0.083	0.801	**
Compared to students who enrolled in a public research university (zenroll)				
Other four-year college	-0.039	0.096	0.962	
Two-year college	0.244	0.112	1.276	**
Compared to students who received no financial aid (zaid2)				
21st Century Scholar with aid	0.091	0.215	1.096	
Other aid recipient	-0.050	0.103	0.952	
Comparison group for enrollment outcome is nonpersisters				
****p<0.001, ***p<0.01, **p<0.05, *p<0.10				
N of cases= 24,062; 1790 cases were excluded from the regression due to missing values.				
-2 Log likelihood= 37,1916.855				
Chi-square= 14.955**				
McFadden= 0.160				
Nagelkerke= 0.350				

First, relatively few of the individual background variables were associated with attainment of two-year degrees compared to dropping out. Gender, race/ethnicity, parents' education level, living situation at home, and language spoken at home were not found to have a statistically significant impact on two-year degree attainment. The results for the only significant background variable—family income—showed that all four categories of family income were negatively associated with attainment of two-year degrees compared to students whose family incomes were not reported (as a result of not having received or applied for aid). This finding may be explained by presupposing that students who have not applied for aid may be more likely to come from affluent backgrounds.

For the first time in the study, some of the high school characteristics were significant. In particular, coming from a high school with a low percentage of minority students increased a student's odds of attaining a two-year degree. Interestingly, coming from a high school with a low percentage of students with honors diplomas was positively associated with the receipt of a two-year degree. This may be because students coming from high schools with a high percentage of honors diploma holders would be more likely to enroll in programs granting bachelor's degrees. Having low grades in ninth grade and in college was negatively associated with attainment of two-year degrees.

In addition, several of the variables related to high school contexts were associated with attainment of two-year degrees. Students who attended high schools with low percentages of minority students were more likely to attain two-year degrees. Similar results were found for students who attended high schools with low percentages of honors graduates. However, coming from a school with a low percentage of students receiving free and reduced-price lunch was not significantly related to two-year degree attainment, nor was high school locale.

Several of the college experience variables were associated with attainment of two-year degrees. Living on campus, a variable typically associated with attending a four-year college, was negatively associated with attainment of two-year degrees. Starting in a two-year college, in contrast, was positively associated with this outcome. Students with C grades, below C grades, and missing grades had lower odds of attaining two-year degrees than their peers with B-average grades.

The fact that student aid was not statistically significant is noteworthy, especially given that students in two-year colleges in Indiana not only tend to come from poorer families but also are less likely to receive aid (probably due to failure to apply for aid) (St. John, Musoba, & Chung, 2004). In Indiana, students are not eligible for state grants unless they apply well in advance. Two-year college students who apply to colleges and apply for aid late in their senior year of high school would be eligible for federal aid but would be too late to receive state aid. However, the fact that all reported income levels were negatively associated with two-year degree attainment also indicates that two-year colleges could take further steps to encourage students to apply early to qualify for state aid.

To summarize, a student with higher grades in high school and college, with unreported family income, aspiring to a two-year degree, attending a two-year college, and from a high school with low percentages of both minority students and honors diploma students would be more likely to attain a two-year degree.

Still Enrolled

The profile of students who were still enrolled but had not graduated after four years was also distinctive. Each category of variables in the model included at least one specific variable found to be at least modestly associated with the likelihood of persistence (Table 2, Part D).

First, both parent education and income were associated with persistence after four years. Students whose parents went to college were more likely to be still enrolled than to have dropped out. In contrast, students in the two lower income quartiles were less likely to be enrolled than students with no reported family income (and who had not received or applied for aid). Living away from parents was negatively associated with continuing enrollment. Race/ethnicity and other background variables were not significantly related to persistence.

Second, the indicators of individual preparation were also associated with persistence among students who had not received degrees. Students in the ninth grade who reported mostly A averages were more likely to be still enrolled than students who reported having As and Bs or mostly Bs. Persistence without a degree was less likely for students whose reported grades were less than a B average. In addition, students who aspired in the ninth grade to any educational level less than four years of college were less likely to persist than students who aspired to attain a four-year degree or higher.

Third, students from urban high schools were more likely to be still enrolled than students from towns and suburbs, controlling for other variables. A possible reason for this result is that students from urban high schools may be more likely in need of academic remediation when entering college; the additional remedial coursework may delay the receipt of a college degree. Other variables related to school context were not significant.

Fourth, most of the variables related to college experience and achievement were significant. Students whose GPAs were below B were less likely than students with a B average to be still enrolled after four years. Those students with A averages were also less likely than their B-average peers to be still enrolled without a degree. Living on campus as a freshman was positively associated with persistence. Students who enrolled initially in two-year colleges were less likely than students who enrolled initially in research universities to be still enrolled in the fourth year.

Finally, being a Twenty-First Century Scholar was negatively associated with continuing enrollment among students who had not received degrees. The likelihood of persistence for students who received other types of aid compared to students who received no aid was not statistically different from zero. Because low-income students were less likely to persist, there are questions about the adequacy of need-based aid.

Table 2. Part D. Multinomial Regression Analysis of Variables Associated with Persisters Who Have Not Completed a Degree, Indiana's Public Colleges, 1999-2003				
Variables	Coefficient	Std. Err.	Odds ratio	Sig.
Female compared to male and unknown (zsex3)	0.033	0.032	1.033	
Compared to White (zxsethn2)				
Missing or prefer not to answer	0.018	0.05	1.018	
Other minorities	-0.079	0.072	0.924	
African American	-0.025	0.079	0.975	
Parents went to college compared to no or unknown parent higher education (zxfirst2)	0.197	0.035	1.218	****
Compared to living with two parents or unknown living situation (zxslive2)				
Live with one parent	-0.031	0.044	0.969	
Do not live with parent	-0.281	0.113	0.755	**
Spanish or other language spoken at home compared to English or unknown language spoken at home (zxlangu2)	0.070	0.169	1.073	
Compared to mixed As and Bs and mostly Bs GPA in the 9th grade (zxgpa2)				
Missing/did not answer	0.083	0.091	1.086	
Mostly As	0.172	0.056	1.188	**
Mixed Bs and Cs and mostly Cs	-0.269	0.039	0.764	****
Mixed Cs and Ds or lower	-0.339	0.075	0.712	****
Compared to families with no reported income (did not apply for financial aid) (zincome)				
Low income (below $30,621)	-0.202	0.069	0.817	**
Lower-middle income ($30,621 - $52,719)	-0.182	0.062	0.834	**
Upper-middle income ($52,719 - $75,316)	-0.109	0.059	0.897	*
High income (above $75,316)	-0.111	0.057	0.895	*
Self-supporting students compared to students dependent on parents or indeterminate dependency status (depend2)	-0.046	0.132	0.955	
Compared to suburban/town/unknown (zlocale2)				
Urban school locale	0.130	0.051	1.138	**
Rural school locale	-0.065	0.042	0.937	
Low (compared to high) percentage students in the student's school who receive free and reduced-price lunch (zlunch)	0.061	0.049	1.063	

Table 2. Part D. Multinomial Regression Analysis of Variables Associated with Persisters Who Have Not Completed a Degree, Indiana's Public Colleges, 1999-2003 (cont.)				
Variables	Coefficient	Std. Err.	Odds ratio	Sig.
Low (compared to high) percentage minority students in high school (zminor)	-0.079	0.048	0.924	
Low (compared to high) percentage honors diploma grads in high school (zhonor)	0.001	0.037	1.001	
Compared to plans for a four-year degree or higher (zedexp2)				
Undecided/other/no response	-0.170	0.053	0.844	**
Aspire to a high school diploma or less	-0.300	0.083	0.741	****
Aspire to less than a two-year degree	-0.333	0.089	0.716	****
Aspire to a two-year degree	-0.218	0.066	0.804	**
Compared to students with a B cumulative college GPA (zcumgpa)				
A	-0.198	0.060	0.821	**
C	-0.101	0.043	0.904	**
Below C	-1.018	0.039	0.361	****
Missing	-1.689	0.108	0.185	****
Students who lived on campus compared to students who lived off campus, with parents or elsewhere (zhousing)	0.358	0.036	1.43	****
Compared to students who enrolled in a public research university (zenroll)				
Other four-year college	-0.058	0.042	0.944	
Two-year college	-1.137	0.057	0.321	****
Compared to students who received no financial aid (zaid2)				
21st Century Scholar with aid	-0.260	0.099	0.771	**
Other aid recipient	-0.007	0.049	0.993	
Comparison group for enrollment outcome is nonpersisters				
****p<0.001, ***p<0.01, **p<0.05, *p<0.10				
N of cases= 24,062; 1790 cases were excluded from the regression due to missing values.				
-2 Log likelihood= 37,1916.855				
Chi-square= 14.955**				
McFadden= 0.160				
Nagelkerke= 0.350				

Attainment Among Low-Income Students

Questions about the most appropriate comparison group for low-income Scholars led to additional analyses of program effects for only the lowest income students. While the tables at the end of the chapter provide the results for all variables included in the model, only the findings regarding the Twenty-First Century Scholars Program are discussed here.

There were no significant differences between Scholars and other low-income students in attainment of four-year college degrees, attainment for students with both two- and four-year degrees, and ongoing enrollment at the end of four years. However, compared to other low-income students, Scholars were twice as likely to have attained a two-year degree (odds ratio of 2.026). While it was hoped that the Scholar's program would have stronger effects for four-year degree attainment, these findings regarding two-year degrees are important. Considering that many Scholars come from families where the parents did not attend college, two-year degree attainment is important economic uplift. Second, considering that the comparison group is other low-income students, the overall dollar amounts of aid may not be substantially different between the groups.

Conclusions and Implications

The analyses of attainment reveal that family background—both income and parents' education—were associated with attainment and persistence. In addition, preparation in high school and achievement in college were associated with degree attainment and persistence. Differences related to school contexts were not consistently related to persistence yet had a strong influence on two-year degree attainment. In most instances gender and race/ethnicity were not statistically significant, but other socioeconomic variables were significant. Taking research on race and gender into consideration in this context, these variables may be "standing in" for or may be correlated with other socioeconomic factors. Twenty-First Century Scholars did not differ significantly in degree attainment from students who did not receive student aid. There was a modest negative association for being a Scholar and still being enrolled at the end of four years in college. In contrast, receipt of other types of aid was positively associated with attainment of bachelor's degrees as well as both two- and four-year degrees four years after high school. However, virtually all categories of family income among financial aid applicants were less likely than students who did not receive aid to have attained degrees or to be still enrolled.

Secondary analyses on low-income students only compared the effects of Twenty-First Century Scholars aid to other forms of financial aid (see Tables 3 and 3.1, Parts A, B, and C). Such comparison is appropriate, given the stated goals of the program: helping low-income students prepare for and attend college through encouragement and financial support. Significant findings included a greater likelihood of two-year degree attainment among Scholars compared to non-Scholars. These findings suggest that academic encouragement along with financial support can influence degree attainment among low-income students, at least with respect to obtaining a two-year degree.

These analyses examined postsecondary attainment after four years and did not consider other possible definitions of persistence. Alternative analyses of persistence would appropriately include variables related to achievement during the intervening years and would require analysis of year-to-year progress, a step not taken in this study but which merits further investigation.

There is reason to be cautiously optimistic about the long-term success of students who participated in the Twenty-First Century Scholars Program. Everything else held constant, these students were more likely to enroll in college than their peers (St. John, Musoba, Simmons, & Chung, 2002) and did not have significantly different odds of degree attainment than students who did not have financial need. This cautious optimism must be tempered with concern about the possible explanations for the intermittent lower odds of persistence by low-income aid recipients, an issue explored further later in this volume (especially

Chapter 10, which examines persistence by Indiana students in the class of 2000).

Appendix
Attainment Analyses for Low-Income Students

Table 3. Descriptive Statistics for Variables in the Multinomial Regression for Enrollment Outcomes for Low-Income Financial Aid Recipients, Indiana's Public Colleges, 1999-2003			
Variable	**Values**	**# Cases**	**%**
Gender	Male and unknown	1,338	42.2
	Female	1,829	57.8
Ethnicity	Missing or prefer not to answer	535	16.9
	Other minority	201	6.3
	African American	435	13.7
	White	1,996	63.0
Parental education level	Parent(s) went to college	2,461	77.7
	No college for parent(s) or unknown parent education	706	22.3
Who the student lived with in ninth grade	Live with one parent	988	31.2
	Do not live with parent	152	4.8
	Live with two parents or unknown living situation	2,027	64.0
Main language spoken in the home	Spanish or other language	26	0.8
	English or unknown	3,141	99.2
GPA in ninth grade	Missing/did not answer	206	6.5
	Mostly As	263	8.3
	Mixed Bs and Cs and mostly Cs	1,081	34.1
	Mixed Cs and Ds or lower	244	7.7
	Mixed As and Bs and mostly Bs	1,373	43.4
Percentage graduates in the student's high school who earned an honors diploma	Low percentage honors graduates	2,370	79.6
	High percentage honors graduates	609	20.4
Locale of high school attended	Urban	650	20.5
	Rural	617	19.5
	Urban fringe, town and unknown	1,900	60.0

Table 3. Descriptive Statistics for Variables in the Multinomial Regression for Enrollment Outcomes for Low-Income Financial Aid Recipients, Indiana's Public Colleges, 1999-2003 (cont.)			
Variable	Values	# Cases	%
Student's aspirations in ninth grade for education completion	Undecided/other/no response	540	17.1
	Aspire to high school diploma or less	177	5.6
	Aspire to less than two-year degree	148	4.7
	Aspire to two-year degree or higher	271	8.6
	Aspire to four-year degree or higher	2,031	64.1
Percentage students in the student's high school who are minorities	Relatively low minority concentration	2,115	70.7
	Relatively high minority concentration	878	29.3
Percentage students in the student's school who receive free and reduced-price lunch	Low percentage students	2,015	66.5
	High percentage students	1,015	33.5
Dependency status	Self-supporting	355	11.2
	Dependent on parents or indeterminate	2,812	88.8
College cumulative GPA	A	225	7.1
	B	1,113	35.1
	C	557	17.6
	Below C	1,111	35.1
	Missing	161	5.1
Living situation while in college	On campus	1,212	38.3
	Live off campus, with parents or elsewhere	1,955	61.7
Institutional type	Other four-year college	1,631	51.5
	Two-year college	1,114	35.2
	Research university	422	13.3
Aid package	21st Century Scholar with aid	391	12.3
	Other aid recipient	2,776	87.7
Enrollment outcomes	Nonpersister, no degree	1,458	46.0
	Persister, no degree	1,148	36.2
	Two-year degree	257	8.1
	Four-year degree, including those w/ both two- and four-year degrees	304	9.6

Table 3.1. Part A. Multinomial Regression Analysis of Variables Associated with Completion of Four-Year Degree, Including Those with Both Two- and Four-Year Degrees, for Low-Income Financial Aid Recipients, Indiana's Public Colleges, 1999-2003

Variables	Coefficient	Std. Err.	Odds ratio	Sig.
Female compared to male and unknown (zsex3)	-0.175	0.165	0.839	
Compared to White (zxsethn2)				
Missing or prefer not to answer	0.582	0.245	1.789	**
Other minorities	-0.686	0.414	0.504	*
African American	0.330	0.327	1.392	
Parents went to college compared to no or unknown parent higher education (zxfirst2)	-0.005	0.185	0.995	
Compared to living w/ two parents or unknown living situation (zxslive2)				
Live with one parent	0.022	0.181	1.022	
Do not live with parent	-0.147	0.404	0.863	
Spanish or other language spoken at home compared to English or unknown language spoken at home (zxlangu2)	-0.535	1.112	0.586	
Compared to mixed As and Bs and mostly Bs GPA in 9th grade (zxgpa2)				
Missing/did not answer	-0.126	0.433	0.881	
Mostly As	0.546	0.236	1.726	**
Mixed Bs and Cs and mostly Cs	0.020	0.206	1.020	
Mixed Cs and Ds or lower	0.068	0.408	1.070	
Self-supporting students compared to students dependent on parents or indeterminate dependency status (depend2)	-0.163	0.303	0.850	
Compared to suburban/town/unknown (zlocale2)				
Urban school locale	0.420	0.238	1.522	*
Rural school locale	-0.247	0.204	0.781	
Low (compared to high) percentage students in the student's school who receive free and reduced-price lunch (zlunch)	0.219	0.223	1.245	
Low (compared to high) percentage minority students in high school (zminor)	0.540	0.273	1.716	**
Low (compared to high) percentage honors diploma grads in high school (zhonor)	0.202	0.190	1.224	

Table 3.1. Part A. Multinomial Regression Analysis of Variables Associated with Completion of Four-Year Degree, Including Those with Both Two- and Four-Year Degrees, for Low-Income Financial Aid Recipients, Indiana's Public Colleges, 1999-2003 (cont.)

Variables	Coefficient	Std. Err.	Odds ratio	Sig.
Compared to plans for four-year degree or higher (zedexp2)				
Undecided/other/no response	-0.250	0.280	0.779	
Aspire to high school diploma or less	-0.074	0.409	0.929	
Aspire to less than two-year degree	-0.571	0.486	0.565	
Aspire to two-year degree	-0.211	0.395	0.810	
Compared to students w/B cumulative college GPA (zcumgpa)				
A	0.661	0.229	1.937	**
C	-0.829	0.206	0.437	****
Below C	-3.955	0.465	0.019	****
Missing††	-21.866	0	0.000	
Students who lived on campus compared to students who lived off campus, w/parents or elsewhere (zhousing)	0.743	0.172	2.102	****
Compared to students who enrolled in a public research university (zenroll)				
Other four-year college	-0.678	0.192	0.508	****
Two-year college	-4.226	0.538	0.015	****
Compared to students who received financial aid but were not Scholars (zaid4)				
Aid recipients who also got Twenty-First Century Scholarship	-0.012	0.238	0.988	
Dependent variable: enrollment outcome by 2003				
****p<0.001, ***p<0.01, **p<0.05, *p<0.10				
N of cases= 2,931; 236 cases were excluded from the regression due to missing values.				
-2 Log likelihood=4,996.503				
Chi-square=273.823				
McFadden=0.181				
Nagelkerke=0.360				

†† The standard error for the variable "missing grades" was substantial. This is largely an artifact of the practice of not reporting grades for students who dropped before the term was ended and grades were reported. Our aim in these analyses was to retain all cases and note all missing cases. Given this goal, this standard error term could not be avoided.

Table 3.1. Part B. Multinomial Regression Analysis of Variables Associated with Completion of Two-Year Degree for Low-Income, Financial Aid Recipients, Indiana's Public Colleges, 1999-2003

Variables	Coefficient	Std. Err.	Odds ratio	Sig.
Female compared to male and unknown (zsex3)	-0.240	0.217	0.787	
Compared to White (zxsethn2)				
Missing or prefer not to answer	0.524	0.317	1.689	*
Other minorities	0.550	0.349	1.732	
African American	0.045	0.425	1.046	
Parents went to college compared to no or unknown parent higher education (zxfirst2)	-0.560	0.306	0.571	*
Compared to living with two parents or unknown living situation (zxslive2)				
Live with one parent	0.523	0.221	1.688	**
Do not live with parent	-0.128	0.552	0.880	
Spanish or other language spoken at home compared to English or unknown language spoken at home (zxlangu2)	-0.045	1.086	0.956	
Compared to mixed As and Bs and mostly Bs GPA in the 9th grade (zxgpa2)				
Missing/did not answer	-0.751	0.524	0.472	
Mostly As	-0.156	0.465	0.855	
Mixed Bs and Cs and mostly Cs	-0.310	0.243	0.733	
Mixed Cs and Ds or lower	-0.649	0.459	0.522	
Self-supporting students compared to students dependent on parents or indeterminate dependency status (depend2)	0.178	0.302	1.195	
Compared to suburban/town/unknown (zlocale2)				
Urban school locale	0.111	0.317	1.117	
Rural school locale	-0.297	0.268	0.743	
Low (compared to high) percentage students in the student's school who receive free and reduced-price lunch (zlunch)	0.315	0.295	1.370	
Low (compared to high) percentage minority students in high school (zminor)	-0.123	0.347	0.884	

Table 3.1. Part B. Multinomial Regression Analysis of Variables Associated with Completion of Two-Year Degree for Low-Income, Financial Aid Recipients, Indiana's Public Colleges, 1999-2003 (cont.)

Variables	Coefficient	Std. Err.	Odds ratio	Sig.
Low (compared to high) percentage honors diploma grads in high school (zhonor)	0.507	0.285	1.661	*
Compared to plans for a four-year degree or higher (zedexp2)				
Undecided/other/no response	0.312	0.311	1.366	
Aspire to a high school diploma or less	0.262	0.455	1.299	
Aspire to less than a two-year degree	-0.268	0.504	0.765	
Aspire to a two-year degree	0.743	0.315	2.103	**
Compared to students with a B cumulative college GPA (zcumgpa)				
A	0.220	0.326	1.247	
C	-0.908	0.300	0.403	**
Below C	-2.069	0.284	0.126	****
Missing	-2.635	0.739	0.072	****
Students who lived on campus compared to students who lived off campus, with parents or elsewhere (zhousing)	-0.252	0.247	0.777	
Compared to students who enrolled in a public research university (zenroll)				
Other four-year college	0.486	0.503	1.626	
Two-year college	0.949	0.507	2.582	*
Compared to students who received financial aid but were not Scholars (zaid4)				
Aid recipients who also got Twenty-First Century Scholarship	0.706	0.280	2.026	**
Dependent variable: enrollment outcome by 2003				
****p<0.001, ***p<0.01, **p<0.05, *p<0.10				
N of cases= 2,931; 236 cases were excluded from the regression due to missing values.				
-2 Log likelihood=4,996.503				
Chi-square=273.823				
McFadden=0.181				
Nagelkerke=0.360				

Table 3.1. Part C. Multinomial Regression Analysis of Variables Associated with Persisting with No Degree for Low-Income, Financial Aid Recipients, Indiana's Public Colleges, 1999-2003				
Variables	Coefficient	Std. Err.	Odds ratio	Sig.
Female compared to male and unknown (zsex3)	-0.013	0.092	0.987	
Compared to White (zxsethn2)				
Missing or prefer not to answer	0.517	0.142	1.676	****
Other minorities	-0.025	0.186	0.976	
African American	0.266	0.165	1.305	
Parents went to college compared to no or unknown parent higher education (zxfirst2)	0.178	0.109	1.195	
Compared to living w/ two parents or unknown living situation (zxslive2)				
Live with one parent	0.219	0.100	1.245	**
Do not live with parent	-0.249	0.225	0.779	
Spanish or other language spoken at home compared to English or unknown language spoken at home (zxlangu2)	0.080	0.490	1.083	
Compared to mixed As and Bs and mostly Bs GPA in 9th grade (zxgpa2)				
Missing/did not answer	-0.641	0.244	0.527	**
Mostly As	0.155	0.176	1.168	
Mixed Bs and Cs and mostly Cs	-0.161	0.107	0.852	
Mixed Cs and Ds or lower	-0.352	0.197	0.703	*
Self-supporting students compared to students dependent on parents or indeterminate dependency status (depend2)	-0.025	0.147	0.975	
Compared to suburban/town/unknown (zlocale2)				
Urban school locale	0.502	0.130	1.653	****
Rural school locale	-0.037	0.118	0.964	
Low (compared to high) percentage students in the student's school who receive free and reduced-price lunch (zlunch)	0.283	0.127	1.327	**
Low (compared to high) percentage minority students in high school (zminor)	-0.055	0.146	0.947	

Table 3.1. Part C. Multinomial Regression Analysis of Variables Associated with Persisting with No Degree for Low-Income, Financial Aid Recipients, Indiana's Public Colleges, 1999-2003 (cont.)

Variables	Coefficient	Std. Err.	Odds ratio	Sig.
Low (compared to high) percentage honors diploma grads in high school (zhonor)	0.330	0.115	1.391	**
Compared to plans for four-year degree or higher (zedexp2)				
Undecided/other/no response	-0.086	0.146	0.918	
Aspire to high school diploma or less	-0.039	0.212	0.962	
Aspire to less than two-year degree	-0.069	0.214	0.933	
Aspire to a two-year degree	0.138	0.164	1.148	
Compared to students with a B cumulative college GPA (zcumgpa)				
A	-0.300	0.194	0.741	
C	-0.247	0.125	0.781	**
Below C	-1.319	0.109	0.267	****
Missing	-1.270	0.241	0.281	****
Students who lived on campus compared to students who lived off campus, with parents or elsewhere (zhousing)	0.156	0.099	1.168	
Compared to students who enrolled in a public research university (zenroll)				
Other four-year college	-0.265	0.145	0.767	*
Two-year college	-1.344	0.162	0.261	****
Compared to students who received financial aid but were not Scholars (zaid4)				
Aid recipients who also got Twenty-First Century Scholarship	-0.055	0.139	0.946	
Dependent variable: enrollment outcome by 2003				
****p<0.001, ***p<0.01, **p<0.05, *p<0.10				
N of cases= 2,931; 236 cases were excluded from the regression due to missing values.				
-2 Log likelihood=4,996.503				
Chi-square=273.823				
McFadden=0.181				
Nagelkerke=0.360				

References

Musoba, G. D. (2004). Postsecondary encouragement for diverse students: A reexamination of the Twenty-First Century Scholars Program. In E. P. St. John (Ed.), *Readings on equal education: Vol. 19. Public policy and college access: Investigating the federal and state roles in equalizing postsecondary opportunity* (pp. 153-180). New York: AMS Press, Inc.

Peng, C. Y. J., So, T. H., Stage, F. K., & St. John, E. P. (2002). The use and interpretation of logistic regression in higher education journals: 1988-1999. *Research in Higher Education, 43*(3), 259-294.

St. John, E. P., Musoba, G. D., & Chung, C. G. (2004). Academic access: The impact of state education policies. In E. P. St. John (Ed.), *Readings on equal education: Vol. 19. Public policy and college access: Investigating the federal and state roles in equalizing postsecondary opportunity* (pp. 131-151). New York: AMS Press, Inc.

St. John, E. P., Musoba, G. D., Simmons, A. B., & Chung, C. G. (2002). *Meeting the access challenge: Indiana's Twenty-First Century Scholars Program.* New Agenda Series, Vol. 4, No. 4. Indianapolis: Lumina Foundation for Education.

St. John, E. P., Musoba, G. D., & Simmons, A. B., Chung, C. G., Schmit, J., & Peng, C. J. (2004). Meeting the access challenge: An examination of Indiana's Twenty-First Century Scholars Program. *Research in Higher Education, 45*(8), 829-871.

SECTION III

State Policies on Postsecondary Education

CHAPTER 9

POSTSECONDARY ACCESS AND ATTAINMENT: REANALYSIS OF THE NATIONAL EDUCATION LONGITUDINAL STUDY

Edward P. St. John and Choong-Geun Chung

While the National Education Longitudinal Study (NELS) of the high school class of 1992 has been extensively analyzed by the National Center for Education Statistics (NCES) and its contractors, many of these studies made serious statistical errors and failed to consider the effects of student financial aid (Becker, 2004; Heller, 2004), leading to a misunderstanding of the role of family income in educational opportunity in the U.S. (Fitzgerald, 2004; St. John, 2003). Research using NELS is important both because it is the most recent cohort for which there is longitudinal information nationally and because analyses of this database continue to be widely referenced. The U.S. Department of Education analyses of NELS continue to be accepted in the policy literature without critical comment (e.g., Martinez & Doniskeller, 2004) and NCES's statistical analyses of NELS are still being replicated (Kazis, 2004). Therefore it is important that NELS be reanalyzed with a focus on family income and public finance.

While NCES and other offices in the U.S. Department of Education continue to focus on academic preparation as a primary explanation for disparity in access (e.g., Adelman, 2004), there is a clear need to build a better understanding of the role of finances in college access and persistence. This reanalysis of NELS illustrates an alternative approach examining student outcomes that explicitly considers differences across income groups and the influence of public finance strategies. Generally accessible information on public finance is used as treatment variables, illustrating an approach that could have been used by NCES, given their argument that self-reported data should not be used in research on access and persistence. After a background on the research approach, this chapter presents a reanalysis of college enrollment and attainment using NELS.

Background

NCES invested hundreds of millions of dollars in the collection and analysis of NELS. A summary report of the NCES studies prepared for the American Council on Education (Choy, 2002) reached the following summative conclusions:

- A young person's likelihood of attending a four-year college increases with the level of his or her parents' education. This is true even for the most highly qualified high school seniors.
- Taking challenging mathematics courses can mitigate the effects of parents' education on college enrollment. The association between taking a rigorous high school math curriculum and going to college is strong for all students, but especially for those whose parents did not go beyond high school.
- More at-risk students apply to college if their friends plan to go. College outreach programs as well as parent and school support with the application process also have proven worthwhile.
- The price of attending college is still a significant obstacle for students from low- and middle-income families, but financial aid is an equalizer to some degree. Low-income

students enroll at the same rate as middle-income students if they take all the necessary steps toward enrollment (p. 5).

These conclusions substantially misguide policy makers who are interested in understanding the impact of federal student aid programs. Consider the following:

- The first conclusion attributes inequality in opportunity to parents' education, a correlate of family income that is also a major determinant of family income. For decades research in economics and sociology have documented that income is related to enrollment opportunity, but the NCES studies systematically overlooked the role and influence of family income (Becker, 1964; Blau & Duncan, 1967; Paulsen, 2001a, 2001b).
- The second conclusion parrots a long line of research that reports on the correlation between advanced math and college enrollment (Adelman, 1995; Pelavin & Kane, 1988, 1990) but does so with a new twist. Choy argues advanced math overcomes the disadvantage of being born into a low-income family (i.e., low parents' education). Yet recent research with NELS that tested this proposition found that minorities did not have the same opportunities to take advanced math courses as Whites (St. John & associates, in review). Could Choy's statement be intended as an argument that only low-income students need math? At best, it is an odd way to state a well-known correlation.
- The third conclusion carries forward a claim that applying to college during the first half of the senior year is highly related to college enrollment (NCES, 1997). The main problems with the decision to emphasize this variable in selection of students to analyze in college enrollment include (a) more students enroll in college than actually apply during their senior year of high school and (b) many colleges allow students to complete applications when

they enroll. This conclusion also implies that students whose friends are privileged—those who have friends who can afford the cost of applying to colleges during the fall—are more likely to be able to pay for these applications themselves.
- The fourth conclusion recognizes two well-known facts: (a) the price of attending college decreases enrollment opportunity for low-income students and (b) student aid, especially need-based aid, can increase opportunity. These facts are well known whether or not the topic is studied. The NCES studies systematically failed to consider the direct effect of student aid, thus avoiding the question whether federal grant aid was adequate to equalize opportunity for equally prepared students with different levels of financial need.

The underlying problem with the NCES studies was that the researchers had to manipulate the data, making fundamental statistical errors, to reach these misleading conclusions. The reviews of the NCES studies (Becker, 2004; Fitzgerald, 2004; Heller, 2004; Lee, 2004) reveal a consistent pattern of statistical errors and misinterpretations in the data analyses. A summary of these reviews drew the following lessons (St. John, 2004; *italics* in original):

- *Lesson 1: Researchers must recognize the limitations of extant databases and of statistical methods* (p. 182).
- *Lesson 2: Theory and prior research should inform the development of statistical models for research on college access when they use statistical analyses to explain the predictors of college enrollment and persistence* (p. 184).
  - *Lesson 2.1: Social theory and research should inform the selection and interpretation of variables related to family background and encouragement* (p. 184).

○ *Lesson 2.2: Economic theory and research should inform research on the effects of financial aid* (p. 185).
○ *Lesson 2.3: Education theory and research can inform the development of statistical models that assess the role of high school curriculum in promoting college access* (p. 185).
○ *Lesson 2.4: Financial aid must be considered in federal policy research that considers college access* (p. 186).
• *Lesson 3: Policy researchers should use balanced approaches in the development of statistical models and the interpretation of the statistics* (p. 187).

The first lesson presents the most serious challenge facing policy researchers. There are two issues that were given special attention in this study. First, NCES arbitrarily eliminated students from their analyses of access based on their high school preparation, a form of selection bias (Becker, 2004; Heller, 2004). The reanalysis considered all high school students, examining enrollment decisions by high school graduates and dropouts as well as controlling for high school math courses. Interestingly, by setting the selection criteria so tightly, NCES excluded a substantial number of college enrollees from some of their enrollment analyses.

The second statistical problem is omitted variable bias resulting from NCES's exclusion of student aid variables from analyses of enrollment and persistence (Heller, 2004), a measurement issue complicated by discretion or arbitrariness in aid applications and awards (Becker, 2004; St. John, 2004). Some eligible students do not apply for aid and some aid awards are arbitrary, complicating efforts to measure aid effects. Failure to consider the direct effects of student aid, the approach used by NCES (1997, 2001), does not resolve the problem. In this reanalysis we used two-level hierarchical models, entering state-level finance variables as a means of measuring the effects of finances on enrollment. Using state finance variables in a two-level model essentially eliminates the selection problem since state residency is not arbitrary.

The second lesson relates to logical construction of statistical models. NCES overlooked long-standing traditions of research on socioeconomic status in both sociology and economics, as the agency used official reports to build the argument that parents' education rather than income explained variation in attainment (Choy, 2002; NCES, 1997, 2001), ignoring the fact that parents' education has a causal relationship with family income and serves as a proxy for income (Becker, 2004; Heller, 2004; St. John, 2004). This reanalysis considers both parents' education and income variables but uses a more theoretically grounded interpretation, considering income and education as a part of socioeconomic status.

In addition, the reanalysis recognizes the contributions NCES and others in the U.S. Department of Education (Adelman, 1995, 2004) have made by discerning the role of math preparation in enrollment and academic success in college. Earlier economic and social research controlled for the type of curriculum students completed (e.g., Jackson, 1978, 1988; Manski & Wise, 1983; St. John, 1991). This reanalysis incorporates variables for advanced math courses—along with high school graduation—into comprehensive models that consider social, economic, and educational explanations for enrollment behavior.[1]

The analyses of attainment also pose other problems for research that uses longitudinal databases like NELS. Since aid packages can vary over time, most early studies of long-term persistence considered receipt of any type of aid (Terkla, 1985). Otherwise, changes in aid packages could result in ambiguous

---

[1] Some research on college access now considers the role of parent involvement variables (e.g., Emeka & Hirschman, Chapter 5). In NELS there are a large number of missing cases in the parent surveys, so no effort was made to include these variables. However, other social and contextual variables were included, as explained below.

findings. For example, Astin (1975) concluded that, although loans were significant in long-term persistence, the findings should be considered an artifact when loans were significant in year-to-year analyses (St. John, 1989). Most subsequent studies have focused on within-year or year-to-year persistence (St. John, Cabrera, Nora, & Asker, 2000), an approach that avoids this measurement problem.

This reanalysis examines educational attainment eight years after high school graduation. For students who had enrolled in college, we compared different types of attainment (two-year degree, four-year degree, advanced degree, and still enrolled) to having dropped out. Since we were interested in the impact of state finance strategies in this study, we could use the average over the eight years for state funding per student on different types of grant aid and tuition within states. This method could be improved upon in future studies because the use of averages reduces variation in public funding. For example, event history analysis can be adapted to consider state-level variables. Alternatively, year-to-year persistence analysis could be conducted (e.g., St. John, Kirshstein, & Noell, 1991).

The third lesson related to the use of appropriate statistical methods and balanced logical models that considered both academic preparation and student financial aid as explanations for enrollment and persistence. This study used hierarchical multinomial logistic regressions to examine enrollment and persistence decisions. The two-level model provides an appropriate means of examining the influence of state finance variables, an appropriate adjustment not only because state funding for grants varies more within a year than federal grant aid but also because state of residence is a relatively unambiguous measure. In addition, the multinomial models provide a means of comparing multiple college destinations to nonenrollment. This study also used a balanced logical model that considers both academic and financial explanations for enrollment and persistence.

Reanalysis of College Access

This reanalysis of NELS responds to the need for balanced research on college access that considers the role of academic preparation and public finance, controlling for family background. After describing the research approach, analyses of enrollment patterns are presented for low-income, middle-income, and upper-income students.

Research Approach

This study used a two-level, hierarchical multinomial model to examine the effect of preparation and state finance variables on college enrollment destinations. The two levels of the model—individual and state—are reviewed below, along with a discussion of statistical methods. The outcome variables in the model used nonenrollment as the comparison variable for enrollment in public two-year colleges, enrollment in public four-year colleges, and enrollment in private (nonprofit and proprietary) institutions.[2]

Individual Level

Variables related to high school graduation, race/ethnicity, parents' education, postsecondary plans, test quartile, entrance exams (i.e., the SAT or ACT), and advanced math courses were used at the individual level. In addition, separate analyses were conducted for low-, middle-, and high-income students to examine the role of parents' education within groups to avoid confusion between the two variables. This means that some students who did not have income reported were excluded from these analyses. However, this group has been considered in another recent

---

[2] An earlier version of this reanalysis (St. John & Associates, in press) considered enrollment in private colleges and proprietary institutions as distinct variables. The findings from this analysis are similar to the earlier findings because a very small percentage of students in the 1992 cohort enrolled in proprietary institutions.

reanalysis of the entire cohort (St. John & associates, in review), which found both income and parents' education were associated with college enrollment. The coding of other variables included mission values, usually in the comparison category (see Table 1).

State Level Variables

This study used the state financial indicators for 1992 (St. John, Chung, Musoba, & Simmons, 2004; St. John, Chung, Musoba, Simmons, Wooden, & Mendez, 2004) in the analysis of state financial indicators (Table 2). Tuition charges for public colleges and universities in states were calculated and weighted, based on the percentage of full-time-equivalent (FTE) students in public institutions,[3] using the Integration Postsecondary Education Data System (IPEDS) financial and enrollment reports. In addition, states' funding for need-based and non-need grants per FTE were calculated using annual total spending divided by undergraduate FTE.[4] The actual amounts of aid were divided by 1,000.

Statistical Methods

These analyses used appropriate state-of-the-art statistical methods. Logistic regression is now widely used in higher education research (Peng, So, Stage, & St. John, 2002). Multilevel and multinomial versions of logistic regression are less commonly used, but these methods are appropriate in this study. We report odds ratios and level of significance for independent variables and present variance for the second-level effect. In addition, descriptive statistics are presented and discussed for each of the analyses.

---

[3] The tuition charge was adjusted for the percentage of FTE in each type of institution to generate a tuition charge that reflected the average tuition a student would expect to pay in a public college.

[4] Total funding for need-based and non-need grant program for 1992.

Table 1. Coding of Individual-Level Variables in Enrollment Models		
Variable	**Coding**	**Comment**
High School Graduation	Graduated	Coded (1)
	Not Graduated (Uncoded)	Comparison Variable
Gender	Male	Coded (1)
	Female	Comparison Variable
Race/Ethnicity	Asian/Pacific Islander	Coded (1)
	Hispanic	Coded (1)
	Black, not Hispanic	Coded (1)
	White, not Hispanic or Native American or Other or Missing	Comparison Variable
Family Income Group	Low (less than $25,000)	Separately Examined
	High ($75,000 or more)	Separately Examined
	Multiple Response or Missing	Not Examined
	Middle ($25,000-$74,999)	Separately Examined
Parent's Highest Education Level	HS, Some College	Coded (1)
	College Grad	Coded (1)
	M.A., Ph.D., M.D., Other	Coded (1)
	Didn't Finish HS or HS Grad or GED or Don't Know or Missing	Comparison Variable
Postsecondary Education Plans	VOC, TRD, BUS after HS	Coded (1)
	Will Attend College	Coded (1)
	Will Finish College	Coded (1)
	Advanced Degree	Coded (1)
	Won't Finish HS or Will Finish HS or Missing	Comparison Variable
Standard Test (1992 NELS Test) Quartile	Quartile 1 Low	Coded (1)
	Quartile 2	Coded (1)
	Quartile 3	Coded (1)
	Quartile 4 High	Coded (1)
	Missing or Test Not Comp	Comparison Variable
Indicator If Took SAT or ACT	Took SAT or ACT	Coded (1)
	Took Neither SAT nor ACT, or Missing or Refusal or Don't Know	Comparison Variable
Advanced Math Course Taking	Trigonometry/Precalculus only	Coded (1)
	Calculus	Coded (1)
	No Trigonometry/Precalculus or Calculus, or Missing	Coded (1)

Table 2. Coding of State-Level Variables		
Financial Indicators	Need-based grant in 1,000 dollars	Actual $/1,000
	Non-need grant in 1,000 dollars	Actual $/1,000
	Public system undergraduate in-state tuition in 1,000 dollars	Actual $/1,000

Enrollment by Low-Income Students

There were some notable differences in enrollment patterns among low-income students the year after high school (Table 3). Nearly two-thirds (64%) did not enroll in college after high school. However, slightly more than half of the high school graduates enrolled in college, with 22 percent enrolling in four-year colleges, 21 percent in public or for-profit two-year colleges, and 9 percent in private colleges. About one-third of Asian/Pacific Islanders did not enroll in some type of college, while about two-thirds of each racial/ethnic group did not enroll in college. Higher percentages of Asian/Pacific Islanders and African Americans who enrolled went to four-year colleges, while a higher percentage of Hispanic enrollees were in two-year colleges.

While the NCES analyses concluded that parents' education had a substantial association with enrollment (Choy, 2002; NCES, 2001), this analysis reveals that about one-third of the low-income students whose parents had four-year and advanced degrees did not enroll (Table 4), further illustrating problems with NCES's methods. In addition, nearly half of the low-income students who planned to finish college did not enroll immediately after high school. Thus, aspirations and parental attainment did not appear to be as important as previously asserted.

NCES (1997) argued that students who took advanced math courses and the SAT/ACT were more likely to enroll. However, it should be noted that 41 percent of the low-income students who took the SAT did not enroll in college after high school. Only 30 percent of low-income students who took the SAT enrolled in four-year colleges. However, taking advanced math did appear to be important: 52 percent of the low-income students who had completed calculus enrolled in four-year colleges, while only 13 percent of this group did not enroll. In addition, 47 percent of low-income students who took trigonometry enrolled in four-year colleges, and 21 percent did not enroll at all. Nearly three-quarters of the students who did not complete these advanced courses did not enroll in any college after high school. It should also be noted, however, that some students who did not graduate from high school went to college, although 96 percent of the low-income nongraduates did not enroll at all.

Low-income students lived in states that funded need-based grants at an average of $207 per FTE and funded merit grants at an average of $26 per FTE in 1992. The average full-time tuition charge was $2,279. In addition to considering the effects of individual-level variables, this analysis considers the influence of state financing strategies.

The analysis of enrollment patterns for low-income students (Table 4) is consistent with the findings reported by NCES (Choy, 2002), but also provides insight into the influence of variables omitted in the NCES studies. An individual-level variable not considered by NCES was high school graduation. In this analysis, graduation had a very substantial association with enrollment in all types of colleges. Questions should be raised about the association between education policies and high school dropout rates. Many of the accountability reforms had negative associations with graduation in time-series analyses (St. John, Musoba, & Chung, 2004). Other individual-level findings in the analysis of low-income students included the following (controlling for other variables in the analysis):

Table 3. Descriptive Statistics for Variables Included in Enrollment Analyses, Low-Income Students Only PSE Destination Model: Low Income Only

INDIVIDUAL		PSE Choice							
		Public 4-Year		Public 2-Year or Less/Private For-Profit Combined		Private Nonprofit		Not Attending or Missing	
		Count	Row %	Count	Row %	Count	Row %	Count	Row %
High School Graduation	Graduated	600	21.9	564	20.6	244	8.9	1,330	48.6
	Not Graduated	9	0.7	29	2.3	8	0.6	1,212	96.3
Gender	Male	258	13.4	251	13.1	105	5.5	1,309	68.1
	Female	351	16.9	342	16.5	147	7.1	1,233	59.5
Race/Ethnicity	Asian/Pacific Islander	81	30.9	60	22.9	31	11.8	90	34.4
	Hispanic	99	12.3	128	16.0	24	3.0	551	68.7
	Black, not Hispanic	128	16.3	92	11.7	57	7.3	507	64.7
	White, not Hispanic or Native American or Other or Missing	301	14.0	313	14.6	140	6.5	1,394	64.9
Family Income Group	Low (less than $25,000)	609	15.2	593	14.8	252	6.3	2,542	63.6
	High ($75,000 or more)								
	Multiple Response or Missing								
	Middle ($25,000-$74,999)								
Parent's Highest Education Level	HS, Some College	286	18.5	249	16.1	106	6.8	907	58.6
	College Grad	70	32.7	40	18.7	34	15.9	70	32.7
	M.A., Ph.D., M.D., Other	22	23.9	12	13.0	26	28.3	32	34.8
	Didn't Finish HS or HS Grad or GED or Don't Know or Missing	31	10.8	292	13.6	86	4.0	1,533	71.6

Table 3. Descriptive Statistics for Variables Included in Enrollment Analyses, Low-Income Students Only PSE Destination Model: Low Income Only (cont.)

		Public 4-Year		Public 2-Year or Less/Private For-Profit Combined		Private Nonprofit		Not Attending or Missing	
		Count	Row %	Count	Row %	Count	Row %	Count	Row %
INDIVIDUAL									
Postsecondary Education Plans	VOC, TRD, BUS after HS	32	6.9	59	12.8	10	2.2	360	78.1
	Will Attend College	62	10.1	105	17.1	29	4.7	418	68.1
	Will Finish College	308	24.1	229	17.9	107	8.4	635	49.6
	Advanced Degree	157	26.5	94	15.9	84	14.2	258	43.5
	Won't Finish HS or Will Finish HS or Missing	50	4.8	106	10.1	22	2.1	871	83.0
Std Test (1992 NELS Test) Quartile	Quartile 1 Low	52	5.1	146	14.3	23	2.3	797	78.3
	Quartile 2	125	14.4	167	19.2	42	4.8	536	61.6
	Quartile 3	169	27.0	114	18.2	53	8.5	291	46.4
	Quartile 4 High	178	43.1	46	11.1	96	23.2	93	22.5
	Missing or Test Not Comp	85	8.0	120	11.2	38	3.6	825	77.2
Indicator If Took SAT or ACT	Took SAT or ACT	568	30.1	323	17.1	233	12.3	765	40.5
	Took Neither SAT nor ACT, or Missing or Refusal or Don't Know	41	1.9	270	12.8	19	0.9	1,777	84.3
Taking Advanced Math Courses	Trigonometry/Precalculus Only	191	47.2	66	16.3	64	15.8	84	20.7
	Calculus	92	52.3	13	7.4	48	27.3	23	13.1
	No Trigonometry/Precalculus or Calculus, or Missing	326	9.5	514	15.1	140	4.1	2,435	71.3

STATE		Mean
Financial Indicators	Need-Based Grant in 1,000 Dollars	0.207
	Non-need Grant in 1,000 Dollars	0.026
	Public System Undergraduate In-state Tuition in 1,000 Dollars	2.279

Table 4. Multilevel, Multinomial Analysis of College Enrollment by Low-Income Students PSE Destination Model: Low Income Only					
	Public 4-Year		Public 2-Year or Less/Private For-Profit Combined		Private Nonprofit	
LEVEL 1: INDIVIDUAL	Odds Ratio	Sig.	Odds Ratio	Sig.	Odds Ratio	Sig.
High School Graduation						
Graduated	21.272	***	13.759	***	10.906	***
Not Graduated						
Gender						
Male	0.879		0.781	**	0.827	
Female						
Race/Ethnicity						
Asian/Pacific Islander	2.197	***	1.722	**	1.945	**
Hispanic	1.355		1.005		0.871	
Black, not Hispanic	2.247	***	0.954		2.734	***
White, not Hispanic or Native American or Other or Missing						
Parent's Highest Education Level						
HS, Some College	1.152		1.155		1.175	
College Grad	2.079	***	1.622	**	2.750	***
M.A., Ph.D., M.D., Other	1.738		1.251		5.313	***
Didn't Finish HS or HS Grad or GED or Don't Know or Missing						
Postsecondary Education Plans						
VOC, TRD, BUS after HS	1.366		1.332		0.916	
Will Attend College	1.488	*	1.443	**	1.628	
Will Finish College	2.594	***	1.754	***	2.023	**
Advanced Degree	2.493	***	1.742	***	2.862	***
Won't Finish HS or Will Finish HS or Missing						

Table 4. Multilevel, Multinomial Analysis of College Enrollment by Low-Income Students PSE Destination Model: Low Income Only (cont.)

	Public 4-Year		Public 2-Year or Less/Private For-Profit Combined		Private Nonprofit	
	Odds Ratio	Sig.	Odds Ratio	Sig.	Odds Ratio	Sig.
LEVEL 1: INDIVIDUAL						
Std Test (1992 NELS Test) Quartile						
Quartile 1 Low						
Quartile 2	0.700		0.953		0.786	
Quartile 3	1.110		1.001		0.950	
Quartile 3	1.776	***	1.008		1.302	
Quartile 4 High	2.700	***	0.897		3.572	***
Missing or Test Not Comp						
Indicator If Took SAT or ACT						
Yes	13.854	***	1.981	***	10.918	***
No or Missing or Refusal or Don't Know						
Taking Advanced Math Courses						
Trigonometry/Precalculus Only	2.741	***	1.193		2.024	***
Calculus	3.831	***	0.804		3.877	***
No Trigonometry/Precalculus or Calculus, or Missing						
LEVEL 2: STATE						
Financial Indicators						
Need-Based Grant in 1,000 Dollars	1.711		3.380	***	2.305	**
Non-need Grant in 1,000 Dollars	0.152		2.289		0.026	*
Undergraduate In-state Tuition in 1,000 Dollars	0.840		0.772	**	1.247	
Random Effect	Variance	Sig.				
Level 2 Effect: Category 1 (Public 4-Year)	0.165	***				
Level 2 Effect: Category 2 (Public 2-Year or Less/Private For-Profit)	0.115	***				
Level 2 Effect: Category 2 (Private Nonprofit)	0.134	***				

Note: *** $p<0.01$, ** $p<0.05$, * $p<0.1$

- Males had lower odds than females of enrolling in two-year colleges than of not enrolling in college.
- Asian/Pacific Islanders had higher odds than Whites of enrolling in all types of institutions than of not enrolling, while African Americans had higher odds than Whites of enrolling in public four-year colleges and private colleges.
- Students whose parents had graduated from college had higher odds of enrolling in all types of colleges, while students whose parents had attained advanced degrees had higher odds of enrolling in private colleges and did not differ significantly on enrollment in other types of colleges.
- Students with test scores in the highest two quartiles had higher odds of enrolling in public four-year colleges, while student in the highest quartile had higher odds of enrolling in private colleges.
- Taking the SAT/ACT had a substantial significant association with enrollment in public four-year colleges and in private colleges.
- Advanced math courses were also associated with enrollment in four-year colleges and private colleges, but the odds ratios for these variables (an indicator of effect size) were lower than for taking the exam and much lower than for graduating from high school.

In addition, the state-level variables had a significant association with enrollment patterns. State funding for need-based grants was positively associated with enrollment by low-income students in public two-year colleges and in private colleges. State funding for non-need (mostly merit) grants was modestly (.1 alpha) and negatively associated with enrollment in private colleges by low-income students. In contrast, public sector tuition charges were negatively associated with enrollment in two-year colleges. Clearly, state finance strategies have an influence on enrollment opportunities for low-income students.

Enrollment by Middle-Income Students

Sixty percent of middle-income students in the 1992 sample enrolled in college the year after high school (Table 5). However, most middle-income high school dropouts did not enroll in college (92%). A higher percentage of males (44%) than females (35%) did not enroll in college, although the percentages of males and females enrolled in public four-year colleges were similar.

Most middle-income students whose parents had graduated from college or had attained advanced degrees enrolled in college. Students whose parents had attained college and advanced degrees also enrolled in public four-year colleges and private colleges at higher rates than students whose parents had lower levels of education. In addition, a relatively high percentage of middle-income students who expected to complete college and graduate degrees enrolled in public four-year colleges and private colleges. Unlike the analysis of low-income students, the analysis of middle-income students was consistent with the general patterns of parent education and aspirations described by Choy (2002).

In addition, the relationships between enrollment patterns and preparation were similar to Choy's summary of NCES studies. Most students with advanced math preparation went to four-year colleges, most students who took the SAT/ACT enrolled, and so forth. Clearly, the general pattern of preparation described by Choy (2002) was evident in the analyses of middle-income students.

The multinomial logistic regression (Table 6) indicated a more complex pattern of relationships than the NCES pattern described by Choy. High school graduation, one of the variables NCES omitted, had significant and positive associations with enrollment in public four-year and private colleges. Among middle-income high school students, high school graduates had higher odds than nongraduates of enrolling in two-year colleges.

Table 5. Descriptive Statistics for Variables Included in Enrollment Analyses, Middle-Income Students Only PSE Destination Model: Middle Income Only

INDIVIDUAL		Public 4-Year		Public 2-Year or Less/Private For-Profit Combined		Private Nonprofit		Not Attending or Missing	
		Count	Row %	Count	Row %	Count	Row %	Count	Row %
High School Graduation	Graduated	1,576	30.3	1,150	22.1	799	15.4	1,675	32.2
	Not Graduated	11	1.5	37	4.9	7	0.9	699	92.7
Gender	Male	764	25.7	544	18.3	339	11.4	1,325	44.6
	Female	823	27.6	643	21.6	467	15.7	1,049	35.2
Race/Ethnicity	Asian/Pacific Islander	133	34.0	90	23.0	63	16.1	105	26.9
	Hispanic	129	24.7	121	23.1	43	8.2	230	44.0
	Black, not Hispanic	122	25.8	65	13.7	64	13.5	222	46.9
	White, not Hispanic/Native American/Other/Missing	1,203	26.3	911	19.9	636	13.9	1,817	39.8
Family Income Group	Low (less than $25,000)								
	High ($75,000 or more)								
	Middle ($25,000-$74,999)	1,587	26.7	1,187	19.9	806	13.5	2,374	39.9
Parent's Highest Education Level	Multiple Response or Missing								
	HS, Some College	705	25.2	657	23.5	294	10.5	1,145	40.9
	College Grad	384	37.6	182	17.8	190	18.6	264	25.9
	M.A., Ph.D., M.D., Other	283	40.2	91	12.9	215	30.5	115	16.3
	Didn't Finish HS/HS Grad/GED/Don't Know/Missing	215	15.0	257	18.0	107	7.5	850	59.5
Postsecondary Education Plans	VOC, TRD, BUS after HS	40	9.2	103	23.7	14	3.2	278	63.9
	Will Attend College	113	16.6	162	23.8	39	5.7	368	54.0
	Will Finish College	841	31.5	580	21.7	402	15.1	848	31.7
	Advanced Degree	537	38.8	217	15.7	320	23.1	310	22.4
	Won't Finish HS/Will Finish HS/Missing	56	7.2	125	16.0	31	4.0	570	72.9

Table 5. Descriptive Statistics for Variables Included in Enrollment Analyses, Middle-Income Students Only PSE Destination Model: Middle Income Only (cont.)

		PSE Choice						
		Public 4-Year		Public 2-Year or Less/Private For-Profit Combined		Private Nonprofit		Not Attending or Missing	
INDIVIDUAL		Count	Row %	Count	Row %	Count	Row %	Count	Row %
Std Test (1992 NELS Test) Quartile	Quartile 1 Low	62	7.8	166	20.9	29	3.6	539	67.7
	Quartile 2	184	16.3	320	28.3	71	6.3	554	49.1
	Quartile 3	440	32.0	329	23.9	193	14.0	412	30.0
	Quartile 4 High	685	46.9	180	12.3	391	26.8	203	13.9
	Missing or Test Not Comp	216	18.1	192	16.1	122	10.2	666	55.7
Indicator If Took SAT or ACT	Took SAT or ACT	1,518	38.2	794	20.0	769	19.3	894	22.5
	Took Neither SAT nor ACT, or Missing/Refusal/Don't Know	69	3.5	393	19.9	37	1.9	1,480	74.8
Taking Advanced Math Courses	Trigonometry/Precalculus only	576	48.5	207	17.4	262	22.1	142	12.0
	Calculus	296	52.7	34	6.0	179	31.9	53	9.4
	No Trigonometry/Precalculus/Calculus/Missing	715	17.0	946	22.5	365	8.7	2,179	51.8
STATE		Mean							
Financial Indicators	Need-Based Grant in 1,000 Dollars	0.207							
	Non-need Grant in 1,000 Dollars	0.026							
	Public System Undergraduate In-State Tuition in 1,000 Dollars	2.279							

Table 6. Multilevel, Multinomial Analyses of College Enrollment by Middle-Income Students					
	Public 4-Year		Public 2-Year or Less/Private For-Profit Combined		Private Nonprofit	
	Odds Ratio	Sig.	Odds Ratio	Sig.	Odds Ratio	Sig.
Level 1: Individual						
High School Graduation						
Graduated	19.562	***	8.011	***	14.410	***
Not Graduated						
Gender						
Male	0.821	**	0.709	***	0.631	***
Female						
Race/Ethnicity						
Asian/Pacific Islander	1.021		0.992		0.847	
Hispanic	1.632	***	0.897		1.210	
Black, not Hispanic	1.523	**	0.643	***	1.476	**
White, not Hispanic/Native American/Other/Missing						
Parent's Highest Education Level						
HS, Some College	1.512	***	1.518	***	1.345	**
College Grad	2.007	***	1.334	**	2.028	***
M.A., Ph.D., M.D., Other	2.704	***	1.602	***	4.117	***
Didn't Finish HS/HS Grad/GED/Don't Know/Missing						
Postsecondary Education Plans						
VOC, TRD, BUS after HS	0.804		1.240		0.593	
Will Attend College	1.772	***	1.235		1.185	
Will Finish College	2.696	***	1.583	***	2.498	***
Advanced Degree	3.152	***	1.332	*	3.307	***
Won't Finish HS/Will Finish HS/Missing						

Table 6. Multilevel, Multinomial Analyses of College Enrollment by Middle-Income Students (cont.)

	Public 4-Year		Public 2-Year or Less/Private For-Profit Combined		Private Nonprofit	
	Odds Ratio	Sig.	Odds Ratio	Sig.	Odds Ratio	Sig.
Level 1: Individual						
Std Test (1992 NELS Test) Quartile						
Quartile 1 Low	0.505	***	1.200		0.547	**
Quartile 2	0.708	**	1.573	***	0.596	***
Quartile 3	1.270	*	1.601	***	1.153	
Quartile 4 High	1.724	***	1.215		1.894	***
Missing or Test Not Comp						
Indicator If Took SAT or ACT						
Yes	12.215	***	2.153	***	9.869	***
No or Missing/Refusal/Don't Know						
Taking Advanced Math Courses						
Trigonometry/Precalculus Only	3.556	***	1.603	***	2.959	***
Calculus	3.626	***	0.653	*	3.518	***
No Trigonometry/Precalculus/Calculus/Missing						
Level 2: State						
Financial Indicators						
Need-Based Grant in 1,000 Dollars	0.865		2.248	**	1.450	
Non-need Grant in 1,000 Dollars	0.743		4.933		0.249	
Undergraduate In-state Tuition in 1,000 Dollars	1.048		0.751	***	1.409	***

Random Effect	Variance Component	Sig.
Level 2 Effect: Category 1 (Public 4-year)	0.173	***
Level 2 Effect: Category 2 (Public 2-year or Less/Private For-Profit Combined)	0.132	***
Level 2 Effect: Category 2 (Private Nonprofit)	0.139	***

Note: *** $p<0.01$, ** $p<0.05$, * $p<0.1$

Unlike the analysis of low-income students, middle-income male students were less likely to enroll in all types of colleges than were middle-income females. High levels of parents' education and high expectations were significantly and positively associated with enrollment in all types of colleges, consistent with the general pattern described by NCES (Choy, 2002).

Academic preparation variables had a substantial association with enrollment but had a complex pattern. High test scores were positively associated with enrollment in all types of colleges, as was taking the SAT/ACT. Calculus was positively associated with enrollment in public four-year colleges and private colleges but negatively associated with enrollment in two-year colleges. In contrast, trigonometry was positively associated with enrollment in all three types of institutions.

The state-level finance variables also helped explain variance in enrollment behavior. Funding for need-based grants was positively associated with enrollment in two-year colleges, while public-sector tuition charges had a negative association. In contrast, public tuition charges were positively associated with enrollment in private colleges, indicating that in high-tuition states more middle-income students chose to enroll in private colleges. However, none of the finance variables were significantly associated with enrollment in public four-year colleges by middle-income students. This supports the conclusion that there were also structural limitations on access to public four-year colleges during this period.

Enrollment by High-Income Students

For high-income students (Table 7), as for their low- and middle-income peers, most students who do not graduate from high school also do not go on to college (85%). Nearly three-tenths of high-income Hispanics did not go to college the first year after high school (29%), and a similar percentage went to public four-year colleges (29%), with one-quarter going to two-year colleges (25%) and a smaller percentage attending private colleges (19%). In contrast about four-tenths of all racial/ethnic groups enrolled in public four-year colleges, and about three-tenths enrolled in private colleges. Thus, high-income students of all races attended college at higher rates than their peers with lower incomes, but Hispanics in this population were enrolling at lower rates than other high-income students.

Most high-income students with low aspirations—those who had vocational aspirations or did not plan to go on to college—did not attend colleges. Among high-income students, there were differences in college enrollment by variables related to academic preparation. In addition, wealthy students with low scores on the standardized tests and those who did not take the SAT did attend college at high rates. However, more than two-thirds of the high-income students who had taken advanced math actually went on to college.

In level one of the logistic regression analysis (Table 8), high school graduation was strongly associated with enrollment in all types of colleges. However ethnicity and gender were not associated with college choice among wealthy students. Yet having parents with college degrees or advanced degrees was positively associated with enrolling both in public four-year colleges and in private colleges, compared to not enrolling. In addition, aspiring to four-year and advanced degrees were positively associated with enrollment both in public four-year colleges and in private colleges, as were high test scores and advanced math courses.

Two of the second-level variables were also significant for high-income students. The amount of state funding for need-based aid was negatively associated with enrollment in public four-year colleges. This is logical because need-based grants create competition for limited slots in public four-year colleges by expanding opportunity for qualified middle- and low-income students. In addition, high public-sector tuition was negatively associated with enrollment in two-year colleges for high-income students.

Table 7. Descriptive Statistics for Variables Included in Enrollment Analyses, High-Income Students Only PSE Destination Model: High Income Only

		PSE Choice							
		Public 4-Year		Public 2-Year or Less/Private For-Profit Combined		Private Nonprofit		Not Attending or Missing	
		Count	Row %	Count	Row %	Count	Row %	Count	Row %
INDIVIDUAL									
High School Graduation	Graduated	62	39.8	156	11.0	503	35.6	192	13.6
	Not Graduated	4	5.4	6	8.1	1	1.4	63	85.1
Gender	Male	96	38.7	83	10.9	242	31.7	143	18.7
	Female	70	37.3	79	10.9	262	36.2	112	15.5
Race/Ethnicity	Asian/Pacific Islander	69	40.1	15	8.7	62	36.0	26	15.1
	Hispanic	20	29.0	17	24.6	12	17.4	20	29.0
	Black, not Hispanic	23	40.4	5	8.8	18	31.6	11	19.3
	White, not Hispanic/Native American/Other/Missing	454	38.2	125	10.5	412	34.7	198	16.7
Family Income Group	Low (less than $25,000)								
	High ($75,000 or more)	566	38.1	162	10.9	504	33.9	255	17.1
	Multiple Response or Missing								
	Middle ($25,000-$74,999)								
Parent's Highest Education Level	HS, Some College	95	36.7	50	19.3	35	13.5	79	30.5
	College Grad	159	39.5	53	13.2	128	31.8	63	15.6
	M.A., Ph.D., M.D., Other	290	38.9	48	6.4	333	44.6	75	10.1
	Didn't Finish HS/HS Grad/GED/Don't Know/Missing	22	27.8	11	13.9	8	10.1	38	48.1
Postsecondary Education Plans	VOC, TRD, BUS after HS	4	14.3	3	10.7	3	10.7	18	64.3
	Will Attend College	22	28.6	15	19.5	9	11.7	31	40.3
	Will Finish College	242	37.5	92	14.3	209	32.4	102	15.8
	Advanced Degree	283	42.6	41	6.2	272	40.9	69	10.4
	Won't Finish HS/Will Finish	15	20.8	11	15.3	11	15.3	35	48.6

Table 7. Descriptive Statistics for Variables Included in Enrollment Analyses, High-Income Students Only PSE Destination Model: High Income Only (cont.)

		PSE Choice						
		Public 4-Year		Public 2-Year or Less/Private For-Profit Combined		Private Nonprofit		Not Attending or Missing	
		Count	Row %	Count	Row %	Count	Row %	Count	Row %
INDIVIDUAL									
Std Test (1992 NELS Test) Quartile	Quartile 1 Low	10	15.9	11	17.5	10	15.9	32	50.8
	Quartile 2	41	28.3	32	22.1	26	17.9	46	31.7
	Quartile 3	130	43.5	47	15.7	74	24.7	48	16.1
	Quartile 4 High	276	41.8	40	6.1	293	44.4	51	7.7
	Missing or Test Not Comp	109	34.1	32	10.0	101	31.6	78	24.4
Indicator If Took SAT or ACT	Took SAT or ACT	549	42.3	116	8.9	486	37.4	148	11.4
	Took Neither SAT nor ACT, or Missing/Refusal/Don't Know	17	9.0	46	24.5	18	9.6	107	56.9
Taking Advanced Math Courses	Trigonometry/Precalculus Only	206	45.3	43	9.5	165	36.3	41	9.0
	Calculus	126	37.3	9	2.7	185	54.7	18	5.3
	No Trigonometry/Precalculus or Calculus, or Missing	234	33.7	110	15.9	154	22.2	196	28.2
STATE		Mean							
Financial Indicators	Need-Based Grant in 1,000 Dollars	0.207							
	Non-need Grant in 1,000 Dollars	0.026							
	Public System Undergraduate In-state Tuition in 1,000 Dollars	2.279							

Table 8. Multilevel, Multinomial Analysis of College Enrollment by High-Income Students
PSE Destination Model: High Income Only

	Public 4-Year		Public 2-Year or Less/Private For-Profit Combined		Private Nonprofit	
	Odds Ratio	Sig.	Odds Ratio	Sig.	Odds Ratio	Sig.
Level 1: Individual						
High School Graduation						
Graduated	19.283	***	6.271	***	50.473	***
Not Graduated						
Gender						
Male	1.167		1.096		0.903	
Female						
Race/Ethnicity						
Asian/Pacific Islander	0.869		0.784		0.672	
Hispanic	0.768		1.389		0.599	
Black, not Hispanic	1.532		0.912		1.260	
White, not Hispanic/Native American/Other/Missing						
Parent's Highest Education Level						
HS, Some College	1.276		1.562		1.397	
College Grad	1.520	*	1.810		3.137	**
M.A., Ph.D., M.D., Other	1.842	*	1.405		5.103	***
Didn't Finish HS/HS Grad/GED/Don't Know/Missing						
Postsecondary Education Plans						
VOC, TRD, BUS after HS	0.779		0.520		0.939	
Will Attend College	1.377		1.031		0.818	
Will Finish College	2.636	**	1.663		2.784	**
Advanced Degree	3.190	***	1.106		2.949	**
Won't Finish HS/Will Finish HS/Missing						

Table 8. Multilevel, Multinomial Analysis of College Enrollment by High-Income Students PSE Destination Model: High Income Only (cont.)

Level 1: Individual	Public 4-Year		Public 2-Year or Less/Private For-Profit Combined		Private Nonprofit	
	Odds Ratio	Sig.	Odds Ratio	Sig.	Odds Ratio	Sig.
Std Test (1992 NELS Test) Quartile						
Quartile 1 Low	0.693		1.013		1.217	
Quartile 2	0.538	**	1.504		0.511	**
Quartile 3	1.123		1.524		0.868	
Quartile 4 High	1.025		1.023		1.046	
Missing or Test Not Comp						
Indicator If Took SAT or ACT						
Yes	8.968	***	1.188		5.669	***
No or Missing/Refusal/Don't Know						
Taking Advanced Math Courses						
Trigonometry/Precalculus Only	2.135	***	1.481		2.598	***
Calculus	2.331	***	0.760		4.719	***
No Trigonometry/Precalculus/Calculus/Missing						
Level 2: State						
Financial Indicators						
Need-Based Grant in 1,000 Dollars	0.315	**	1.434		0.691	
Non-need Grant in 1,000 Dollars	0.431		0.044		0.085	
Undergraduate In-state Tuition in 1,000 Dollars	0.920		0.551	***	1.123	
Random Effect			Variance Component		Sig.	
Level 2 Effect: Category 1 (Public 4-Year)			0.260		***	
Level 2 Effect: Category 2 (Public 2-Year or Less/Private For-Profit Combined)			0.325		***	
Level 2 Effect: Category 2 (Private Nonprofit)			0.024		***	

Note: *** $p<0.01$, ** $p<0.05$, * $p<0.1$

Reanalysis of Postsecondary Attainment

Degree attainment is an important measure of long-term academic success, and many of Choy's conclusions from NCES studies related to long-term effects of preparation. Therefore, it was important to reconsider the impact of background and preparation on college success in addition to considering the impact of public finance variables.

Research Approach

The analyses of attainment used a similar two-level multinomial model as used in the enrollment models, with a few adaptations at the two levels. At the individual level, we added family income to the model, since a single model was used rather than breakouts by income groups. At the state level we used the average student grant and funding per-FTE tuition charges across the eight years. In addition, we considered college of origin in the descriptive breakdown but could not consider this in the logistic model because of the strong correlation between starting in a two-year college and attaining a two-year degree. The outcome variables in this model used nonenrollment as the comparison for enrollment in (a) public two-year colleges and for-profit colleges, (b) public four-year colleges, and (c) private nonprofit colleges.

While this approach was appropriate for comparison with the NCES studies, it has limitations. One is that it does not consider whether students transferred. This is not necessarily a limitation from the perspective of college attainment research. Second, the use of averages for state grant funding and tuition charges substantially reduces variations in these treatment variables. Future studies should examine year-to-year transitions.

Analysis of Attainment

Persistence Rates. While the number of non-high-school graduates who enrolled in college was small, almost half (46%) persisted—attained a degree or were still enrolled after eight years—in 2000 (see Table 9). While the number is too small for analysis of persistence using the full model, these statistics further illustrate the problems with setting selection for enrollment analysis so tightly as to exclude these students.

There were relatively substantial differences in persistence rates among students based on background. African Americans and Hispanics persisted at substantially lower rates than Asian Americans and Whites/others. There were also differences related to parents' levels of educational attainment. Given the interrelationships among income, race, and parents' education in American society, it is illogical to attribute inequalities to only one of these variables—parents' education—as was the theme of the NCES studies summarized by Choy (2002).

There were also differences in college persistence in relation to variables concerning high school preparation: taking SAT/ACT exams, having high scores on standardized tests, and taking advanced math courses. In addition, the most substantial differences were related to advanced math. The dropout rates were 8 percent of the students who had completed calculus and 16 percent of the students who had completed trigonometry compared to 37 percent for students who had not completed either of these courses. However, the majority of students who did not complete either advanced math course persisted. So it is definitely misleading to conclude it is essential to take advanced math in high school if the majority of college students who did not attain this level of math education were successful.

Further, the type of colleges students attended after high school also appeared to be related to persistence rates. Slightly more than half (56%) of the students who began in community colleges did not persist. However, only about one quarter (26%) of the students who started in proprietary schools did not persist.

Table 9. Descriptive Analyses of Persistence (Degree Attainment or Current Enrollment) in 2000 by Students in the NELS Cohort Enrolling During the Fall Term of 1992 Descriptive Statistics for Variables in HLM Logistic Regression for PSE Persistence

INDIVIDUAL		PSE Persistence			
		Enrolled or Earned Degree(s)		Dropout	
		Count	Row %	Count	Row %
High School Graduation Status	Graduated	5,736	71.7	2,259	28.3
	Not Graduated	32	45.7	38	54.3
Gender	Male	2,531	69.1	1,130	30.9
	Female	3,237	73.5	1,167	26.5
Race/Ethnicity	Asian/Pacific Islander	547	82.3	118	17.7
	Hispanic	534	58.3	382	41.7
	Black, not Hispanic	435	64.9	235	35.1
	White, not Hispanic/Native American/Other/Missing	4,252	73.1	1,562	26.9
Family Income Group	Low (less than $25,000)	1,085	62.5	651	37.5
	High ($75,000 or more)	1,083	88.5	141	11.5
	Multiple Response or Missing	815	68.4	376	31.6
	Middle ($25,000-$74,999)	2,785	71.2	1,129	28.8
Parent's Highest Education Level	HS, Some College	1,946	66.1	997	33.9
	College Grad	1,087	79.2	286	20.8
	M.A. or Equal	760	88.0	104	12.0
	Ph.D., M.D., Other	496	93.2	36	6.8
	Didn't Finish HS/HS Grad/GED/Don't Know/Missing	1,479	62.9	874	37.1
Postsecondary Education Plans	VOC, TRD, BUS after HS	281	58.5	199	41.5
	Will Attend College	497	58.2	357	41.8
	Will Finish College	2,684	73.0	993	27.0
	Advanced Degree	1,873	81.2	434	18.8
	Won't Finish HS or Will Finish HS or Missing	433	58.0	314	42.0

Table 9. Descriptive Analyses of Persistence (Degree Attainment or Current Enrollment) in 2000 by Students in the NELS Cohort Enrolling During the Fall Term of 1992 Descriptive Statistics for Variables in HLM Logistic Regression for PSE Persistence (cont.)

		PSE Persistence			
		Enrolled or Earned Degree(s)		Dropout	
		Count	Row %	Count	Row %
INDIVIDUAL					
Std Test (1992 NELS Test) Quartile	Quartile 1 Low	435	52.0	401	48.0
	Quartile 2	886	63.1	519	36.9
	Quartile 3	1,345	72.7	506	27.3
	Quartile 4 High	2,033	85.0	359	15.0
	Missing or Test Not Comp	1,069	67.6	512	32.4
Indicator if Took SAT or ACT	Took SAT or ACT	4,748	78.0	1,337	22.0
	Took Neither SAT nor ACT/Missing/Refusal/Don't Know	1,020	51.5	960	48.5
Taking Advanced Math Courses	Trigonometry/Precalculus Only	1,583	84.5	291	15.5
	Calculus	979	91.6	90	8.4
	No Trigonometry/Precalculus/Calculus/Missing	3,206	62.6	1,916	37.4
Sector for Most Recent PSE Attended	Don't Know or Missing	76	86.4	12	13.6
	Public, 4-Year or Above	2,686	80.8	640	19.2
	Private Nonprofit	1,482	88.6	191	11.4
	Private For-Profit	457	74.4	157	25.6
	Public, 2-Year or Less	1,067	45.1	1,297	54.9
STATE		Mean			
Financial Indicators	90s Average Need-Based Grant in 1,000 Dollars	0.257			
	90s Average Non-need Grant in 1,000 Dollars	0.062			
	90s Average Public System Undergraduate In-state Tuition in 1,000	2.751			

Students who started in other types of colleges had higher persistence rates.

The average public tuition charge during the eight years was higher than was the average in the year of initial enrollment. State funding for need-based grants also increased. Future studies should examine annual funding on year-to-year transitions as a means of untangling how policy changes influenced persistence.

Regression Analysis

The regression analysis indicates there were differences in attainment related to all of the variables included in these models. Given the themes emphasized in the NCES research, it is important to consider background, preparation, and finance.

First, there were significant differences in the opportunity to attain degrees based on background:

- Males were less likely than females to attain degrees of any type.
- Asian Americans and African Americans were more likely than were Whites/others to be currently enrolled, while Hispanics were less likely to have attained either bachelor's or advanced degrees. In addition, Asian Americans had modestly higher odds (.1 alpha) of attaining a bachelor's degree and Hispanics were modestly less likely to have attained an advanced degree.
- High-income students had significantly higher odds than middle-income students to have attained either bachelor's or advanced degrees. In contrast, low-income students had modestly lower odds (.1 alpha) than middle-income students of having a B.A. and modestly higher odds of being currently enrolled.
- Students whose parents had college degrees were more likely than students whose parents had not finished college to have attained bachelor's or master's degrees, but less likely to have attained two-year degrees/ certificates. In addition, compared to students whose

parents did not have degrees, students whose parents had advanced degrees were more likely to have attained a bachelor's or advanced degree or to be still enrolled.
- In addition, compared to students who did not aspire to attend college, students who aspired to complete college and to get advanced degrees were more likely to have attained both bachelor's and advanced degrees.

The question is which background variables should be emphasized. NCES studies clearly zeroed in on parents' education and deemphasized income and ethnicity (Choy, 2002). Statistically, all of the variables noted above are significant, so the choice of emphasis is value based. What seems compelling, relative to the intent of federal Title IV programs, is that income is significant even when several of the correlates with income (parents' education, race/ethnicity, and so forth) are also significant. In addition, readers are reminded that these analyses control for the effects of preparation and state funding policies.

Second, there were also significant differences in attainment related to preparation:

- Scores on standardized tests were associated with attainment. Compared to students without a reported test score, students in the lowest quartile were less likely to have attained bachelor's or advanced degrees and to be still enrolled, students in the low-middle quartile were more likely to have associate's degrees/certificates and less likely to have advanced degrees, and students in the highest quartile were less likely to have associate's degrees/certificates and more likely to have bachelor's and advanced degrees.
- Compared to students who did not take SAT/ACT exams, students who took these tests were more likely to have completed bachelor's and advanced degrees.

- Compared to students who had not taken advanced math, students who took trigonometry were more likely to have attained a bachelor's or advanced degree and to be currently enrolled and students who completed calculus were more likely to have bachelor's and master's degrees and less likely to have associate's degrees/certificates.

The attainment patterns are consistent with the role of preparation in college enrollment, so it is difficult to untangle the relative importance of these same variables in attainment. Nevertheless, it is appropriate to conclude that, controlling for background and state finance, academic preparation contributed to educational attainment. However, there is not a solid statistical reason to limit the emphasis to advanced math, which was the consistent pattern in the NCES studies (Choy, 2002).

Finally, the second-level variables were not significant. During the eight-year period, variations across states in the amounts of public-sector tuition charged or in state funding for grants were not significant. However, it is essential that we interpret findings in college enrollment in relation to the role and influence of these variables on enrollment. We also need to interpret findings on persistence in relation to the impact of background variables (these analyses).

It is crucial to note the substantial role that state funding for need-based grants played in enrollment by low- and middle-income students in four-year year public and private colleges. College costs and low funding for need-based grants created substantial barriers to access—even to getting into this analysis group. And it is reasonable to expect that states with funding that enables enrollment also have funding sufficient to promote persistence, controlling for preparation.

Table 10. HLM Multinomial Regression Analysis of Attainment Outcomes
HLM PSE Persistence Outcomes

Level 1: Individual	Associate/Certificate		B.A./B.S.		M.A., Ph.D., Professional		Still Enrolled	
	Odds Ratio	Sig.	Odds Ratio	Sig.	Odds Ratio	Sig.	Odds Ratio	Sig.
Gender								
Male	0.788	***	0.749	***	0.546	***	1.096	
Female								
Race/Ethnicity								
Asian/Pacific Islander	0.947		1.298	*	1.348		1.608	***
Hispanic	0.946		0.683	***	0.655	*	1.163	
Black, not Hispanic	0.982		0.977		0.897		1.470	***
White, not Hispanic/Native American/Other/Missing								
Family Income Group								
Low (less than $25,000)	1.029		0.859	*	0.778		1.187	*
High ($75,000 or more)	0.934		1.746	***	2.208	***	1.262	
Multiple Response or Missing	0.971		1.159		1.379	*	1.270	**
Middle ($25,000-$74,999)								
Parent's Highest Education Level								
HS, Some College	0.914		1.134		0.904		1.059	
College Grad	0.778	**	1.783	***	1.616	**	1.031	
M.A. or Equal	0.907		2.982	***	3.351	***	1.561	**
Ph.D., M.D., Other	0.774		3.963	***	4.596	***	1.903	**
Didn't Finish HS/HS Grad/GED/Don't Know/Missing								
Postsecondary Education Plans								
VOC, TRD, BUS after HS	1.169		0.797		0.399		0.909	
Will Attend College	0.895		1.135		0.666		0.869	
Will Finish College	0.906		1.771	***	2.002	**	0.960	
Advanced Degree	0.881		1.873	***	2.859	***	1.145	
Won't Finish HS/Will Finish HS/Missing								

Table 10. HLM Multinomial Regression Analysis of Attainment Outcomes HLM PSE Persistence Outcomes (cont.)

Level 1: Individual	Associate/Certificate		B.A./B.S.		M.A., Ph.D., Professional		Still Enrolled	
	Odds Ratio	Sig.	Odds Ratio	Sig.	Odds Ratio	Sig.	Odds Ratio	Sig.
Std Test (1992 NELS Test) Quartile								
Quartile 1 Low	1.043		0.526	***	0.158	***	0.741	**
Quartile 2	1.214	**	0.838	*	0.631	**	0.840	
Quartile 3	1.094		1.169	*	0.851		0.869	
Quartile 4 High	0.697	***	1.446	***	1.482	**	0.869	
Missing or Test Not Comp								
Indicator If Took SAT or ACT								
Yes	0.961		4.702	***	8.097	***	1.104	
No or Missing or Refusal or Don't Know								
Taking Advanced Math Courses								
Trigonometry/Precalculus only	0.997		2.607	***	3.142	***	1.345	***
Calculus	0.620	**	4.105	***	6.665	***	1.361	*
No Trigonometry/Precalculus/Calculus/Missing								
Level 2: State								
State Financial Indicators								
90s Average Need-Based Grant in 1,000 Dollars	1.103		1.329		1.614		1.068	
90s Average Non-need Grant in 1,000 Dollars	1.233		1.334		1.582		1.057	
90s Average Public System Undergraduate In-state Tuition in 1,000 Dollars	1.083		1.054		1.035		0.957	
Random Effect	Variance	Sig.						
Level-2 Effect: Category 1 (Associate/Certificate)	0.017	***						
Level-2 Effect: Category 2 (B.A./B.S.)	0.071	***						
Level-2 Effect: Category 2 (M.A., Ph.D., Professional)	0.070	***						
Level-2 Effect: Category 2 (Still Attending)	0.015	***						

Note: *** $p<0.01$, ** $p<0.05$, * $p<0.1$

From these analyses (Table 10, as summarized above), we know that background variables were significant, indicating a pattern of inequality in attainment. In addition, income variables and the correlates with these variables (e.g., parents' education and race/ethnicity) were significantly associated with patterns of attainment. Thus, given the role of finance in initial enrollment, we must hypothesize that *the levels of public funding were not sufficient to equalize opportunity for attainment by low- and middle-income students, controlling for preparation.* However, future research on the year-to-year transitions would be needed to test this hypothesis.

Conclusions and Implications

This reanalysis of NELS was necessary because of the systematic pattern of statistical errors and misinterpretations in the NCES studies. The reanalysis reported here corrects for many of the statistical errors made in the NCES studies. Our findings are summarized below in relation to the four central claims made in the NCES studies. Then, we consider the implications for policy and research.

Claims in NCES Studies Reconsidered

Claim 1: Parents' education is the most important background variable in access and persistence. This was the first conclusion in the summary of the report on the NCES studies (Choy, 2002), and parents' education was a central issue in the NCES research (NCES, 2001). Our reanalysis did not screen out students who had not taken required courses or who had not graduated from high school. Rather, dichotomous and design coding was used to retain all possible students in the analysis. Controlling for preparation, there were major differences across income groups in college destinations. And parents' education was associated with the enrollment patterns of low-income students, but the effect of parents' education was not substantially greater than that of race/ethnicity or other background variables. In other words, there was not a statistical reason to emphasize parents' education in enrollment.

In addition, the attainment analysis of students who had enrolled after high school revealed that most background variables were significant in the extent of attainment. Race/ethnicity and income, in addition to parents' education, were statistically significant. The most compelling statistical finding was that high-income students had substantially higher opportunity than middle-income students, controlling for preparation and other background variables. Therefore, the NCES conclusion about the centrality of parents' education was not correct.

Claim 2: Advanced math courses are the most important indicator of academic preparation. For decades economists and policy researchers have considered the role of preparation in access and attainment (Jackson, 1978; Manski & Wise, 1983; Perna, 2005; St. John & Noell, 1989). What distinguished the education research sponsored by the U.S. Department of Education (Adelman, 1999, 2004; NCES, 1997, 2001; Pelavin & Kane, 1988) was the consideration of the courses students actually took in higher school, rather than self-reports of academic track. This represented a step forward. However, the NCES studies misused this powerful data tool. In particular, the construction of an index of multiple variables related to preparation (i.e., NCES, 1997) is replete with statistical errors, including selection bias (Becker, 2004; Heller, 2004).

This reanalysis considered variables related to test scores, to taking the SAT/ACT, and to taking advanced math courses. All of these variables were associated with whether and where students enrolled in college as well as with their success in college. These findings confirm understandings of preparation that have been well known for decades. However, these findings do not support the argument that advanced math courses are the best indicator of preparation. The facts that nearly two-thirds of the students entered college without advanced math as part of their preparation and that more than half of these students persisted should dispel this myth.

It is important to recognize that there are multiple indicators of preparation. Further, all of the indicators of preparation used in this study were statistically related to enrollment, persistence, and attainment.

Claim 3: Plans to attend college and college applications are important indicators of enrollment. The NCES research has confirmed a long-standing understanding that enrollment and persistence are related to student aspirations (Jackson, 1978; Manski & Wise, 1983; Paulsen & St. John, 2002; St. John, Kirshstein, & Noell, 1991). In these analyses students' aspirations were associated with enrollment, the type of college attended, persistence, and degree attainment (St. John & associates, in review).

Claim 4: College prices do not deter enrollment by low-income students who take the necessary steps toward enrollment. This conclusion was reached and repeated in NCES studies based on manipulations of variables related to application. In NELS and prior longitudinal studies, high school seniors were asked a battery of questions about whether they applied, why they applied, and what factors were considered important in applications. NCES (1997a) used self-reports of application during the senior year to screen students out of their analyses. NCES concluded that among the students who took the steps to prepare (including applying for college) there were no racial/ethnic or income inequalities. There are serious problems with this approach (Becker, 2004; Heller, 2004; St. John, 2002, 2003), so we do not reexamine this self-reported variable.

It should be noted that prior studies of college using longitudinal databases had developed appropriate means for contending with this ambiguity. For example, several studies had treated both students who reported applying and students who had enrolled as applicants because some students who did not self-report on the survey actually enrolled in college (e.g., Jackson, 1978; St. John & Noell, 1989). Thus, NCES had means available to make appropriate adjustments to self-reported application information. More sophisticated techniques of adjustment are now being tested by researchers (Becker, 2004), but the problem has been well understood for decades, and NCES chose to use a biased treatment of application variables.

In this study, we used state finance variables in two-level models to assess the effects of public finance on enrollment and attainment. Since students have well-defined states of residence, it was possible to assess the effects of public-sector tuition charges and funding for state grants on enrollment and attainment. The findings indicated that both tuition and need-based grants had significant associations with college enrollment by both low-income and middle-income students. In addition, high-income students were substantially more likely to attain degrees than middle- or low-income students, controlling for other variables. Thus, *there were financial inequalities in opportunity for enrollment and attainment for low- and middle-income students compared to high-income students.* Equally prepared students with low and middle incomes had significantly reduced postsecondary opportunity compared to their wealthier peers.

Implications

Building on prior efforts to reanalyze NELS (e.g., Fitzgerald, 2004; Lee, 2004), the analyses in this chapter correct for major errors made by NCES. When these corrections are made, it is apparent that the NCES studies promoted unsupported myths, much as an ideologically based set of novellas might do. However, in this case, many millions of public dollars were used to collect and manipulate data to tell this mythical story. The major theme running through these misanalyses and narratives has been that there is equal educational opportunity in the U.S. for students who take the steps to prepare for college. This rationale, along with multiple manipulations, was used to disguise fundamental inequalities in educational opportunity. It is important to take a step back and consider the implications of this story telling for the policy research community and policy makers.

The policy research community is comprised of government researchers and contract officers, researchers in the private sector who contract with the government, researchers within public interest groups and lobby groups, and university researchers. The NCES studies illustrate that researchers can make errors when they try to conform their research to policy positions. The ideological argument that preparation is the greatest equalizer was promoted by politicians and lobby groups (e.g., Finn, 2001; King, 1999; Paige, 2003). However, it was unfortunate that so many researchers failed to consider both preparation and financial aid. Many of the limitations of the longitudinal databases have been known and appropriately treated (e.g., Jackson, 1978, 1988; Manski & Wise, 1983). There was no reasonable justification for the systematic pattern of errors and omissions in the NCES studies (Becker, 2004; Fitzgerald, 2004; Heller, 2004).

Instead of testing alternative explanations and setting out to prove the null hypothesis, the NCES researchers designed research to document and illustrate a belief. The fact that commonly accepted statistical methods were used in these studies seems largely inconsequential because so little care was taken in the design of the research. The alternative to testing a single hypothesis and the null of the hypothesis is designing research to test multiple hypotheses or claims, an approach that is particularly relevant to research on student choice and higher education finance (St. John, 2003; St. John & Hossler, 1998; St. John & Paulsen, 2001).

While it is may not be easy for researchers to stand up to political power, it is necessary that they do so, at least with respect to the design of research and the testing of political claims. Faculty members in public policy schools and education programs must rethink the content and methods used in their professional programs so as to enable their graduates to be prepared to design research to test claims rather than to build evidence supporting positions. This distinction is crucial and should not be overlooked by policy researchers or faculty in graduate programs.

In contrast to policy researchers, people who become legislators, government officials, and executives in universities have a wide range of backgrounds. Typically, politicians and bureaucrats are not trained in statistics and research design. When confronted with evidence contradicting strongly held beliefs, they may seek confirmatory evidence. It is crucial that researchers who provide evidence avoid falling into the trap of building a case for a policy position at the expense of quality research.

Both academic preparation and higher education finance are clearly important issues. Two decades of focusing on preparation and ignoring public finance have been costly with respect to equal opportunity in this country. In the middle 1970s, there was nearly equal opportunity across racial/ethnic groups for high school graduates to enroll in college—a condition not evident in the decades since (St. John, 1993). For the 1992 cohort, there was not equal opportunity for equally prepared students across income groups.

The two key findings of this study were

- State funding for need-based grants had a significant influence on enrollment opportunities for low- and middle-income students, and both groups had lower odds of attaining degrees, controlling for preparation, compared to high-income students.
- Preparation is crucial for students' success, as can be documented by a number of indicators. However, advanced math courses are not the most important indicator of academic preparation as the majority of the students who do not complete these courses have success in college.

Given these findings, policy makers should engage in a process of rethinking both the academic regulations and the financial policies used to promote college access. While outreach can help, if students lack the opportunities to prepare and to pay for college, then outreach cannot work for the majority of students who have historically been denied access.

References

Adelman, C. (1995). *The new college course map and transcript files: Changes in course-taking and achievement, 1972-1993.* Washington, DC: National Center for Education Statistics.

Adelman, C. (1999). *Answers in the tool box: Academic intensity, attendance patterns, and bachelor's degree attainment.* Washington, DC: National Center for Education Statistics.

Adelman, C. (2004). *Principle indicators of student academic histories in postsecondary education, 1972-2000.* Washington, DC: U.S. Department of Education, Institute of Education Sciences.

Astin, A. W. (1975). *Preventing students from dropping out.* San Francisco: Jossey-Bass.

Becker, G. S. (1964). *Human capital: A theoretical and empirical analysis with special reference to education.* New York: Columbia University Press.

Becker, W. E. (2004). Omitted variables and sample selection in studies of college-going decisions. In E. P. St. John (Ed.), *Readings on equal education: Vol. 19. Public policy and college access: Investigating the federal and state roles in equalizing postsecondary opportunity* (pp. 65-86). New York: AMS Press, Inc.

Blau, P. M., & Duncan, O. D. (1967). *The American occupational structure.* New York: Wiley.

Choy, S. P. (2002). *Access & persistence: Findings from 10 years of longitudinal research on students.* Washington, DC: American Council on Education.

Finn, C. E., Jr. (2001, February 21). College isn't for everyone. *USA Today*, A4.

Fitzgerald, B. (2004). Federal financial aid and college access. In E. P. St. John (Ed.), *Readings on equal education: Vol.*

19. Public policy and college access: Investigating the federal and state roles in equalizing postsecondary opportunity (pp. 1-28). New York: AMS Press, Inc.

Heller, D. E. (2004). NCES research on college participation: A critical analysis. In E. P. St. John (Ed.), *Readings on equal education: Vol. 19. Public policy and college access: Investigating the federal and state roles in equalizing postsecondary opportunity* (pp. 29-64). New York: AMS Press, Inc.

Jackson, G. A. (1978). Financial aid and student enrollment. *The Journal of Higher Education, 49,* 548-574.

Jackson, G. A. (1988). Did college choice change during the seventies? *Economics of Education Review, 7,* 15-27.

Kazis, R. (2004). Introduction. In R. Kazis, J. Vargas, & N. Hoffman (Eds.), *Double the numbers: Increasing postsecondary credentials for underrepresented youth.* Cambridge: Harvard Education Press.

King, J. E. (1999). Conclusion. In J. E. King (Ed.), *Financing a college education: How it works, how it's changing* (pp. 198-202). Westport, CT: American Council on Education/Oryx Press.

Lee, J. B. (2004). Access revisited: A preliminary reanalysis of NELS. In E. P. St. John (Ed.), Readings on equal education: Vol. 19. Public policy and college access: Investigating the federal and state roles in equalizing postsecondary opportunity (pp. 87-96). New York: AMS Press, Inc.

Manski, C. F., & Wise, D. A. (1983). College choice in America. Cambridge, MA: Harvard University Press.

Martinez, M. R., & Doniskeller, C. (2004). Theme schools: A model for restructuring high schools. In R. Kazis, J. Vargas & N. Hoffman (Eds.), *Double the numbers: Increasing postsecondary credentials for underrepresented youth* (pp. 189-195). Cambridge: Harvard Education Press.

National Center for Education Statistics. (1997). *Access to higher postsecondary education for the 1992 high school graduates.* NCES 98-105. By L. Berkner & L. Chavez. Project Officer: C. D. Carroll. Washington, DC: Author.

National Center for Education Statistics. (2001). *Students whose parents did not go to college: Postsecondary access, persistence, and attainment.* By S. Choy. Washington, DC: Author.

Paige, R. (2003, January 10). More spending is not the answer. Opposing view: Improving quality of schools calls for high standards, accountability. *USA Today,* A11.

Paulsen, M. B. (2001a). The economics of human capital and investment in higher education. In M. B. Paulsen & J. C. Smart (Eds.), *The finance of higher education: Theory, research, policy & practice* (pp. 55-94). New York: Agathon Press.

Paulsen, M. B. (2001b). The economics of the public sector: The nature and role of public policy in higher education finance. In M. B. Paulsen & J. C. Smart (Eds.), *The finance of higher education: Theory, research, policy & practice* (pp. 95-132), New York: Agathon Press.

Paulsen, M. B., & St. John, E. P. (2002). Social class and college costs: Examining the financial nexus between college choice and persistence. *The Journal of Higher Education, 73*(3), 189-236.

Pelavin, S. H., & Kane, M. B. (1988). *Minority participation in higher education.* Prepared for the U.S. Department of Education, Office of Planning, Budget and Evaluation. Washington, DC: Pelavin Associates.

Pelavin, S. H., & Kane, M. B. (1990). *Changing the odds: Factors increasing access to college.* New York: College Board.

Peng, C. Y. J., So, T. H., Stage, F. K., & St. John, E. P. (2002). The use and interpretation of logistic regression in higher education journals: 1988-1999. *Research in Higher Education, 43*(3), 259-294.

Perna, L. W. (2005). The key to access: Rigorous academic preparation. In W. G. Tierney, Z. B. Corwin, & J. E. Colyar,

Preparing for college: Nine elements of effective outreach (pp. 113-134) Albany: State University of New York Press.

St. John, E. P. (1989). The influence of student aid on persistence. *Journal of Student Financial Aid, 19*(3), 52-68.

St. John, E. P. (1991). What really influences minority attendance? Sequential analyses of the high school and beyond sophomore cohort. *Research in Higher Education, 32*(2), 141-158.

St. John, E. P. (2002). *The access challenge: Rethinking the causes of the new inequality.* Policy Issue Report No. 2002-01. Bloomington, IN: Indiana Education Policy Center.

St. John, E. P. (2003). *Refinancing the college dream: Access, equal opportunity, and justice for taxpayers.* Baltimore, MD: Johns Hopkins University Press.

St. John, E. P. (2004). Conclusions and implications. In E. P. St. John (Ed.), *Readings on equal education: Vol. 20. Improving access and college success for diverse students: Studies of the Gates Millennium Scholars Program* (pp. 265-282). New York: AMS Press, Inc.

St. John, E. P., & Associates. (in press). *Education and the public interest: School reform, public finance, and access to higher education.* Dordrecht, The Netherlands: Springer.

St. John, E. P., Cabrera, A. F., Nora, A., & Asker, E. H. (2000). Economic influences on persistence reconsidered: How can finance research inform the reconceptualization of persistence models? In J. M. Braxton (Ed.), *Reworking the student departure puzzle* (pp. 29-47). Nashville: Vanderbilt University Press.

St. John, E. P., Chung, C. G., Musoba, G. D., & Simmons, A. B. (2004). Financial access: The impact of state financial strategies. In E. P. St. John (Ed.), *Readings on equal education: Vol. 19. Public policy and college access: Investigating the federal and state roles in equalizing postsecondary opportunity* (pp. 109-129). New York: AMS Press, Inc.

St. John, E. P., Chung, C. G., Musoba, G. D., Simmons, A. B., Wooden, O. S., & Mendez, J. (2004). *Expanding college access: The impact of state finance strategies.* Indianapolis: Lumina Foundation for Education.

St. John, E. P., & Hossler, D. (1998). Higher education desegregation in the post-*Fordice* legal environment: A critical-empirical perspective. In R. E. Fossey (Ed.), *Readings on equal education: Vol. 15. Race, the courts, and equal education: The limits of the law* (pp.123-156). New York: AMS Press, Inc.

St. John, E. P., Kirshstein, R., & Noell, J. (1991). The effects of student aid on persistence: A sequential analysis of the high school and beyond senior cohort. *Review of Higher Education, 14*, 383-406.

St. John, E. P., Musoba, G. D., & Chung, C. G. (2004). Academic access: The impact of state education policies. In E. P. St. John (Ed.), *Readings on equal education: Vol. 19. Public policy and college access: Investigating the federal and state roles in equalizing postsecondary opportunity* (pp. 131-151). New York: AMS Press, Inc.

St. John, E. P., & Noell, J. (1989). The impact of financial aid on access: An analysis of progress with special consideration of minority access. *Research in Higher Education, 30*(6), 563-582.

St. John, E. P., & Paulsen, M. B. (2001). The finance of higher education: Implications for theory, research, policy and practice. In M. B. Paulsen & J. C. Smart (Eds.), *The finance of higher education: Theory, research, policy & practice* (pp. 11-38). New York: Agathon.

Terkla, D. G. (1985). Does financial aid enhance undergraduate persistence? *The Journal of Higher Education, 15*(3), 11-18.

CHAPTER 10

DIVERSITY AND PERSISTENCE IN INDIANA HIGHER EDUCATION: THE IMPACT OF PREPARATION, MAJOR CHOICES, AND STUDENT AID

Edward P. St. John, Deborah F. Carter, Choong-Geun Chung, and Glenda Droogsma Musoba

The concept of the K-16 pipeline, a major focus in the policy literature on education, proposes a strong relationship between high school curriculum and college enrollment. Stimulated by reports from the U.S. Department of Education that used descriptive and correlation statistics to examine the relationship between high school curriculum and college enrollment (Choy, 2002; National Center for Education Statistics [NCES], 1997a, 1997b, 2001a, 2001b), many states, including Indiana (Indiana Commission for Higher Education, 2003), have used this logic to promote new requirements for high school graduation and admission to public colleges and universities. The NCES reports focused in particular on the relationship between taking advanced mathematics courses in high school and enrollment in college but also pointed to parent education and the high school peer group. These policy arguments raise a number of complex questions for higher education institutions related to outreach, admissions, and retention.

These efforts to reform high schools have potential implications for diversity on college campuses. This chapter takes a step forward in the research-based conversation about pathways for diverse students in K-16 systems by analyzing the impact of a high school curriculum and other policy-related variables on persistence by African Americans, Hispanics, and Whites enrolled in a state system of higher education. Using a class of students who graduated from Indiana's public high schools in 2000 and enrolled in college the next academic year, this study examines the impact of academic preparation, student aid, and college academic experience on persistence in college. As background, we first describe the logical model used in the study in relation to the policy context for this study. This is followed by a discussion of research methods, findings, and a conclusion that considers implications for policy and practice in higher education.

Background

The policy debate on K-16 education is one of three major issues facing states and institutions of higher education as they adapt to the education policy environment of the early 21st century. The other crucial issues include concerns about public financing of students and public institutions, accountability of public institutions, and accountability for students' achievement.

The K-16 Pipeline

Federal efforts to define a college preparatory curriculum could be a boon for higher education if the changes in curriculum really do enable more students to prepare for college. However, the efforts to transform high schools from the old comprehensive model to fit the new preparatory model raise questions about pathways into and through college. Do students preparing for the arts need the same type of preparatory curriculum as student preparing for math and science? Is it possible that the academic pathways into higher education are far more complex than conceptualized by the narrow pipeline concept?

Another *critical question,* and a focal point in this study, is *how might the efforts to change high school curriculum and graduation requirements influence educational opportunities for diverse groups?* Indiana has been in the forefront nationally on curriculum reform (St. John, Musoba, & Chung, 2004a); therefore, it makes good sense to address this critical question by examining Indiana students. There is a great deal of evidence that minority students in general attend high schools that offer fewer advanced courses but that high achieving minority college students often have had the opportunity to acquire these courses (Trent, Gong, & Owens-Nicholson, 2004). From this perspective, there could be advantages in extending advanced curriculum to all high schools.

Efforts to reform the high school curriculum face many obstacles. There has been a historic problem with ensuring that predominantly minority high schools have teachers who are prepared to teach advanced courses, especially the advanced math courses that are central to the new rationale for academic preparation. Is it possible that these new policies, coupled with limitations in teacher preparation, could push more students out of the educational system altogether, causing higher dropout rates? Indeed, a recent trend analysis of the impact of K-12 education policies on high school graduation rates in the states revealed that many of the new policies, including the requirement of more math courses for graduation and the implementation of math standards, were associated with lower high school graduation rates in states (St. John, Musoba, & Chung, 2004a).

Therefore, studies of the relationships between academic preparation in high schools and success in colleges are important from a policy perspective in states. They can inform policy makers who are interested in promoting these new policies about alternative conceptions of the policies as well as provide information to college faculty and administrators who are trying to adapt to these new initiatives.

The Underlying Problem of Public Finance
Higher education in most states has been adapting to the decline in public support of colleges and college students. Over the

past two decades, the purchasing power of federal Pell grants has declined by more than half, leaving large numbers of prepared students without financial access to four-year colleges (Advisory Committee on Student Financial Assistance [ACSFA], 2001, 2002; Fitzgerald, 2004; Lee, 2004; St. John, 2002). Tuition charges have also climbed in public colleges as a response to the decline in tax subsidies per student (Hauptman, 1990; St. John, 1994, 2003).

Some states have responded to these conditions by implementing merit-based grant programs (Heller, 2004). These programs remain controversial for a couple of reasons. A few studies have found that merit aid programs improve access for Whites and middle-income students, but not for minorities (Dynarski, 2002). Further, a recent time-series analysis of the impact of state grant programs confirmed that state funding for non-need grants was associated with improvement in college enrollment rates for high school graduates but also revealed that funding for these programs was associated with higher high school dropout rates (St. John, Chung, Musoba, Simmons, Wooden, & Mendez, 2004), an undesirable consequence.

In addition, most states have failed to make sufficient investments in need-based grants to equalize opportunity for enrollment and persistence. The recent time-series study of state grant programs found that funding for need-based grants was substantially and positively associated with college enrollment rates in the states without the negative influence on high school graduation rates (St. John et al., 2004). So it is crucial that states maintain a sufficient investment in grants to equalize enrollment and persistence rates for all students. There is substantial evidence that Indiana, the state being used as a basis for this study, has maintained equal opportunity for low-income students to enroll in four-year colleges (St. John, Musoba, Simmons, & Chung, 2002; St. John, Musoba, Simmons, Chung, Schmit, & Peng, 2004) and to persist (Hu & St. John, 2001; St. John, Hu, & Weber, 1999, 2000, 2001).

Thus, research on the academic pipeline to higher education should consider the role of finances along with the role of preparation. Indeed, a balanced approach to research is needed in persistence just as it is needed in access studies (St. John, 2002, 2003; St. John & Hu, 2004). This chapter addresses these concerns by integrating variables related to student financial aid and high school persistence into a comprehensive persistence model.

The Push Toward Public Accountability
There has been relatively rapid movement toward accountability systems in public higher education in recent years (Zumeta, 2001). Most states have implemented some form of a reporting or accountability system for higher education that includes reporting on persistence rates (Zumeta, 2001), a pattern of policy practice that will probably accelerate if the federal government requires more emphasis on public accountability to maintain funding in student aid programs authorized under Title IV of the Higher Education Act.

The prospect that states will use accountability systems for funding further complicates efforts to untangle the effects of K-12 reforms and public finance strategies. If institutions receive more funding because they attract students who are already prepared for college, then this unintended consequence of public policy could undermine efforts to maintain or improve diversity in public higher education. It is crucial, therefore, that efforts be made to understand the effects of education and public finance policies on persistence by diverse students and low-income students of all types (St. John, Kline, & Asker, 2001).

The Pathways Project, funded by the Lumina Foundation for Education, includes an assessment of the effects of preparation and student financial aid on the educational choices by students in the 2000 high school cohort in Indiana (St. John, Musoba, & Chung, 2004b). The Pathways analyses provide an alternative to accountability systems that rely on persistence rates and other narrow indicators without adjusting for the complexity of the educational choice process of diverse groups. This chapter provides analyses of continuous enrollment by African Americans, Hispanics, and Whites in the Indiana 2000 cohort and compares the results to the analyses of the population as a whole.

Situating the Pathways Approach

There has long been interest in research on the impact of financial aid and other public policies on persistence by college students (Astin, 1975; Leslie & Brinkman, 1988; Murdock, 1989). In fact, studies that examine the impact of finances on persistence, appropriately referred to as financial impact models (St. John, Cabrera, Nora, & Asker, 2000), predate the person-institution fit or involvement models proposed by Tinto and Bean.

The fit models proposed by Tinto (1975, 1987, 1993) and Bean (1980, 1983, 1985, 1990) have been widely tested and replicated (Braxton, 2000; Pascarella & Terenzini, 1991). These fit models have been adapted to include the role of perceptions of finances—the ability to pay or the financial reasons for choosing a college—along with financial effects (Cabrera, Nora, & Castaæda, 1992, 1993; St. John, Cabrera, Nora, & Asker, 2000; St. John, Paulsen, & Starkey, 1996).

More recent studies have extended the inquiry into the relationships between fit, or involvement, and finances (St. John, 2004). Analyses that examine the effects of finances and perceptions of finances on academic and social involvement in college for high achieving students of color reveal that involvement is substantially influenced by finances. Further, the effects of variables related to finances and perceptions of finances on persistence were largely unaltered by the inclusion of variables related to academic and social involvement.

However, the adapted models that integrate consideration of finances and fit are not adequate to address the policy issues discussed above. To be useful for this task, a reconceptualization was needed. In this context, the student choice construct (St. John, Asker, & Hu, 2001) was used as the logical guide for the development of a new set of analyses of student education choices

(St. John, Musoba, & Chung, 2004b). For traditional-age college students, these analyses examine

- The impact of student background, academic preparation, and SAT scores (base variables for the cohort) and student aid packages on college choice;
- The impact of the base variables for the cohort plus the types of colleges they attended, their college academic experiences, and student aid packages on major choices; and
- The impact of the base variables for the cohort, their college choices, their college academic experiences, their major choices, and student financial aid packages on persistence (in analyses of within-year, freshman-to-sophomore-year, and continuous enrollment).

By analyzing this sequence of choices, it is possible to untangle the diverse ways curriculum and finance policies influence the educational choices students make. This type of comprehensive study of student cohorts is necessary, given the complex set of issues facing educational researchers who are concerned about K-16 policy. This chapter presents the analyses of the continuous enrollment of three racial/ethnic groups and compares the results to the findings in the basic analysis of the entire population.

The easiest way for public institutions to raise persistence rates in response to new accountability standards, given the expected increase in the size of the traditional-age cohort (NCES, 2003), is by tightening admissions standards. However, not only would this approach overlook the most critical challenge in persistence, but it would increase inequalities in access. The model used in this study provides a mechanism that institutions can use to respond to this challenge. The persistence model used for the academic pathways analyses provides an alternative way of responding to political pressures for accountability, a way which examines the factors that influence educational opportunities, including persistence, for diverse students.

Research Approach

This study used a database on the 2000 college cohort of Indiana high school graduates constructed from College Board questionnaires and SAT scores for all seniors in the cohort, student records reported by public and private colleges, and student aid records. These sources of information are generally available to colleges and universities, if they take steps to protect human subjects, and, therefore, the models used here can be replicated by other institutions and states.

In this study the persistence model (with variables outlined above) was used to examine continuous enrollment by African Americans, Hispanics, and Whites. There were substantially fewer Asians, Native Americans, and students in other racial/ethnic groups in this sample, so these groups could not be separately examined.

Persistence Model Specifications

For the past several years, first-to-second-year persistence has been widely used in persistence studies, in part because institutions are concerned about retaining students. However, within-year persistence has provided a more viable approach to assessing the impact of public policies on retention, particularly finance policies. Using continuous enrollment during the first two years of college as a persistence outcome combines features of both approaches, responding to institutional concerns about retaining students with an explicit concern about examining the impact of public policies on attainment. The academic pathways analyses in this chapter examine the influence of variables related to student background, high school preparation, SAT scores, the types of institution attended, major choices, college academic experiences, and student aid. The database was constructed from College Board questionnaires and college student records from public and private colleges and state agencies in Indiana. An attempt was made to code variables in a way that would retain all possible cases by including categorical variables with a "missing value" category.

Background variables relate to gender, family income, parents' education, and high school locale (Table 1). Income was derived from college enrollment records and state student financial aid records and, as a secondary source, from student self-reports on College Board questionnaires. Students with low incomes, high incomes, and missing incomes were compared to students in the middle group.[1] Parents' education was derived from College Board data and student aid records. Students with missing information and parents' education of a high school diploma or less were compared to students whose parents had attained at least some college, an approach that allows us to consider claims about first-generation college students (e.g., Choy, 2002). Students who went to high school in urban or rural areas were compared to students from suburbs, towns, or missing locale information.

Academic Preparation variables relate types of high school diplomas (an indicator of the level of advancement of high school courses) and grades (an indicator of achievement). Students who completed Core 40 diplomas (a basic college preparatory curriculum), who received honors diplomas (requiring additional advanced math, language, and science), and who had missing information on curriculum were compared to students with regular diplomas. College Board questionnaires on courses taken and college or financial aid application reports on the students' high school curriculum were used to derive diploma types. Students with A grades (3.66 GPA) or higher, C grades (2.33 GPA) or lower, and missing grades in high school were compared to students with B grades.

Data for variables related to *SAT scores* were derived from College Board reports of actual scores for Indiana high school

---

[1] Approximately three equal-sized groups were created with low income defined as below $30,000, middle income as between $30,000 and $70,000, and high income as over $70,000 per annum.

students, and college enrollment records on SAT scores were a secondary source. Students with high scores (half a deviation above the mean on the combined score), low scores (half a deviation below the mean on the combined score), and missing scores were compared to students in the mid-range (within one-half of a standard deviation). Because the College Board provided records for all public high school students, missing SAT scores probably mean the student did not take the SAT.

College Types compared students enrolled in different types of public colleges to students enrolled in two-year colleges. The types of four-year colleges in Indiana were state universities, regional campuses of the two public systems, the urban university, public research universities, and private colleges (most of the independent colleges, excluding the University of Notre Dame). The two-year colleges were in the process of merging into a community college system in 2000, the base year of enrollment for this study.

Majors were coded from institutional reports for the freshman year using the Classification of Instructional Programs (CIP) codes, which were collapsed into 11 general categories. Students in the humanities, arts, science/math, social science, health, business, education, computers, engineering, and other major fields were compared to students who were undeclared as freshmen.

College Academic Experiences variables relate to college grades, remedial education, enrollment status, and living on or off campus. Students with A grades, C grades or below, or missing grades were compared to students with B averages in college, using GPAs reported at the end of the freshman year. Students who had taken only remedial math, only remedial language, or both types of remedial courses were compared to students who did not take any remedial courses. Students who were full time in the first semester were compared to others. Students who delayed entry until the second semester of the freshman year were compared to fall starters. And students who lived on campus were compared to others who did not.

Student Aid variables were coded as packages. Students with grants but not loans, loans but not grants, grants and loans, or packages without loans or grants (usually including work-study) were compared to students who did not receive student aid. In addition, traditional-age students who were legally self-supporting, according to student aid regulations, were compared to others as a means of controlling for differences in the amount of aid students were eligible to receive.

Statistical Methods

The persistence analyses include both breakdown statistics and regression analyses. The breakdowns compare basic statistics—means or rates—for persisting students and nonpersisting students in each racial/ethnic group. Logistic regression analyses used generally accepted methods (Cabrera, 1994; Peng, So, Stage, & St. John, 2002). The logistic analyses present a sequential set of logistic regression analyses. Variables related to background, high school preparation, SAT scores, the types of institution attended, major choices, college academic experiences, and student aid were entered in seven steps for each racial/ethnic group. This approach allows for comparison of the significance of variables across models, providing a basis for exploring the meaning of changes in significance as confounding relationships (Peng et al., 2002).

Given that we present 21 logistic regression models, we decided to limit the statistics presented here for each model. We present the odds ratios because they provide a reasonable measure of relative probabilities. In addition, we present three levels of significance (.01, .05, and .1). The last of these measures indicates a weak association and is discussed as such.

Three model statistics are presented for each logistic analysis (model chi square, Nagelkerke R^2, and percentage correctly predicted). The Nagelkerke R^2s are pseudo measures[2] of the amount of variance explained, provided by SPSS. The percentage

---

[2] It is not possible to calculate a true R^2 in logistic regression.

correctly predicted provides an additional indicator of the quality of the model. The chi square indicates model fit. We used the pseudo R^2 as the general indicator of model quality as this measure is more generally understood among educational researchers.

Limitations

The analysis of extant data sources in persistence research was once rare in higher education research because of incomplete data and small samples, but it has become more generally accepted. The workable models approach (St. John, 1991, 1999; St. John & Somers, 1997; Somers, 1992; Somers & St. John, 1997), which uses extant data sources, has gained acceptance. Initially the workable models approach was developed to examine the relationship between financial aid and student attainment while controlling for related variables such as student background, academic preparation, and college experience.

While the original proposal for the workable models approach to institutional research focused on the variables needed to estimate the effects of student aid on persistence, it also recommended the option of including majors, remedial courses, and interventions intended to improve persistence. This study extends the workable models approach to build a cohort of students to track from high school through their first two years of college. There are three limitations associated with the use of large-scale analyses using extant data sources.

First, there is usually a relatively large amount of missing data elements. For example, while the majority of Indiana high school students take SAT exams, some students who enroll in college do not. In addition, colleges may not report grades of students who drop out during their first term and in other cases (e.g., courses that are not given letter grades). We often coded missing values in their own category in order to retain all possible cases. This approach provides persistence rates that are reasonable, relative to other types of commonly reported rates. If we excluded student cases with missing information, we would overestimate persistence because institutions collect and retain more information for students who persist than for students who drop out. Further, if we limited our analyses to cases with no missing data we would seriously misestimate the effects of independent variables on persistence. We use our understanding of these reporting anomalies in the discussion. However, we do not know all of the reasons for missing values, so readers should be cautious in their own interpretations of the meaning of missing data.

Second, there can be anomalies in the reporting of data by different types of institutions. For example, community colleges are less likely to have undeclared majors (St. John, Musoba, & Chung, 2004b). In addition, there are variations in grading policies, major programs, and aid packages along with variations in the reporting of these data across institutions. The combination of coding choices and the sequential method of analyses reveal some of these anomalies. We discuss these anomalies but cannot fully resolve inconsistencies.

Finally, the quality of state-level data collections could be improved, as is the case with federal-level data collections. Data collections are generally more likely to be improved over time if they are used. As part of the Pathways study and subsequent work, we have provided analytic reports to collaborating colleges and universities and this could encourage improvement of databases over time.

Findings

The persistence analyses for Whites, Hispanics, and African Americans are presented separately. African Americans were discussed last because of the distinctive patterns evident in the group. Both breakdown statistics and regression results are presented and discussed.

Whites

The descriptive statistics on persistence rates for each variable in the model are presented in Table 1 for Whites. Sixty-five percent (65.4%) of that population persisted. Whites who attended state universities (72.8%), research universities (77.9%), and private colleges (67.8%) persisted at higher rates than those in other types of institutions, i.e., the urban university, regional campuses, and community colleges. The persistence rates for Whites at regional campuses and two-year colleges were similar (about 54%), and the urban university had the lowest rate (51.3%). These statistics suggest that the type of institution attended is significantly associated with persistence for Whites.

Whites in most major fields persisted at higher rates than those who were undeclared. More than 60 percent of the students in all major categories enrolled continuously, except for other majors (57.1%). These differences suggest that most declared, compared to undeclared, majors are positively associated with persistence. Relatively large percentages of Whites were undeclared or had declared majors in business, education, and other majors. Science/math (72.8%), education (71.7%), arts (71.0%), and humanities (70.7%) had the highest persistence rates, and we would intuitively expect these majors to be positively associated with persistence.

Background variables had expected differentials in persistence rates for White students. High-income Whites persisted at a higher rate (72.7%) than other income groups. Students whose parents had at least some college persisted at a higher rate (71.8%) than students whose parents were less well educated. Students whose parents' education was missing or whose parents had less than a high school diploma persisted at lower rates (51.4% and 49.5% respectively). From these statistics we might expect that both income and parents' education would be associated with persistence.

Variable	Category	Persistence of Fall to Spring Freshman			
		Persisters		Nonpersisters '	
		N	Row %	N	Row %
College Destination in Freshman Year	State Universities	3,356	72.8	1,251	27.2
	Regional Campuses	2,835	54.2	2,393	45.8
	Urban University	1,183	51.3	1,121	48.7
	Research Universities	6,335	77.9	1,793	22.1
	Private	2,356	67.8	1,118	32.2
	2-year '	2,681	54.6	2,228	45.4
Major in Freshman Year	Humanities	618	70.7	256	29.3
	Arts	764	71.0	312	29.0
	Science and Math	1,419	72.8	529	27.2
	Social Science	1,080	69.6	472	30.4
	Health	1,401	65.5	739	34.5
	Business	2,501	67.5	1,205	32.5
	Education	2,277	71.7	897	28.3
	Computer	530	61.4	333	38.6
	Engineering	1,205	68.1	565	31.9
	Others	2,757	57.1	2,072	42.9
	Undecided '	4,194	62.4	2,524	37.6
Composite Gender	Male	8,565	63.8	4,854	36.2
	Female '	10,181	66.9	5,048	33.1
	Missing '			2	100.0
Composite Ethnicity	Native American				
	Asian American Pac. Islander				
	African American				
	Hispanic				
	White	18,746	65.4	9,904	34.6
	Other				
	Missing				
Composite Parent Income Level	Low (below $30,000)	2,755	61.0	1,760	39.0
	Mid ($30,000-$70,000) '	6,825	65.5	3,587	34.5
	High (over $70,000)	7,020	72.7	2,632	27.3
	Missing	2,146	52.7	1,925	47.3
Composite Parent Education Level	Middle/Jr high school or less	95	49.5	97	50.5
	High school	5,770	64.2	3,214	35.8
	College or beyond '	10,118	71.8	3,983	28.2
	Missing	2,763	51.4	2,610	48.6
Composite Locale	City	3,346	66.0	1,727	34.0
	Suburban and town '	8,525	66.6	4,267	33.4
	Rural	5,391	66.4	2,734	33.6
	Missing	1,484	55.8	1,176	44.2

Table 1. Breakdown of Persistence Rates for Variables in Analysis of Continuous Enrollment of Fall or Spring Freshman thru Spring Sophomore for White Students

Table 1. Breakdown of Persistence Rates for Variables in Analysis of Continuous Enrollment of Fall or Spring Freshman thru Spring Sophomore for White Students (cont.)

Variable	Category	Persistence of Fall to Spring Freshman			
		Persisters		Nonpersisters '	
		N	Row %	N	Row %
Composite High School Diploma	Honors	6,954	81.5	1,583	18.5
	Core 40	6,665	66.7	3,327	33.3
	Regular or Missing '	5,127	50.7	4,994	49.3
Composite High School GPA	A	5,383	82.0	1,178	18.0
	B '	7,790	67.9	3,681	32.1
	C or Lower	2,714	56.1	2,120	43.9
	Missing	2,859	49.4	2,925	50.6
Composite SAT Scores	High	5,780	75.9	1,835	24.1
	Mid '	6,252	69.1	2,801	30.9
	Low	3,803	58.7	2,677	41.3
	Missing	2,911	52.9	2,591	47.1
College Freshman GPA	A	5,241	81.6	1,179	18.4
	B '	9,502	77.9	2,700	22.1
	C or Lower	3,873	42.2	5,294	57.8
	Missing	130	15.1	731	84.9
Remedial Coursework in Freshman Year	Remedial Math only	1,500	52.6	1,353	47.4
	Remedial Lang. Arts only	420	49.9	421	50.1
	Remedial Math & Lang. Arts	826	51.9	765	48.1
	No Remedial Coursework '	16,000	68.5	7,365	31.5
Enrollment Status in First Semester	Full-time	17,332	68.2	8,083	31.8
	Part-time '	1,414	43.7	1,821	56.3
Delayed Enrollment in Spring as Fresh.	Delayed	1,294	49.0	1,347	51.0
	Not delayed '	17,452	67.1	8,557	32.9
Housing Status in Freshman Year	On-campus	8,134	75.1	2,701	24.9
	Others '	10,612	59.6	7,203	40.4
Dependency Status	Indeterminate status '	6,143	61.3	3,883	38.7
	Self-supporting	219	43.8	281	56.2
	Dependent '	12,384	68.3	5,740	31.7
Aid Packages	Grants only	5,347	68.9	2,408	31.1
	Loans only	2,425	66.1	1,245	33.9
	Grants and Loans	3,656	69.7	1,590	30.3
	Other Packages	1,083	68.3	502	31.7
	None '	6,235	60.0	4,159	40.0
Total		18,746	65.4	9,904	34.6

' is the reference category in regression.

Academic preparation and SAT scores also had the expected association with persistence rates for White students. Students with honors diplomas had higher persistence rates than students with Core 40, whose rates were higher than those of students with regular diplomas. In addition, grades and test scores were hierarchically associated with persistence, with higher persistence rates associated with high achievement on these indicators.

Similarly, college experiences were associated with persistence in expected ways, given the findings of the NCES studies (Choy, 2002; NCES, 1997a, 1997b, 2001a, 2001b). Whites with higher college grades had higher persistence rates. Students with remedial courses persisted at lower rates, as did students who delayed enrollment, attended part time, and so forth. In addition, students with grants only and loans only persisted at slightly higher rates than students who did not have aid.

If our goal were merely to use descriptive statistics to reach conclusions about educational attainment, then we might conclude that educational attainment is explained by parents' education and high school courses, as has been a central finding of federally funded research (Choy, 2002). However, it is crucial to control for events in the lives of students when examining student attainment, something NCES has failed to do (Becker, 2004; Heller, 2004). The sequential logistic regression analyses provide a means of examining the relative effects of background, preparation, and other variables on attainment, which are highly related to continuous enrollment during the first two years of college.

The logistic regression analyses of continuous enrollment by White students revealed some expected relationships along with some that were not predicted from the descriptive statistics (Table 2). The discussion below considers each block of variables, looking across the sequence.

Family background variables of White students had the expected relationship with persistence, but there were some interesting nuances. Males were less likely to persist than females, but only before academic preparation variables were added to the equation (Model 2). Similarly, low-income students were less likely to persist than middle-income students only before preparation was considered. However, high-income students were consistently more likely to persist. Students with missing income were less likely to persist after college choice was considered.[3] Finally, students whose parents had a high school education or less or who had missing values on this variable were less likely to persist than those whose parents had at least some college—an expected relationship.

High school preparation and test scores had expected relationships with persistence by Whites. Students with honors and Core 40 diplomas were more likely to persist than students with regular diplomas. Students with A grades were more likely to persist than those with B grades or with low or missing grades. However, the combination of background and preparation explained a relatively small portion of total variance, about one-third of the full model. So the claim that parents' education and high school curriculum are the primary causes of college persistence (Choy, 2002) seems off base.

The addition of SAT scores of White students to the model did not contribute much to its predictive quality, raising the R^2 by only .002. High SAT scores were positively associated with persistence and low scores had a negative association, both in comparison to mid-range scores, but only before college experiences were added. College achievement clearly had a more substantial influence than SAT scores on postenrollment success. Interestingly, students who did not take the SAT were more likely to persist after college achievement entered the model, further discrediting the NCES (1997a) claim that taking SAT exams is necessary for higher education (see also St. John, 2002, 2003).

The type of college attended had a substantial influence on college persistence by White students. Attending state universities, private colleges, and research universities—the state's residential

---

[3] This finding is probably an artifact of institutional reporting. Community colleges were less likely to report incomes because their students were less likely to apply for student aid and enroll full time.

campuses—was positively associated with persistence in every step. In contrast, attending the urban university and regional campuses reduced the odds of persisting compared to being enrolled in community colleges.

Business and education major choices were positively associated with persistence compared to being undeclared, for Whites. However, adding major choice to the model did not add substantially to its predictive power, increasing the R^2 by only .003.

Academic experiences in college substantially improved the predictive power of the model, more than doubling the R^2 (by .141, from .135 to .276). High grades were positively associated with persistence, while low grades had a negative association. Compared to not taking remedial courses, taking both remedial math and language arts had a positive association with persistence.

Finally, student financial aid was not significantly related to continuous enrollment. While coefficients for all but grants were negative, none were significant. It is apparent from these analyses that financial aid tends to equalize persistence opportunities for low- and middle-income students, controlling for other variables.

Hispanics

The overall persistence rate for Hispanics (59.4%, see Table 3) was lower than for Whites. Similar to Whites, Hispanics who enrolled in state universities (70.1%) and research universities (73.6%) persisted at higher rates than Hispanic students enrolled in other types of institutions.

There were substantial differences in persistence rates for Hispanics across majors. Arts (71.0%), business (70.8%), science/math (70.0%), and all majors other than computer science (44.0%) had higher persistence rates than undeclared majors. Therefore, logic would predict most declared majors to be positively associated with persistence in the regression.

Table 2. Logistic Regression Analyses of Persistence of Continuous
Enrollment of Fall or Spring Freshman thru Spring Sophomore for White Students

	Model 1		Model 2		Model 3		Model 4		Model 5		Model 6		Model 7	
	Odds R	Sig.	Odds R	Sig.	Odds R	Sig.	Odds R	Sig.	Odds R	Sig.	Odds R	Sig.	Odds R	Sig.
Male	0.876	***	0.982		0.952	*	0.941	**	0.959		1.104	***	1.101	***
Family Income Low	0.885	***	0.973		0.977		0.965		0.965		1.016		1.018	
Family Income High	1.319	***	1.220	***	1.207	***	1.167	***	1.165	***	1.142	***	1.129	***
Family Income Missing	0.969		1.002		1.021		1.064		1.067		1.237	***	1.232	***
Parent Ed. HS or less	0.751	***	0.806	***	0.824	***	0.858	***	0.855	***	0.895	***	0.897	***
Parent Education Missing	0.488	***	0.794	***	0.775	***	0.716	***	0.714	***	0.590	***	0.596	***
Locale City	0.974		0.962		0.955		0.932	*	0.934	*	0.994		0.994	
Locale Rural	0.985		0.971		0.973		0.958		0.960		0.969		0.970	
Locale Missing	0.888	**	1.242	***	1.243	***	1.207	***	1.203	***	1.107	*	1.119	**
HS Diploma Honors			2.820	***	2.610	***	2.286	***	2.286	***	1.815	***	1.811	***
HS Diploma Core 40			1.773	***	1.720	***	1.608	***	1.607	***	1.469	***	1.469	***
HS GPA A			1.619	***	1.508	***	1.440	***	1.447	***	1.130	***	1.129	***
HS GPA C or lower			0.773	***	0.793	***	0.820	***	0.823	***	0.883	***	0.880	***
HS GPA Missing			0.869	***	0.865	***	0.859	***	0.868	***	0.860	***	0.858	***
SAT Score High					1.122	***	1.054		1.065		0.948		0.944	
SAT Score Low					0.846	***	0.911	**	0.911	**	1.021		1.023	
SAT Score Missing					0.893	***	1.000		1.005		1.123	**	1.132	***
State Universities							1.276	***	1.230	***	1.211	***	1.216	***
Regional Campuses							0.769	***	0.763	***	0.820	***	0.823	***
Urban University							0.671	***	0.652	***	0.716	***	0.721	***
Research Universities							1.517	***	1.482	***	1.420	***	1.424	***
Private							1.213	***	1.174	***	1.196	***	1.202	***
Humanities									1.060		0.990		0.991	
Arts									1.304	***	1.074		1.076	
Science and Math									1.014		0.976		0.977	
Social Science									1.066		1.053		1.056	

Table 2. Logistic Regression Analyses of Persistence of Continuous Enrollment of Fall or Spring Freshman thru Spring Sophomore for White Students (cont.)

	Model 1		Model 2		Model 3		Model 4		Model 5		Model 6		Model 7	
	Odds R	Sig.	Odds R	Sig.	Odds R	Sig.	Odds R	Sig.	Odds R	Sig.	Odds R	Sig.	Odds R	Sig.
Health									1.008		0.959		0.963	
Business									1.176	***	1.094	*	1.091	*
Education									1.327	***	1.171	***	1.174	***
Computer									1.020		1.097		1.100	
Engineering									1.020		0.976		0.979	
Others									1.017		1.008		1.007	
College GPA A											1.218	***	1.212	***
College GPA C or lower											0.229	***	0.229	***
College GPA Missing											0.072	***	0.072	***
Remedial Math only											1.033		1.034	
Remedial Lang. Arts only											1.029		1.033	
Rem. Math & Lang. Arts											1.490	***	1.492	***
Full-time First Semester											1.545	***	1.545	***
Delayed Enrollment											0.744	***	0.744	***
On-campus Housing											1.012		1.042	
Self-supporting													0.787	**
Grants only													1.025	
Loans only													0.979	
Grants and Loans													0.935	
Other Packages													0.908	
Number of Cases	28,650		28,650		28,650		28,650		28,650		28,650		28,650	
Model χ^2	870		2,450		2,500		2,890		2,944		6,393		6,404	
Nagelkerke R^2	0.041		0.113		0.115		0.132		0.135		0.276		0.276	
% Correctly Predicted	65.1		66.8		67.0		67.3		67.4		74.0		73.9	

Note: *** $p<0.01$, ** $p<0.05$, * $p<0.1$

Background variables had expected associations in persistence rates of Hispanic students in many instances, but not all. Females had higher persistence rates than males. High-income students had higher persistence rates than other income groups. The persistence rates for the three levels of parent education were nearly equal (just above 60%), a somewhat surprising finding, but students with missing values, a small number of students, persisted at a lower rate (46.8%). Hispanics from towns and suburbs persisted at a higher rate (65.5%) than their peers from other locales.

Academic preparation and achievement tests also had expected relationships with persistence for Hispanic students. Students with A grades persisted at a higher rate (83.8%) than those with Bs or lower. Students with honors (81.2%) or Core 40 (65.4%) diplomas persisted at a higher rate than others (46.4%), and those with high SAT scores persisted at a high rate (75.0%).

Academic experiences in college also had expected relationships with persistence. Hispanic students with As (85.3%) and Bs (75.8%) had high persistence rates. However, Hispanic students who took remedial math courses persisted at lower rates than those who did not, although students with only remedial language arts courses persisted at a higher rate than those without any remedial courses (66.7% and 61.4% respectively).

Hispanics with all types of aid packages persisted at higher rates than students who did not have aid. However, students with grants and loans persisted at a similar rate (59.4%) to the average for all Hispanics (59.4%), lower than for other aid recipients.

The regression analyses reveal patterns that are related to the descriptive statistics, but with some unexpected twists (Table 4). While background variables explained more variance for Hispanics than for Whites (R^2 of .065 for Hispanics in Model 1 in Table 4 compared to .041 for Whites), only four variables were significant in any of the models. High incomes were consistently and positively associated with persistence for Hispanics. In contrast, Hispanic students from urban and rural locales did not persist as well as students from suburban and town locales.

High school courses had a more substantial association with persistence for Hispanics than did high school grades. Both honors and Core 40 diplomas substantially improved the odds of persisting compared to regular diplomas. High school A grades were not significant once college experience was considered. SAT scores were not significantly associated with persistence. The first three steps explained less than half of the total variance explained by the model (R^2 in step 3 of .152 compared to .366 for Model 7), casting further doubt on the NCES interpretations of national data (Choy, 2002; NCES, 1997a, 1997b, 2001a, 2001b), given their many specification problems (Heller, 2004).

None of the variables related to college type was significant. Thus, while Hispanic students in research universities and state universities had high rates of persistence, there was not a significant causal association with the outcome.

Three of the majors were significantly and positively associated with persistence of Hispanic students. Majoring in the arts was positively associated with persistence before college academic experiences were considered. Business majors and other majors were more likely to persist than undeclared majors across the final three steps. These findings are somewhat in contrast to the descriptive analyses (Table 3) that showed science/math majors with a higher persistence rate. Apparently, high school curriculum was associated with the choice of science/math majors.

The addition of academic experiences in colleges explained a substantial portion of the variance in persistence of Hispanic students (increasing the R^2 from .188 to .361). Only a slight positive association with persistence was found for A grades (.1 alpha), while low grades substantially reduced the odds of persistence. Taking remedial math and language arts courses substantially improved these odds of persisting.

Table 3. Breakdown of Persistence Rates for Variables in Analysis of Continuous Enrollment of Fall or Spring Freshman thru Spring Sophomore for Hispanic Students					
Variable	Category	Persistence of Fall to Spring Freshman			
		Persisters		Nonpersisters '	
		N	Row %	N	Row %
College Destination in Freshman Year	State Universities	47	70.1	20	29.9
	Regional Campuses	161	54.0	137	46.0
	Urban University	20	44.4	25	55.6
	Research Universities	134	73.6	48	26.4
	Private	24	53.3	21	46.7
	2-year '	58	52.7	52	47.3
Major in Freshman Year	Humanities	16	66.7	8	33.3
	Arts	22	71.0	9	29.0
	Science and Math	21	70.0	9	30.0
	Social Science	26	65.0	14	35.0
	Health	27	54.0	23	46.0
	Business	68	70.8	28	29.2
	Education	36	67.9	17	32.1
	Computer	11	44.0	14	56.0
	Engineering	20	58.8	14	41.2
	Others	118	55.4	95	44.6
	Undecided '	79	52.3	72	47.7
Composite Gender	Male	171	55.3	138	44.7
	Female '	273	62.3	165	37.7
	Missing '				
Composite Ethnicity	Native American				
	Asian American Pac. Islander				
	African American				
	Hispanic	444	59.4	303	40.6
	White				
	Other				
	Missing				
Composite Parent Income Level	Low (below $30,000)	111	60.7	72	39.3
	Mid ($30,000-$70,000) '	169	57.5	125	42.5
	High (over $70,000)	115	71.4	46	28.6
	Missing	49	45.0	60	55.0
Composite Parent Education Level	Middle/Jr High school or less	42	63.6	24	36.4
	High school	170	64.2	95	35.8
	College or beyond '	151	62.1	92	37.9
	Missing	81	46.8	92	53.2
Composite Locale	City	100	55.6	80	44.4
	Suburban and town '	253	65.5	133	34.5
	Rural	54	54.5	45	45.5
	Missing	37	45.1	45	54.9

Variable	Category	Persistence of Fall to Spring Freshman			
		Persisters		Nonpersisters '	
		N	Row %	N	Row %
Composite High School Diploma	Honors	108	81.2	25	18.8
	Core 40	176	65.4	93	34.6
	Regular or Missing '	160	46.4	185	53.6
Composite High School GPA	A	88	83.8	17	16.2
	B '	156	60.5	102	39.5
	C or Lower	113	60.8	73	39.2
	Missing	87	43.9	111	56.1
Composite SAT Scores	High	63	75.0	21	25.0
	Mid '	139	64.7	76	35.3
	Low	136	59.9	91	40.1
	Missing	106	48.0	115	52.0
College Freshman GPA	A	93	85.3	16	14.7
	B '	232	75.8	74	24.2
	C or Lower	111	37.6	184	62.4
	Missing	8	21.6	29	78.4
Remedial Coursework in Freshman Year	Remedial Math only	39	45.9	46	54.1
	Remedial Language Arts only	10	66.7	5	33.3
	Remedial Math and Lang. Arts	34	57.6	25	42.4
	No Remedial Coursework '	361	61.4	227	38.6
Enrollment Status in First Semester	Full-time	408	61.5	255	38.5
	Part-time '	36	42.9	48	57.1
Delayed Enrollment in Spring as Freshman	Delayed	41	43.6	53	56.4
	Not delayed '	403	61.7	250	38.3
Housing Status in Freshman Year	On-campus	167	73.6	60	26.4
	Others '	277	53.3	243	46.7
Dependency Status	Indeterminate status '	179	57.2	134	42.8
	Self-supporting	13	46.4	15	53.6
	Dependent '	252	62.1	154	37.9
Aid Packages	Grants only	145	63.6	83	36.4
	Loans only	62	63.3	36	36.7
	Grants and Loans	79	59.4	54	40.6
	Other Packages	42	71.2	17	28.8
	None '	116	50.7	113	49.3
Total		444	59.4	303	40.6

Table 3. Breakdown of Persistence Rates for Variables in Analysis of Continuous Enrollment of Fall or Spring Freshman thru Spring Sophomore for Hispanic Students (cont.)

' is the reference category in regression.

Table 4. Logistic Regression Analyses of Persistence of Continuous Enrollment of Fall or Spring Freshman thru Spring Sophomore for Hispanic Students

	Model 1		Model 2		Model 3		Model 4		Model 5		Model 6		Model 7	
	Odds R	Sig.	Odds R	Sig.	Odds R	Sig.	Odds R	Sig.	Odds R	Sig.	Odds R	Sig.	Odds R	Sig.
Male	0.762	*	0.764	*	0.766		0.757	*	0.719	*	0.741		0.757	
Family Income Low	1.201		1.223		1.215		1.158		1.192		1.284		1.168	
Family Income High	1.863	***	1.744	**	1.721	**	1.685	**	1.782	**	2.006	***	2.104	***
Fam. Income Missing	0.944		0.969		0.971		0.993		0.949		1.297		1.303	
Parent Ed. HS or less	1.247		1.385	*	1.390	*	1.372		1.417	*	1.369		1.309	
Parent Ed. Missing	0.763		1.149		1.169		1.068		1.214		0.843		0.849	
Locale City	0.651	**	0.584	***	0.580	***	0.578	***	0.561	***	0.539	***	0.505	***
Locale Rural	0.613	**	0.547	**	0.535	**	0.510	***	0.535	**	0.565	**	0.557	**
Locale Missing	0.578	**	0.858		0.871		0.822		0.802		0.789		0.732	
HS Diploma Honors			3.228	***	3.262	***	3.171	***	3.093	***	2.221	**	2.365	**
HS Diploma Core 40			1.903	***	1.914	***	1.936	***	1.919	***	1.609	*	1.647	**
HS GPA A			2.431	***	2.421	***	2.333	**	2.300	**	1.628		1.662	
HS GPA C or lower			1.245		1.277		1.338		1.264		1.358		1.392	
HS GPA Missing			0.938		1.008		1.077		1.034		0.905		0.954	
SAT Score High					1.135		1.110		1.124		1.134		1.143	
SAT Score Low					1.128		1.187		1.172		1.211		1.232	
SAT Score Missing					0.939		1.032		0.959		0.955		0.952	
State Universities							1.117		1.353		1.162		1.171	
Regional Campuses							0.672		0.748		1.114		1.149	
Urban University							0.511	*	0.595		0.735		0.785	
Research Universities							1.091		1.228		1.173		1.151	
Private							0.676		0.710		1.106		1.137	
Humanities									1.364		1.336		1.297	
Arts									2.371	*	1.887		1.736	
Science and Math									1.460		1.411		1.508	

Table 4. Logistic Regression Analyses of Persistence of Continuous
Enrollment of Fall or Spring Freshman thru Spring Sophomore for Hispanic Students (cont.)

	Model 1		Model 2		Model 3		Model 4		Model 5		Model 6		Model 7	
	Odds R	Sig.	Odds R	Sig.	Odds R	Sig.	Odds R	Sig.	Odds R	Sig.	Odds R	Sig.	Odds R	Sig.
Social Science									1.176		0.935		0.876	
Health									0.738		0.805		0.737	
Business									2.101	**	2.434	***	2.417	**
Education									1.510		1.414		1.409	
Computer									0.950		1.332		1.322	
Engineering									1.288		1.237		1.203	
Others									1.648	**	1.852	**	1.859	**
College GPA A											1.887	*	1.847	*
College GPA C or lower											0.202	***	0.200	***
College GPA Missing											0.107	***	0.109	***
Remedial Math only											0.891		0.858	
Remedial Lang. Arts only											2.748		2.948	
Rem. Math & Lang. Arts											2.543	**	2.526	**
Full-time First Semester											1.123		1.130	
Delayed Enrollment											0.882		0.928	
On-campus Housing											1.563		1.571	
Self-supporting													1.238	
Grants only													1.302	
Loans only													1.010	
Grants and Loans													0.905	
Other Packages													1.755	
Number of Cases	747		747		747		747		747		747		747	
Model χ^2	37		88		89		99		112		232		236	
Nagelkerke R^2	0.065		0.151		0.152		0.167		0.188		0.361		0.366	
% Correctly Predicted	62.2		64.5		65.5		66.8		67.7		74.7		74.8	

Note: *** $p<0.01$, ** $p<0.05$, * $p<0.1$

The final step improved the model modestly (raising the R^2 by .005), but there were no significant aid variables for Hispanic students. The types of packages tended to equalize the odds for aided students compared to students who did not receive aid.

African Americans

African American undergraduates in Indiana (Table 5) had a substantially lower rate of continuous enrollment (53.3%) than the other groups. African Americans in state universities (66.7%), research universities (67.8%), and private colleges (60.4%) persisted at higher rates than students in the other institution types—a pattern consistent with the groups examined above.

In contrast to the other groups, however, African Americans with undeclared majors persisted at a higher rate (59.1%) than their peers in all majors except social science (60.3%), science/math (59.3%), and the humanities (61.5%). Therefore, there is reason to hypothesize a positive association for these majors with higher persistence of African American students but a negative association for other majors. Interestingly, it is other majors and business majors that have the largest number of African American students.

The differences in persistence rates of African Americans were not substantial for most background variables, at least compared to Whites and Hispanics. Females persisted at a higher rate (54.2%) than males, but the gender gap was not as large as that for Hispanics and was similar to that for Whites. The differences in persistence by income groups, from 63.4 percent for high income to 50.3 percent for low income (and 44.0% for missing), was similar to the other groups. Students with missing income persisted at a lower rate (39.3%), possibly indicating they should have applied for aid. Yet the variability among the groups with reported parents' education was relatively modest, from 54.6 percent for students whose parents had high school education to 58.0 percent for those with college-educated parents. Given the differences across groups in variability by family background, there is reason to question using a single set of metrics as an explanation for variation in enrollment rates. NCES concluded parents' education provides substantial explanation for variance in attainment (Choy, 2002; NCES, 2001a, 2001b), but the present analysis suggests that for African Americans this is not an especially strong predictor.

There were substantial differences in the rates for high school academic preparation variables for African Americans. Honors graduates persisted at 79.1 percent, while 75.2 percent of students with A grades persisted. African Americans with low grades and regular diplomas persisted at substantially lower rates. There was also variation across the SAT groups with particularly low persistence among students who did not take the SAT. Therefore, there was reason to expect that preparation was influential in attainment, as NCES claimed (NCES, 1997a, 2001a, 2001b). However, there were also substantial differences in rates for the variables related to college academic experiences for African Americans. There was particularly high variation for A grades (77.2%) and B grades (75.8%) compared to C or lower grades and missing grades (39.2% and 30.4% respectively). Students with all types of remedial courses had lower rates than students who did not take remedial courses. Consistent with the other groups, students who enrolled full time persisted at a higher rate than those who enrolled part time, and students who lived on campus also persisted at a higher rate than students who did not. Students who delayed enrollment persisted at lower rates.

African American students with financial aid packages persisted at higher rates than their peers who did not receive aid. Self-supporting students persisted at lower rates.

Table 5. Breakdown of Persistence Rates for Variables in Analysis of Continuous Enrollment of Fall or Spring Freshman thru Spring Sophomore for African American Students					
		Persistence of Fall to Spring Freshman			
Variable	Category	Persisters		Nonpersisters '	
		N	Row %	N	Row %
College Destination in Freshman Year	State Universities	244	66.7	122	33.3
	Regional Campuses	154	47.5	170	52.5
	Urban University	114	41.5	161	58.5
	Research Universities	257	67.8	122	32.2
	Private	93	60.4	61	39.6
	2-year '	252	42.6	339	57.4
Major in Freshman Year	Humanities	32	61.5	20	38.5
	Arts	29	53.7	25	46.3
	Science and Math	54	59.3	37	40.7
	Social Science	73	60.3	48	39.7
	Health	86	49.4	88	50.6
	Business	188	54.8	155	45.2
	Education	72	51.4	68	48.6
	Computer	43	44.3	54	55.7
	Engineering	38	55.9	30	44.1
	Others	237	46.8	269	53.2
	Undecided '	262	59.1	181	40.9
Composite Gender	Male	440	52.1	405	47.9
	Female '	674	54.2	570	45.8
	Missing '				
Composite Ethnicity	Native American				
	Asian American Pac. Islander				
	African American	1,114	53.3	975	46.7
	Hispanic				
	White				
	Other				
	Missing				
Composite Parent Income Level	Low (below $30,000)	496	50.3	490	49.7
	Mid ($30,000-$70,000) '	336	56.8	256	43.2
	High (over $70,000)	187	63.4	108	36.6
	Missing	95	44.0	121	56.0
Composite Parent Education Level	Middle/Jr High school or less	12	57.1	9	42.9
	High school	407	54.6	339	45.4
	College or beyond '	516	58.0	374	42.0
	Missing	179	41.4	253	58.6
Composite Locale	City	773	54.9	635	45.1
	Suburban and town '	209	53.5	182	46.5
	Rural	35	47.9	38	52.1
	Missing	97	44.7	120	55.3

Table 5. Breakdown of Persistence Rates for Variables in Analysis of Continuous Enrollment of Fall or Spring Freshman thru Spring Sophomore for African American Students (cont.)					
		Persistence of Fall to Spring Freshman			
Variable	Category	Persisters		Nonpersisters '	
		N	Row %	N	Row %
Composite High School Diploma	Honors	200	79.1	53	20.9
	Core 40	454	59.0	315	41.0
	Regular or Missing '	460	43.1	607	56.9
Composite High School GPA	A	124	75.2	41	24.8
	B '	454	60.7	294	39.3
	C or Lower	343	48.9	359	51.1
	Missing	193	40.7	281	59.3
Composite SAT Scores	High	74	64.3	41	35.7
	Mid '	208	65.4	110	34.6
	Low	516	55.2	419	44.8
	Missing	316	43.8	405	56.2
College Freshman GPA	A	122	77.2	36	22.8
	B '	516	75.8	165	24.2
	C or Lower	427	39.2	662	60.8
	Missing	49	30.4	112	69.6
Remedial Coursework in Freshman Year	Remedial Math only	144	41.6	202	58.4
	Remedial Language Arts only	45	35.2	83	64.8
	Remedial Math and Lang. Arts	187	46.8	213	53.3
	No Remedial Coursework '	738	60.7	477	39.3
Enrollment Status in First Semester	Full-time	999	55.5	801	44.5
	Part-time '	115	39.8	174	60.2
Delayed Enrollment in Spring as Freshman	Delayed	126	43.4	164	56.6
	Not delayed '	988	54.9	811	45.1
Housing Status in Freshman Year	On-campus	545	59.3	374	40.7
	Others '	569	48.6	601	51.4
Dependency Status	Indeterminate status '	214	50.6	209	49.4
	Self-supporting	62	39.2	96	60.8
	Dependent '	838	55.6	670	44.4
Aid Packages	Grants only	386	52.1	355	47.9
	Loans only	92	54.1	78	45.9
	Grants and Loans	319	54.7	264	45.3
	Other Packages	163	63.9	92	36.1
	None '	154	45.3	186	54.7
Total		1,114	53.3	975	46.7
' is the reference category in regression.					

The sequential persistence regression analyses (Table 6) revealed some patterns similar to those for other groups as well as some that differed. Interestingly, background variables had much less association with persistence for African Americans than for Whites and Hispanics. Only two variables had anything other than modest associations in any step. In the first model, before preparation entered the equation, missing parents' education was negatively associated with persistence and it remained significant.[4] In the last model, after the effects of student aid were considered, African American aid applicants with high incomes were more likely to persist than those with middle incomes. Given these findings, the NCES claim that background and parents' education explain a substantial portion of variation in enrollment and attainment for minorities (Choy, 2002; NCES, 1997a) seems especially misleading.

Two academic preparation variables were significant. African Americans who had completed the honors curriculum or Core 40 were more likely to persist than those who did not. This indicates that efforts to expand preparatory curriculum could influence access and success in college. However, grades were mostly insignificant with only a modest negative association for low grades in the early steps of the regression model. Nor were SAT scores significant, further debunking the notion that taking the exam is somehow an explanation for differentials in attainment rates (e.g., Choy, 2002; NCES, 1997a).

Similar to the earlier analyses, attending the urban university reduced the odds of persisting compared to attending a two-year college—controlling for preparation and background. When first considered, African Americans at state universities and research universities were more likely to persist than African Americans at

---

[4] This could be related to reporting peculiarities on College Board surveys, given that these questionnaires were the primary source of information on high school courses. Further, financial aid data was the secondary source, and some campuses showed lower aid applications.

two-year colleges, but the significance disappeared once college experience was taken into account.

The biggest difference in the analyses of persistence by African Americans compared to other groups was for academic majors. Controlling for background, preparation, and college choice, African Americans who majored in business, health, education, and computers were less likely to persist than their peers. In addition, majors such as science/math or arts that were positively related to persistence for Whites were not significant, with negative coefficients for African Americans. These findings raise serious questions about engagement in learning within academic fields for African American students.

In most respects, the findings for variables on academic experiences in college for African Americans were comparable to those for other groups. Grades of C or lower and missing grades were negatively associated with persistence compared to B grades, controlling for other variables. Taking both remedial math and language was positively associated with persistence.

The findings for African Americans living on campus were different than those for Whites and Hispanics. While this variable had been significant and positive in the prior analyses, for African Americans, living on campus as a freshman was negatively associated with persistence. When coupled with the findings on major choices, it is apparent that African Americans engaged with their campus environments differently than most other students.

Finally, student aid had a more substantial influence on persistence by African Americans than by other groups. All types of packages except loans without grants raised the odds of persistence compared to not having an aid package. This finding is in contrast to prior research which has found African Americans but not Whites to be negatively influenced by loans in persistence (Kaltenbaugh, St. John, & Starkey, 1999). Overall, this analysis shows that financial aid continued to support uplift in the millennial class of African Americans in Indiana.

Table 6. Logistic Regression Analyses of Persistence of Continuous Enrollment of Fall or Spring Freshman thru Spring Sophomore for African American Students

	Model 1		Model 2		Model 3		Model 4		Model 5		Model 6		Model 7	
	Odds R	Sig.	Odds R	Sig.	Odds R	Sig.	Odds R	Sig.	Odds R	Sig.	Odds R	Sig.	Odds R	Sig.
Male	0.920		1.037		1.034		0.987		0.963		1.044		1.053	
Family Income Low	0.817	*	0.895	*	0.907	*	0.928	*	0.927	*	0.991		0.933	
Family Income High	1.330	*	1.315		1.297	*	1.353	*	1.351	*	1.317	*	1.433	**
Family Income Missing	1.020		1.153		1.160		1.220		1.197		1.153		1.408	
Parent Ed. HS or less	0.939		0.987		1.002		0.992		1.000		1.026		1.011	
Parent Ed. Missing	0.549	***	0.721	**	0.747	*	0.675	**	0.684	**	0.617	***	0.639	***
Locale City	1.071		1.035		1.053		1.057		1.058		1.129		1.113	
Locale Rural	0.816		0.814		0.810		0.783		0.802		0.846		0.821	
Locale Missing	0.921		1.177		1.207		1.217		1.206		1.314		1.321	
HS Diploma Honors			3.445	***	3.370	***	2.940	***	3.015	***	2.685	***	2.636	***
HS Diploma Core 40			1.659	***	1.635	***	1.434	***	1.447	***	1.463	***	1.442	***
HS GPA A			1.412	*	1.382		1.336		1.348		1.102		1.091	
HS GPA C or lower			0.785	**	0.804	*	0.828	*	0.819	*	0.905		0.894	
HS GPA Missing			0.763		0.816		0.819		0.812		0.815		0.807	
SAT Score High					0.848		0.798		0.781		0.625	*	0.616	*
SAT Score Low					0.908		0.945		0.934		1.121		1.117	
SAT Score Missing					0.783		0.886		0.862		1.006		0.985	
State Universities							1.838	***	1.730	***	1.397		1.411	
Regional Campuses							0.963		0.916		0.759		0.735	
Urban University							0.647	***	0.627	***	0.627	**	0.619	**
Research Universities							1.500	**	1.496	**	1.382		1.338	
Private							1.398	*	1.380		1.582	*	1.484	
Humanities									1.014		1.097		1.119	
Arts									0.845		0.602		0.594	
Science and Math									0.594	**	0.715		0.733	

Table 6. Logistic Regression Analyses of Persistence of Continuous
Enrollment of Fall or Spring Freshman thru Spring Sophomore for African American Students (cont.)

	Model 1		Model 2		Model 3		Model 4		Model 5		Model 6		Model 7	
	Odds R	Sig.	Odds R	Sig.	Odds R	Sig.	Odds R	Sig.	Odds R	Sig.	Odds R	Sig.	Odds R	Sig.
Social Science									0.934		0.884		0.883	
Health									0.675	**	0.683	*	0.665	**
Business									0.842		0.709	**	0.698	**
Education									0.659	**	0.641	**	0.647	**
Computer									0.731		0.671		0.649	*
Engineering									0.897		0.823		0.795	
Others									0.848		0.772		0.758	
College GPA A											1.101		1.099	
College GPA C or lower											0.227	***	0.229	***
College GPA Missing											0.167	***	0.171	***
Remedial Math only											0.789		0.784	
Remedial Lang, Arts only											0.841		0.855	
Remedial Math & Lang.											1.457	**	1.453	**
Full-time First Semester											1.132		1.070	
Delayed Enrollment											1.015		1.044	
On-campus Housing											0.718	**	0.648	***
Self-supporting													0.670	*
Grants only													1.458	**
Loans only													1.380	
Grants and Loans													1.540	**
Other Packages													1.854	***
Number of Cases	2,089		2,089		2,089		2,089		2,089		2,089		2,089	
Model χ^2	49		155		158		204		214		442		452	
Nagelkerke R^2	0.031		0.095		0.097		0.124		0.130		0.255		0.260	
% Correctly Predicted	56.6		61.0		61.0		62.8		62.5		69.5		69.6	

Note: *** $p<0.01$, ** $p<0.05$, * $p<0.1$

Conclusions

These analyses reveal substantial similarities and a few very important differences among the three ethnic groups in the factors that influence persistence. The differences are most easily understood if viewed as being related to differences in the situated contexts of the lives of college students (St. John, 2003), an alternative to the more usual vantage point of seeking to uncover universal patterns (Braxton, 2000; Pascarella & Terenzini, 1991). By revealing differences in persistence patterns across diverse groups, we can illuminate factors that inhibit equal opportunity as well as highlight policy "levers" that might improve opportunity. While it is apparent that the block of variables, or factors, are associated with attainment by all three groups, the variations in findings about each group reveal critical issues.

First, background variables were associated with persistence by all three groups, but there were substantially different patterns among the groups. In these analyses, Whites followed the general pattern espoused by NCES more closely than other groups. For Whites, having parents who had not attained a college education decreased the odds of academic success in college, while being from families with high incomes improved these odds. For Hispanics and African Americans, high income was a positive factor, but parents' education was simply not significant.

These differences are appropriately interpreted within the Indiana context, a state that has made an effort to place preparatory curriculum in all high schools, has implemented a major postsecondary encouragement program, and has provided and fulfilled a guarantee of adequate grant aid to eighth graders who took a pledge to prepare for college (St. John, Chung, Musoba, & Simmons, 2004)—a program that has had especially substantial effects on opportunities for African Americans (Musoba, 2004). For African Americans and Hispanics, an adequate aid guarantee enables students to overcome barriers related to parents' education and income, a condition that is not met nationally (ACSFA, 2001, 2002; NCES, 1997a, 2001a, 2001b; St. John, 2002, 2003).

Second, there was a consistent pattern of association between high school curricula and persistence in colleges. For all three groups, completing preparatory Core 40 or honors curricula had a sustained positive influence on persistence. High school grades did not have as substantial an influence for White students and had no significant relationship for African American or Hispanic students, indicating that increasing the availability of advanced courses can expand opportunity, an interpretation that would be consistent with the outcomes following the increase in opportunity in Indiana during the 1990s (St. John, Musoba, & Chung, 2004a).

Third, taking the SAT and having high scores on this test had an effect on educational opportunity for Whites in the earlier models but was not significant in the final model. For African Americans or Hispanics there were no significant gains from taking the SAT. Because the majority of high school students take the SAT in Indiana, the state provided a good sample for examining the influence of taking the SAT (St. John, Musoba, & Chung, 2004b). Further, taking advanced courses was associated with high SAT scores in Indiana. These findings about the significance of curriculum as contrasted to grades and scores may be noteworthy for policy makers in other states as well.

Fourth, college choices influenced persistence for White and African American students. Attending state universities, private colleges, and research universities was consistently and positively associated with persistence compared to enrollment in two-year colleges, while attending regional campuses and the urban campus did not have this positive association for Whites. This was also significant in the early African American models, but only the negative association with the urban campus was significant in the final model, while for Hispanics, none was significant. In Indiana, the research universities, the private colleges, and the state universities have substantial residence halls, while the regional campuses and the urban campus do not. It is possible that the opportunity to live on campus makes a positive difference for White students. However, living on campus was negatively associated with persistence for African Americans and not significant in the other models, so readers should hesitate to conclude that on-campus residence is the answer. Other explanations merit consideration, including explanations related to engagement in the academic side of the college experience.

Fifth, there were very substantial differences in the association between major choices and persistence across the three groups. For Whites and Hispanics a few majors were positively associated with persistence. However, for African Americans, several academic majors were negatively associated with persistence and there were no positive associations. These findings raise questions about engagement in academic programs and whether the content of major programs meets the expectations of African Americans. Since these analyses control for preparation and achievement, it simply is not possible or appropriate to reduce these findings to ability or preparation differences. Instead, these findings point to serious academic problems in Indiana higher education. Faculties in health, business, education, and computer science in particular need to consider why their majors do not support persistence by diverse students.

We hope that prejudice, however subtle or covert, is not the explanation for these differences in students' experience of academic programs in Indiana. These findings recall James Comer's (1989) autobiography, in which he describes how stereotyping by faculty at Indiana University induced him to transfer to Howard University, a historically Black university. If this reflected past conditions of education in the state, we hope that these practices have changed or will change. At the very least, it is crucial that faculties at colleges and universities examine whether their major programs are discouraging African Americans and, if they are, to explore alternative explanations for these differences and to pilot test new academic strategies for creating more engaging curricula and academic experiences.

Sixth, there were many common patterns in the effects of college experiences across the three sets of analyses. High college grades were positively associated and low grades were negatively associated with persistence. Yet African American and Hispanic students may not distinguish between A and B averages as precisely in the decision to persist. In addition, taking remedial courses in both math and language was consistently and positively associated with persistence. This means that achievement is important but support services can help students who have additional academic needs. These findings point to the fact that interventions aimed at improving student engagement in the learning environment can make a difference in educational opportunities for students across racial/ethnic groups.

Coupled with the findings on academic majors, these results suggest that faculty should not only assess whether minorities persist at lower rates in their programs but should also engage in experiments to improve the odds of success. Students who have declared majors are generally the more able or prepared students with less need for remedial courses. Since African American students, like others, benefited from remedial courses in Indiana, the challenge is not only at the low end of the achievement continuum, but it is even more critical to engage high-ability minority students. James Comer went on to medical school and became an endowed professor at Yale (Comer, 1989). He found an engaging learning environment at Howard and went on to achieve his goals and to fulfill his grandmother's dream of cross-generation uplift. Interventions that create more engaging learning environments for diverse students appear long overdue in Indiana.

Finally, there were differences in the effects of student financial aid across racial/ethnic groups in Indiana, at least for the entering collegiate class of 2000. For Whites and Hispanics there were no significant financial aid variables, suggesting aid may help equalize opportunity, yet high-income students were more likely to persist in all three ethnic groups. Because of the Twenty-First Century Scholars Program in Indiana, aid appears adequate for low-income students. Specifically, for African Americans, with a high percentage of low-income students, all types of packages with grant aid, including loans and grants, were positively associated with persistence. These findings on the impact of student financial aid packages further reinforce the interpretive approach of situated contexts (St. John, 2003; St. John, Asker, & Hu, 2001). Public finance policies influence different groups in different ways. Because of their high poverty rate in Indiana, African Americans can benefit from Indiana's Scholars program more than Whites (Musoba, 2004). Further, excessive loans can be problematic for middle-income families, who may question whether their expected earnings will grow sufficiently to justify continued borrowing. At the very least, these differences merit further and wider consideration, given the ongoing challenges facing educational opportunity for high-achieving students of color (St. John, 2003).

Implications

These analyses provide further evidence for considering the situated contexts influencing the ways students engage in their learning environments. There has been strong emphasis in higher education on finding best practices for *all* students—which can be decoded to mean *White* students because of their dominant position. This is not to argue that racism and stereotyping are intentional acts. Rather, it is to assert that it is possible inadvertently to construct curricula and learning environments that discriminate, where the assumption of race neutrality is false, and where practices support majority better than minority students.

This atmosphere of unintended discrimination may exist in Indiana higher education. The fact that, controlling for preparation, college grades, and remedial courses, African Americans in several applied majors—business, education, health, and computer science—do not persist as well as their peers with undeclared majors reveals a serious problem with the engagement of the best and the brightest minority students. The causes cannot be cast off on the lack of parental education or low achievement. The challenge resides within the colleges and universities in the state.

Turner (1994) studied the racial climate for students of color at the University of Minnesota and found that although that university "provides supportive programs and implements policies intended to serve students of color, the campus climate continued to be 'unwelcoming' to students of color" (p. 356). Turner further quoted Ron Wakabayashi (Daniels, as cited in Turner, 1994), who expressed the sense of exclusion many students of color experience: "We feel that we're a guest in someone else's house, that we can never relax and put our feet up on the table" (p. 356). Daniels extends the analogy by saying that guests must follow the house rules, must be on their best behavior, and do not have the freedoms that family members enjoy.

However, African American students often experience treatment that is much worse than the treatment experienced by typical houseguests. Feagin, Vera, and Imani (1996) detailed some of the negative experiences African Americans have in predominantly White institutions. A central theme in their study is Black invisibility. Much like the main character of Ralph Ellison's book (1995), African American students in this study were not seen by "[W]hite professors, students, staff members and administrators . . . as full human beings with distinctive talents, virtues, interests and problems" (p. 14).

Related to the research of Feagin, Vera, and Imani are the findings of Smedley, Myers, and Harrell (1993) that most severe negative impacts to student performance were minority-status stressors that "undermined students' academic confidence and ability to bond to the university" (p. 435). Therefore, it may be that in certain majors, African American students do not feel comfortable in the environment and are not seen as full human beings. All of these elements impact the African American students' academic confidence and ability to bond with the institution.

Indiana is surely not alone in facing the challenge of improving opportunities for persistence by high-achieving minority students. This is the first state-level study to explore the role of preparation and achievement for a cohort of students within a state. It is possible that if other states take the steps to compile and analyze longitudinal databases, they too will find serious challenges that impede the academic success of their students. The challenges they face may or may not be related to diversity. However, given the national shame of blaming low attainment of minorities on the preparation of their parents and the quality of schools students can attend (e.g., Choy, 2002; NCES, 1997a, 2001a, 2001b), it is time to reconsider what the challenges are and how they can be resolved.

When financial aid is adequate for low-income students, which has been the case in Indiana, then parents' education is no longer a major factor for African Americans. The value of cross-generation uplift is very highly held among African Americans (Allen-Haynes, St. John, & Cadray, 2003; Walker & Snarey, 2004). This study shows that when adequate financial aid is provided, parents' education is not the barrier for African Americans and Hispanics that it is for Whites. It is time to put aside stereotypes about parents' education and underachievement of African Americans and address the challenge of creating engaging curricula and encouraging academic environments for African American undergraduates.

References

Advisory Committee on Student Financial Assistance. (2001). *Access denied: Restoring the nation's commitment to equal educational opportunity.* Washington, DC: Author.

Advisory Committee on Student Financial Assistance. (2002). *Empty promises: The myth of college access in America.* Washington, DC: Author.

Allen-Haynes, L., St. John, E. P., & Cadray, J. (2003). Rediscovering the African American tradition: Restructuring in post-desegregation urban schools. In L. F. Mirn & E. P. St. John (Eds.), *Reinterpreting urban school reform: Have urban schools failed, or has the reform movement failed urban schools?* (pp. 249-275). Albany, NY: SUNY Press.

Astin, A. W. (1975). *Preventing students from dropping out.* San Francisco: Jossey-Bass.

Bean, J. P. (1980). Dropouts and turnover: The synthesis of a causal model of attrition. *Research in Higher Education, 12,* 155-187.

Bean, J. P. (1983). The application of a model of turnover in work organizations to the student attrition process. *Review of Higher Education, 6,* 127-148.

Bean, J. P. (1985). Interaction effects based on class level in an explanatory model of college student dropout syndrome. *American Educational Research Journal, 22,* 35-64.

Bean, J. P. (1990). Why students leave: Insights from research. In D. Hossler, J. P. Bean, & Associates (Eds.), *The strategic management of enrollment* (pp. 147-169). San Francisco: Jossey-Bass.

Becker, W. E. (2004). Omitted variables and sample selection problems in studies of college-going decisions. In E. P. St. John (Ed.), *Readings on equal education: Vol. 19. Public policy and college access: Investigating the federal and state roles in equalizing postsecondary opportunity* (pp. 65-86). New York: AMS Press, Inc.

Braxton, J. M. (Ed.). (2000). *Reworking the student departure puzzle.* Nashville, TN: Vanderbilt University Press.

Cabrera, A. F. (1994). Logistic regression analysis in higher education: An applied perspective. In J. C. Smart (Ed.), *Higher education: Handbook of theory and research,* Vol. 10. New York: Agathon Press.

Cabrera, A. F., Nora, A., & Castaæda, M. B. (1992). The role of finances in the persistence process: A structural model. *Research in Higher Education, 33*(5), 571-594.

Cabrera, A. F., Nora, A., & Castaæda, M. B. (1993). College persistence: Structural equations modeling test of an integrated model of student retention. *Journal of Higher Education, 64*(2), 123-139.

Choy, S. P. (2002). Access *& persistence: Findings from 10 years of longitudinal research on students.* Washington, DC: American Council on Education.

Comer, J. (1989). *Maggie's American dream: The life and times of a Black family.* New York: Plume Books.

Dynarski, S. (2002). *The consequences of merit aid.* Working Paper No. 9400. Cambridge, MA: National Bureau of Economic Research.

Ellison, R. (1995). *Invisible man* (2nd ed.). New York: Vintage.

Feagin, J. R., Vera, H., & Imani, N. (1996). *The agony of education: Black students at White colleges and universities.* New York: Routledge.

Fitzgerald, B. (2004). Federal financial aid and college access. In E. P. St. John (Ed.), *Readings on equal education: Vol. 19. Public policy and college access: Investigating the federal and state roles in equalizing postsecondary opportunity* (pp. 1-28). New York: AMS Press, Inc.

Hauptman, A. M. (1990). *The college tuition spiral.* New York: Macmillan.

Heller, D. E. (2004). State merit scholarship programs. In E. P. St. John (Ed.), *Readings on equal education: Vol. 19. Public policy and college access: Investigating the federal and state roles in equalizing postsecondary opportunity* (pp.99-108). New York: AMS Press, Inc.

Hu, S., & St. John, E. P. (2001). Student persistence in a public higher education system: Understanding racial/ethnic differences. *Journal of Higher Education, 72*(3), 265-286.

Indiana Commission for Higher Education. (2003, February 12). *Long-term development policies for Indiana postsecondary education.* Indianapolis, IN: Author.

Kaltenbaugh, L. S., St. John, E. P., & Starkey, J. B. (1999). What difference does tuition make? An analysis of ethnic differences in persistence. *Journal of Student Financial Aid, 29*(2), 21-31.

Lee, J. B. (2004). Access revisited: A preliminary reanalysis of NELS. In E. P. St. John (Ed.), *Readings in equal education: Vol. 19. Public policy and college access: Investigating the federal and state roles in equalizing postsecondary opportunity* (pp. 87-96). New York: AMS Press, Inc.

Leslie, L. L., & Brinkman, P. (1988). *The economic value of higher education.* New York: Macmillan.

Murdock, T. A. (1989). Does financial aid really have an effect on student retention? *Journal of Student Financial Aid, 19*(1), 4-16.

Musoba, G. D. (2004). Postsecondary encouragement for diverse students: A reexamination of the Twenty-First Century Scholars Program. In E. P. St. John (Ed.), *Readings on equal education: Vol. 19. Public policy and college access: Investigating the federal and state roles in equalizing postsecondary opportunity* (pp. 153-177). New York: AMS Press, Inc.

National Center for Education Statistics. (1997a). *Access to higher postsecondary education for the 1992 high school graduates.* NCES 98-105. By L. Berkner & L. Chavez. Washington, DC: Author.

National Center for Education Statistics. (1997b). *Confronting the odds: Students at risk and the pipeline to higher education.* NCES 98-094. By L. J. Horn. Washington, DC: Author.

National Center for Education Statistics. (2001a). *Bridging the gap: Academic preparation and postsecondary success of first-generation students.* NCES 2001-153. By E. C. Warburton & R. Bugarin. Washington, DC: Author.

National Center for Education Statistics. (2001b). *Students whose parents did not go to college: Postsecondary access, persistence, and attainment.* By S. Choy. Washington, DC: Author.

National Center for Education Statistics. (2003, October). *Projections of education statistics to 2013.* NCES 2004013. By D. E. Gerald & W. J. Hussar. Washington, DC: Author.

Pascarella E. T., & Terenzini, P. T. (1991). *How college affects students.* San Francisco: Jossey-Bass.

Peng, C. Y. J., So, T. H., Stage, F. K., & St. John, E. P. (2002). The use and interpretation of logistic regression in higher education: 1988-1999. *Research in Higher Education, 43,* 259-294.

St. John, E. P. (1991). What really influences minority attendance? Sequential analyses of the high school and beyond sophomore cohort. *Research in Higher Education, 32,* 141-58.

St. John, E. P. (1994). *Prices, productivity, and investment.* ASHE/ERIC monograph, No. 3. San Francisco: Jossey-Bass.

St. John, E. P. (1999). Evaluating state grant programs: A study of the Washington State grant programs. *Research in Higher Education, 40*(2),149-170.

St. John, E. P. (2002). *The access challenge: Rethinking the causes of the new inequality.* Policy Issue Report No. 2002-01. Bloomington, IN: Indiana Education Policy Center.

St. John, E. P. (2003). *Refinancing the college dream: Access, equal opportunity, and justice for taxpayers.* Baltimore: Johns Hopkins University Press.

St. John, E. P. (Ed.). (2004). *Readings on equal education: Vol. 20. Improving diversity on campus: Research on the Gates Millennial Scholarship Program.* New York: AMS Press, Inc.

St. John, E. P., Asker, E. H., & Hu, S. (2001). The role of finances in student choice: A review of theory and research. In M. B. Paulsen & J. C. Smart (Eds.), *The finance of higher education: Theory, research, policy & practice* (pp. 419-436). New York: Agathon.

St. John, E. P., Cabrera, A. F., Nora, A., & Asker, E. H. (2000). Economic influences on persistence reconsidered: How can finance research inform the reconceptualization of persistence models? In J. M. Braxton (Ed.), *Reworking the student departure puzzle* (pp. 29-47). Nashville: Vanderbilt University Press.

St. John, E. P., Chung, C. G., Musoba, G. D., & Simmons, A. B. (2004). Financial access: The impact of state financial strategies. In E. P. St. John (Ed.), *Readings on equal education: Vol. 19. Public policy and college access: Investigating the federal and state roles in equalizing postsecondary opportunity* (pp. 109-129). New York: AMS Press, Inc.

St. John, E. P., Chung, C. G., Musoba, G. D., Simmons, A. D., Wooden, O. S., & Mendez, J. (2004). *Expanding college access: The impact of state finance strategies.* Indianapolis: Lumina Foundation for Education.

St. John, E. P., & Hu, S. (2004, April). *The impact of guarantees of financial aid on college enrollment: an evaluation of the Washington State Achievers Program.* Paper presented at the annual meeting of the American Educational Research Association, San Diego, CA.

St. John, E. P., Hu, S., & Weber, J. (1999). *Affordability in public colleges and universities: The influence of student aid on persistence in Indiana public higher education.* Policy Research Report No. 99-2. Bloomington, IN: Indiana Education Policy Center.

St. John, E. P., Hu, S., & Weber, J. (2000). Keeping public colleges affordable: A study of persistence in Indiana's public colleges and universities. *Journal of Student Financial Aid, 30*(1), 21-32.

St. John, E. P., Hu, S., & Weber, J. (2001). State policy and the affordability of public higher education: The influence of state grants on persistence in Indiana. *Research in Higher Education, 42,* 401-428.

St. John, E. P., Kline, K. A., & Asker, E. H. (2001). The call for public accountability: Rethinking the linkages to student outcomes. In D. E. Heller (Ed.), *The states and public higher education: Affordability, access, and accountability* (pp. 219-242). Baltimore: Johns Hopkins University Press.

St. John, E. P., Musoba, G. D., & Chung, C. G. (2004a). Academic access: The impact of state education policies. In E. P. St. John (Ed.), *Readings on equal education: Vol. 19. Public policy and college access: Investigating the federal and state roles in equalizing postsecondary opportunity* (pp. 131-151). New York: AMS Press, Inc.

St. John, E. P., Musoba, G. D., & Chung, C. G. (2004b). *Academic preparation and college success: Analyses of Indiana's 2000 high school class.* Report prepared for the Indiana

Commission on Higher Education and the Lumina Foundation for Education. Bloomington, IN: Indiana Project on Academic Success.

St. John, E. P., Musoba, G. D., Simmons, A. B., & Chung, C. B. (2002). *Meeting the access challenge: Indiana's Twenty-First Century Scholars Program.* New Agenda Series, Vol. 4, No. 4. Indianapolis: Lumina Foundation for Education.

St. John, E. P., Musoba, G. D., Simmons, A. B., Chung, C. G., Schmit, J., & Peng, C. J. (2004). Meeting the access challenge: An examination of Indiana's Twenty-First Century Scholars Program. *Research in Higher Education, 45*(8).

St. John, E. P., Paulsen, M. B., & Starkey, J. B. (1996). The nexus between college choice and persistence. *Research in Higher Education, 37,* 175-220.

St. John, E. P., & Somers, P. (1997). Assessing the impact of aid on first-time enrollment decisions. In J. S. Davis (Ed.), *Student aid research: A manual for financial aid administrators* (pp. 101-126). Washington, DC: National Association of Financial Aid Administrators.

Smedley, B. D., Myers, H. F., & Harrell, S. P. (1993). Minority-status stresses and the college adjustment of ethnic minority freshmen. *Journal of Higher Education, 64*(4), 434-452.

Somers, P. (1992). *A dynamic analysis of student matriculation decisions in an urban public university.* Unpublished doctoral dissertation. University of New Orleans, LA.

Somers, P. A., & St. John, E. P. (1997). Analyzing the role of financial aid in student persistence. In J. S. Davis (Ed.), *Student aid research: A manual for financial aid administrators* (pp. 127-138). Washington, DC: National Association of Financial Aid Administrators.

Tinto, V. (1975). Dropout from higher education: A theoretical synthesis of recent research. *Journal of Higher Education, 45,* 89-125.

Tinto, V. (1987). *Leaving college: Rethinking causes and links of student attrition.* Chicago: University of Chicago Press.

Tinto, V. (1993). *Leaving college* (2nd ed.). Chicago: University of Chicago Press.

Trent, W. T., Gong, Y., & Owens-Nicholson, D. (2004). The relative contribution of high school origins to college access. In E. P. St. John (Ed.), *Readings on equal education: Vol. 20. Improving access and college success for diverse students: Studies of the Gates Millennium Scholars Program* (pp. 45-70). New York: AMS Press, Inc.

Turner, C. S. V. (1994). Guests in someone else's house: Students of color. *The Review of Higher Education, 17*(4), 355-370.

Walker, V. S., & Snarey, J. (Eds.). (2004). *Race-ing moral formation: African American perspectives on care and justice.* New York: Teachers College Press.

Zumeta, W. (2001). Public policy and accountability in higher education: Lessons from the past and present for the new millennium. In D. E. Heller (Ed.), *The states and public higher education policy: Affordability, access and accountability* (pp. 155-197). Baltimore: Johns Hopkins University Press.

SECTION IV

Conclusion

CHAPTER 11

UNDERSTANDING AND INTERPRETING RESEARCH ON EDUCATIONAL OPPORTUNITY

Edward P. St. John

This volume of *Readings on Equal Education* provides a comprehensive, although incomplete, view of finance and education policies and reforms in the U.S. The three spheres of educational opportunity—achievement and equity outcomes of K-12 education (Section I), transitions from high school to college (Section II), and academic success and attainment in college (Section III)—have largely been addressed independently, in distinct streams of discourse. This volume has been comprehensive in the sense that it includes policy studies in each of the spheres. Yet this task of building an understanding of educational opportunity that cuts across these policy domains is new and far from complete. Policy researchers from across fields—and especially from economics, sociology, and public policy—who share interest in educational opportunity should be encouraged to engage in research that builds understanding across the spheres of opportunity. As the body of cross-cutting research develops, it should be possible to reinterpret the research to illuminate the ways public policies influence and shape educational improvement and equalize opportunity.

411

This concluding chapter takes two further steps toward the goal of contributing to a policy literature that looks across the spheres of educational opportunity. First, I summarize the studies, focusing on building an understanding of the roles of education and finance policies across sectors. Then, I use theories of justice as a basis for reinterpreting the findings to further illuminate the challenges facing education in the U.S.

Understanding the Spheres of Educational Opportunity

When discussing the influence of public policy on educational practice and outcomes, it is necessary to consider the role of policy in both financing education and in education delivery. We need to understand both types of policies within each sphere before articulating understandings reached about the effects of reforms looking across the spheres of opportunity.

Whether they are rationalized as means of improving quality or equity, reforms like vouchers, charters, and student grants to college students are primarily finance reforms that emphasize privatization. Historically the costs of attending educational institutions in the U.S. were subsidized by direct funding of schools and colleges. Charters and vouchers have changed the means of institutional subsidy provided to schools. Charters alter the flow of funds within public or quasi-public schools, allowing funds to follow students who choose schools. In contrast, vouchers function as grants to individuals, enabling students to attend private schools. Most of the current voucher programs do not fully subsidize the cost of attending private school. Most state and federal grants and private scholarship programs for college students (like Washington State Achievers) are portable, and they, too, subsidize only a portion of the costs of attendance. Both charters and vouchers in K-12 education have been rationalized based on arguments that they would improve the quality of education outcomes, while need-based grants for college students were rationalized based on potential improvements in equity, and new merit-based government grants and scholarships have been rationalized based on arguments about economic development and retention of college graduates in state (Heller & Marin, 2002). To build an understanding of these sorts of reforms, it is important to consider their roles as financing mechanisms.

In contrast, government influences education policies through requirements, as is the case with the plethora of accountability policies in K-12 education that are unrelated to funding policy. However, some education reforms have financial incentives. For example, Comprehensive School Reform (CSR) provides large grants to schools. In these instances, it is important to consider the role and influence of funding when interpreting findings. When interpreting research on the effects of reforms that aim to alter educational delivery, it is also important to recognize the autonomy of teachers in their classroom practices. Even in highly regulated educational systems, teachers usually have freedom to teach using their own knowledge and skills as part of their classroom practice. Some K-12 reforms, like some CSR models, focus explicitly on teaching practices. Educational standards and other accountability mechanisms impose external requirements on educational practice. In higher education, in contrast, there is a history of faculty and institutional autonomy which usually limits government intrusion into teaching practice.

With this brief background on the mechanisms currently in use in education policy and finance, it is possible to summarize across studies within spheres of opportunity. The three spheres of reform are examined below.

School Reforms
All four of the chapters on school reforms (Section I) provide evidence related to the consequences of reform financing mechanisms and arguments of policy linkages to educational practice. It is important to consider the government role in funding as part of the design of reform because the changes in financial incentives embedded in reforms—from vouchers to school grant funding incentives—remain one of the major ways that

governments influence educational practice, in spite of arguments to the contrary.

Vouchers and charters alter the flow of funding. Charters redirect the funding of schools by allowing school dollars to follow students to new schools that are exempted from some of the educational requirements imposed on normal public schools by states and districts, while the voucher gives money to students to alter their choice between public and private schools. Eckes and Rapp (Chapter 1) indicate that access to charter schools has been extended across racial/ethnic and income groups. While charter schools as a whole (or as a category of schools) have attracted diverse students, the new schools themselves are not necessarily desegregated. Similarly, Metcalf and Paul discuss how vouchers have been created to provide access for low-income students to private schools. However, Metcalf and Paul also note attrition of more of the lowest income children from private schools, an outcome that could be related to the fact that vouchers usually pay only a portion of the cost of attending private schools. They argue that parents with very low incomes are apparently not able to pay the extra costs. Readers are cautioned, however, that more and different types of research would be needed to test this proposition.

There could be slight difference in the achievement effects of these two school finance reforms, but evidence is far from conclusive. Eckes and Rapp report that evidence is uneven with respect to the achievement effects of charter schools compared to common public schools. While public schools are confronted by common requirements and teachers are faced with choices about accepting or resisting standards and other requirements, charter schools are much more variable in their missions and curricula than public schools. The variability in missions of charter schools complicates efforts to compare them as a class of schools to public schools. Metcalf and Paul report only very modest differences between achievement by students with vouchers who attend private schools and by students in public schools. They also report substantial differences in satisfaction. Both of these outcomes could be attributable to the unique features of private schools, which have been founded and maintained based on missions that emphasize religious and/or academic values. It is also possible that parents feel more satisfied because they have exercised choice about the schools their children attend. If parents are satisfied with their choices about enrolling their children in private schools and charter schools, then there could continue to be political support for these types of reforms for some years to come, until new forms of education are realized.

Musoba (Chapter 3) explicitly examined the effects of state education policies and public funding on SAT scores using a two-level model for a national sample of 2000 high school seniors who took the exam. She tested the hypothesis that accountability—and not funding—influences student achievement (e.g., Finn, 1990, 2001; Paige, 2003). Her findings contradict this claim. At the very least, her research raises questions about whether the consequences of education regulations can really be untangled from the consequences of funding. In a time series analysis, Hanushek and Raymond (2004) found that accountability reform with financial consequences has an effect on achievement while other accountability mechanisms do not, a finding that is similar to other studies using similar time series methods (St. John, Musoba, & Chung, 2004b).

Finally, the CSR study in Michigan (St. John, Hossler, Musoba, C-G. Chung, & Simmons, Chapter 4) examined the role and influence of large grants on classroom outcomes. While the CSR schools were required to select and implement a reform model, there was a great deal of variation in the types of models schools selected. Overall, there were higher failure rates reported by teachers, which indicates that the reforms did not enable more students to achieve at grade level, at least after the first two years of implementation. However, the study indicted that teachers' practices, including collaboration on curriculum, had a more substantial influence on classroom outcomes than did the types of reforms chosen. This suggests that the educational aspects of CSR reforms are more important than the grant administration and compliance processes.

It is also possible to examine the educational aspects of these reforms. Interestingly, neither charter schools (Chapter 1), nor accountability reforms (Chapter 3), nor CSR (Chapter 4) significantly improved student outcomes although all three of these reform strategies were rationalized based on this type of logic. Only vouchers have some modest evidence of achievement effects, and these findings are often disputed, as Metcalf and Paul report. The findings that classroom practices and teacher collaboration on curricula were significantly associated with classroom outcomes may be noteworthy (Chapter 4), but hardly a basis for redefining or revising policy, at least from this one study alone.

Transitions to College

Three of the chapters on college transitions examined one program, Washington State Achievers (WSA). In addition, one chapter examined Indiana's Twenty-First Century Scholars program. The two programs are the distinctive hybrid programs that include features normally associated with merit and need-based programs (St. John, 2004). This review considers the research relating to the financial and educational features of the two programs.

The WSA and Twenty-First Century Scholars programs both combine financial commitments made to students—the financial aid guarantees—with obligations students must fulfill to receive the awards. In WSA, students were selected by noncognitive criteria (Sedlacek & Sheu, Chapter 6). Although merit was not explicitly considered in their selection, students who received the scholarship were academically well prepared (St. John & Hu, Chapter 7). Students who received awards agreed to apply for state grants as well as to prepare for college. They also had mentors and other forms of support. In addition, while minorities were more likely to receive awards, family also played a role (Emeka &

Hirschman, Chapter 5). In contrast, to be eligible for the Twenty-First Century Scholars, students had to be eligible for free and reduced-price lunch programs in eighth grade. Students of color were more heavily represented in the program than White students (Musoba, 2004b). The Twenty-First Century Scholars signed up for the program in the eighth grade and made a commitment to complete high school, to maintain at least a 2.0 GPA, to remain drug free, and to apply for student aid. In both programs, the combination of early commitments and aid guarantees was positively associated with enrollment (Chapter 7; St. John, Musoba, Simmons, & Chung, 2002). Chapter 8 provides further evidence that the Twenty-First Century Scholars program provides sufficient support to retain students who enroll because of the program and even improves the odds of attaining two-year degrees for low-income students.

These scholarship programs also have embedded academic features in the sense that students have financial incentives to prepare academically. There is strong reason to assume that availability of student aid encourages preparation, and there is empirical evidence from time series analyses of the states to support this proposition (St. John, Chung, Musoba, & Simmons, 2004). However, the Twenty-First Century Scholars and WSA programs make this link explicit, providing strong encouragement for students to prepare, and the research confirms that this aspect has a measurable effect.

It is also important not to isolate the features of the financial aid components of these initiatives. While the WSA program had not implemented the features of this program in time for the students in these studies to benefit from the education reforms, the teachers and administrators in their schools had been engaged in planning for these reforms, a process that may have influenced their teaching and the culture in the schools. In addition, students had active mentors while they were in high school to encourage their preparation and to help them prepare for college. In Indiana, the Twenty-First Century Scholars program was implemented in a state that has several other reform initiatives (St. John, Musoba, &

Chung, 2004a). For example, the state had provided incentive funding for all high schools in the state to graduate students with college preparatory and honors diplomas. Research on the Washington and Indiana programs has not yet shown the influence of financial incentives on educational performance in high school, but there is substantial evidence of effects from financial incentives on college enrollment and college choice nonetheless.

The findings from the study of the long-term effects of the Twenty-First Century Scholars program indicate that Scholars did not differ from other traditional-age students in persistence (Chapter 8). The good news is that opportunity for persistence is relatively equal for these low-income students once they prepare. However, additional grant money did not increase persistence among Scholars compared to other low-income students.

Academic Success in College
The studies of college student success (St. John & C-G. Chung, Chapter 9; St. John, Carter, C-G. Chung, & Musoba Chapter 10) also provide compelling information about the roles of academic preparation and financial aid, along with a relatively comprehensive view of access and persistence and the challenges facing reformers and policy makers. In addition to considering the roles of education policy in preparing students for college and public funding in ensuring and equalizing opportunity, I consider the role of universities in providing academic and support programs that enable students to reach their goals.

First, both studies further confirm the argument that there is a relationship between high school curricula and college success. The reanalysis of NELS (Chapter 9) examined the influence of high school graduation and advanced math courses on college enrollment after high school and degree completion or current enrollment after eight years. The analyses of enrollment revealed substantial differences in the role and influence of math courses across groups in four-year colleges, especially for low- and middle-income students. However, high school graduation also had a substantial influence on college enrollment for all income groups. In addition, the analyses left little doubt that background variables, including race and income, had an influence on enrollment in four-year colleges, controlling for the influence of preparation. In other words, the NCES claim that enrollment disparities across groups was explained by preparation (NCES, 1997) was not only based on a flawed analysis (Becker, 2004; Heller, 2004); additionally, the reanalysis of educational attainment (Chapter 9) revealed that both advanced math courses and student background influenced college success. Controlling for math courses, high-income students were more likely than middle-income students to have attained degrees while low-income students were more likely to be still enrolled. Clearly a decade of NCES research, summarized by Choy (2002) in a report published by the American Council on Education, has distorted the roles of background and math preparation.

The study of the Indiana 2000 cohort focused more explicitly on the role of state curricula policy (Chapter 10) by considering the influence of diploma types. These analyses are important because Indiana and other states are in the process of changing graduation requirements to encourage or require college preparation. For the 2000 cohort, Indiana had required high schools to offer Core 40 (college preparatory) and honors (more advanced) diploma curricula, but the regular diploma required for graduation did not have as many requirements. The analyses found that having a preparatory curriculum (either Core 40 or honors) was positively associated with continuous enrollment for Whites, Hispanics, and African Americans, but there was a difference across racial/ethnic groups that merits note. While high SAT scores were not significantly associated with persistence by Whites and Hispanics, African Americans with SAT high scores were significantly less likely to persist than their peers who did not have SAT scores reported. Therefore, there is reason for concern about the loss of high ability African Americans, at least in Indiana.

Second, these studies also added to the general understanding of the role of financial aid in equalizing the opportunity for college enrollment and persistence. Research that considers roles of both academic preparation and financial aid is important because many of the official reports over the past few decades, especially those published by NCES, have overlooked the role and influence of student financial aid (Becker, 2004; Fitzgerald, 2004; Heller, 2004).

The reanalysis of NELS (Chapter 9) found that state funding for student financial aid helped promote enrollment in different ways across income groups. For low-income students, state funding for grants was positively associated with enrollment in two-year colleges and private colleges, and public tuition charges were negatively associated with enrollment in two-year colleges and private colleges. For middle-income students, state funding for need-based grants was positively associated with enrollment in two-year colleges, and public tuition was negatively associated with enrollment in two-year colleges and positively associated with enrollment in private colleges. For high-income students, need-based grants were negatively associated with enrollment in public four-year colleges, and tuition charges were negatively associated with enrollment in public four-year colleges. These findings illustrate that high tuition and high grants can have a role in equalizing opportunity across income groups for enrolling in four-year colleges and private colleges. In addition, the findings on attainment indicate that there are still inequalities in the opportunity to persist across income groups, controlling for the influence of academic preparation. This indicates the aid available may not have been enough to equalize opportunity to persist.

The analyses of the 2000 college cohort in Indiana (Chapter 10) found that aid was significant and positively associated with persistence by African Americans but was not significant for Whites and Hispanics. For all three racial/ethnic groups, middle- and low-income students had similar odds of persisting. Financial aid played a role in equalizing opportunity, given that aid was positive or neutral for each group. However, the positive findings about grants are important given the significance of all types of aid packages for African Americans.

Third, the findings from the Indiana study (Chapter 10) provide insight on some of the academic barriers to student success for minority students in higher education. African Americans were the only group for which high SAT scores were negatively associated with persistence. In addition, several major choices were also negatively associated with persistence by African Americans, another pattern not evident for the other groups. Specifically, African Americans in business, education, health, and computer science were less likely to persist than their peers with undeclared majors, controlling for background, preparation, and other factors. The answers to these challenges lie within higher education and are not byproducts of preparation.

Policy and Educational Opportunity

Looking across these studies, it is apparent that public policies on education and finance exert an influence on education outcomes. Finances play a central role in equalizing opportunity, a proposition supported by studies of vouchers (Chapter 2), SAT preparation (Chapter 3), postsecondary encouragement (Chapters 7 and 8), and college success (Chapters 9 and 10). It is also evident that K-12 policies have some influences, but the influences are contradictory and less substantial than implied by NCES and other research groups that focus on the academic pipeline. Moreover, the influences of education policies are mitigated by educational practices in both schools and colleges, and educational practices are crucial to both expanding and equalizing educational opportunity. However, the role of educational practice has not received sufficient attention in the policy debates about educational opportunity.

Reinterpreting the Roles of Public Policy

It is important that education reforms both improve the quality of education available to all students preparing for and enrolling in college and also that they not disadvantage some groups of students. However, since in higher education students can make choices about whether and where to enroll and whether to persist, college success is not always determined by prior qualifications. Yet given the growing emphasis on improving college preparation and expanding college enrollment in the U.S., it is important to think about the criteria used to judge success.

Standards for Public Policy on Education

Most of the conversation about standards and accountability in education has focused on specific areas of content and learning. While the linkages between curricular content and test results are important, centering the standards debate in these areas misses the larger issues related to educational opportunity that are of central importance to policy and society. Education improvement and attainment are appropriately viewed in their social and economic contexts, with an emphasis on fair and just access to education and to a livelihood in the emergent global economy. Before reinterpreting the findings of the studies in this volume by looking across spheres of opportunity, it is appropriate to view the problem of standards for public accountability from the just societies framework.[1] I suggest three standards as criteria for understanding the efficacy of public policy on education.

---

[1] In my recent books (Mirⁿh & St. John, 2003; Priest & St. John, in review; St. John, 2003; St. John & Associates, in press; St. John & Parsons, 2004), I have used John Rawls's theory of justice (1971, 2001) as a starting point for reframing the policy debates in education. This section summarizes and extends the understanding reached in these earlier works.

It is important to define a basic standard of education to which all youth should have fair and equal access, a standard related to the basic rights of citizens (Nussbaum, 1999, 2000; Rawls, 1971, 2001; Sen, 1999; Walzer, 1983). In the United States, mandatory K-12 education has evolved as a standard. However, there is now a strong push to provide universal postsecondary access, a new threshold based on economic considerations. It now seems appropriate to view the attainment of a postsecondary qualification as a threshold of the basic capabilities citizens need to provide for their families, at least in the U.S. (St. John & Associates, in press). This is a perspective based on the arguments about human capabilities advanced by Nussbaum (1999, 2000) and Sen (1999). Three standards of justice in educational opportunity can be proposed.

Standard 1 (The Basic Capabilities Standard): At each level of education—elementary school, middle school, high school, and college—equally prepared students should have equal access to quality educational opportunities.

Current choice schemes like charters and vouchers are appropriately viewed as means of providing this type of equal access to K-12 education (elementary, middle, and secondary school). In higher education, the shift toward privatization of the public system (Priest & St. John, in review) complicates efforts to ensure equal access. In addition, efforts to raise K-12 educational standards and to require college preparatory curricula for high school graduation can be viewed as efforts to raise the standard of quality education contributing to human capabilities at each level of the education system.

Standard 2 (The Equity Standard): Public policies that promote and ensure access to basic and advanced education should deviate from equal treatment only when family and life circumstances create unfair disadvantages.

This standard is akin to Rawls's difference principle (Rawls, 1971, 2001) but is also compatible with critiques by Walzer (1983) and Nussbaum (1999). There is a great deal of evidence in this volume and others cited by the contributing authors that poverty and other factors, including race, contribute to inequalities in access to both K-12 schools and to public four-year colleges. Citizens in democratic societies should, at a minimum, expect their government agencies to help equalize access.

Policies that are aimed at equalizing opportunity for those with disadvantages have included supplemental programs for high poverty schools (i.e., Title I of the Elementary and Secondary Education Act, as amended), desegregation and affirmative action policies that attempt to rectify past patterns of discrimination, remedial and supplemental education during college, and need-based financial aid that enables low-income students to pay the costs of attendance. In spite of such policies, inequalities in educational opportunity persist. One recent study illustrates that Whites benefited more substantially from the new K-12 policies (Musoba, 2004a). In addition, there is growing evidence that higher education privatization in the 1980s and early 1990s—the rise in tuition, decline in grants, and rise in loans—has created unequal access to four-year colleges (Fitzgerald, 2004; St. John, 2003). Thus, not only has the commitment to the older equalization strategies waned, but the new K-12 and higher education policies have also had unintended, negative effects on equity outcomes.

Standard 3 (The Public Finance Standard): Public finance strategies should use tax dollars to meet the basic education standard, emphasizing equalizing opportunity as a first priority when inequalities are evident, given availability of tax revenue and public willingness for just taxation.

This standard provides a conservative reinterpretation of Rawls's concepts of cross-generation equity and just savings

(Rawls, 1971, 2001). Privatization shifts some of the burden for funding education from the public to consumers, especially in higher education. As Musoba's analysis of SAT scores reveals, public funding is more central to quality improvement in K-12 education than are accountability schemes that lack financial support. Higher education has proven easier to privatize than K-12 education because there is a history of individual payment of tuition and living costs. Shifting a higher percentage of educational costs to students and their families in public colleges has not generally been viewed as taxation, but this type of privatization substitutes tuition for tax dollars. Therefore, public tuitions should be viewed as a targeted form of taxation. Those from low-income families deserve the subsidies needed to make these payments or meet these tax obligations, given their families' ability to pay and borrow.

The chapters in this volume add to our understanding of how public policies can be rebalanced to reach these standards. Further, public officials in education and in state and federal legislative positions should be held accountable for their ability to meet and balance these standards. Holding public officials accountable for meeting these standards may be more appropriate than the current emphasis on holding schools and educators accountable for meeting new politically constructed content standards if those standards do not enable educators to meet the larger goals of ensuring basic capabilities and equitable education.

Improving Educational Opportunity

For two decades, the efforts to improve educational opportunity in the U.S. have emphasized the quality of basic education by raising standards and requirements. However, these efforts are better understood as an attempt to raise the level of expectation for basic capabilities. Efforts to raise the standard for basic capabilities have not been sufficiently considered for high school reform. Uneven outcomes in all three spheres of opportunity—K-12 education, transitions to college, and college success—are related to the difficulties in high school reform.

Reforming high school education in ways that respond to the implicit expectation of higher educational requirements for human capabilities as a standard for high school education should be at center stage of policy debates about all three spheres of educational opportunity. Viewing the problem of reforming high schools as being related to changing expectations about human capabilities—recognizing the need to attain at least some college as a threshold for supporting a family—can help us untangle the complexities of high school reform. The current arguments for increasing the number and level of high school math courses required for graduation seem misguided, given that many college majors do not require knowledge of calculus. For example, students in music, history, applied engineering, and nursing might benefit from other advanced courses more than from calculus. Further, the research on attainment (Chapter 9) revealed that high school math is not as highly predictive of college success as has often been argued in NCES studies (1997, 2001).

In spite of the problems created by researchers who focus on correlations between high school math courses and college success, the issue of high school improvement is even more important than assumed by some of the myopic proponents of advanced math education. At the core of the issue is whether comprehensive high schools should be transformed into preparatory high schools in the European model (St. John & Associates, in press). If we assume the pathway to college success is narrow and related primarily to high prestige fields that require advanced math preparation—like engineering, science, medicine, and economics—then the pipeline argument seems reasonable. However, if the problem is that the older vocational and regular tracks of high school education are no longer appropriate for the level of preparation needed for a broader range of collegiate fields, including a large number of new technical fields that may not require prior calculus for degree or certificate completion, then the issue of reforming high schools has been misidentified.

The fact that graduating from high schools in suburbs and towns is often associated with collegiate success (Chapter 10) means that high schools in these locales, which are mostly comprehensive high schools, are doing well compared to high schools in other locales. Urban areas are more likely to have specialized high schools, including vocational high schools that are usually not strongly oriented toward college preparation even in the new vocational fields. And rural high schools generally lack the capacity to offer advanced curricula. Thus, the comprehensive high school may be able to respond to the new basic capabilities standard better than educational systems that lack this model of education. Clearly, there is a need to rethink the meaning of high school reform relative to the shifting expectations about college enrollment, but this rethinking probably should not be defined so narrowly as it is in the pipeline rationale. With this background, then, it is possible to reconsider the relative effectiveness of both education policies and finance reforms at meeting the basic capabilities standard.

There are three reasons why changes in accountability seem to have failed to meet the basic capabilities standard (Chapters 3 & 10; St. John & Associates, in press; St. John, Musoba, & Chung, 2004a, 2004b). First, accountability policies have not sufficiently considered the range of collegiate pathways that should be developed in middle schools and high schools to prepare students for the choice of major fields—a challenge that seems to have gone unrecognized with the overemphasis on advanced math. Second, too frequently, new accountability policies are implemented without financial support, under the supposition that improvement is unrelated to funding, when the research does not support this supposition (e.g., Musoba, 2004a). Third, reform methods being implemented do not give sufficient consideration to the educational practices of school teachers and collegiate educators. The analysis of CSR indicates that classroom practices and teacher collaboration are more directly related to classroom outcomes than is the type of reform model implemented (Chapter 4). In addition, some of the persistence challenges for African

American college students appear to be related to the practices of collegiate education within their fields (Chapter 10), rather than to preparation or financial aid.

Finance policies that emphasize a market approach may provide viable ways of redesigning educational systems. The evidence here indicates that high tuition with high grants can expand college access and degree completion for majority and minority students, but adequate need-based grants are necessary to ensure equal opportunity for low-income students (Chapter 9; St. John, 2003). The problem is that most states do not adequately fund need-based grants, given the decline in federal funding for grants (St. John & Associates, in press; St. John, Chung, Musoba, & Simmons, 2004). The early evidence from charter schools and vouchers indicates satisfaction among these students and their parents (Chapters 1 & 2), even if the achievement outcomes remain ambiguous. However, Metcalf and Paul speculate that the cost of attending after vouchers was too high for many low-income children. Additionally, there is strong evidence that test scores are linked to funding for education, at least when there are controls for student background and other state-level reforms (Chapter 3).

Equalizing Educational Opportunity

Given the long history of inequality in U.S. education, it is important to remember that the vestiges of unequal access and opportunity for success have not been mitigated. The arguments made to end affirmative action and redirect the focus of education policy from inputs to outcomes seemed to have made the opposite assumption (Finn, 1990, 2001). The changes in federal policies in the 1980s and 1990s also shifted the focus of the U.S. Department of Education from emphasizing equal education to emphasizing improving opportunity for all. But how well have these new reforms maintained equity?

Before addressing this question, it is important to look at how the newer education policies rationalize inequalities and their resolution. Interestingly, two of the publicly funded voucher programs were rationalized as strategies to extend private school choice for low-income students. In addition, some of the early CSR reforms grew out of efforts to improve schools for low-income students (e.g., Success For All, School Development Program, and Accelerated Schools) and these reforms were often funded through Title I, before the Comprehensive School Reform Program, and the No Child Left Behind Act. These reform models were focused on low-income serving schools but used a market model to remedy problems within schools. The appraisal of newer reforms is relatively positive (see Chapters 1, 2, & 4) even though it is incomplete. What is different about the newer reforms like choice schemes and CSR is that they favor market solutions to educational challenges. Parental satisfaction with having choices about schools may be an important factor in the eventual judgments about the efficacy of these reforms.

The privatization of public higher education has had some positive outcomes, at least with respect to the rising basic capabilities standard and public finance standard. Taxpayer costs for higher education on a per-student basis went down in the 1980s and early 1990s while the number of students served went up (St. John, 2003). Consumers paid a larger share of the cost of attendance and taxpayers paid less per student. However, a large gap between Whites and minorities in college enrollment opportunities opened in the 1980s and has persisted, narrowing only slightly since then (St. John, 2003, 2005).

The more complex issues pertain to equal education opportunity and to the improvement of educational practices. The research on both school reform (Chapter 4) and higher education success (Chapter 10) indicate that educational practices play an important role in promoting education outcomes. The types of accountability policies that have been implemented in K-12 education have increased dropout and have not substantially improved test scores (Chapter 3; Musoba, 2004a, St. John, Musoba, & Chung, 2004a), and the types of merit-grant policies being proposed for higher education seem to have similar flaws (St. John & Associates, in press).

Rethinking Privatization and Accountability

The two dominant patterns of policy in education in the U.S. and internationally are privatization and accountability in schools (Henry, Lingard, Rizvi, & Taylor, 2001; Rizvi, in review; St. John & Associates, in press). This volume adds to the understanding of the consequences of both strategies in the U.S.

Privatization has probably worked better than most liberal educators would have predicted two decades ago. College enrollments are higher than predicted (St. John, 2003), and there are strong indications that charters and vouchers are workable strategies for urban schools (Chapters 1 & 2). If we use the basic capabilities standard and the public finance standard as evaluative criteria, then the privatization patterns implemented to date seem to have worked reasonably well. However, if we use the equity standard as a basis for evaluating the course of policy over the past 20 years, then these finance strategies—especially vouchers and the privatization of public higher education—seem to fall short of a reasonable expectation.

However, the efficacy of accountability schemes is questionable. Hanushek and Raymond (2004) found a positive association between accountability with consequences and test score gains. Our time series study of the effects of accountability schemes had similar findings about test scores but found the same practices were negatively associated with high school completion rates (St. John, Musoba, & Chung, 2004). However, since the consequences of these particular accountability strategies pertain to funding mechanisms—funding for performance or threats to remove funding or close schools—it is possible that the analyses of Hanushek and Raymond (2004) actually measured the effects of financial incentives and not accountability per se. In other words, linking funding and accountability may be more effective than implementing accountability without sufficient funding.

Musoba's two-level analysis of SAT scores raises further doubts about the linkages between accountability policies and test scores. At the very least, accountability without funding linkages is an ineffectual strategy with respect to the basic capabilities standard and is highly suspect, if not a failure, with respect to the equity standard.

Thus, the success of the new schemes—privatization of higher education, accountability with consequences, and school choice—seems linked to the financial aspect of these policies rather than to accountability and standards per se. Hybrid schemes that combine academic and financing features, such as the comprehensive encouragement programs (Section II), may be a step forward. However, of the reforms examined in this volume, only the encouragement programs appear to be related to improvement in the equity standard. Therefore, greater emphasis on equity is needed in policy development to reach a better balance among goals.

Another concept of accountability involves holding bureaucrats and elected officials accountable for their successes and failures with education reform (St. John & Associates, in press). If we view the reforms of the past few decades through this lens, then there is an apparent need for change. However, rather than throwing out the whole set of reforms, it may be wise to adapt these strategies as appropriate to improve equity while emphasizing improvement in educational practices.

Implications

Looking across research on the effects of school reform, postsecondary encouragement programs, and state higher education policies, three new understandings emerge: (1) finances play a central role in educational improvement across the three spheres of opportunity, (2) the inequalities in educational opportunity have worsened as a consequence of the new accountability and privatization schemes, and (3) changes in the capabilities required for employment may necessitate a rethinking of education and finance strategies. Each understanding has implications for policy research as well as for policy development.

First, it is apparent that financial incentives have a more substantial influence on education outcomes than education policies without funding linkages. The chapters in this volume demonstrate that charters and vouchers improve parent satisfaction, need-based student grants improve access and college success, and programs that combine grant guarantees with encouragement for preparation have an influence on opportunities to enroll and persist. School funding has a direct and substantial influence on test scores, controlling for the influence of accountability reforms. Overall, accountability reforms without financial consequences appear relatively ineffectual with respect to either test scores or equal opportunity to progress academically. The accountability reforms that influence student outcomes appear to be the ones that include financial and other incentives.

New emphasis on market strategies and other privatization reforms along with voter resistance to taxation complicates efforts to refine public finance strategies. There is ample reason, based on the research in this volume and elsewhere, to conclude that market strategies provide workable approaches to the delivery of both K-12 and higher education. However, while market strategies have political advantages because of family preferences to make educational choices, these approaches can increase inequalities if they do not provide sufficient opportunity for low-income students to pay the higher costs. In the sphere of collegiate opportunities, market strategies in the 1980s and early 1990s coincided with a widening gap in opportunity as a consequence of the decline in the purchasing power of federal grants.

Second, the erosion of equal opportunity—the national decline in high school graduation rates and the gap across races in college opportunity—presents a crucial challenge. While it is possible that improved funding of Pell grants and state grants reduced the gap in the early 2000s (St. John, 2005), inequalities remain problematic, given the new emphasis on market strategies in both K-12 and higher education. Between two- and four-million college-qualified students were denied access in the 1990s due to financial barriers (Fitzgerald, 2004; Lee, 2004; St. John, Chung, Musoba, Simmons, Wooden, & Mendez, 2004). Based on the history of Pell grants, there are substantial risks to educational opportunity in the U.S. if market strategies are widely implemented without sufficient funding.

Third, the challenge of developing workable approaches to finance that are integrated with appropriate educational incentives is especially critical. There is a clear need for improvement in high school graduation rates, college enrollment rates, and completion rates for college certificates and degrees. Individuals who do not attain at least some postsecondary education are at some risk of being unable to support their families or to survive economically in the new global economy. The rising level of educational attainment required for employment also has substantial implications for high school reform, which remains at center stage in policy debates about education.

References

Becker, W. E. (2004). Omitted variables and sample selection in studies of college-going decisions. In E. P. St. John (Ed.), *Readings on equal education: Vol. 19. Public policy and college access: Investigating the federal and state roles in equalizing postsecondary opportunity* (pp. 65-86). New York: AMS Press, Inc.

Choy, S. P. (2002). *Access & persistence: Findings from 10 years of longitudinal research on students.* Washington, DC: American Council on Education.

Finn, C. E., Jr. (1990, April). The biggest reform of all. *Phi Delta Kappan, 71*(8), 584-592.

Finn, C. E., Jr. (2001, February 21). College isn't for everyone. *USA Today,* 4A.

Fitzgerald, B. (2004). Federal financial aid and college access. In E. P. St. John (Ed.), *Readings on equal education: Vol.*

19. Public policy and college access: Investigating the federal and state roles in equalizing postsecondary opportunity (pp. 1-28). New York: AMS Press, Inc.

Hanushek, E. A., & Raymond, M. E. (2004). *Does school accountability lead to improved student performance?* [Working Paper 10591]. Cambridge, MA: National Bureau of Economic Research.

Heller, D. E. (2004). NCES research on college participation: A critical analysis. In E. P. St. John (Ed.), *Readings on equal education: Vol. 19. Public policy and college access: Investigating the federal and state roles in equalizing postsecondary opportunity* (pp. 29-64). New York: AMS Press, Inc.

Heller, D. E., & Marin, P. (Eds.). (2002). *Who should we help? The negative social consequences of merit scholarships.* Cambridge, MA: The Civil Rights Project, Harvard University.

Henry, M., Lingard, B, Rizvi, F., & Taylor, S. (2001). *The OECD, globalization, and education policy.* Amsterdam: Pergamon Press.

Lee, J. B. (2004). Access revisited: A preliminary reanalysis of NELS. In E. P. St. John (Ed.), *Readings on equal education: Vol. 19. Public policy and college access: Investigating the federal and state roles in equalizing postsecondary opportunity* (pp. 87-96). New York: AMS Press, Inc.

Mir⊓n, L. F., & St. John, E. P. (Eds.). (2003). *Reinterpreting urban school reform: Have urban schools failed, or has the reform movement failed urban schools?* Albany, NY: SUNY Press.

Musoba, G. D. (2004a). *The impact of school reform on college preparation: A multilevel analysis of the relationship between state policy and student achievement.* Unpublished doctoral dissertation. Bloomington, IN: Indiana University.

Musoba, G. D. (2004b). Postsecondary encouragement for diverse students: A reexamination of the Twenty-First Century Scholars Program. In E. P. St. John (Ed.), *Readings on equal education: Vol. 19. Public policy and college access: Investigating the federal and state roles in equalizing postsecondary opportunity* (pp. 153-180). New York: AMS Press, Inc.

National Center for Education Statistics. (1997). *Access to higher postsecondary education for the 1992 high school graduates.* NCES 98-105. By L. Berkner & L. Chavez. Project Officer: C. D. Carroll. Washington, DC: Author.

Nussbaum, M. C. (1999). *Sex and social justice.* Oxford, UK: Oxford University Press.

Nussbaum, M. C. (2000). *Women and human development: The capabilities approach.* New York: Cambridge University Press.

Paige, R. (2003, January 10). More spending is not the answer. Opposing view: Improving quality of schools calls for high standards, accountability. *USA Today*, 11A.

Priest, D., & St. John, E. P. (Eds.) (In review). *Privatization in public universities: Implications for the public trust.* Bloomington, IN: Indiana University Press.

Rawls, J. (1971). *A theory of justice.* Cambridge, MA: Belknap Press of Harvard University Press.

Rawls, J. (2001). *Justice as fairness: A restatement.* Cambridge, MA: Belknap Press of Harvard University Press.

Rizvi, F. (In review). The ideology of privatization in higher education: A global perspective. In D. M. Priest & E. P. St. John (Eds.), *Privatization in public universities: Implications for the public trust.* Bloomington, IN: Indiana University Press.

St. John, E. P. (1993). Untangling the web: Using price-response measures in enrollment projections. *The Journal of Higher Education, 64*(6), 676-695.

St. John, E. P. (2003). *Refinancing the college dream: Access, equal opportunity, and justice for taxpayers.* Baltimore, MD: Johns Hopkins University Press.

St. John, E. P. (2004). The impact of financial aid guarantees on enrollment and persistence: Evidence from research on Indiana's Twenty-First Century Scholars and Washington State Achievers Programs. In D. E. Heller & P. Marin (Eds.), *State merit scholarship programs and racial inequality* (pp. 124-140). Cambridge, MA: The Civil Rights Project, Harvard University.

St. John, E. P. (2005). *Affordability of postsecondary education: Equity and adequacy across the 50 states*. Prepared for Renewing Our Schools, Securing Our Future, National Task Force on Public Education, Center for American Progress.

St. John, E. P., & Associates. (in press). *Education and the public interest: School reform, public finance, and access to higher education*. Dordrecht, The Netherlands: Springer.

St. John, E. P., Chung, C. G., Musoba, G. D., & Simmons, A. B. (2004). Financial access: The impact of state financial strategies. In E. P. St. John (Ed.), *Readings on equal education: Vol. 19. Public policy and college access: Investigating the federal and state roles in equalizing postsecondary opportunity* (pp. 109-129). New York: AMS Press, Inc.

St. John, E. P., Chung, C. G., Musoba, G. D., Simmons, A. B., Wooden, O. S., & Mendez, J. (2004). *Expanding college access: The impact of state finance strategies*. Indianapolis: Lumina Foundation for Education.

St. John, E. P., Musoba, G. D., & Chung, C. G. (2004a). Academic access: The impact of state education policies. In E. P. St. John (Ed.), *Readings on equal education: Vol. 19. Public policy and college access: Investigating the federal and state roles in equalizing postsecondary opportunity* (pp. 131-151). New York: AMS Press, Inc.

St. John, E. P., Musoba, G. D., & Chung, C. G. (2004b, July 21). *Academic preparation and college success: Analyses of Indiana's 2000 high school class.* [Report prepared for the Indiana Commission on Higher Education and the Lumina Foundation for Education.] Bloomington, IN: Indiana Project on Academic Success.

St. John, E. P., Musoba, G. D., Simmons, A. B., & Chung, C. G. (2002). *Meeting the access challenge: Indiana's Twenty-First Century Scholars Program.* [New Agenda Series, Vol. 4, No. 4.] Indianapolis: Lumina Foundation for Education.

St. John, E. P., & Parsons, M. D. (Eds.). (2004). *Public funding of higher education: Changing contexts and new rationales.* Baltimore: Johns Hopkins University Press.

Sen, A. (1999). *Development as freedom.* New York: Anchor Press.

Walzer, M. (1983). *Spheres of justice: A defense of pluralism and equality.* New York: Basic Books.

INDEX